Orientation to the History of Roman Judaea

Orientation to the History of Roman Judaea

Steve Mason

CASCADE *Books* · Eugene, Oregon

ORIENTATION TO THE HISTORY OF ROMAN JUDAEA

Copyright © 2016 Steve Mason. All rights reserved. Except for brief quotations in critical publications or reviews, no part of this book may be reproduced in any manner without prior written permission from the publisher. Write: Permissions, Wipf and Stock Publishers, 199 W. 8th Ave., Suite 3, Eugene, OR 97401.

Cascade Books
An Imprint of Wipf and Stock Publishers
199 W. 8th Ave., Suite 3
Eugene, OR 97401

www.wipfandstock.com

PAPERBACK ISBN: 978-1-4982-9447-8
HARDCOVER ISBN: 978-1-4982-9449-2
EBOOK ISBN: 978-1-4982-9448-5

Cataloguing-in-Publication data:

Names: Mason, Steve, 1957–.

Title: Orientation to the history of Roman Judaea / Steve Mason.

Description: Eugene, OR: Cascade Books, 2016 | Includes bibliographical references and index.

Identifiers: ISBN 978-1-4982-9447-8 (paperback) | ISBN 978-1-4982-9449-2 (hardcover) | ISBN 978-1-4982-9448-5 (ebook)

Subjects: LCSH: Josephus, Flavius. | Jews—History—168 B.C.–135 A.D—Historiography.

Classification: BR129 M377 2016 (print) | BR129 (ebook)

Manufactured in the U.S.A.   12/01/16

For my father

Contents

List of Illustrations | viii
Preface | ix
List of Abbreviations | xiii

Part 1: Doing History | 1

1. Popular vs. Academic History | 3
2. Social Scientists and Humanists: Debates among Historians | 19
3. Special Problems in the History of Ancient Judaea | 57
4. Method and Procedure: Ancient vs. Modern History | 65

Conclusion to Part I | 84

Part 2: Mapping Peoples | 87

5a. The Classical Paradigm: *Ethnos* and *Polis* | 97
5b. The Classical Paradigm: Sacrificial Cult and Voluntary Association | 147
6. The End of the Classical Paradigm | 175
7. Geography: The World, the Homeland, the Mother-*Polis* | 221

Summary and Conclusions | 275

Bibliography | 281

Illustrations

Figure 1. Graphic representation of the difference between tradition and history. Author. | 15

Figure 2. Map of Palestine (Map 8) from S. A. Mitchell, *Mitchell's Ancient Atlas, Classical and Sacred*. Philadelphia: Butler, 1873 (1844 original). Public domain. | 235

Figure 3. Map of Palestine (pp. 6–7) from W. R. Shepherd, *Historical Atlas*, 5th ed. New York: Holt, 1926 (1911 original). Public Domain. | 236

Figure 4. The classic reconstruction of first-century Jerusalem's Herodian temple mount. © and rights reserved by L. Ritmeyer, used with permission. | 257

Figure 5. Cutaway view of the building stages of the temple mount, the largest area being Herod's retaining wall, showing the bedrock. © and rights reserved by L. Ritmeyer, used with permission. | 257

Figure 6. Model of first-century Jerusalem at the Israel Museum, from the south: Lower City and temple with Antonia in the background to the right, Upper city centre left, and New City in the distance northward. Author © 2013. | 258

Figure 7. Plan of Jerusalem ca. A.D. 66, with the area of the modern Old City shaded more darkly. The diagram is © with rights reserved by L. Ritmeyer. Annotations by the author with Ritmeyer's permission. | 258

Preface

This book is not a history of ancient Judaea. Several good ones are readily available. This book is about often-overlooked problems that face us when we first form an intention to study the history of ancient Judaea. The best word I can suggest for this is *Orientation*. The study in your hands takes up matters that I sometimes wish had been raised more explicitly during my academic formation. Coming to grips with them in some measure has turned out to be important for the way I approach my work: for the questions I ask and the ways I go about answering them. It is part of the mystery of scholarship that we all find ourselves asking quite different questions of roughly the same material, and perhaps talking past each other as a result. I have no wish to puncture any mysteries, but it has occurred to me that greater clarity about what we are actually doing, and why, might facilitate communication, which is not the same thing as agreement.

It is possible, to be sure, that these only become pressing matters after we have been engaged in research and publication for a while. We find ourselves mired in debates and, wondering how on earth we got there, retrace our intellectual steps. Why do respected colleagues see things so differently? Are we sure of our foundations? I am not sure when these orientation questions normally arise for others, much less when they *should*. But I reflected that advanced students today, when so much information and so many viewpoints about Roman Judaea and Christian origins are at our fingertips, might value another person's effort to work through a couple of fundamental questions.

In truth I developed this material over a decade of work on *A History of the Jewish War, A.D. 66 to 74* (hereafter *HJW*).[1] I needed to clarify what I thought about the nature of history, in general and in our field, and

---

1. Mason 2016.

about the language and categories we use for mapping ancient people(s). Other preliminary matters included Roman provincial administration outside Syria and the many revolts of various kinds that occurred elsewhere, as comparative material. The main investigation of that book turned out to be large without this material, however, and its publisher wisely encouraged me not to include more (cf. Josephus, *Ant.* 1.6–7). The question then was whether it might be of value for others. Could I rewrite it as a self-contained study, with advanced students and interested others in view? I approached Wipf & Stock editor K. C. Hanson because I thought that this rapidly growing publisher could produce a high-quality but affordable book that would remain available, for students in particular. I am grateful to K. C. and to Brian Palmer at Wipf & Stock for accepting and then enthusiastically supporting this modest project.

So I set about rewriting the material, enjoying the challenge of "repurposing" it for students. Teaching is the most enjoyable job in the world, because you get to constantly re-examine the basics, together, and the ancient texts and other remains are full of surprises, no matter how often you may have read them. The stimulus of student questions can knock you over with new and simple angles. In general, simple is good for all of us. We can easily become entangled in highly complex interpretations built on a mountain of forgotten assumptions and unexamined categories. Whether any students would read the book or benefit from it lay beyond my control. But the work itself would be hugely satisfying.

From everything I had prepared for *HJW*, two large question sets emerged with enough coherence for a book, it seemed. The rest could be left in the drawer for now, as having served its purposes for me. These two problem sets complement each other from historical and human-geographical directions, namely: What does it mean to do the history of Roman Judaea? And how can we orient ourselves to ancient ways of mapping peoples and places? The person we call "the geographer Strabo" (early first century A.D.) actually wrote a *History*, which has been lost, before his famous *Geography*. He had many other irons in the fire too, and was neither a historian nor a geographer in our sense. His linkage of his two major works is unimaginable from the pen of a modern geographer or historian, and it already provides an intriguing entry-point to ancient ways of thinking:

> So, after we had made our *Historical Outlines*—beneficial, we reckon, for moral and political philosophy—we resolved to supplement them with the present composition [the *Geography*]. It has the same form and is written for the same men, particularly

those in high positions. Still another similarity is that, just as that other work [*History*] brings to memory the lives of illustrious men and leaves aside what is small and inestimable, so also here we must disregard what is trivial and inconspicuous, and concern ourselves with what is distinguished and grand, wherever we find that which is practically useful, conducive to memory, and pleasurable . . . This is a sort of colossus in the making, explaining large matters and wholes, except where some small item is able to stimulate the lover of learning and the practical leader. These remarks were made in order to say that the work at hand is serious, and suitable for a philosopher.

Although we no longer write for important men in our town, in some ways we have returned to the ancient insights that research in all genres comes from a basic philosophical perspective and that when we write up our work some kind of shared rhetorical values (in the broadest sense) govern what we produce. These are questions that will come up in various guises throughout this book. Perhaps I may cite Strabo in support of my broaching two large areas that stretch the limits of my disciplinary competence. (I would not attempt to publish in specialized journals on many of these matters.) But we do need efforts at painting big pictures, and someone has to attempt it from time to time.

The fact that I first prepared much of the content here in connection with *HJW* means that I sometimes refer to it for examples, rather than repeating its content here.

While I was preparing this, my friend and colleague of more than thirty years, Prof. Daniel Schwartz at the Hebrew University of Jerusalem, published two books on related matters: historical method (Schwartz 2013) and the question of religion and Judaism in the first century (2014). For students in particular I recommend both of these clear and succinct studies. I say "for students" only because colleagues will already know them; Schwartz is a prominent scholar in these areas. Students faced with mountains of potential reading, who want to isolate debated issues and see how two people of good will can look at much the same material, to some extent in dialogue with each other, might find it useful to compare our very different (and yet philosophically related) questions and procedures.

In the process of testing bits of *HJW*'s argument in academic conferences, I included as methodological context some paragraphs of Part I in this book. Those papers became chapters in two fine collections, edited respectively by Mladen Popović and by Joshua Schwartz and Peter Tomson.[2]

---

2. Mason 2011a and 2014b.

The second chapter of *HJW* also tightly compresses a few points (pp. 88–91) from chapters 5 and 6. I divided Chapter 5 of this book out of consideration for the reader, though it is a conceptual whole.

My father Terry is turning 88 as I send this book to production. Born and raised in India, the oldest son of a British Warrant Officer's nine children, he took his wife and first child to Canada, where I appeared after a while. Once we had reached our full complement of seven, he led the family back to England and to Australia for some years, before England and Canada again—just in time for the children to broach adulthood and begin our own wanderings. Those early cross-cultural experiences, albeit within the long shadow of Britain's former colonies and using varieties of English, meant exciting life aboard ships for weeks at a time and ports of call that a boy could only find exotic. Those experiences gave me an abiding fascination, shared by a large proportion of the world's migrating population, with (ships and) questions of human identity. In gratitude for his courage in leading our little band around the planet, for showing by example that everything was open to be discovered, and for much that cannot be said, I dedicate this book to my father.

Abbreviations

CIL *Corpus Inscriptionum Latinarum, Consilio et Auctoritate Academiae Litterarum Regiae Borussicae Editum*. Berlin: Reimer, 1863–1974

IBerenike J. Reynolds, "Inscriptions," In *Excavations at Sidi Khrebish Benghazi (Berenice). Vol. 1: Buildings, Coins, Inscriptions, Architectural Decoration*, edited by J. A. Lloyd, 233–254. Supplements to Libya Antiqua 5. Libya: Department of Antiquities, Ministry of Teaching and Education, People's Socialist Libyan Arab Jamahiriya, 1977.

IDelos Roussel, P. and M. Launey. *Inscriptions de Délos: Décrets postérieurs à 166 av. J.-C. (nos. 1497–1524). Dédicaces postérieures à 166 av. J.-C. (nos. 1525–2219)*. Académie des Inscriptions et Belles-lettres. Paris: Librairie Ancienne Honoré Champion, 1937

IEph H. Engelmann, H. Wankel, and R. Merkelbach. *Die Inschriften von Ephesos. IGSK 11–17*. Bonn: Habelt, 1979–1984

SEG *Supplementum Epigraphicum Graecum*. Leiden: Brill, 1923–

Part I

Doing History

> But to attempt to paint the ancients; to elaborate in this way the development of their minds; to regard events as characters in which we may accurately read the most sacred feelings and intents of their hearts—this is an undertaking of no ordinary difficulty and discrimination, although as frequently conducted, both childish and trifling.
>
> —Voltaire, *Philosophical Dictionary*, "History" section III

> I know it will work very well in practice, but tell me John, how will it work in theory?[1]

Historians are famously impatient with theory.[2] History is not, after all, rocket science. It may require long days poring over archival documents or texts, in difficult languages, trying to decipher inscriptions and coins, or waking at 4:00 a.m. to work on a dig. Endless reflection only postpones the necessary labor. Why not get on with it?

---

1. This version of a quip, attributed to a number of scientists and economists, is credited to Irish Taoiseach Garret Fitzgerald by Séamus Martin, citing A. J. F. O'Reilly, in *The Irish Times*, 6 July 1985, p. 14 col. 5 (http://quoteinvestigator.com/2015/08/30/practice/#return-note-11897-10).

2. See Clark 2004: 9–28; Jenkins 1995: 64–66 (on G. R. Elton).

The problem with getting on with it becomes clear when we ask: What are we trying to achieve? What are we supposed we do with all this evidence, once we have cleaned it up? What does it mean to understand it, and how does that bear on history? In short: What *is* history?

In recent months I have heard professional colleagues (some no doubt speaking loosely) express such views as these. History is *the past* or some authoritative account of it such as *the historical record*. Historians must follow evidence and avoid speculation. If we have no evidence for a fact, we should exclude it from consideration: "There's no evidence" means more or less "That did not happen." Or it is proposed that ancient history concerns itself only with elite texts, whereas archaeologists explore the lives of common people. Or historians are grouped in ideological camps: maximalists vs. minimalists, realists vs. postmodernists, radicals vs. conservatives, or some other two-kinds-of-people scheme. Because these conceptions are common, and some readers may think that at least one of them sounds fine, I invite the reader to think with me about the historian's task, for the study of ancient Judaea but also in general.

There is no yield in trying to characterize what all historians do or think, or should do or think. Like other disciplines, history presents considerable diversity, and for good reasons. All the same, it cannot be whatever we wish it to be. Rethinking first principles should help us at least to gain some bearings. Confusion and outright disagreement about history's nature and purpose come from at least three directions: popular versus professional perceptions, disputes among practicing historians or philosophers of history, and peculiarities connected with Roman Judaea. The first three chapters in this section take these up in order. The fourth tries to extract from that discussion a method and a rough procedure, taking account of the difference between ancient and modern history.

1

Popular and Academic: Tradition vs. History

We all understand that words can have technical senses at odds with common use. Most of us do not think of tomatoes, cucumbers, or peppers as fruits, even if botanists must. Medical language is a world of its own, removed from the popular categories of shin splints or heart attacks. When university students enroll in the ancient myth course offered by the Classics Department, they are not intending to learn old falsehoods, as the popular meaning of myth might suggest, but rather durable and meaning-charged stories. Specialists in all disciplines, if they are to communicate with colleagues, require a lexicon that is robust enough to hold for all cases of a type and yet precise enough to distinguish one type from another. History is also a word with senses more technical than those in common use.

In ordinary speech we use history to mean either the past or an authoritative record of it, or at the very least a creditable effort in that direction: *a* history of England if not *the* history.[1] For this impression we have the support of a Columbia University Professor of History in 1922: "the word 'history' has two meanings. It means either the record of events or the events themselves." Most of us who took history in school gained the impression that it happened some time ago, created by history-making people and events, and so it is now there to be learned. Since history is this blended pudding of events and "the record," knowing it means being able to recall the important players, achievements, events, and dates. Someone who cannot cite the dates of the Battle of Hastings or the French Revolution, we say, "does not know her history." From this perspective, the history of

---

1. Shotwell 1922: 2. Cf. the old student handbook, Garraghan and Delanglez 1946, which derives historical knowledge from trustworthy authorities.

India under Ashoka (third century B.C.), Judaea under the Romans, or Italy under German occupation in the 1940s can all be studied in the same way. A more cynical view may hold that "the winners [get to] write history," but this strongly reinforces that picture of history as an authoritative account. One has only to locate the record, to be found in the history books—much of which has found its way into *Wikipedia* entries. Historians are people who can rattle this off without looking, at least the sections pertaining to their specializations.

If in school we were expected to learn some chosen facts of history, as adults we wear a heavier mantle of guilt. For it turns out that the record does not merely sit there waiting for us. History apparently has a mind and even a personality. It must be going somewhere because people say it is best to be on "the right side of history." Every week pundits appear on television discussing whether "history will be kind" or not to a certain politician, specifying what "history will remember" her for, and deferring to history for the hard decisions: "History will decide . . ." And history's mind is not merely content to sit and observe us. It is nearly bursting to tell us what it knows, the facts but especially the lessons it would love to teach us, if *only* we would listen. "History tells us . . . ," declares the politician, preacher, or pundit.[2] Alas, most of us rudely ignore history's efforts, avoiding even eye contact. That is why, self-destructively, we keep "repeating the mistakes of the past."[3] Our leaders assure us that history shows whatever they believe at the moment: that greed and inequality bring down empires, that troublesome foreign leaders must never be appeased, that a populace must be armed if it is to avoid tyranny, or that weapons have never resolved anything. Whatever exactly history teaches, if we would just learn those lessons we would spare ourselves endless grief.

---

2. E.g., T. Stone 2016 ("History Tells Us What Will Happen with Trump and Brexit"). What history seems to "teach" is that life will be hard for many at times, but humanity will come through. Astrology and fortune cookies teach the same lessons.

3. The saying most often cited in this regard has nothing actually to do with history. In the first volume of his book *The Life of Reason or The Phases of Human Progress* (1920), George Santayana explores (on Darwinian foundations) the relationship between flux and species progress, making the point that progress has more to do with "retentiveness" than change, which would be random if it did not learn by experience. Both infants and the very old, lacking a serviceable memory (like "savages"), act only from impulse and thus do the same things repeatedly. One can progress past infancy only if one remembers previous actions and their consequences. Hence, "Those who cannot remember the past are condemned to repeat it" (1920: 284). This trite observation (e.g., children do learn not to touch hot stoves or irons) is hardly applicable to research or history in particular. It cannot straightforwardly apply to "remembering" bad experiences with Neville Chamberlain or Hitler and avoiding them in the future.

This image of history as teacher had a partial Roman counterpart. A famous line credited to Thucydides expressed the neat idea that "history is philosophy from examples."[4] Thucydides probably said nothing of the sort, but Roman historians put great stock in using human lives as instructive *exempla*, as we see in Livy or Josephus.[5] But notice two differences from our time. First, the view of history involved here had more to do with good stories capable of carrying moral lessons, without excessive concern about whether they happened just so. Second, the ancients did not pretend to derive moral lessons from past stories inductively, as our leaders sometimes do. They knew what virtue was through philosophical reflection, and this is what allowed them to look for stories that illustrated these known traits. Our pretense that "the historical record" teaches us by itself is perhaps a reflex of nervousness about deductive norms, which we cover with history's blanket—while in fact noticing only the "lessons" that our conditioning and existing values highlight. We are not learning them from the past as such or from research into it.

At any rate, if we call the bluff of the people who say such things and respond, "You have persuaded me! I do want to learn history's lessons. Where do I go for that?" we shall find them suddenly speechless. If we are concerned about foreign immigration or urban blight or joblessness, there is no catalogue of history's lessons that we can consult and follow. The many people who suggest there is such a thing have no theory of history.

That so many people continue to talk of history's facts and lessons is understandable, and it exposes a real problem. In most disciplines we study things that exist: dung beetles, bacteria, mango trees, our solar system, or the floor of the North Sea. Some deal with aspects of present human society by using models, for such large aggregations as the economy, the market, or business, or criminal psychology or legislative systems. Historians are in the rare position of devoting themselves to the study of the one thing—the human past—that no longer exists now and cannot exist in the future. This difference has been known to make history professors feel uncomfortable.

Such considerations have led some to conclude that if knowledge-generating history is possible, that can be only in relation to the recent past. Ancient history is a mirage because it is not possible to acquire confident

---

4. Ps-Dionysius, *Ars rhet.* 11.2. Although we may not have all that Thucydides wrote and surely not all he said, it is unlikely that he spoke of *historia* (below), or in this way. The later author compares this alleged sentiment with a passage in Plato (*Phaedr.* 245a), that only poets inspired by the Muses educate future generations by dressing up the deeds of ancient figures for moral instruction. The equivalence of poetry and history makes clear the literary, non-investigative nature of the idea.

5. See Livy, 1.pr.10 with Kraus and Woodman 1997: 53–56; Hölkeskamp 1996.

knowledge about human actions in remote times from the scarce, scattered, and unverifiable sources that have reached us. In the ancient world already Thucydides (1.1.3, 22.3), Polybius (9.2.1–7), and Josephus at times (*War* 1.13–16) expressed similar views: people who claim to know the ancient past are just telling tales.

In the mid-1700s, Voltaire would insist that only the period since about 1500, when the printing press made reliable texts available, could possibly repay historical investigation.[6] Although the sometime Professor of Modern History in Cambridge, J. B. Bury, had been a successful classicist, he came to think that modern history "offered the only period in which the records were abundant and certain . . . Only abundant records enable the historian to see with the eyes of contemporaries."[7] In many university departments, accordingly, pre-modern history is absent. The ancient world finds a home, if anywhere, in Classics, though scholars there have most often devoted their work to the ancient languages and interpreting the surviving literature.

Whether it is worthwhile to explore the ancient past will depend on what we require from history. If we need comprehensiveness and/or near certainty, we shall be out of luck. But the reflections above also make such an expectation absurd. They put us on a fast train to uncertainty in relation to *all* history. In place of the boring comfort of learning facts, we realize that history—all history—will require us to *think* and *imagine*. The past of any period does not come to us of its own volition. If we are interested in aspects of what happened at some time, we must launch an intellectual expedition to go after it. And if we are prepared to do that, why specify that the voyage must yield certain conclusions? Why is it not enough to make the voyage: to pursue a problem and, in coming to grips with the evidence and imagining scenarios, experience aspects of the past again in our imaginations? Ancient history can be worthwhile, I suggest, if we are willing to accept its limits.

We shall return to this question in Chapter 4, but we may recap before proceeding. For historians, history cannot be the past itself, which is not available to be studied, or an authoritative record, which does not exist. History is not something out there that imposes itself on us. It is something we do: the investigation of problems we pose about aspects of past human life that interest us. About *human life* because astronomy, geology, and biology also deal with dimensions of the past, but these have never been considered the province of history. By old convention history restricts its purview still further, to the tiny part of the human past since the invention of writing,

---

6. See Force 2009: 457–84. Voltaire apparently became partly reconciled to ancient history when he learned of archaeological finds, which closed the distance with vivid remains.

7. So editor H. Temperley in Bury 1930: xxii, summarizing one of his essays.

ceding "pre-historic" humanity to anthropology. That division is hard to justify, since many populations we study in the period after writing left no literature either. For present purposes it does not matter because Hellenistic-Roman Judaea falls well within the literate period.[8]

History's Origins

A look at history's beginnings will show why methodical inquiry lies at the heart of the enterprise.

Students learn that Herodotus, the fifth-century B.C. author, was history's father, a label he earned already in antiquity.[9] But *what* did Herodotus father? Not the past, obviously, or writing or talking about the past. None of his contemporaries doubted there was a Greek past. Like them, he grew up hearing all sorts of stories (Greek: *mythoi, logoi*) about preceding centuries. Most of the texts that related the stories were in verse form, as Homer's epics or Hesiod's account of the gods. These tales were much discussed. They provided a fund for thinking about society's values and self-image. They provided themes and events for the sculpture found everywhere in Greek cities, the texts for education, and the plots and characters for stage drama. But when Herodotus decided to write about the Persian–Greek wars that had devastated Athens and northern Greece in recent times (490–479 B.C.), a subject on which others had written predictable things,[10] he faced a question that has confronted historians ever since: Can I say something new, which will improve people's knowledge?

Herodotus realized that if he wanted a better picture he could not merely recycle what people had already heard. He would need to investigate the background and events of the wars for himself—or be able to say convincingly that he had. For this purpose he would exploit the mindset, language, and techniques of exploration that others had been using for philosophical or scientific study, in the Greek Enlightenment of the preceding century. Rather than allowing the past come to him ready-made through circulating stories, he would launch his own energetic investigation even into the human past.

---

8. Collingwood (1994: 372, 490) argues that the concept of a human prehistory is a relic of the untenable view that history comes to us pre-made in written authorities. No written authorities, no history. But if everything depends on investigation that barrier disappears.

9. So Cicero (*Leg.* 1.1.5), citing a commonplace in the mid-first century B.C. He himself claims that Herodotus' narrative is full of fabulous tales.

10. Dionysius (*Pomp.* 3.7) mentions two predecessors.

During the sixth century B.C. the Persians had expanded from their Iranian heartland westward over the Asian continent to the Aegean Sea, across which lay Greece and Europe. Coming from Halicarnassus (mod. Bodrum in western Turkey), a Dorian-Greek city under Persian rule, where he admired a Persian queen but was expelled for resisting a current ruler, Herodotus was fascinated by the cultural conflict that the Persian–Greek wars represented. Although these wars were triggered by the recent Ionian Revolt (494 B.C.), he saw them as the culmination of a primal conflict between Asia and Europe. After his expulsion he travelled extensively through Persia's vast empire, from Egypt through Syria-Palestine eastward, before returning to the Greek islands, Athens, Sparta, and various colonies. During two decades or more of research, he claims to have interviewed a range of exotic witnesses and cross-examined their testimony (Greek *elenchos*; cf. 1.24.7; 2.22–23).

Herodotus' project fused many intellectual currents of his time. He was steeped in both Homeric epic and tragic ways of thinking. He shared with contemporaries the assumption that the world's diverse nations or peoples (plural *ethnē*) acted in keeping with their distinctive characters. The nature of each *ethnos* (singular) was shaped by the environment in which it found its definitive shape (see Chapter 2), and then by its peculiarly evolving customs, ways of worship, dress, diet, laws, values, and political constitution. He takes the first half of his work to discuss the varied cultures of the Persian world.

Whereas we can be impatient with these digressions, if we expect from history a conclusive account of names and dates, Herodotus' project implies that the investigative journey, the inquiry, is *the point*. He is often cautious or agnostic about conclusions, apparently hoping that his audiences will rather share the excitement of the investigation. That new method of sustained inquiry is what he presents.[11] Herodotus is called the father of history, then, not because he was the first to think about the past, but because he saw the need for a new approach. His peer audiences are invited to participate virtually in his travels, hear the stories, observe the surviving evidence, and reason with him. In one place Herodotus even declares it a general principle that he feels compelled to pass along everything he heard, even though he does not believe much of it (7.152.3)—the ultimate in seeming to let others decide, though of course they cannot without independent access. This again suggests that a desire for admiration from audiences who could travel vicariously with him was a large part of his aim.

---

11. 4.30 (before an ethnographic digression): "for my work has proceeded from the start by way of digression."

POPULAR AND ACADEMIC: TRADITION VS. HISTORY

The word-group that Herodotus used to distinguish his method, rendered by "inquiry, inquire" in the following excerpts, was *historia* (*historiē* in his dialect). It was such an important word that he put it in the title to define the whole project (1.1.1): "Here is the presentation [*epideixis*] of *the inquiry* [*historiē*] by Herodotus of Halicarnassus." Having finished an inquiry that he alone could conduct, that is to say, he describes it with apparent fullness for others to share. Throughout the narrative, he makes many remarks such as these:[12] "I have *acquired knowledge* about the Persians, as follows ..." (1.131.1); "None of the Egyptians could give me any information, *when I inquired of them*, as to what power the Nile possesses ..." (2.19.3); "I did learn as much as I could by travelling to the city of Elephantine and seeing it for myself, *but I investigated* the region beyond that point through hearsay alone" (2.29.1–2); "All that can possibly be learned about its [the Nile's] course *by means of inquiry* has been stated here" (2.34.1); "Since I wished to *know something definite* about all this, . . . when *I asked* the priests . . . I discovered that they did not agree with the Hellenes . . . And so *this research* shows clearly that . . ." (2.44.1–5); "The Egyptians tell this story . . . When I asked them *how they knew that this had really happened*, they replied . . ." (2.54.1); "To this point *my own observation, judgment, and inquiry* are doing the talking. From here on I record Egyptian stories, according to *what I heard*, with some of my own *observation* added" (2.99.1); "When I inquired into the stories concerning Helen [of Sparta/Troy], the priests told me ..." (2.113.1).

Before Herodotus, the philosophers of nearby Ionia up the coast had practiced rigorous inquiry (*historiē*)—into nature.[13] From that same area, Hecataeus of Miletus had anticipated Herodotus, two generations before, opening his lost work with the line: "I write what seems to me truthful. Many sayings of the Greeks are, to my mind, laughable."[14] He too had travelled much and showed a particular interest in ethnography. So Herodotus did not invent inquiry, and both his scientific-medical language and ethnographical orientation were also part of his time.[15] His innovation was to apply this methodical way of thinking to the human past. Like Plato's version of Socrates, rather than trusting authorities or confident beliefs, he postured as an investigator who would go to any lengths to understand. He took

---

12. Translations are basically those of Purvis 2007, which I have lightly adapted to highlight terms of interest for us, adding emphasis.

13. Heraclitus reportedly said of Pythagoras that he "practiced inquiry more than all others" (in Diogenes Laertius 8.6).

14. Recalled by Ps-Demetrius, *De eloc.* 12 (second cent. A.D.).

15. On Herodotus' affinities and possible debts see Fowler 2006, Thomas 2006, and Luraghi 2006.

statements from people who claimed to know something, subjected their evidence to hard questioning or dialectic, and finally—*if* he felt confident enough—propounded a conclusion. Like Socrates, however, he redirected people's attention from conclusions to the *basis* of knowledge.

Herodotus' efforts were not universally admired. The problem with setting a high standard is that failure is conspicuous. It is revealing of ancient values, however, that the one explicit critique of him that survived, and that from half a millennium later, faults him for misplaced *moral allegiances* rather than for errors of fact. According to his critic, Herodotus had been too sympathetic to foreign easterners: happy to give them the benefit of the doubt while believing the worst of his Greek compatriots.[16] That essay may be a student exercise exploring possible lines of attack on a writer of unquestioned stature, though perceived disloyalty or partisanship toward foreigners could be dangerously culpable.[17] Whether history has an obligation to patriotism is a question that has not left us even today.[18]

Herodotus' effort at least provoked those who thought they could do better at the same sort of enterprise. Most famous of these was Thucydides, himself exiled from Athens for military failure, whose terse analysis of the Peloponnesian War (431–411 [404] B.C.)[19] would become history's gold standard. Without naming Herodotus, Thucydides criticizes him implicitly by presenting himself as the truly rigorous investigator.[20] His avoidance of *historia* language, perhaps because of a taint from Herodotus, shows incidentally that "inquiry" (*historia*) was not yet decisively linked with investigating *the past*. With a stinging rebuke of those who pass along stories uncritically (1.20.1, 3; 21.1), Thucydides insists on tough standards. He frequently uses words related to eyewitness testimony, proof, and cross-examination.[21] The tough soldier allows that some readers might find unappealing his exclusion

---

16. Plutarch, *On the Malice of Herodotus*, e.g., 857a: the historian was a *philobarbaros*.

17. On betrayal of native customs see Chapter 2. On criticism for loving outsiders see Polybius 2.56, 61, on Phylarchus. This alleged pro-Spartan failed to see the excellence of Polybius' people, and Polybius declares that he prefers to follow a historian (Aratus) who had the right sympathies.

18. As I write, during the U.S. presidential election of 2016, it is common to hear President Obama and Democrat candidate (former Secretary of State) Hillary Clinton accused of loving foreigners more than the homeland and, while allegedly apologizing for America's behavior, failing to respect "American exceptionalism." See below for history-textbook wars.

19. The war lasted to 404 but the narrative stops in 411.

20. See Hornblower 1987: 7–33.

21. *Martyrion*: Thucydides 1.8.1, 33.1, 73.3; 3.11.4, 53.4; 6.82.2. *Tekmērion*: 1.1.3, 20.1, 21.1, 34.3, 73.5, 132.5; 2.15.4, 39.2, 50.2; 3.66.1; 6.28.2. *Elenchos* and cognate verb: 1.132.1, 135.2; 3.38.4, 53.3, 61.1, 86.1. For analysis see Hornblower 1987:100–107.

of charming stories—about ethnography, Gods, and oracles—but this is his badge of honor.

Thucydides postures as a cold analyst for serious men, diagnosing the behavior of states and offering cures (1.22.2-4). In place of Herodotean speculations about fate and cosmic justice, he focuses on the supposed laws or realities of political behavior. He is probably most famous for his sophisticated explorations of a conflict between abstract notions of justice and the grim reality of politics that states with power will act in their self-interest.[22] His work has therefore been the Bible of political realism, though it seems that he was actually critiquing the exercise of raw power—especially by Athens, which had exiled him and would lose the war against Sparta.

Whereas Herodotus traced causal chains going back to mythical times, Thucydides replaces such folklore with razor-sharp insight into present-day conditions and states' motives. He underscores the difference between leaders' asserted motives and the diagnosable realities underlying their claims (e.g., 1.23.6, 88). For him, investigating the past is definitely not about simply gathering evidence and presenting that to the reader. The historian must be a man of affairs, who can use his insight to penetrate through to the underlying conditions of city-states and the repeatable conditions of all *polis* life. This provides a basis for predicting how things will go, depending on the actions taken by states. His forbidding style, in contrast to Herodotus' languid narrative, supports the clinical feel. Thucydides demands that his audience trust his ability as a diagnostician. He has no intention of providing the raw material for others to second-guess him.

Subsequent Greek and Roman historians would regard Thucydides as the master, though his example was intimidating. They would try to display analytical insight and imply their unique moral excellence, without divulging sources. Herodotus' legacy did not simply shrivel in fealty to the somber Athenian, however. Later historians were heirs to both, as we see in the perennial appeal of ethnographical and geographical digression, quasi-tragic plots, otherworldly episodes, and appealing style. Josephus' *Judaean War*, half a millennium after both men, exhibits Thucydidean pretensions common in his time but also, more quietly, Herodotean influences.[23] Herodotus' term *historia*, in particular, would win out as the undisputed word for

---

22. E.g., Thucydides 1.67-88; 5.84-115. See Chapter 4 on realism.

23. On Thucydides' unique standing see Dionysius, *Thuc.* 2-3; Diodorus 1.37.4; and Lucian, *Hist. conscr.* 15, 18-19, 39, 42. He was an inspiration for Josephus in both *War* (see Mader 2000) and *Antiquities* (Richards 1939: 37, 39). Josephus reports (*Apion* 1.18) that some contemporaries have accused *even* Thucydides of lying, though he is thought the most accurate historian. Dionysius' essay finds fault with Thucydides' *style*, another reflection of prevailing values.

methodical study of the human past, and even in a secondary sense for the kind of text that preserved such research.

Modern approaches to history have changed in countless ways from those of the ancient world, of course. I have spent time with Herodotus and Thucydides because their shared notion of history as investigator-driven inquiry (with or without *historia*), and requiring critical thinking, skepticism, and doubt, would be revived with the birth of the modern university discipline in the early nineteenth century.[24] The idea that historians are people who go out and search for the human past, as distinct from people who focus on learning "the historical record," remains universally shared in university departments of history.

History vs. Tradition

Now let us return to an important distinction we have left hanging. I mentioned that Herodotus knew many stories about the past before he embarked on his new program of *historia*. He had known the past, that is, the way we all do before we encounter history,[25] through what is *handed down* by others. This is *tradition*. Every human being encounters traditions because, unlike history, they greet us whether we like it or not, long before we are able to think about such matters. Tradition is eager to speak to those in its group. Its whole reason for being is didactic: to teach and shape.

Not only is there nothing wrong with tradition; it is a necessary part of life in society. We grow up learning the traditions of our families, religious communities, and the countries we live in. They are reaffirmed constantly through holidays, calendar markers, rituals, and festivals: Canada Day in Ottawa, the American Pledge of Allegiance and July 4th celebrations, or memorial days and military tattoos in London and Edinburgh. Still further any group we join as adults, whether professional, educational, military, commercial, social, benevolent, or religious, will have its own traditions and rituals, which we must absorb if we are to function harmoniously in the group. By preserving certain defining events and characters from the past, tradition provides crucial guidance about what it means to belong to this group. Tradition thus has a necessary socializing function.

---

24. See Iggers 1968; 1997; Bentley 1997: 395–506.

25. For the study of the ancient past, our personal memory is obviously irrelevant. Although I realize that colleagues often speak warmly of social, cultural, or collective memory (from Halbwachs 1950; Assman 1988), these seem to overlap almost entirely with what I prefer to call tradition, since it is passed along by a community and not "remembered" in the usual senses.

Tradition absorbs the elements of the past most suited to its needs. But, as Michael Oakeshott observes, this organic way in which we first encounter the past is "not significantly past at all":

> It is the present contents of a vast storehouse into which time continuously empties the lives, the utterances, the achievements and the sufferings of mankind. As they pour in, these items undergo a process of detachment, shrinkage, and desiccation which the less interesting of them withstand and in which the rest are transformed . . . into emblematic actions and utterances.[26]

All of the popular perceptions of history I mentioned above (winners write it; it is an authoritative record; it has a mind and is going somewhere; it decides people's legacies; it wants to teach lessons) seem to describe tradition—or emblematic preservation—rather than history or investigation.[27]

Even what we learn in school under the name of history is nearly always tradition. It is what society's elders in a given locale think their young should know about the past: what is most productive for value-formation and citizenship. School-level history *can* rarely involve open inquiry,[28] for the good reason that pupils lack the necessary background for independent investigation. But to the extent that they are expected to internalize what government ministries, school boards, and parent representatives consider important, they are learning tradition.[29]

To be sure, school history depends on the inquiries of professional historians, and textbooks are regularly updated in conversation with evolving research. Tradition also evolves because of changing social tastes and norms of decency. That is why the Puritans, once the embodiment of Pilgrim virtues, faded from American tradition as their image of intolerance became less appealing.[30] Disgust for racism, misogyny, or brutality can make even former presidents and other icons look repulsive, perhaps quite suddenly if criticism of them rapidly crystallizes.[31] Notwithstanding its capacities

---

26 Oakeshott 1999: 43–44.

27. Not everyone would make the distinction so sharply. Pompa 1993 is particularly valuable for stating the problems; his effort to find warrants for history in tradition, however, I find rather strained.

28. I can only admire the efforts of school teachers I have known who have tried with some success to involve students at all levels in problem-solving and thinking for themselves about the past, with graduated exercises.

29. For critical reflections on issues in teaching school history, see Ferro 2003: 356–63.

30. Dawson 1984. Kammen 1991 is a lively treatment of the general issue of history and tradition, if not with that language.

31. The academic year 2015–2016 saw a sharp rise in overt student hostility to the

for absorbing historical research and evolving with changing social norms, when a history curriculum is understood as the morally educative preservation of the past, indeed as something that needs to be learned, it is tradition.

It is precisely the character of school history as tradition that makes governments, totalitarian regimes most obviously, anxious about curricula. Richard Evans writes of the period following Adolf Hitler's rise to power in Germany:[32]

> History, ruled a directive issued on 9 May 1933 by the Reich Minister of the Interior, Wilhelm Frick, had to take a commanding position in the schools.... *The purpose of history was to teach people that* life was always dominated by struggle, that race and blood were central to everything that happened in the past, present and future, and that leadership determined the fate of peoples. *Central themes* in the new teaching included courage in battle, sacrifice for a greater cause, boundless admiration for the Leader and hatred of Germany's enemies, the Jews.[33]

On a less dramatic scale, school-board controversies remain alive from the U.S. to East Asia, and history occupies a central place in these debates, alongside the science vs. religion conflicts in the U.S.[34] Whenever we see history harnessed to socialization or hear debates about which history should be taught, we are again dealing with traditions rather than open-ended, problem-driven inquiry or history in its proper sense. I am not suggesting that it could be otherwise, but wish simply to distinguish between ingrained perceptions of history and what most historians actually do.

Figure 1 is an attempt to represent visually the difference between tradition and history.

---

continuing presence of Woodrow Wilson, John C. Calhoun, and Thomas Jefferson in statues and building names that had been in place for perhaps a century; see Jaschik 2015.

32. Evans 2005: 263. Emphasis added.

33. Cf. Schimmeck 2013, on the initiative of the Zimbabwean government to produce a history of their activity after colonial days—for public education and citizenship.

34. See e.g., Birnbaum 2010.

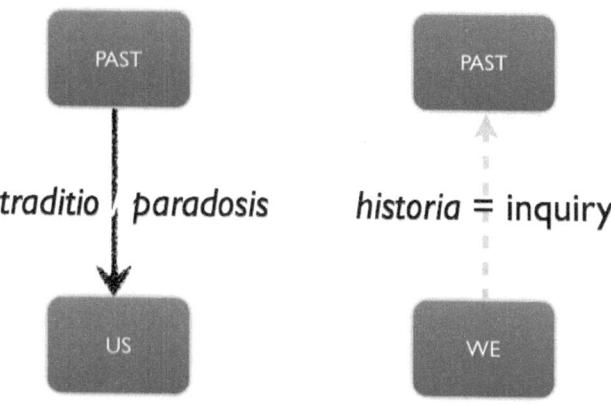

Figure 1. Graphic representation of the difference between tradition and history.

Traditions can also serve the historian, especially one seeking to understand a society's language and values. Historians of Republican Rome or Rabbinic Judaism will certainly need to study the traditions cherished by those societies. That is different, obviously, from simply embracing one's own tradition, from the inside, *as* the authoritative guide to the past, as members of religious and political communities often do.[35] In R. G. Collingwood's paraphrase of Giambattista Vico: "All traditions are true, but none of them mean what they say; in order to discover what they mean [*sc.* for the

---

35. I do not claim to understand Hans-Georg Gadamer's important contribution to hermeneutics, but realize that his rejection of "methodologism" and all pretenses to objectivity, especially the Enlightenment call to free oneself from tradition, entails a very different estimation of tradition (1989: 283–84 [his emphasis]): "*At the beginning of all historical hermeneutics, then, the abstract antithesis between tradition and historical research, between history and the knowledge of it must be discarded.* The effect (Wirkung) of a living tradition and the effect of historical study must constitute a unity of effect, the analysis of which would reveal only a texture of reciprocal effects." As far as I can tell from his examples, however, he is working at a higher level of abstraction and talking chiefly about the interpretation or "hearing" of the past or certain kinds of texts (285 [my emphasis]: "Our historical consciousness is *always filled with a variety of voices* in which the echo of the past is heard. Only in the multifariousness of such voices does it exist: this *constitutes the nature of the tradition in which we want to share* . . . . Modern historical research itself is not only research, but the handing down of tradition"). I value tradition, do not imagine history to be objective, and realize that traditions often stimulate questions for historical investigation. But when we explore historically such events as the career of King Herod, causes of the war against Rome, or the actions of a specific Roman provincial governor, traditional impressions have no standing as far as I can see.

historian], we must know what kind of people invented them and what such a kind of people would mean by saying that kind of thing."[36]

In the religious realm, the contrast is clear in the difference between traditional Christian language about Christ, based on creeds (crucified and risen, seated at the right hand of God, returning to judge), and the scholars' "historical Jesus" research, which is going strong after about three centuries. In the political domain we may contrast how nations present their births, formative generations, or traumas such as wars with historical research on similar questions. Tradition remembers Winston Churchill's unwavering determination to fight the Nazis, the nearly miraculous evacuation of British and French forces from Dunkirk (May–June 1940), the altruism shown in subway shelters during the *Blitz* (intense bombing of London), and the selfless efforts of European resistance movements. Tradition begins with real episodes of life but interprets them and reuses them in a process that produces a streamlined narrative emblematic of British values. Historical investigation of the same episodes has a different purpose and way of thinking. Asking open questions and investigating available evidence, it recovers a picture that includes human complexities, contradictions, and obnoxious behavior, even among the "greatest generation."[37]

Exploring the past through inquiry will inevitably, though this is not its aim, sit awkwardly with traditional perceptions of the same material. Either tradition will absorb enough research to become more robust and accommodating of diversity or, in less secure environments, it will steamroll the free thinking that history requires.

The confusion between tradition and history is so ubiquitous, however, that basic communication can be difficult. On my shelf is a book called *Bad History: How We Got the Past Wrong*.[38] Although one would imagine it to be an exposé of poorly executed history, it is actually and simply a correction of popular notions, which people heard from tradition, by historical investigation. It is not a critique of history at all. Perhaps the most famous conflation appeared in the third installment of a 1917 interview in *The Chicago Daily Tribune* with carmaker Henry Ford. This was shortly before America's entry into World War I (1917), and the interviewer was insisting that surely the U.S. should rapidly expand its navy, because *history*

---

36. Collingwood 1994: 70.

37. On the Blitz see Beckett 2010; Gardiner 2010; Mortimer 2010: esp. 119–25. On the resistance movements, Burleigh 2010: 268–86. On Churchill's first uncertain months, Reynolds 2006: 75–98. In the following chapter Reynolds provides a clinic in historical method, penetrating the fog of Churchill's legacy or tradition by investigating three questions of his devising as an investigator (101–2).

38. Marriott 2011.

showed that only a strong navy had kept Britain secure. Ford dismissed such "historical" argumentation:

> History is more or less bunk. It's tradition. We don't want tradition. We want to live in the present . . . That's the trouble with the world. We're living in *books and history and tradition* . . . The men who are responsible for the present war in Europe know all about history. Yet they brought on the worst war in the world's history.[39]

I mention this anecdote because Ford's main point seems to me correct, and his conflation revealing. The past (let us say) indeed does not speak for itself, much less divulge lessons for all time, and those who think that it does are apt to create problems by failing to understand the unique conditions of each new situation. Likewise, research into the past cannot by its nature (as hypothetical reconstruction) teach lessons uni-directionally. Tradition wants to teach lessons about the past, but we have a right to be skeptical—to think historically.

Having distinguished history from the creation of authoritative narratives I must now concede that the reality is messier. Already in the centuries following Herodotus, writers began to use *historia* for the narratives that were said to result from inquiry, more than for the inquiry itself.[40] By the first century B.C., literary-genre expectations marginalized rigorous investigation as history's hallmark.[41] Whereas the quality of an author's research was not available for scrutiny, the aesthetics and moral tone of the literary product could be examined. So it was easiest to declare all narrations of the past *histories*, and evaluate them by prevailing criteria: fairness (to those who mattered), depth of insight, fineness of analysis, eyewitness credentials, literary balance, dignity, and appropriateness. In the late first century A.D., Josephus poses as a champion of old-fashioned investigative rigor, the rare historian still worthy of the name. He mocks his word-obsessed contemporaries: "they have the gall to label their works *historiai*, though there is nothing sound in them" (*War* 1.7). Preoccupation with style and effect did not go away. A couple of generations later, the satirist Lucian expresses contempt for the nincompoops of his day who claim the prestige of historian

---

39. Wheeler 1916: 10 (emphasis added).

40. Aristotle; Polybius.

41. Dionysius of Halicarnassus (60–7+ B.C.) was a historian and author of a twenty-volume history of Roman antiquity. But study of that work and especially of his critical essays shows that he saw literature mainly as literature, and judged it (even Thucydides) by literary standards.

but merely throw together pretentious nonsense in inflated language (*Hist. conscr.* 1–2, 15, 18–19, 25–26).

In sum, the ancient world saw a shift from the original sense of *historia* as inquiry (into anything) to a new prose genre developed to accommodate research into the human past. Modern popular usage has moved from history as a genre—forgetting the inquiry part almost completely—to the inchoate fusion of an imagined authoritative record with the events themselves. It often attributes the human capacities of mind and will to this fusion. These developments are understandable, but the common perceptions of history are not very useful for anyone attempting to undertake historical work. Although they rarely discuss the foundations of what they do, university departments of history depend on the original notion of history as methodical investigation into the human past, a view reborn in the post-Enlightenment atmosphere of the German research university.

2

Social Scientists and Humanists: Debates among Historians

If most practitioners would agree on this much, profound differences remain with respect to both philosophy and practice. In the history department of a public university, colleagues work across many periods and regions, the modern history of the host country usually being most prominent field. Scholars trained in various countries under doctoral advisors with distinctive approaches, and with their own unique research interests, naturally pursue different sorts of questions: about political and institutional history, prosopography (the careers of prominent figures), economic, military, or religious history, the history of ideas or discourse, a social history dealing with families, women, and slaves. Some may focus for a time on a particularly important (for them) decade, war, popular movement, revolution, or even an individual's career or family's life. Also the practical nature of their work may look quite different. A specialist in modern Britain, America, or Japan might spend her research time in the archives of London, Washington, or Tokyo, whereas the investigator of ancient Rome or Judaea will need to visit archaeological sites, museums, and coin and papyrus collections in scattered locations.

If these were the only differences they could happily coexist. But lurking beneath them are differences of philosophy over which historians have sometimes parted company in a marked manner. This is not the place for a history of history. Detailed accounts are easy to find, many of them illustrated with sizeable excerpts from contributors to the debates.[1] Scouting

1. Among many fine surveys are Collingwood 1994: 14–231; Hale 1967; Iggers 1968; 1997; Bambach 1995: 138–51. Momigliano 1966 is a collection of essays by this master. Stern 1973 and Hughes-Warrington 2008 are sourcebooks with well-chosen excerpts from key thinkers with brief context. Jenkins 1995 offers four lively essays on

a few important fissures and the reasons for them will, however, help to show why I prefer some approaches to others for the study of the eastern Mediterranean under Rome.

Basic questions include the following. What can *knowledge* mean when it comes to the distant past? Is it the same as knowledge of the world around us now, and what do we mean by *that*? How might accepted paths to knowledge in the present—especially observation and reason—function, if they do, when we study the past? What do we mean when we say that one event or thing *causes* another, either in present experience or in the past? Do events occur predictably in keeping with principles or laws, or do they depend on inscrutable individual choices in unrepeatable situations (E.g., Would Nazism or the Final Solution have come about without Hitler?)? What do we mean by social and political and economic *trends*, now and in the past? In what sense were such trends *there* in antiquity, if the ancients did not know about them, or are they a function of modern-observer categories? What kinds of meaning can the past in general, or thinking about the past, generate for us? Another set of problems arises from language, both that of past figures we hope to understand and our own language, when we try to represent the past somehow. Can language be objective, and is objectivity desirable?

Problems of historical understanding are of course part and parcel of those connected with human understanding generally. During the seventeenth and eighteenth centuries many vigorous thinkers began to marginalize the ecclesiastical authorities that had shaped or constricted human understanding for a millennium and a half, cultivating a growing sense of intellectual freedom. Much like their counterparts in the ancient Greek Enlightenment, these men questioned all received wisdom, integrating the rapidly changing views of nature and the cosmos made possible by the rise of science.[2]

---

postmodernist historians and their detractors. Bentley 1997 has thirty-nine compact essays by a range of experts from historiography's ancient beginnings to the present. Bentley's book-length contribution, on history in modern thought and as a university discipline (1997: 395–506), is a gem. Clark 2004 is a nuanced investigation of seminal thinkers. A slim but elegant—and standard—overview is Gilderhus 2010 (7th edition). The difficulty of the philosophical issues connected with history is reflected in such journals as *Clio, History and Theory*, and the *Journal of the Philosophy of History*.

2. Important figures included Francis Bacon (1561–1626), René Descartes (1596–1650), Giambattista Vico (1668–1744), Immanuel Kant (1724–1804), and G. W. F. Hegel (1770–1831). See Bacon 1605, with Collingwood (1994: 269) on the application of Bacon's insights to history; Vico 1990 [1708], 1993 [1699–1707], and (via Pompa) 2002 [1725], with Caponigri 1953; Kant 1881 [1781] and 1950 [1783] (also via Carus 1909); Hegel 1900 [122–1831]; Beiser 2011 and Houlgate 2011 on Hegel and Ranke; McCarney 2000 on Hegel and history. Bentley 1997: 395–506 provides a superb

I mention this because of our natural need to simplify or caricature the insights of great contributors to historical thinking, such as G. W. F. Hegel and Leopold von Ranke. We should always remember the likelihood that we do not understand them well. How could we—given their very different and long past working environments? In my high school history class, when studying standard large-scale views of history (linear, cyclical, etc.), we learned about "Hegel's dialectic," according to which history progressed as one direction met opposition from another (thesis and antithesis), their conflict producing a synthesis that became a new thesis. Although it sounded quite good, when I was finally able to read some of Hegel himself I found it rather alien—and still do. It became clear that his views about the gradual unfolding of absolute spirit among human peoples were intricately connected with the philosophical inclinations of his time, long before there was a Germany, while Napoleon's armies were overrunning Europe, and pantheism was appealing to many thinkers. To understand any such author even minimally would require patient and detailed contextual study.

So the following effort to clarify a few conceptual problems in history is not intended to say much about these thinkers' larger views in their own contexts. I hope that it will not seem like the exercises in sheep and wool classification at my Australian agricultural high school, which required us to identify staples from a pile (superfine, cross-breed, Marino) and toss them in the correct bin.[3] I group some thinkers only to spotlight a particular question of importance for us, not to suggest that this explains the thinker. I quote a few extracts only for a taste of the person's energy and style, to suggest that there is much more worth exploring, for all of us. Health warning: Use of what follows for anything other than its intended purpose may cause lasting conceptual injury.

E. H. Carr, What Is History?

An appealing gateway to some enduring scholarly debates is E. H. Carr's *What Is History?* Comprising the G. M. Trevelyan lectures on history at Cambridge University in 1961, this little book has been reprinted for decades and is still assigned as a basic text.[4] It would be a mistake, however, to see it as a simple manual. Carr begins by acknowledging deep rifts among

---

overview of modern historical thought from its philosophical origins.

3. I was certified hopeless, as also in the compulsory wood- and metalworking classes.

4. Carr 2001 [1961]. For an overview of the book's impact see Evans in pp. ix–xlvi of this (Jubilee) edition.

historians, before turning to fight his corner.⁵ His wit and style attract us to his views, but we should realize that he is taking particular positions in controversial territory.

Carr makes two propositions, for example, that would preclude the sort of investigation I pursued in *HJW*.⁶ First, he considers *social forces* alone to be history's proper object and dismisses any concern with individuals as such:⁷

> But I think we are entitled by convention ... to reserve the word 'history' for the process of inquiry into the past of man *in society* ... The facts of history are ... facts about *the relations of individuals to one another in society* and about *the social forces* which produce from the actions of individuals results often at variance with, and sometimes opposite to, the results which they themselves intended ... What seems to me essential is to recognize in the great man an outstanding individual who is at once a product and *an agent of the historical process, at once the representative and the creator of social forces* which change the shape of the world and the thoughts of men.⁸

Carr thought it acceptable to study selected individuals, then, but only if they embodied *their age* as he saw it—a repackaged legacy of Hegel's idea of an unfolding spirit in history, in which each age *has* an identity. A history of social forces only, however, would not allow us to examine the unique situations and actions of a Gessius Florus, Cestius Gallus, John of Gischala, Josephus, or Simon bar Giora, all crucial individuals of unique aims and actions in my view.

Equally difficult is Carr's view that only what endures from a given age *in retrospect* is truly worthy of historical investigation. Agreeing with J. Burckhardt that history is "the record of *what one age finds worthy of note in another*"⁹—note the similarity to what I have called tradition—he dispenses with so-called *chance events*, on the ground that whatever happened as a result of chance cannot reflect important social forces:

> Just as from the *infinite ocean of facts* the historian selects those which are significant for his purpose, so from the multiplicity of sequences of cause and effect he extracts those, and only those, which are *historically significant*; and the standard of historical

---

5. Carr 2001 [1961]: 3–4.
6. Mason 2016.
7. Carr 2001: 25–49.
8. Carr 2001: 42, 46, 49 (emphasis added).
9. Carr 2001: 49.

significance is his ability to fit them into *his pattern of rational explanation and interpretation*. Other sequences of cause and effect have to be *rejected as accidental* . . . because the sequence itself is irrelevant. The historian can do nothing with it; it is not amenable to *rational interpretation*, and *has no meaning either for the past or the present*. It is true that Cleopatra's nose, or Bajazet's gout, or Alexander's monkey-bite, or Lenin's death, or Robinson's cigarette-smoking,[10] had results. But it makes no sense *as a general proposition* to say that generals lose battles because they are infatuated with beautiful queens, or that wars occur because kings keep pet monkeys, or that people get run over and killed on the roads because they smoke cigarettes.[11]

Although Carr has makes everything sound like pure common sense, this is a position worth pondering: that only events capable of supporting general laws of predictable relations, such as "Wars begin for reasons X, Y, an Z," are truly historical.

Carr illustrates his claim. In a northern industrial town in 1850 England, "a vendor of gingerbread, as the result of some petty dispute, was deliberately kicked to death by an angry mob. Is this a fact of history?" Although we might say "Of course, if it happened," by Carr's criteria for history it cannot be. Writing a century after the event, he allows that it might still *become* historical, but that would only happen if a historian could show why the incident was important for nineteenth-century England. Failing that, it must "relapse into the limbo of *unhistorical facts* about the past"[12]—a paradoxical concept.

Carr's justly famous book is no simple guide, therefore, but a valuable statement nonetheless. It shows that one cannot do history without a view of what history is, and Carr lays out his position with verve. In the process he exposes basic problems of communication. He assumes an "ocean" of existing *facts* from which the historian *selects*, and says that "history means interpretation" of these.[13] But where do we find such ready-made facts to interpret and assemble as history?

10. Carr had used this fictional figure to illustrate chance: a man who leaves his home to buy cigarettes is struck by a car.

11. 2001: 99–100 (emphasis added).

12. 2001: 6 (emphasis added in both quotations); cf. Evans in Carr 2001 (xxxv) in the ironies involved in this choice.

13. 2001: 18. Cf. 24: "The historian starts with a provisional selection of facts."

Facts Anyone?

Speaking of facts leads us to a problem that Carr treats ambiguously. Etymology does not define meaning, but it is worth recalling that English "fact" comes from Latin *factum* (plural *facta*): something "done, given, hence unchangeable." This definition remains implicit in the English word, as when we say "You are entitled to your opinion, not your own facts"—facts being something given for all alike. So let us begin with the idea of facts as things done and no longer changeable, to clarify their possible relevance for history. In opening this question I am assuming our discussion (Chapter 1) of popular views that cannot withstand scrutiny: of history as a collection of facts that are somehow known and fixed.

Most obviously and precisely, we may call everything that has happened, including among humans of the past, facts. All of that is indisputably done and past, and it cannot now be changed. We may be confident in speaking of facts (*facta*) in this way. The central problem of history, however, is that those past actions are not being done now, so that we may observe them, and most have left no trace. Untold billions of things have been done, but knowing that only defines our predicament: If we are interested, how can we possibly recover them? Still, it helps us to keep some clarity in our language if we recognize that history indeed rests on facts in this most basic sense: we want to investigate what was truly done in the past. This is not a naïve quest, for we are making no judgments about problems of representation and perception. We are simply recognizing that people did things, *facta*, and we are permitted to be interested in them.

Second, although most people's actions were washed away like proverbial sandcastles on the beach, we do have some survivals even from the ancient past: literary texts continuously preserved by copying, coins, inscriptions, building sections, pottery, and so on discovered by excavation or chance. When placed on a table, a hoard of such pottery or coins may seem large, but in relation to what once existed it is of course a minuscule trace, not necessarily representative of much beyond its find-spots. It will need interpretation and explanation. Nevertheless, these survivals are also *facta*. Out of the billions of things that were ever done or made, these few have survived long past the animated world that brought them into being. To distinguish them from the countless lost *facta* (situations, intentions, and actions) mentioned above, we might call them artifacts ("made by humans"). In the context of an investigation some of them will become our evidence, or evidentiary facts.

It is worth stressing that whereas both of these kinds of *facta* were real, the only kind that exists now from the past are artifacts. We can and should debate the meaning of each survival, such as the symbols on Herod's Year 4 coins or their date (Year 4 *of what?*), but still they exist. We can debate what Pliny or Tacitus or Josephus meant by a certain phrase, but its existence and the frequency of its occurrence (assuming a largely reliable text) is a fact for all of us alike. We can debate the meaning of Judaism(s), but cannot deny that the Greek word assumed to correspond to it (*Ioudaismos*) was not part of general ancient discussion. We can all be too quick to throw out the baby of factual evidence with the bathwater of interpretations that we reject.

We still possess facts from the past, then, in the sense of these survivals. But now it is up to us to figure out what they mean and how they came into existence. Their meaning has at least two general senses: (a) understanding the thing before our eyes, which involves interpreting the language, structures, themes, and meanings of texts or of inscriptions, coin symbols and legends, papyri, pottery, or partial building remains; and (b) hypothetically *reimagining* the completely lost world of human beings, social interactions, and intentions that produced these survivals. We may subdivide the latter into: (i) the general question about how this coin or text came into being, which every scholar might have an interest in discussing, and (ii) the relevance of this survival for a particular investigation of something, which the thing itself cannot declare. For example, trying to figure out the legends and symbols on Jerusalem's wartime coins is a general question, worth answering for itself; what we might make of that for hypothetical scenarios of groups and interests during the war would depend on the contours (question, assumptions, framework) of a particular investigation into that kind of problem.

Although our hypothetical scenarios (under b) mark the concluding phase of historical research, which we publish in order to bring them into general discussion, neither sort can ever become *facts*, no matter how convinced we may be of them and indeed no matter how widely accepted some of these scenarios may become. They can never transform themselves into *givens* or things simply done, which anyone must recognize in the way that anyone can see the same legend and symbol on a coin. Scenarios are products of our imagination and reasoning.

I admit to being as attracted as anyone to the rejoinder, "Oh please! Everyone knows that there *are basic accepted facts* about the past, for example that Herod ruled from 37 to his death in 4 B.C. or that the three Jewish–Roman wars lasted, respectively, from A.D. 66 to 73, 115 to 117, and 132 to 135." As a student I memorized all these facts, taking them to be secure hooks for hanging all the more debated matters. Since then, however, every single one of these dates has been vigorously disputed, and some of the alternatives appear to be winning (66 [if not 65] to 74, 116–117, 132–136).[14] Since the defining trait of facts is that they are done and unchangeable, these cannot be facts. They are hypothetical constructions, which used to be almost universally accepted, for explaining surviving evidence. As assumptions and questions and angles of vision change, however, new constructions take over—or present a challenge without being widely accepted.

If this is so, then historical inquiry cannot be as Carr describes it: a process of selecting *some facts* from an ocean of them, and then interpreting them and joining up these facts to create history. Carr marginalized, in my view, the fundamental importance of the question that drives an inquiry (below). Other critics have wondered where his criteria would leave those pioneering historians interested in the submerged voices of the past: women, slaves, children, minorities, and outliers. Such people never had the chance to define their ages in their own time; we have only become interested in them because of developments in our ways of thinking, our questions. Even the notion that ages *have* representative voices might seem quaint in our multicultural, upwardly mobile, cosmopolitan and migrant-rich societies.[15]

Further, if we were to stipulate that the social forces of an age were moving in a single direction, how could we understand the agonies faced by political and military leaders making gut-wrenching decisions about war, alliance, or economics?[16] Why did they not simply recognize the spirit of the age and go with it? Carr's fourteen-volume *History of Soviet Russia* also met criticism on such points.[17] I mention him not to offer fresh criticism now but because his lectures, which might be thought to constitute a handbook, are valuable instead because they expose basic fissures among practicing historians.

Carr's outlook puts the spotlight on one basic division in the modern study of history: between a broadly social-scientific and a humanistic trajectory. Shortly before he gave his Cambridge lectures, Fernand Braudel published an essay that established a programmatic distinction between

14. See for example Kokkinos 1998 for revised dates from Herod through his great-grandson Agrippa II; Mahieu 2012 for a still more radical revision of dates in Herod's career and the near aftermath; Mason *HJW* 561–65 for a discussion of scholars' proposals about the date of Masada's fall (hence the notional end of the war).

15. See Gilderhus 2010: 50–69.

16. Isaiah Berlin, Carr's frequent target, was a trenchant critic on this point above all (2002: 18–30; cf. 94–165). E.g., 26: "[A]nyone concerned with human beings is committed to consideration of motives, purposes, choices, the specifically human experience that belongs to human beings uniquely . . ."

17. Carr 1950–1978. Hugh Trevor-Roper objected to Carr's "ruthless dismissal" of those who did not participate, or succeed, in history's ongoing progress. Cf. Evans 1997: 224–33 (227–28); also Evans in Carr 2001: ix–xlvi.

the then-traditional history of political events, great leaders, and their decisions (*l'histoire événementielle*), and the social historian's concern with longer-term conditions of life, shared by all society in its various classes and groups (*l'histoire de la longue durée*), in which individuals and particulars played little role. Braudel saw room for a productive dialectical relationship between the two, each being needed to explain the other, a position I fully support.[18] But in practice historians tend to work in one stream, sometimes harboring suspicions of the other. Because there is more at stake than just one's chosen object of study (events or conditions), and the choice often goes with larger philosophical commitments, it is worth exploring this divide more fully.

To help lay bare some philosophical underpinnings, I shall associate the social-scientific track with "positivism." This comes at some risk because there are few terms more negative than *positivist*, but this is part of my point. We tend to ignore what seemed positive about positivism, and use it now as a term of disdain.[19] But its program had much to do with the origins of social-scientific approaches to history. And the other side of the table may not be happy with the term *historicist*, which I shall apply there for similar reasons.

As soon as we assign more than one thinker to a family we are unavoidably grouping incompatibles, and again readers should take any label as provisional at best. Carr illustrates the problem. I have baptized him into the positivist family, though he mentions positivists only with distaste. That is because he rejects the positivist notion that all facts are equally valuable, given his view (above) that the historian *selects and interprets* those facts that are "on the side of history."[20] Though we must respect his disavowal when we are trying to understand his ideas and reasons, his preoccupation with social forces, predictive laws, societal progress, and humanity in the aggregate, as well as his harsh critique of historians who favor particulars and individual thought, put him at least in the suburbs of positivism.[21]

---

18. Braudel 1958: 725–53 (translated in Stern 1973: 404–29). For the dialectic see Stern 1973: 406–408. 417–19.

19. Cf. S. Schwartz 2011: 210: "Steve Mason may be battled effectively on his own positivistic turf," and 222: "Mason is a straightforward positivistic empiricist." If I can attract these labels, when most others criticize my work for leaning toward post-modernism, they have no stable content.

20. Carr 2001: 2–4.

21. Cf. (historicist) Isaiah Berlin (2002: 20): "Carr is . . . essentially a late positivist, in the tradition of Auguste Comte, Herbert Spencer and H. G. Wells."

History as Social Science: Positivism's Heirs

Perhaps the largest group of working historians today in a standard history department studies societies, groups of various kinds (central and peripheral, ethnic groups and families), economic forces, and typical relationships among these. This kind of history is broadly social and often social-scientific, using types and models formulated across times and places, at least heuristically: to help understand human behavior in particular times and places. It is not much interested in individuals or their thoughts. Rethinking positivist origins might both illuminate the original rationales for such an approach and help restore some useful meaning to the label.

In the early nineteenth century the prestige of natural science, with its rapid advances in human knowledge after breaking out from clerical domination, was making scholars in the humanities nervous. The new type of research- and seminar-based university that was spreading from Berlin, Paris, and Oxbridge had taken bold scientific research to its heart. Broadly speaking, science (German *Wissenschaft*) expected its professors to be conducting original research that would continuously advance human knowledge, in a decisive break from centuries of pointless opinion masquerading as sacred authority. In that heady atmosphere of rapid change in our understanding of the universe, nature, and humanity's place, which often had practical consequences for engineering and medicine, scholars of history, philosophy, and literature were apt to look like useless ornaments. If they continued to recycle tired debates about Plato, Virgil, or Shakespeare, spinning new stories out of old ones and publishing yet more unprovable notions, why should they have a protected place in the research university? Universities wanted from their professors words about real things that made a difference, not words about words.[22] What were humanists, who had for so long dominated the university curriculum, to do now?

The main options appeared to be resistance, which was futile, or accommodation with some new direction. Many scholars in the humanities (now sciences of the mind/spirit: *die Geisteswissenchaften*) began to introduce language and principles that sounded more rigorous and publicly accessible—not issuing from the mind of an unanswerable authority—with methods arguably comparable to those of the sciences. For historians there were various possibilities.

---

22. Ridder-Symoens and Rüegg 1992–2010: 3.3–32. For "words about words" see Berlin 2002: 95.

For the late medieval and modern past, historians sought new evidence, uncontaminated by great social-political authorities, from documentary archives. For the ancient and early medieval past, even better, hard evidence could be extracted from the ground via excavation. The nineteenth century witnessed an explosion of such discovery and the resulting production of magnificent catalogues and reference works that we still use (and update) today. Even in the first decades of rather careless excavation, the most remarkable finds found their way to the museums of colonial powers or the new world through an unregulated trade in antiquities. Over the following century, methods of observation and recording would become highly refined and precise, adding scientific credibility to the method as well as the result. Scholars began with a particular discovery (a site, coin, inscription, or papyrus) and, through the gradual collection, classification, and interpretation of all similar objects, made many generalizations possible.

This kind of historical activity looked much more like other sciences than traditional humanistic research. Archaeology continues to enjoy special prestige today for similar reasons. But what about the great mass of existing "knowledge" and its basis in ancient texts?

Another scientific-seeming option was to work the logical-deductive side of historical knowledge by applying what could seem a more hard-edged, scientific analysis to the *data* of the past, making use of rapid advances in statistics. History might then be as respectable as the (other) sciences, the idea was, if it could dissociate itself from the realm of subjective opinion. A new generation of scientific historians could process its data, reveal its underlying patterns, and even make predictions from these generalizations.

It was in this new spirit that Auguste Comte (1798–1857) introduced "the positive philosophy" in an ambitious work of six volumes.[23] The interest of the Romantic movement of his day in individuals and their unique characters—itself a reaction to the Enlightenment schematization of whole epochs and civilizations—left Comte unimpressed, as did any Hegelian notion of a spirit or mind expressed by a nation or in a given era. Comte tried to develop a coolly scientific method that would hold for all disciplines, and thus place the "human sciences" on the same plane as the natural sciences with respect to the respectable hardness of their knowledge claims.

No matter what we study as academics, Comte argued, we shall never understand objects *per se* (or *in se*)—in their internal selves. We cannot get inside plants, other animals, or even humans. We can study only the observable and typical *relations* among objects, whether plants or animals of all

23. Comte 1830–1842. Comte produced this rapid draft in marathon sessions from a prodigious memory of his lectures. He welcomed Martineau's elegant (if often free) three-volume English condensation (1896 [1853]).

kinds. And we can do this much with confidence, if we use the scientific tools of observation and deduction. It does not matter, then, whether our chosen objects are planets or plants, animals or atoms. Whatever we study, their *relations* become visible to us in the same way, as we classify like with like and see how they behave. For those who know how to do this, such study will yield comparable laws of relations in all fields alike.

Comte divided the existing branches of knowledge in two groups: inorganic (astronomy, physics, and chemistry) and organic (physiology and "social physics"). Mathematics was not a science for him, but rather the indispensable tool undergirding all logic and statistics.[24] History was similar: a supporting discipline that presented no conceptual problems of its own but rather the data for analyzing human societies. History was the record of the past, which needed only to be rescued from boring opinion-blarers and exploited in a scientific way.

What was "positive" about positivism was its vision of large-scale human progress.[25] The mind, in Comte's view, had evolved through three main states: from the ancient or primitive-theological/fictitious (moving from fetishism to polytheism and then monotheism) to the metaphysical or abstract to the scientific or *positive*—in his own happy time:

> In the final, the positive state, the mind has given over the vain search after Absolute notions, the origin and destination of the universe, and the causes of phenomena, and applies itself *to the study of their laws,—that is, their invariable relations of succession and resemblance.* Reasoning and observation, duly combined, are the means of this knowledge.[26]

For Comte, the only respectable sources of knowledge, reason and experience (not faith or tradition), were thus the foundations of human and natural sciences alike. He devoted the latter half of his master-work to *sociology* as the ultimate form of knowledge, because it deals with relations among human groups. Here are representative remarks from his triumphant sixth volume, which reviews human history from this positivist perspective (emphasis added):

> The best way of proving that my principle of social development will ultimately regenerate social science, is to show that it affords *a perfect interpretation* of the past of human society,—at least *in its principal phases* . . . In this department of science, as in

---

24. Martineau 1896: 1.27–30.
25. Cf. Croce on "the positivity of history," 1921: 83–93.
26. Martineau 1896: 1.2. See also Mill 1891: 6.

every other, *the commonest facts are the most important.* In our *search for the laws of society* we shall find that *exceptional events and minute details must be discarded as essentially insignificant*, while science lays hold of *the most general phenomena which everybody is familiar with*, as constituting the basis of ordinary social life . . . Our employment of history in this inquiry, then, must be essentially abstract. It would, in fact, be *history without the names* of men, or even if nations, if it were not necessary to avoid all such puerile affectation.[27]

What kinds of laws could Comte discover in this way? The finale was anti-climactic. He found that bored dissatisfaction (*ennui*), the limited duration of human life, and steady population growth were among the most constant stimuli to progress.[28]

But it was Comte's vision of a scientific way to do history, abandoning a Romantic concern with individuals, that captured others' imaginations and won impressive converts. John Stuart Mill (1806–1873) wrote in tribute: "From this time [the 1860s], any political thinker who fancies himself able to dispense with *a connected view of the great facts of history, as a chain of causes and effects*, must be regarded as below the level of the age."[29] Henry T. Buckle's three-volume *History of Civilization in England* (1857) was an important heir. I mention it partly because J. G. Droysen, whom we shall consider below, would single out Buckle for debate.

Buckle openly lamented that history lagged behind other disciplines, where "the necessity of generalization is universally admitted." Historians were too often people who had merely read "a certain number of books."[30] Even the best of them "are manifestly inferior to the most successful cultivators of physical science." Buckle was committed to advancing the prestige of history, then, and he was sure that he could do it by exposing its "fixed and universal laws."[31]

Buckle thought that the ancient debating chestnut, whether human actions were caused by "the state of the society in which they occur" or by "some capricious and personal principle peculiar to each man, such as

27. Comte 1896: 3.1–5 (emphasis mine). Comte's sixth volume was important enough that, though she condensed the other five into two, Martineau preserved it whole as her third.

28. Comte 1896: 2.299–333. Like many thinkers of the time, Comte would not imitate writers who vaunted their erudition by considering "India and China and others that have not aided the process of human development" (3.2).

29. Mill 1891 [1865]: 86 (emphasis mine).

30. Buckle 1903 [1857]: 1.2, 4.

31. Buckle 1903: 1.7, 6.

free will or the like," could be settled once and for all.[32] Consider actions that we usually attribute to strictly personal motives, such as murder and suicide. These are the most personal decisions imaginable, and we naturally connect them with extreme psychological states (of anger or depression) arising from purely individual situations. If that impression were scientifically valid, Buckle asked, how could it be that the incidence rates for such actions—now reliably countable in municipal records—were remarkably consistent over the years? Indeed, they were much *more* consistent than phenomena we attribute to forces beyond our control, such as the incidence of disease. How could disease fluctuate considerably, while supposedly volitional actions were predictable in frequency?

Buckle concluded that murder and suicide, along with all supposedly "free" actions, must in fact be "determined, not by the temper and wishes of individuals, but by large and general facts, over which individuals can exercise no authority."[33] Individual free will was a doubtful, unnecessary, and entirely unproven tenet.[34] The consequence for historians was that individuals, with their proud ideas and intentions, did not matter much to the development of the human species.

Herbert Spencer (1820–1903), the evolutionary sociologist known for the phrase "survival of the fittest," was an important contributor to the positivist heritage. His article on "The Study of Sociology" opened the inaugural issue of *The Popular Science Monthly* (now *Popular Science*) in 1872. Dismissing old-style histories of monarchs and their ambitions, the stuff of older history, as so much gossip, he declared:

> The only history that is of practical value is, what may be called Descriptive Sociology. And the highest office which the historian can discharge is that of so narrating *the lives of nations* as to furnish materials for a Comparative Sociology, and for the subsequent determination of *the ultimate laws* to which social phenomena conform.[35]

Spencer fiercely attacked the Romantic "great-man" approach, on the ground that no individual is an island. Just as Aristotle could not have come from cannibal parents, so every person is a product of their race and society: "Before he can re-make his society, his society must make him."[36] To study the human past scientifically, therefore, was to remove the names

32. Buckle 1903: 1.22–23.
33. Buckle 1903: 1.24–32 (32).
34. Buckle 1903: 1.9–12.
35. Spencer 1896: v (emphasis mine).
36. Spencer 1896: 31 (emphasis mine).

SOCIAL SCIENTISTS AND HUMANISTS: DEBATES AMONG HISTORIANS 33

and personalities, which are irrelevant to the big movements and relations. Human beings are after all a herd like any other species, in spite of our misplaced conceit.

Whereas Buckle saw evolving intellect as the propeller of change, and Spencer found it in physical evolution, Karl Marx (1818–1883) and Friedrich Engels (1820–1895) famously turned to economic conditions as the real and analyzable drivers of human affairs. Marx's "materialist conception of history" held that the individual's place was determined by economic relationships, which rendered personal thought or intention insignificant. When the impersonal forces of production (of material) and the social relations involved in that production came into conflict, as they inevitably do, the result will be a revolution that moved events forward in steps, ultimately reaching a state of socialism. Socialism would reconcile the means (e.g., mines and factory work) with the relations (capitalists and workers) of production, bringing harmony to the age-old conflict. For Marx, ideology could only ever be a superstructure grounded (consciously or not) in this materially rooted conflict: "It is not the consciousness of men that determines their existence, but, on the contrary, their social existence determines their consciousness . . . *this consciousness must be explained from the contradictions of material life*, from the conflict existing between the social forces of production and the relations of production."[37]

Because he saw the world moving steadily toward that end, Marx's historical interest was in charting it. He identified economic antagonisms that were specific to each period and type of older society: slaves vs. free, patricians vs. plebeians, barons or lords vs. serfs, and recently bourgeois vs. proletariat.[38] Like others of the positivist family, he did not think that history itself presented any serious problems of *knowing*. The familiar historical record, known in the history books, would furnish the competent analyst with material.

The scientific historians who arguably had the greatest impact on the early twentieth century are those we would rather forget about, but I must mention them to show how far this approach to history *could* go. Their ideas were very prominent across the West for the better part of a century. For them, a scientific view of the human race and "races" was the main thing.[39] Race-based histories were for them the perfection of a history finally treated on purely scientific principles. This kind of history was often written by men

---

37. Marx 1904 [1859]: 11–12 (emphasis mine).
38. Marx 1904: 13. Cf. Schätzl 2003: 171.
39. Overviews in Adams 1990.

with natural-science credentials, who openly chided humanist counterparts for being squeamish in the face of nature's facts.[40]

Opposed to notions of an equally shared human evolution and social progress, they believed that only one of the world's four or five principal races was the real driver of progress. This conveniently happened to be their supposed Teutonic–Nordic–Aryan race, which thus needed protection from others. The Frenchman Count Gobineau was among the first to write in this vein (1853): "everything great, noble, and fruitful in the works of man on this earth ... belongs to one family alone, the different branches of which have reigned in all the civilized countries of the universe."[41]

Though we would rather forget about it, this kind of scholarship was all but ubiquitous and growing in confidence through the later nineteenth and early twentieth centuries, among those who considered themselves part of the great race. Even Lord Acton, later to be Regius Professor of Modern History in Cambridge, was sure that Persians, Greeks, Romans, and Germans were "the only makers of history," all others—their "character" unchanged since antiquity—being passive and parasitic.[42] In 1904, the German periodical *Archive for Racial and Social Biology, Including Racial and Social Hygiene* began to cast its light over the benighted world of humanists and theologians. Each issue was packed with contributions from the world's most eminent scientists, anthropologists, and philosophers. One could read about the relative weights of brains and the cephalic (length-to-width) indexes of various races, the Jews—viewed as a racial mixture—always attracting disproportionate attention, given their increasingly problematic position among Europe's nation-states.[43] The forerunner of the American

---

40. Chamberlain 1910: xcvii, 2.200–211; Grant 1916: 7–14, 59, 79, 100. The editors of the *Archiv für Rassen- und Gesellschafts-Biologie* (2 [1905]: foreword) regretted the absence of input from scholars of "the so-called Humanities," attributing this to the latter's lamentable ignorance of natural science and resistance to the flow of "modern thinking," which they hoped would change soon.

41. Gobineau 1915 [1853]: xv. Cf. Chamberlain 1910: lxvi: "all those who from the sixth century onwards appear as genuine shapers of the destinies of mankind ... belong to the Teutonic race."

42. In a disdainful review of a book on the Irish (1862): "Other races possessing a highly developed language, a copious literature, a speculative religion, enjoying luxury and art, attain to a certain pitch of cultivation ... Their existence is either passive, or reactionary and destructive ... The Chinese are a people of this kind ... So the Hindoos ... So the Huns ... So the Slavonians ... To this class of nations also belong the Celts of Gaul. The Roman and the German conquerors have not altered their character [as "authors of advancement"] as it was drawn two thousand years ago" (Dalberg-Acton 1907: 240–41).

43. *Archiv für Rassen- und Gesellschafts-Biologie, einschliesslich Rassen- und Gesellschafts-Hygiene* 2 (1905), 76–85 [degenerative traits in 'isocephalics'], 153–54, 450–51

Popular Science magazine carried many articles on race in its early decades. In the closing years of the nineteenth century, MIT and Harvard Professor William Ripley justified racial anti-semitism in the U.S. on the same basis as that in Germany.[44]

This boldly *scientific* racial history, with a worldwide subscription among the white races, had eugenic implications.[45] The forerunner of the *American Popular Science magazine* carried many articles on race in its early decades (from 1872). The MIT / Harvard professor William Ripley gave a distinguished lecture series in 1896 Boston on the races of Europe, in which he compared American fear of Jewish migration from eastern Europe with its German counterpart.[46] And it was in the *American Journal of Sociology* (1908) that Samuel Z. Batten championed hard-headed eugenics. Considering himself a champion of Christian and civilized values over against the harsh prescriptions of scientists and sociologists for "defectives" now living, Ripley nevertheless believed that social engineering was the only solution: "Modern society, motived by the Christian spirit, and working in a scientific way, must declare that there shall be no unfit and defective members in the state."[47]

The American Madison Grant's 1916 book on *The Great Race* prompted the U.S. Congress to curtail immigration, in order to prevent the degeneration of what Grant called the "native American," by which remarkably he meant the Nordic-Teutonic, master race.[48] Grant was no crackpot, but

---

[reviewing books on Jewish brain weight/size and Jewish income vs. philanthropy—deduced from the response to a flood—as though a racial trait]. The journal's sub-subtitle specified "research into the essence of race and society and their mutual relations, for the biological conditions of their persistence and evolution . . ." The foreword to the second issue (1905), while disavowing political motives, admitted that the editors had accepted methodologically weak contributions if they offered stimulating hypotheses or factually rich material (*anregende Hypothesen oder . . . reiches Tatsachenmaterial*).

44. Ripley 1898–1899: 54, p. 166: "Germany shudders at the dark and threatening cloud of population of the most ignorant and wretched description which overhangs her eastern frontier. Berlin must not, they say, be allowed to become a new Jerusalem. . . . That also is our American problem. This great Polish swamp of miserable human beings . . . threatens to drain itself off into our country as well. . . . "

45. See Adams 1990, with Turda and Weindling 2007: 283–98 on early Zionist interest.

46. Ripley 1899: 166 ("Germany shudders at the dark and threatening cloud of population of the most ignorant and wretched description which overhangs her eastern frontier . . . That also is our American problem. This great Polish swamp of miserable human beings . . . threatens to drain itself off into our country as well, unless we restrict its ingress.")

47. Batten 1908: 242. Cf. Michaud 1908; Nearing 1912.

48. Grant 1936: xxviii, i.e., to "adopt discriminatory and restrictive measures."

Chairman of the New York Zoological Society and a trustee of the Natural History Museum. It was the Professor of Zoology at Columbia University who wrote (without irony) in the preface to his book:

> the author [Grant], never before a historian, has turned this historical sketch in the current of a great biological movement ... The moral tendency of the hereditary interpretation of history is ... in strong accord with the true spirit of the modern eugenics movement in relation to patriotism, namely, the conservation and multiplication for our country of the best spiritual, moral, intellectual, and physical forces of heredity ... certainly more widely and uniformly distributed in some races than in others ... Thus conservation of that race, which has given us the true spirit of Americanism, is not a matter either of racial pride or of racial prejudice; it is ... a true sentiment which is based upon knowledge and the lessons of history.[49]

As a rule of thumb, I suggest again, we should run from anyone who trots out *the lessons of history*.

H. S. Chamberlain was the scion of British military aristocracy, who moved to Germany and married the daughter of the composer Richard Wagner. Chamberlain saw himself as only the humblest scientist and servant of facts.[50] In arguing strenuously that Jesus was not a (racial) Jew, he complained that humanists were stubbornly ignoring the racial realities exposed by science: "To think that at the close of the nineteenth century a professor could still be ignorant that the form of the head and the structure of the brain exercise quite decisive influence upon the form and structure of the thoughts... O Middle Ages! When will your night leave us?"[51] Indeed.

More infamously still, the lavishly illustrated German texts by H. F. Günther became virtual handbooks for helping everyone to identify racial mixtures in European society. Along with their distinctive anatomical and mental-psychic (*seelisch*) characteristics, Günther claimed, each race had a particular gait, repertoire of gestures, and smell.[52] The "science" espoused in many of these places was obviously intuitive, anecdotal, and kitchen-sinkish. It combined real anatomy with gossip, religion, psychology, politics, and moral opprobrium. When the white-coated men of facts could not agree what a race was, where the borders among races lay, or what the supposedly resistant racial traits were, they gave the game away. Those decades

---

49. Grant 1916: vii–ix.
50. Chamberlain 1910: lx–lxi.
51. Chamberlain 1910: 1.210.
52. Günther 1930a, 1930b.

preceding the Nazis' rise to power, were surely the most consequential period of academic bad faith, though hardly the only one, in western history.[53]

Such zealous varieties of *history as science* have run their course in our day.[54] Evolutionary history never recovered from injuries sustained in the First World War, as Europe's most evolved peoples nearly destroyed each other, or from the later political efforts to realize Utopian collectivist theory. The racial strain, we continue to hope, died by 1945.[55]

Few historians today would deny that even our most individual decisions have material, economic, social, and political contexts, or that similar human societies and groups behave in comparable ways when faced with similar circumstances. The more humane branches of the positivist tradition today support historical research in rigorous and extremely productive ways. Their distinctive interest remains, however, in various kinds of collectives and aggregates (societies, classes, trades, families—certainly no longer races), more than in individuals: in data that can be analyzed statistically. Since the world wars nearly everyone accepts that we are dealing with human beings, who deserve some special value as our own, and not with mere herds.

The most enduring contribution of the extended positivist historical family was probably the *Annales* school in late-1920s Strasbourg, later in Paris. These scholars called for a history "from below"—that is, from the perspective of non-elite, ordinary people and their daily lives, also with attention to their shared values and ways of understanding (*mentalités*). What were the conditions in which members of a given society married, raised children, found food and shelter, supported themselves financially, and dealt with illness and death? How did they think about what they were doing? Socially oriented history seems to me the dominant strain in western

---

53. *Archiv* editors came to provide the National Socialists with a respectable-seeming science: Friedlander 1995: 9–11.

54. A late-comer was philosopher of science C. G. Hempel in 1942, who seems to have been blissfully innocent of most preceding debates. He optimistically wished to show "the methodological unity of empirical science" on the premise that history was another "branch of empirical inquiry"; indeed, "general laws have quite analogous functions in history and in the natural sciences" (1942: 35). Cf. Roberts, *Logic*, 1–15.

55. Even racial science did not necessarily advocate genocide. Most often it called for apartheid: segregation and/or the rule of the allegedly inferior races by the superior (Grant). But the belief in ineradicable inequality meant that those deemed not to be fully part of the human family could become expendable under certain conditions. As Chamberlain's book already made clear (1910: 1.116), Europe's Jews were seen as a special case, seen (with remarkable tolerance of self-contradiction) as degenerate and uncreative and yet as terrifying rivals through their supposed domination of capitalism, communism, trades, press, politics, and commerce.

departments of history today.[56] Historians of the modern past can often apply statistics to state records, surveys, and other representative data, to clarify the real conditions of ordinary life in particular times and places: mortality rates, incidence of disease, causes of death, types of employment, diet, and much else.

Many historians in this trajectory would not call themselves by the old-fashioned term positivist, so I should reiterate why I have used this genealogical framework. From Comte onward, positivism was marked by a thesis and ambition, a method, and a technique. The thesis was that human societies were evolving toward a finally positive mentality, free of inhibiting superstitions, fears, and passions. This was embodied in the research itself, which required analysts skilled in logic, mathematics, and statistics. That was because the method, second, was aggregative, dealing with humans in social groups. Only when groups were studied as such could one ascertain types, patterns, and predictive laws. The procedure, therefore, involved the gathering and mainly computational analysis of data. This has become a very sophisticated procedure, especially for modern history. As also in some religious studies departments, fieldwork is the heart of research because it is the only way that investigators can control their data, by understanding the rules of representative sampling and error margins, when it comes to human groups, or establishing strict procedures for the study of material remains.

Whereas positivism took its name from its evolutionary thesis, which did not survive the world wars in its purest form, one might argue that a vaguer notion of scientific progress (in the advancement of civil, personal, and women's rights, marriage equality) are still assumed, along with the scientific aspiration. I am connecting positivism mainly with the aggregative method, which flows directly from the notion of scientific progress. At bottom, humans are another component of nature and capable of being studied in the aggregate and by class, like plants or other animals. Paradoxically, however, the term seems to be most often connected, at least in ancient-historical and religious-studies circles, with the procedure of naïve data collection.

This last has always been the Achilles heel of social approaches to the ancient past. The social sciences depend on the representative nature of their data sampling, and go to great lengths to control that process. How can this be replicated in long-dead societies when we can no longer interview even the famous people who left written legacies, let alone representatives of the groups that interest us most (women, slaves, children, foreign minorities)?

---

56. E.g., Zunz 1985.

On the material side, how can we weld lucky finds from pinpointed locations in France or Jordan into a representative picture of conditions? And where we are fortunate to have some written texts, how are we to use the highly literary and normally sly productions of ancient elite writers to generate countable facts. The serious danger, which one sees in Comte and many of his successors until now, is that analysts will grab whatever "data" they can from any source, riding roughshod over the nature of the thing they are dealing with.

We are seeing, however, ever more resourceful and impressively plausible efforts to analyze Roman-era demographics, natural resources and crops, manufacturing and trade, land yields, slave prices, income levels and purchasing power, education and literacy, patron-client relations, voluntary associations, and other such *longue-durée* conditions.[57] Especially when scholars can come up with ingenious ways of cross-checking estimates, these studies are enormously valuable for all historians.

Some branches of history are more explicitly social-scientific, using sociological methods to deal with types of societies (e.g., hunter-gatherer, pastoral, agrarian, industrial, industrializing), standard groups found within each type, and the typical or predictable relations among them.[58] The study of "ethnicity" in antiquity has taken a decidedly social-scientific turn, scholars being more concerned to define the modern analytical category or "ethnic group"—some using DNA to track ancient group affiliations—than to investigate the use of *ethnos* language in ancient texts as a separate task.[59] For ancient Judaea, Simon Dubnow was a pioneer in the early twentieth century, bringing a sociological approach to Jewish history that included such specific issues as the Pharisee–Sadducee conflict or the significance of Yavneh.[60] Anthony Saldarini sought to explain the place of Pharisees, Scribes, and Sadducees in Judaean society with the aid of Gerhard Lenski's

---

57. E.g., Saller 1982, 1984; Hopkins 1983; Edmondson 1987; Harris 1989; Parkin 1992; Cribiore 2001; Harlow and Laurence 2002; Harland 2003; Scheidel 2004, 2005; Scheidel and Friesen 2009.

58. A classic study is Nolan and Lenski 2015.

59. McInerney 2014: 1–16, esp. 4–8. See further Chapter 2.

60. Dubnow 1903 presents seven periods from the biblical to the enlightened (e.g., 42–45): "The central problem is to unfold the meaning of Jewish history, . . . to state the universal laws and philosophic inferences deducible from the peculiar course of its events" (42). "Our task is to arrive at the laws underlying this growth" (44). Cf. 1958: 336–37 on the "synthetic" task of the historian ("to uncover the organic connections") and 340–41: on national and social antagonisms as the real issue between Pharisees and Sadducees, and on Yavneh as a national and social reorganization (not an academy resulting from any individual's design).

model of the nine classes found in agrarian societies.[61] Albert Baumgarten used the typology of "sect" across the millennia ("a voluntary association of protest") and millenarianism to explore the origins and nature of ancient Pharisees, Sadducees, Essenes, and Qumraners.[62] Seth Schwartz eschewed concerns with what Judaeans of the Hellenistic-Roman period knew to say or think when he investigated the *longue-durée* structures of their societal norms, grounded in group preservation and solidarity, over against the reciprocity standard assumed in Mediterranean cities.[63] Showing a similar concern for broad structural patterns in Jewish-Roman relations, much research into the Judaean War's causes has social-historical or social-scientific tendencies.[64] Even without an investment in hard-core social-science, many scholars assume that long-span socio-economic conditions, or the characteristic ideas of the age (putative messianism or anti-imperialism), rather than individual motives, situations, or actions, were the main drivers of revolt against Rome.[65]

Tessa Rajak's landmark monograph, *Josephus: The Historian and His Society* (1983), provided a bridge from the social-science family to its main, humanist alternative (below). Her book has contributed much to our understanding of the individual Josephus and his particular works, but its (often overlooked) primary concern is social-historical.[66] Rajak declares herself to be mainly interested in groups, models, and typical behaviors, and is reticent about become entangled in one person's oddities. Josephus' perspective is her subject, but he serves mainly as the best-evidenced voice of the "upper echelons of the Palestinian priesthood, an outward looking, flexible group."[67] Rajak's main concern comes forward in such remarks as these:

> Yet we need to be sure that we are not dealing with *one man's highly personal, perhaps eccentric opinions* . . . There is no question of describing the actual outbreak of revolt against Rome in a simple way to the *activities of influential individuals* . . . A scheme of social classification usually *has its exceptions;*

---

61. Saldarini 1988: 37–41.

62. Baumgarten 1997; quotation on p. 7.

63. Schwartz 2010: 1–20.

64. See especially the Marxist analysis by Kreissig 1970: 17–87; 54–55, 73, 80–82, who defines classes in relation to the means of production.

65. Horsley and Hanson 1988; Horsley 2003, 2008; Faulkner 2004. For large-scale ideas and social trends, see Farmer 1973; Rhoads 1976; Hengel 1989.

66. Rajak 1983: 7 (emphasis mine).

67. Rajak 1983: 8; cf. 21, 42.

and upper-class idealists are not a rarity. They are often found among the young . . ."[68]

The militant and prophetic figures in Josephus, in her analysis, fit sociologist Max Weber's "charismatic" type.[69] And she tries to understand the war itself in terms of structure and model, developing Crane Brinton's work on revolutions via Cecil Roth to describe the Judaean Revolt as one of a predictable and repeatable type.[70] In the course of such a systemic analysis, however, she also investigates much of Josephus' unique corpus and makes fundamental contributions to their interpretation (concerning his life and ancestry, his role as propagandist, the lost Aramaic version of his work, and his knowledge of Greek and use of assistants). This is a particularly productive marriage of social and individual history.

History as Humanistic Inquiry: Historicism in Action and Thought

The main alternative to the social-scientific stream in historical research is the trajectory that insists on *historicizing*: looking down from models and typical patterns, irrespective of personal names or specific cases, to the spatially and temporally particular.

This interest in individual characters and lives is ancient. Although Thucydides and Polybius drew out prescriptive patterns in the lives of *poleis*, offering to diagnose their disease or health, they were far from positivism's ambitions or methods and put great stock in the actions of crucial individuals. During the Hellenistic and Roman periods history became ever more biographically focused. Even as individual lives often served as examples of generic virtue or its opposites, they could be portrayed in surprisingly complex and rounded ways, highlighting challenges and tensions that the virtue imperative created in the face of fortune's turns. Josephus' *War* has some of this, especially in the extended opening volume on Herod, while his *Antiquities* is basically history as serial biography. It moves from Moses and Joshua through David, Solomon, and later kings to Alexander and his successors, the Hasmoneans, King Herod, Tiberius, Gaius, Claudius, and Nero's governors—many figures receiving a volume or more of close attention. The whole work departs from the proposition that "more or less everything turns on the wisdom of our law-giver Moses" (1.18). Josephus' own

68. Rajak 1983: 84, 105, 116, 120–21, 129 (emphasis mine).
69. Rajak 1983: 113.
70. Rajak 1983: 126–43.

autobiography thus provides a fitting capstone.[71] He shares the assumptions of Sallust, Livy, Tacitus, and Plutarch about the value of individual lives for important political and moral themes.

The view that history advanced or things happened because important people—kings and queens, popes, and generals—intended them may in this sense be considered a simple and old-fashioned kind of history, though even ancient authors greatly complicated matters by introducing fortune (*tychē*) and the contrary intentions of others.[72] Part and parcel of this view was that the thoughts of the great (nearly always men) were worthy of study, as we see in Josephus' exposition of Moses' thought as foundation for the history (*Ant.* 1.18–26) and in the use of long speeches, in which authors allowed the great to put their best foot forward with incisive perceptions. The history of ideas has always been part of the individual, textual-interpretative, or humanistic stream of history.

Although we should not disregard these ancient roots, the modern humanist trajectory in history was no mere innocent preservation of old prejudices. It was in part a historical expression of the so-called Romantic reaction—across art and literature—against the Enlightenment's rationalist conceit that whole societies and periods could be usefully characterized. More particularly it reacted against the movement to apply the principles of natural science to historical research (above).

I use the English word historicism to capture this historicizing reaction, the turn toward the specific and particular, following the standard rendering of German *Historismus*.[73] Much as with positivism, *Historismus* narrowly refers to a now-dead movement. Even characterizing that movement is a controversial enterprise requiring a knowledge of nineteenth-

---

71. See Mason 2001 for introduction, context, and commentary.

72. For the unsettling role of *tychē* in human affairs, see Polybius 1.1.2, 4.5, 35.2; 39.8.2 [40.12.19]. He therefore denies that Roman success was merely a matter of fortune. It was often in spite of fortune: 1.63.9; cf. 10.2.5, 5.8, 7.3, 9.2–3; cf. Dionyius, *Ant. rom.* 1.7.2. Cf. Eckstein 1995: 254–71.

73. Because Greek and Latin *historia* (verb: *historein*) lack medial c, German, which tends in its borrowings to stay closer to the classical languages, used simply *Historismus*. A classic study of the German historical school is Meinecke 1972 [1936], though it should be read with Iggers 1968 and Beiser 2011a. Pois 1970 shows how different (yet similar) scholars considered "historicist" can be. Popper confused matters by devoting a book to attacking positivist-systemic history as "historicism," which he seems to think he created for that phenomenon, so that his readers would not quibble over terminology (1957: 3–4). "New historicism" complicates matters further, though one can see lines of connection. This is a North American-European movement in the 1980s concerned, in alliance with postmodernism, to demolish hegemonic notions of timeless truths about human nature, and therefore cultural-literary canons, by drawing attention to cultural embeddedness, materiality, and relativism. See Veeser 1989.

SOCIAL SCIENTISTS AND HUMANISTS: DEBATES AMONG HISTORIANS 43

century German philosophy that I do not possess.[74] It would be easy to become tangled up in knots if we tried for a definition that everyone would accept or if we imagined a single pure school called historicism. So let us not do those things.

The men's bathroom in the basement of McMaster's University Hall, when I was a graduate student, sported a stall that some wag had reserved for "Historicists Only." That would be a thin justification for speaking of the ongoing importance of historicism. A better justification is that it remains the most useful umbrella term for an admittedly motley queue, beginning in the nineteenth century, of historians who have (a) rejected the natural-science model, taking generalization as the only valid aim of research, and (b) called for historical investigation to begin from specific cases in unique time-space contexts.[75] These tendencies remain a live alternative to the social-scientific stream. As C. G. Rand put it in 1964, long after the death of *Historismus* proper: "the historian . . . is directed to look upon each person, event, nation, or era as a unique individual . . ."[76]

In its nineteenth-century origins, this approach was no less concerned than positivism with scientific respectability in the modern university. But whereas positivism burnished its credentials by mirroring the natural sciences to explore de-personalized aggregate patterns, quantitative analysis, and predictability, historicism staked its claim on the scientific virtues of precise observation and accounting for detail, ahead of theorizing. For antiquity this proved particularly attractive because evidence had survived only for a few moments and individuals in scattered times and places. Whereas positivists tended to need all such survivals as comparable *data* for their generalizations, even if they found some of these data more telling or useful than others, historicists thought that ignoring the specific nature and limitations of each survival in its context was a betrayal of scientific responsibility. Understanding a particular case might reveal it to be useless for generalizations. Momigliano conveys the spirit of historicism when he writes:

> Every document is the product of a specific situation and tells us something about it. After all, even a word has different meanings when used in different contexts, by different speakers . . . or at different moments. The goal of the historian is to discover the

---

74. See Bambach 1995 and Howard 2000 for influences on German historicism.

75. Hume 1999 is a spirited defense of (archaeo-) historicism as method and Hamilton 2003 treats historicism in an unbroken line from its origins to New Historicism.

76. Rand 1964: 507.

specific situation that allows the placement of a document in its precise context in space and time.[77]

Historicists were not necessarily against generalization, *if* general statements could be supported by a representative range of cases, a condition rarely met. Nor were they uninterested in prevailing ideas or conditions. But in place of the grand ideas of ages or epochs or peoples, they preferred to start from the outlooks and intentions of individuals. Many were *idealists*, then, in the sense that human ideas were their ultimate concern and in the sense that they saw the ancient past existing now only as an *idea*—a construction in the minds of historians. History could not be a matter of observing, reporting, and analyzing real-life data, as the positivists and the social sciences generally assumed. These humanists wanted to recover individuals and their unique circumstances as the best, most stable entry points to the past.

I have suggested that history departments generally favor the social-scientific (even statistical) trajectory of research, particularly in modern fields. That same limited experience suggests that historicist-idealist tendencies are found disproportionately in research on ancient Judaism and Christian origins. Several factors might help to explain that: the special nature of sustained archaeology in the Holy Land, which has made possible stratified narratives of specific locations such as Iotapata, Gamala, Masada, and Caesarea, or old tendencies of classical, biblical, New Testament, and related studies to examine texts in contexts. Scholars' efforts to locate and interpret 2 Maccabees, *Joseph and Aseneth*, Philo, Paul, Josephus, or the Qumran Scrolls' authors, or debates about the varieties of Judaism, voluntary associations, and one's preferred translation of *Ioudaios* (Jew or Judaean) usually reflect typically historicist concerns with locations, the meaning of texts, and contexts.

When we think of modern historians who have insisted on studying particulars, Leopold von Ranke (1795–1886) leaps to mind. Ranke is most often disparaged nowadays, as someone we should not emulate, because of a memorable phrase from his Preface to *Histories of the Latin and Germanic Peoples*.[78] Whereas history since antiquity had been expected to teach timeless lessons, he said, his book would exploit newly researched primary sources to show only *wie es eigentlich gewesen* (usually: "how it really was"). The phrase is now cited as though Ranke advocated a naïve approach. Like the 1950s TV detective Joe Friday (this too is misattributed), he is thought to be asking for "Just the facts, Ma'am." But the distinguished Berlin his-

---

77. Momigliano 1974 in Schwartz 2013: 185.
78. Ranke 2011: 564–565.

torian Ranke was thoroughly familiar with the philosophy of his day after Kant, and with Hegel's philosophy of the unfolding divine spirit embodied in different peoples. He simply disagreed, thinking that Hegel's world spirit "runs counter to the truth of individual consciousness."[79] Historians ought to work from specific evidence, he insisted, trying to encounter and truly understand the deep reality of each separate situation. Even his famous quotation should probably be interpreted this way: *eigentlich* meaning not what *simply* happened, as distinct from interpretation, but rather what *essentially* happened: the heart or essence of an event in the specific consciousness behind it.[80]

Ranke's English contemporary Thomas Carlyle (1795–1881) humorously labeled as *valetism* the view that only collective social forces mattered. In a time when gentlemen had valets, attendants who helped them with the complicated process of dressing for society, he was alluding to the maxim: "No man is a hero to his valet." *Valetism* was thus the notional valet's impression, by this maxim, that at bottom everyone puts his trousers on the same way, and although those outside the household may admire someone as above the common herd, the valet knows better. Carlyle was mocking, in other words, the kind of history that would treat humans as mere members of a herd. According to such a view, he thundered, we are all predictably "selfish Digesting-machines."[81] If the quip about valets had any truth to it, Carlyle said, that was a result of limited imagination:

> the fault is at least as likely to be the valet's as the hero's. For it is certain that to the vulgar eye, few things are wonderful that are not distant. It is difficult to believe that the man, the mere man whom they see ... toiling at their side through the poor jostlings of existence, can be made of finer clay than themselves.[82]

Carlyle was sure that some people *were* made of finer clay. Whereas Hegel or Marx or Carr could envision a great person, but only in the sense that the collective found in this person the embodiment of social forces, mirroring society's own values and crystallizing what it already believed, for Carlyle the great man was the truly unique and indispensable person. Society awaited and *needed* this person, different from themselves, to lead the way. If they did not get him, they suffered. In spite of the obvious class

---

79. Ranke 2011: 276; cf. 203, 251–52.

80. See Iggers 1968: 63–89 (also Bentley 1999: 38–39), and Ranke 2011: 33–36, 82–83 (Iggers' analysis).

81. This is from Carlyle's review of a new edition of Boswell's *Life* of Johnson, in Boynton 1896: 83–84.

82. Of many examples, see Boynton 1896: 2 (on Robert Burns, written in 1828).

bigotry and sexism of such writers, from our perspective today, it is worth reading them for their understanding of history's justification and plausible objects of study.

Carlyle used a sticks-and-fire analogy. Whereas valetism saw everyone as the same kind of stick, some of which would periodically catch fire under natural conditions as their aspirations and ideas took form, Carlyle thought that something entirely other was necessary, which was neither natural nor predictable:

> But I liken common languid Times, with their unbelief, distress, perplexity . . . to dry dead fuel, waiting for the lightning out of Heaven that shall kindle it. The great man, with his free force direct out of God's own hand, is the lightning . . . The dry mouldering sticks are thought to have called him forth . . . Those are critics of small vision [i.e., positivists & co.], I think, who cry 'See, is it not the sticks that made the fire?' No sadder proof can be given by a man of his own littleness than disbelief in great men.[83]

It will come as no surprise that Carlyle, with most others in a time before either most men or any women had voting rights, favored aristocracy over growing demands for democratic participation in government, which he called "swarmery."[84]

Because Carlyle saw society as "the aggregate of all the individual men's Lives who constitute society," history was for him the distillation of "innumerable biographies."[85] This was not mere naïveté or thoughtless preservation of ancient ways. With many post-modernist thinkers, on this point alone, he saw the real past as an impossible, unmanageable chaos of interactions, stimuli, and responses, with no real or intrinsic shape. Since that past had vanished and left hardly a trace, the best that historians could reasonably do was to pool their resources, with each one taking up just one tiny aspect of the whole—a single life in its context—and "aiming at only some picture of the things acted, which picture itself will at best be a poor approximation." Even for a single life, the creation of a plotline with a beginning, middle, and end would be artificial in relation to the lost reality. But it was a start. Any attempt to spell out general causes and effects was doomed

---

83. In Boynton 1896: 166 (emphasis mine). Later, however, those arguing for "covering laws" would use the same analogy to argue that when a spark falls into a wastebasket, under certain predictable conditions, a fire *will* result. Cf. M. White 1965: 15–16; cf. C. Roberts 1996: 96–99; L. Krieger 1968: 1094.

84. E.g., Carlyle 1900–1901: 5.4–7, where he also exhibits the widespread but profound racism of his time.

85. Boynton 1896: 69 ("On History").

by the need, which could never be satisfied, to understand each particular in its full complexity:

> Actual events are nowise so simply related to each other as parent and offspring are; every single event is the offspring not of one, but of all other events, prior or contemporaneous, and will in its turn combine with all others to give birth to new: it is an ever-living, ever-working Chaos of Being, wherein shape after shape bodies itself forth from innumerable elements.[86]

Carlyle's approach to history was based on a certain intellectual humility—leaving aside the social bigotry—that linked him with Ranke. Whereas the social scientists had shown their caution in not pretending to understand the essence of things in themselves but confining their investigation to external relations and patterns, Ranke and Carlyle showed theirs in rejecting claims to large-scale social understanding. The historian's business cannot be to recover laws, Carlyle thought, but only to learn (and unlearn) whatever was necessary to place himself authentically in the world of his chosen human subject(s), to re-enact in the imagination something significant of that person's thought and existence.[87]

Johann Gustav Droysen (1808–1884) is of interest because his work was highly influential and, for us, because his acute critique of Buckle gets to some central issues. Droysen had no doubt that history was a science (*Wissenschaft*), but rejected the assumption that *natural* science offered the only model. History's material is simply different, and so there is no point trying to make it resemble natural science.[88] Historians cannot begin with facts observed in front of us and seek to explain them, but must instead set out from some formulated *problem* (*die historische Frage*) about the lost past. Only an inquiry into a problem will enable us to spot potential evidence and, in the best case, allow us to create a plausible picture of the lost reality. Without inquiry, evidence does not even declare itself to *be* evidence, let alone tell us what it might mean in relation to our problem.[89]

Droysen could sound like Hegel when he said that history was humanity's consciousness or knowledge of itself. Anticipating sociology, he

---

86. Boynton 1896: 72.

87. Boynton 1896: 82–83 (speaking of Samuel Johnson).

88. Given the number of German editions and translations of Droysen's *Outline* with different pagination, and his own use of paragraph numbers, I cite the latter instead of page reference. The 1893 English translation I have used claims to be based on the third German edition (1881), which I have not been able to see. Even paragraph numbers can cause problems. Those of the second German edition (1875), which I could consult, depart from the English towards the end.

89. Droysen 1893: §§8, 5, 20.

also recommended the use of statistics for the study of civilizations. But he believed that individual "acts of will" (*Willensacte*) were the most important drivers of events, comparable to cells in organic matter—where the real action takes place.[90] Like Carlyle, he assumed that nearly everyone is trapped in a world of daily work and survival. Only exceptional individuals are able to break out of this, to actualize the truly free will needed to produce independent thoughts and move things forward.[91] Droysen's first major work was thus a *History of Alexander the Great* (1833), which fused history with biography. His later multi-volume *History of Prussian Politics* (1855–1886) was also largely biographical, treating key figures in detail.

Droysen's emphasis on the individual is especially clear in his review of Buckle, which he entitled "The Elevation of History to the Level of a Science."[92] There he points out that until recently it was the "sciences" of theology and philosophy that dominated both history *and* natural science. Now that natural science is in the ascendant and enjoying prestige, Buckle wants to assimilate history to *it*. But why? "Is there only one way, one method of knowing? Are not the methods different and varied, each according to its objects of study?" Forcing all sciences to adopt the method of the natural sciences, Droysen offers, would be like trying to smell with the hands.[93] Why not let each scientific discipline go its own way, according to the nature of its material and logic?

Buckle must never have thought about what it could really mean to apply "empiricist" principles to history, Droysen charges, for if he had done:

> He would have had to realize that not past events, not the infinite confusion of 'facts' (*Thatsachen*) which constituted them, now lie before us as materials for investigation; that instead these facts vanished forever with the moment to which they belonged, and that we in the human way have only the here and now, albeit with the motive and capacity to develop the ephemeral point [of study] in unlimited ways by applying learning, insight, and will.[94]

Moreover, given that "everything is accessible to our understanding, from the least significant love story to the great affairs of state, from the solitary spirit-work of the poet or thinker to the immeasurable combinations

---

90. Droysen 1893: §§74, 83, 86, 53, 72, 77.
91. Droysen 1893: §§75, 79.
92. Droysen 1893: 61–89. I switch here to page numbers.
93. Droysen 1893: 68–69 (here my translation; 1875: 47).
94. Droysen 1893: 71 (partly my translation, influenced by 1875: 49).

SOCIAL SCIENTISTS AND HUMANISTS: DEBATES AMONG HISTORIANS 49

of world commerce," Buckle's effort to abstract large-scale scientific laws misses the point.[95]

Droysen offers the sixteenth-century artist Raphael as an example. Suppose (on Buckle-like assumptions) that Raphael himself was of little consequence for history, because everything he was and did he shared with his environment: his education, artistic materials, and influences from other artists. He was generic in this sense. But, Droysen asked, how would this common stock explain anything important about Raphael, such as his world-famous painting of the Sistene Madonna, so widely admired as an enduring contribution to the human spirit?[96] Obviously, it was his unique genius that distinguished him from most people and allowed him to make his singular contributions.

Stipulate, Droysen conceded to historical calculation, that a human life might be expressed by the formula $\alpha + x$, where α is everything contributed by one's environment and x is the unique sphere of the individual. Stipulate even that x is "vanishingly small" by comparison with α. The positivists claim on this basis that α alone is worth discussing in respectable history, as in Buckle's use of generic and predictable murder, suicide, and childbirth rates, which have nothing to do with individual thoughts or motives. Droysen insists, by contrast, that no person who has been involved in childbirth or murder or suicide ever saw things in such terms. Rather, "the vanishingly small x is of immeasurable weight, . . . it embraces the entire moral value—that is, the entire and sole value—of the human being."[97] His historicizing is also the humanizing of history over against social-scientific assimilation of humanity to the status of all other natural phenomena.

Another famous historicist made similar points from a more markedly idea-driven perspective. The philosopher Benedetto Croce (1866–1952) was Mussolini's long-lived nemesis. Croce was an avowed Hegelian idealist, who did not think one could separate ideas from the study of the past. For him, history was philosophy incarnate or at least clothed.[98] In his view, people first think and then act to express their thoughts. History is the study of their actions in order to recover their thoughts. Croce would have agreed with Carr that "the history of the world does not depend . . . upon such accidents as the length of Cleopatra's nose, or upon anecdotes."[99] But

---

95. Droysen 1893: 77.

96. A large oil-on-canvas (265 x 196 cm) from 1512, now in Dresden's Gemäldegalerie Alte Meister.

97. Droysen 1893: 78.

98. Croce 1921: 83.

99. Croce 1921: 101.

what scientist-historians failed to see, he thought with Ranke, was that the alternative to accidentalism was not large-scale social forces but the ideas of individuals. Convinced that individuals alone were capable of producing ideas, Croce was baffled that some historians could be interested only in the mentality of an age:

> [T]here must be no talking (save metaphorically) of the wisdom of the Idea and of the folly or illusion of individuals . . . [T]he question which has been for some time discussed, whether history be the history of 'masses' or of 'individuals,' would be laughable in its very enunciation, if we were to understand by 'mass' what the word implies, a complex of individuals . . . Let him who cuts individuals out of history but pay close attention and he will perceive that either he has not cut them out at all, as he imagined, or he has cut out with them history itself.[100]

Again, historicizing idealists agreed with Comte that we cannot know past events in themselves. All we *can* know as human beings, they insisted, is the mind and its products in thought. So also R. G. Collingwood, who worked first as an ancient historian and archaeologist before taking up Oxford's distinguished Waynflete Professorship in Metaphysical Philosophy in the years before his early death in 1943:

> History, then, is not, as it has so often been mis-described, a story of successive events or an account of change. *Unlike the natural scientist*, the historian is not concerned with events as such at all. He is only concerned with those events which are *the outward expression of thoughts*, and is only concerned with these in so far as they express thoughts. At bottom, he is *concerned with thoughts alone*; with their outward expression as events he is concerned only by the way, in so far as these reveal to him the thoughts of which he is in search.[101]

Whereas social-scientific historians looked at Josephus as representative of a class or type, and pre-war social conditions as instances of larger conditions, a historicizing approach would examine Josephus as distinct in viewpoint from his priest-aristocrat colleague Eleazar ben Ananias (apparent founder of the Zealot party) just as it distinguished Cicero from Pompey, and Brutus from Julius Caesar, though members of the same class at the same time. Since they behaved very differently, and their choices had important consequences, it seems pointless to study them only as groups

---

100. Croce 1921: respectively 103, 105–6, 107.
101. Collingwood 1994: 217 (my emphasis).

SOCIAL SCIENTISTS AND HUMANISTS: DEBATES AMONG HISTORIANS   51

and posit group-level patterns for their behavior. In some senses their individual characters, intentions, and decisions drove events.

Whereas positivists hoped to tame the chaos of the past, as scientists brought the chaos of nature to ordered principles, historicists embraced the mess and were suspicious of large-scale explanations. They devoted their energies to figuring out who did what to whom, when, and why, specifically. Details mattered.

If social-scientific history is vulnerable on the question of deciding which data are *historical* on the criteria of large-scale social forces, supposedly age-defining movements, or even fitting models, historicists also invite criticism for what they prefer to ignore: not only the larger conditions that undoubtedly affect us all, but even in individual cases. For Croce and Collingwood, human motives other than thought or ideas are beneath the dignity of history's attention. The historian has no interest in a subject's eating, sleeping, love-making, impulses, or desires *because* they offer no recoverable thought.[102] But if that were so, what should we think about all the events in the social, economic, religious, and political spheres that seem to have come about because of injured pride, greed, and/or sexual desire? Have no modern wars been waged because of emotion? Have no presidencies been shaped by sexual liaisons, no governments brought down or economies brought to the edge by greed or other scandal? The Achaeans' effort to recover Helen of Sparta/Troy in Homer or the affairs of Caesar and Antony with Cleopatra VII of Egypt seem already to put these assumptions in doubt.

That brings us back to Cleopatra's nose, which strangely keeps popping up. Standing for the queen's alleged beauty, the famous nose has become a sort of football, kicked around as a choice example of something truly unique—but accidental and trivial. Blaise Pascal (1623–1662) may have put this ball in motion when he said, anticipating and rejecting the idealists' exclusion of accident:

> He who would thoroughly know the vanity of man, has only to consider the causes and effects of love. The cause is a *je ne sais quoi*—an indefinable trifle; the effects are terrible. Yet this indescribable something, so intangible that one cannot describe, sets the whole earth—princes, armies, multitudes—in motion. If the nose of Cleopatra had been a little shorter, it would have changed the history of the world.[103]

---

102. Collingwood 1994: 216.
103. Pascal (under "Detached moral thoughts" xlvi) 1846: 143.

We have seen that Carr and Croce, from very different perspectives, agreed that the famed sniffer caused nothing worthy or even susceptible of historical study. But J. B. Bury used the same nose to develop a theory of historical contingency. He suggested a category of nose-related events that may be subject to yet unknown laws.[104] At any rate, the more we learn of mind-body connections, the more implausible it seems to follow Croce and Collingwood in separating some pure *thought* from all other human motives.

On the perennial philosophical conundrum of determinism or fate and free will, we have seen that social-scientific history decidedly favors the former. Social sciences rest on the premise that humans act according to type, at both personal (psychological) and group (sociological, anthropological) levels, under certain conditions. Historicism by its nature rests on the premise of human freedom. Individuals are worth studying because they are free to think and act. Isaiah Berlin's 1953 lecture-essay "Historical Inevitability,"[105] opposing positivism, is among the clearest statements.

Given their assumptions about freedom of individual action driven by thought, historicists are reluctant to speak of *causes* in any sense that would sound mechanical or law-like. Even on idealist assumptions, where action comes from thought, nothing truly *causes* the thinker, let alone others, to act in a particular way. Collingwood sees causation more in the way of chess moves. What might be said to cause the other player's moves in fact "only creates a situation in which he exercises his freedom and intelligence" under the conditions your move created.[106] Actions create stimuli for others, but whether and how the other responds remain their choice. So the past reveals no straightforward cause and effect, comparable to flipping a switch and turning on a light. We saw this also with Carlyle's emphasis on the tangled mass of stimuli that prod us to action. But idealists such as Collingwood still focus on the chosen idea or intention: "the historian is not concerned with *events* as such but with actions, i.e. events brought about *by the will and expressing the thought of a free and intelligent agent.*"[107]

When it comes to such complex events as wars, however, which involve vast numbers of individuals with competing claims, thoughts, and aims, the notion that actions proceed directly from someone's thought seems to face insurmountable problems. Michael Oakeshott finds this consideration "fatal to any serious claim of such an historical enquiry to be concerned with

---

104. Goldstein 1977. She charges Collingwood with misinterpreting Bury (902–3).
105. Berlin 2002: 94–165.
106. Collingwood 1994: 474–75.
107. Collingwood 1994: 178 (emphasis mine).

causal relationships,"[108] a radical-seeming proposal, which follows logically from idealist-historicist foundations and marks the final separation from social-scientific concern with precisely such predictable cause and effect. Oakeshott rejects a common assumption that historians earn their keep *by* identifying the true causes of events.

The shortfall between thoughts or intentions and actions need not prevent the historian, I would suggest, from seeking to understand individual intentions in particular circumstances. In studying the Allies' entry into the Second World War, it is surely illuminating to examine the various outlooks, aims, and intentions of Russian, British, and American political and military leaders.[109] This is not because their various individual intentions were fulfilled. On the contrary, they are worth studying because they may offer one of the most securely recoverable dimensions of the past. And once we have an idea of their thoughts, the shortfall between what they wanted and what happened, whether from conscious compromise with others or from unexpected changes in working conditions and evolving goals, provides a fascinating and deeply human way of engaging the past.

I have suggested that ancient Judaism and Christian origins has proven a field congenial for research on individual figures, texts, and situations. Study of the Judaean War, by contrast, has been mainly of the systemic-social or large-scale idea kind (above). Few studies of the war give much weight to such individuals such as John of Gischala, Simon bar Giora, Gessius Florus, Cestius Gallus, or Titus, or such groups as the Zealots.[110] Stephen Dyson's article on revolts under Rome, though written from a largely social-scientific perspective, does draw attention to "the importance of the single leader who to the outsider seems to crystallize and dominate the uprising . . . we are dealing with much stronger leaders than normally would appear."[111] His formulation leaves it an intriguing question whether that crucial individual is a more or less necessary product of the spirit of the time (Hegel, Comte, Marx) or *sui generis* (Carlyle, Droysen). My *HJW* tries to give due consideration to particular situations and individuals, from Cestius Gallus to Agrippa II and Josephus.

---

108. Oakeshott 1999: 95.

109. Roberts 2008 is a particularly insightful study, exploiting diaries to recover the very different outlooks of the individuals working for President Roosevelt and Prime Minister Churchill in planning Allied campaigns. Hastings 2009 examines frustrations of intention and aspiration on every side, not least Churchill's.

110. E.g., Rappaport 1982, 2013; Roth 1960; Michel 1968; Fuks 1985/1988; Bar-Kochva 1976; Gichon 1981; Jones 1989.

111. Dyson 1971: 270–71.

"A plague o' both your houses": Ironic-Tragic History

The problem of causes leads to our last family, which is the least amenable to being called a family at all, though it shows enough of a resemblance for our schematic purposes. When Napoleon III launched the Franco–Prussian War in 1870, apparently from his fear of the increasingly powerful German states next door, he precipitated something that he surely did not intend: a united and more potent Germany under Kaiser Wilhelm (1871). A participant and later historian, Field Marshall Helmuth von Moltke, reflected: "The great wars of recent times have been declared against the wish and will of the reigning powers ... To-day the question is not so much whether a nation is strong enough to make war, as whether its Government is powerful enough to prevent war."[112]

This is a paradoxical thought. Since the time of Homer, warfare has been a rich source of ironic-tragic reflection, especially among its combatants. Could it be that, when it comes to understanding what actually happened in many or most armed conflicts, we are thrown back on fortune or chance, which mocks the human designs that set the conflict in motion?

British historian A. J. P. Taylor championed such a view of nearly all modern conflicts. He seems to have enjoyed overturning the philosophers' tables in history's courtyard.[113] He argued, for example, that the First World War happened precisely *because* no one wanted it, at the time anyway. It was the sheer weight of the instruments designed to prevent war that produced such a calamitous conflict. Once it was underway, the more determined leaders became to end it by throwing everything into "the knockout blow," the more protracted it became. Politicians and generals became tragic figures, driving with futile energy against the unstoppable forces they had unleashed.

His fascination with individuals and specific contexts makes Taylor a historicist, and given his deep interest in actors' intentions we might call him an idealist. He leaves the company of Croce and Collingwood, however, when he completely severs any link between thought or intention and resulting action. To those who insist on knowing the "causes" of the First World War, Taylor offers a surprising buffet of the assassinated Austrian

---

112. Moltke 1907: 1–2.

113. See the introduction to Taylor 1979, surveying the origins of modern wars. He concludes that most acts of aggression that began wars were intended as purely defensive moves: "many of the European wars were started by a threatened Power which had nothing to gain by war and much to lose" (15). See further Chapter 7 on the origins of the Judaean War.

Archduke's love for his wife, European railway timetables, and the strategic plan of a dead German general.[114] He reflects more generally: "Men are reluctant to believe that great events have small causes. Therefore, once the Great War started, they were convinced that it must be the outcome of profound forces. It is hard to discover these when we examine the details. Nowhere was there conscious determination to provoke a war... the statesmen became the prisoners of their own weapons."[115]

The lead article in the *Chicago Daily Tribune* on the day after Archduke Ferdinand's assassination in Sarajevo supports Taylor's view, in real time showing that what followed was hardly obvious or necessary. The newspaper editors hoped that the removal of a hated royal and allegedly grasping wife, unpleasant though the business was, had finally done away with a major irritant and secured Europe's peace.[116]

Among ancient writers, Polybius' programmatic emphasis on chance (*tychē*) anticipated Taylor by two millennia. Polybius everywhere underscores the undoing of human designs by chance. *Tychē* is not merely capricious, however. She deliberately undoes people just at their moment of apparent success and especially after military victories.[117] The Romans learn this repeatedly as their careful military plans are dashed, by weather or other uncontrollable events. What is most admirable about the Romans for Polybius is that they have proven uniquely capable of overcoming chance's reversals because of their indomitable character and discipline, which are reflected in their uniquely effective constitution.[118] He sees the value of a "pragmatic" history such as his in the help it can offer statesmen "to bear nobly the reversals of chance" (1.1.2), learning equally from Rome and from those who have dealt with her growing empire.

More than two centuries before Jerusalem's fall, Polybius described Rome's destruction of Corinth (146 B.C.). As a proud Greek he showed sympathy for his defeated people and an understanding of their old regional conflicts, which had brought in Rome's fateful medicine. Nevertheless, he

---

114. Taylor 2009 [1963]: 13–20. The irony is redoubled in Zuber 2002, which argues that the Schlieffen Plan, cited by Taylor cited as a constraint on any German decision to mobilize against Russia (given its defensive pact with France), did not actually exist; it was invented by the general staff *post factum* to conceal their lack of planning. On rail timetables see Stevenson 1999.

115. Taylor 2009: 16, 255.

116. [Anonymous] Ex-Attaché 1914.

117. E.g., Polybius 1.4.5; 1.35–37 (NB: 1.37.9–10), 39.3–9, 45.14, 48, 50–52, 54–55, 59.4, 61–62, 74.7–8, 87.1; 2.3.3–5; 39.8.2 (40.12.19). Cf. Shorey 1921; Walbank 1972: 60–65; Eckstein 1995: 254–71.

118. Polybius 1.63.9.

condemned the Greek leaders who brought Corinth to such a disastrous end.[119] Older scholarship tended to seek system-level causes for Achaea's conflict with Rome: class revolt in Greece, pro- and anti-Roman factions, or Roman imperialism's relentless march. After reviewing these possibilities, Erich Gruen writes in a Polybian-Taylorian vein: "It is natural to seek rational explanations, whether in social discontents, ideological motivation, or political competition . . . But the event itself mocks reconstructions that assume calculated plans or deliberate provocation . . . [H]istorical events, even those of major consequence, are not always fashioned by purposeful design. Accident and chance have received less than their due."[120]

Compare Josephus, discussing coastal Caesarea's role in igniting the Judaean War (*War* 2.285): "Given the magnitude of the calamities that arose from [the war], it did not have a worthy justification." I call this approach tragic because it breaks with positivism and historicism alike in recognizing the futility of trying to explain events, which are always the intersection of innumerable conscious and unconscious developments, in a purely rational way. The tragedy is ironic because we can see the end result of the events, as those at the time could not. They presumably acted in ways that seemed sensible, even if they were creating disaster.

Fortunately, we do not need a theory of how things *actually work* to undertake historical investigation. I close this review of historians' debates with wise words from Marc Bloch, co-founder of the *Annales* school, who would die a victim of the Gestapo in 1944. Like his colleague Braudel (above), Bloch recognized that: "The word [history] places no *a priori* prohibitions in the path of inquiry, which may turn at will toward either the individual or the social, toward momentary convulsions or the most lasting developments. It comprises in itself no credo; it commits us, according to its original meaning, to nothing more than 'inquiry.'"[121]

---

119. Unfortunately his Book 37, which described the war's origins, is virtually lost; the derivative account in Pausanias (7.12–16) is the key source.

120. Gruen 1976: 46. See also Harris 1985: 240–44; Fuks 1970; Gruen 1984: 520–28; Green 1990: 447–52; Walbank 2002: 269–71.

121. Bloch 1992 [1954]: 17.

3

Special Problems in the History of Ancient Judaea

A final source of confusion about history's meaning is the unique range of academic contexts in which Roman Judaea is studied. Historians of Athens or Sparta, or of Roman Egypt, Syria, Gaul, or Britain share much the same training, terminology, and criteria. They may well move from one sub-area to another. Scholars come to Roman Judaea, however, from much more varied backgrounds: religious studies, Jewish studies, theology, biblical, post-biblical, New Testament, rabbinic, or Near Eastern studies, or "biblical" archaeology. One can see this in the publication outlets, which are rarely journals of ancient history or Classics but mainly books and periodicals in these fields.

Space does not allow us to excavate the academic origins of this situation. It owes something to theology's ancient claims on subjects related to biblical studies, a heritage preserved in Europe, something to the status of Classics and Ancient History in quasi-secular western universities, and something to the particular scene in North America, where universities created religious-studies and Jewish-studies departments or programs in the 1960s and 70s, having left theology to seminaries or church-related universities.[1] The result, in any case, is that scholars in the field come from an unusually diverse range of educational backgrounds and frameworks. Most would not, I suspect, identify themselves as historians first of all, even if they would include history among their methods and insist that it be done properly. Many would consider themselves students of religion first, or text or literature people, or philologists. Without daily involvement in courses,

---

1. Cf. Rashdall 2010 [1895]: 1.3–22; Rüegg in Ridder-Symoens and Rüegg 1992–2010: 3.22–23, 420–28.

seminars, and supervisions devoted explicitly to history, the expectation of teaching historical method, or regular forums on history and the historian's craft, it stands to reason that scholars in this field will differ even more than their counterparts in the history department, not only in their conceptions of history but in their use of language.

Anyone familiar with scholarship on Roman Judaea will, I suspect, recognize the following peculiarities of our field: (1) the unique prestige of archaeology; (2) the extraordinary importance placed on one literary source—Josephus; (3) certain conceptual and terminological idiosyncrasies, deriving partly from the influence of biblical studies; (4) a marked tendency to form polemical camps; (5) the field's uniquely broad constituency at both professional and popular levels.

On the last point: working in a Canadian university department alongside historians of ancient Athens and Rome, it took me years to realize that they did not have the ongoing email and postal interactions with the public that were part of my life, as doctors, lawyers, and business people fulfilled their real passion and sent me their manuscripts on some aspect of the first century. Although there is undoubtedly a large market for documentaries and films on the classical world, and internet gamers or military re-enacters can be dedicated consumers, it is hard to imagine a parallel to the huge constituencies, especially in North America, for research on ancient Judaism and Christian origins. The scale is clear from the hundreds of thousands who pay to attend museum exhibits or public lectures on the Dead Sea Scrolls, and when television series, documentaries, and periodicals find the same large audiences.[2] This unique public, with which we need to communicate effectively about "historical facts," adds a complexity to the already diverse use of language among professionals.

As for the first two factors, archaeology and Josephus have become a sort of tag-team in the study of Roman Judaea, and they can wrestle history right out of the ring. It can seem that there is no need for history, that is to say, when these two conspire. If Josephus tells a story, and we can check him with archaeology, or archaeology turns up something that Josephus

---

2. In email Risa Levitt Kohn, curator of the North American Scrolls exhibits, gives the round figures of 400,000 for San Diego 2007 and between 150,000 and 330,000 for other American cities. The Royal Ontario Museum in Toronto had "an extraordinary" 331,500 visitors to its Scrolls exhibit in 2009–2010 (p. 9 of http://www.rom.on.ca/sites/default/files/imce/annual_report2010.pdf). Mladen Popović reports about 140,000 visitors to the 2013 Scrolls exhibit he hosted in Assen (pop. 67,400). *The Naked Archaeologist* TV series ran for three seasons between 2005 and 2010. It did not follow excavations as such and most of its topics were broadly historical: https://en.wikipedia.org/wiki/The_Naked_Archaeologist.

explains, what more is there to say? If Josephus and archaeology confirm each other, the thinking goes, one can be fairly sure of what happened.[3]

Where history is recognized as "a thing," it is often restricted to the study of *literary accounts*, and most often that means effectively Josephus.[4] Historians are seen from this view as "text people," who are happy to spend their days pondering stories, while archaeologists reconstruct the real past from material remains. They consult what are called "the historical sources" (= literary texts) for orientation, and incorporate them in various ways with their excavation work.[5]

The impression that historians study elite texts would come as a surprise to historians in other fields, where for a good century they have focused on the lives of ordinary people. Already in 1921, the great ancient historian Ulrich Wilamowitz-Moellendorff concluded a survey of the field by saying: "research of this kind entails a descent to the masses from the rarefied atmosphere of polite society in an effort to understand unliterary, irrational, unsophisticated humanity."[6] This was just as the social-historical *Annales* school was taking shape in France. When historians are seen as text people, and contrasted with the real-life explorers of the sunkissed science, the comparison makes history look rather anemic.[7] The popular cachet of archaeology is clear from popular films and from the success of the Biblical

---

3. The subtitle of a chapter in Meyers 1999: 109–22 ("Archaeology and Josephus") is telling. The same dialectic (interpreting archaeology by Josephus and vice versa) appears frequently: Yadin 1966, Broshi 1982: 379–84; Cohen 1982: 385–405; Avigad 1983; ben Zeev 1993: 215–34; Rappaport 1994: 279–89. The related question about whether or not Josephus is "reliable" likewise short-circuits historical inquiry as I am presenting it. Occasional criticism of this common framework (Moehring 1984; McLaren 1998: 178–218, 226–36; Mason 2009: 103–37) has had little impact outside academic circles.

4. Leon 1960: 1–45 and Kadman 1960 devote chapters to "the historical record / background," which summarize the literary accounts before they turn to their main, material evidence.

5. Often Josephus' narrative is taken as a baseline, as in the most prominent archaeological work on Masada. A complete break is rare, as in Goldfus et al. 2016.

6. Wilamowitz-Moellendorff 1982: 177.

7. So Magness (2002: 4–5): "although both archaeologists and historians study the past, they use different methods or sources to obtain their information. Archaeologists learn about the past through the study of the material remains left by humans, whereas historians study written records (texts)." Zunz (1985: 3–10) likewise describes history as commonly practiced—i.e., social history—in a way that sounds very similar to Magness' description of archaeology. Oxford University reverses Magness' categories by distinguishing "Classical languages and literature" from "ancient history and classical archaeology" as two streams within Classics and Ancient History—history there falling decisively on the material side. This fits with the general tendency of history in the past two centuries to undermine familiar texts by seeking out "hard" archival, documentary, and material evidence.

Archaeological Society's admirable flagship periodical and packed conferences for nonspecialists.[8] In our fields, history often seems to be a guest in a house that archaeology built.

I do not say this in criticism of archaeology, of course. Its contributions to the history of Roman Judaea are fundamental, and its popular regard well earned. Archaeology holds out the hope, justified by experience, of a spectacular discovery with each new dig. Problems arise only if it is thought to call the real past to life, whole and immediate before our eyes: Lazarus emerging from the tomb and hungry for dinner. As exciting as archaeological discovery can be, this expectation is a mirage. Even relatively intact discoveries do not explain themselves or declare their meaning, and most are fragmentary. Like texts, all of them require interpretation and explanation.

Another factor in archaeology's prestige is the political import of material culture. A modern state's investment in its ancient past is hardly unusual, as Egypt, Greece, and Italy but also Britain and Germany show in devoting resources to preserving their classical sites. Having been founded in 1948 amidst controversy, the modern State of Israel has a particularly compelling motive to invest in archaeology, and many excavations (Jerusalem, Masada, Caesarea, Gamala, Yodfat/Iotapata) are now prominent national parks.[9]

The problem with the Josephus–archaeology pair bond is that it bypasses the problem of history. We could not speak in the same way of Roman archaeology plus Livy or Tacitus occluding historical work. Perhaps because other provinces of the Roman empire lack a Josephus or the density of archaeological work in Israel-Palestine, and clues about the distant past are relatively scarce, it is clearer elsewhere that the past cannot simply be inferred from, or read out of, either literary or material evidence—or both together—because they are very different kinds of things, which cannot simply be matched up.

That texts do not transparently reflect ancient realities has been clear in principle for a long time. Historians of bygone generations often cited Thucydides, Polybius, Livy, or Tacitus, to be sure, as though they simply mirrored the past. But nowadays every historian sees the problems with

---

8. This is the *Biblical Archaeology Review*, which features recent archaeological discoveries with superb photographs and diagrams, but also often explores issues in the history of ancient Israel/Judaea. It is hard to imagine a magazine being equally popular with the title *Biblical History Review*. Treating historical problems under the umbrella of archaeology can give the impression (surely never intended by the editors) that history is unnecessary.

9. Cf. Hallote and Joffe 2002; also Rabinovich 2011, citing Israel Exploration Society President Y. Aviram: "archaeology was a major instrument of nation-building" already before 1948. See in general Zerubavel 1994.

that.[10] We realize in principle that the interpretation of Polybius, Livy, or Tacitus is a different thing from investigating our own historical questions.[11] In the case of Josephus this distinction has been later in coming. It is not that scholars have simply trusted him; they may have suspected that he was a congenital liar. But even our most critical investigations tend to proceed as though we were attorneys hired to argue for or against Josephus, as though he were in the dock for failing to help us with *our* historical questions.

If we think about it, however, we have no reason to expect Josephus' work to be reliable for *our* problems, or to criticize it when we find it wanting. We should let him rest in peace and take responsibility ourselves for the problems we wish to investigate. Our concerns are up to us and not his problem. When we read his work, our primary task is to understand what he was up to, not to hurl abuse when he fails to do our work for us.

The other two peculiarities of our field—unusual categories and the propensity to form warring camps—are both illustrated in a comprehensive history of ancient Judaism and Christianity (2010) by Leo Sandgren. His methodological introduction explains:

> There are two contemporary and competing approaches to historical investigation that require an introduction. One is called minimalism, the other maximalism. The approaches involve the question of what constitutes evidence, and the quest for certainty of knowledge. The minimalist applies the so-called hermeneutic of suspicion to our sources. Every witness has an ulterior motive, or may be outright lying, unless it can be proven otherwise ... The maximalist leans in the other direction ... Some call this approach a hermeneutic of trust. People (especially religious people?) are prone to tell the truth and not perpetrate falsehood that in their own times can be exposed.[12]

Sandgren is right that this division comes up often; one should not fault him for making the observation.[13] But such terminology would seem strange in other historical sub-fields. We do not hear historians of Ath-

---

10. Woolf (2006: 93): "Modern historians who specialize in the Roman provinces have a bad habit of treating ancient authors as if they are research assistants. ... [O]ur 'witnesses' are not colleagues, their texts are not responses to our research questions, and at least some apparent resemblances between their texts and the products of modern scientific research are profoundly misleading."

11. In general, Woodman 1988; Plass 1988; Kraus and Woodman 1997; Mellor 1999; Luce 1977; Miles 1995; Feldherr 1998; Walbank 1972; Eckstein 1995; Champion 2004; Syme 1958, 1970; Mellor 1993.

12. Sandgren 2010: 3–4.

13. See Garfinkel 2011.

ens, Rome, or Egypt speaking about a hermeneutic of suspicion or about maximalism and minimalism.

Even the phrase "hermeneutic of suspicion" takes on an unusual meaning, as we see when Sandgren, reflecting common use in our field, applies it to the referential accuracy of written sources. The phrase was made famous by Paul Ricoeur, but for him it had nothing to do with the accuracy of texts, or whether one should trust the Bible (or Josephus) or not. His "masters of suspicion" were Nietzsche, Marx, and Freud, who made fundamental contributions to western thought by exposing hypocrisy in relation to power, economic motives glossed as other things, and the role of the unconscious in self-delusion. They were suspicious of the comforting traditional discourses of the West; none was much concerned with the referential correctness of biblical or post-biblical texts.[14]

For history generally, as we have seen, Herodotean suspicion of sources is indispensable and not an option that we can embrace or reject. Marc Bloch's masterful text, *The Historian's Craft*, devoted much space to history's need to reject authority and distrust sources.[15] Collingwood addressed his undergraduates in 1926:

> It is puzzling and rather shocking to face the fact that the writers whom one has regarded as authoritative and incorruptible channels of truth are completely misapprehending the events which they describe, or deliberately telling lies about them; and when experienced historians assure us that all sources are tainted with ignorance and mendacity, we are apt to ascribe the opinion merely to cynicism. Yet this opinion is really *the most precious possession of historical thought*. It is a working hypothesis *without which no historian can move a single step*.[16]

In other words, if we are not suspicious we do not need history; we may happily rely on tradition to convey the useful past to us. There is nothing recent or controversial or minimalist about the need for suspicion. Curiosity about the past and profound suspicion of all proffered claims about it are the foundations of historical inquiry.

A maximalist / minimalist division could not be about method, in any case, but only about *conclusions*. One could not say: "Being a minimalist I prefer to look at only some of the evidence," or "Being a maximalist I include all sorts of extraneous evidence." Competent historians must use all and only the germane evidence, choices they justify to all peers in argument.

14. Ricoeur 1970: 32. Cf. Stewart 1989: 296–307; Leiter 2004: 74–105.
15. Bloch 1992: 66–113.
16 Collingwood 1994: 378 (emphasis added).

The maximalist / minimalist division reflects a deeper assumption in our fields, which is that historians must *believe* things. An old joke runs: "There are two kinds of people in the world: those who think there are two kinds of people in the world and those who don't." Our field of ancient history is definitely in the former camp. We are expected to declare whether we consider Josephus reliable or not; whether we believe that Pharisees dominated first-century Judaean society or were marginal; whether we identify Qumran and the Scrolls as Essene—or insist on their opposition; whether we translate Greek *Ioudaios* as "Judaean" or "Jew."[17] In the study of Christian origins, "two-kinds-of-people" schemes are legion like the demons of Gerasa: Is Acts reliable or not? Was Jesus an apocalyptic prophet or a teacher of wisdom for life? Was Paul "within Judaism" or did he turn away from it? Do you accept the two-document hypothesis or a rival explanation of gospel origins? Are you a conservative or a liberal? Our area of ancient history seems to have a unique propensity to separate the children of light from the children of darkness on the basis of their conclusions.[18] One could readily speculate about the reasons why areas of ancient history connected with religion tend this way—if indeed my experience reflects a real character perceived by others—but we may leave the question of causes here.

It is enough to state the obvious: that open-ended investigation and debate about evidence, without speculation about others' motives, interests, or affiliations, is necessary for historical work. Lord Acton stated the principle in 1862: "The absence of a definite didactic purpose is the only security for the good faith of a historian."[19]

Conclusion

One of my reasons for writing this book is to appeal for a closer integration of research on Hellenistic-Roman Judaea with the history of other parts of

---

17. I have found myself involuntarily assigned to one such camp or another. McLaren (2003: 150–51) divides Josephus scholars into camps that consider Josephus basically reliable or not, and puts me in the former—though my research as much as anyone's divorces Josephus' narrative from real events and rejects "reliability" as a criterion. For my involuntary enrollment in other camps, see Sanders 1992: 532 n. 9; Atkinson and Magness 2010: 318–19; Klawans 2012: 8. I mention my experience only for illustration and to avoid speculating about others. But this logic of binary choice and camp allegiance appears often.

18. Cf. Garfinkel (2011: 47) on the "minimalists": their approach comprises "groundless arguments, masquerading as scientific writing through footnotes, references and publication in professional journals."

19. Dalberg 1922 [1907]: 236.

the Roman world. It is wonderful that our field enjoys such a large public constituency, such diverse academic contributions, uniquely dense archaeological excavation, and the extraordinarily helpful narratives of Josephus, not to mention the Scrolls, the library of other post-biblical texts, and early rabbinic literature. At the same time, we risk isolation from the other harbors of ancient history, with the loss of potential insight and testing for our proposals, if we do not work hard to maintain lines of communication. This means in part deciding whether we are historians above all and, if so, what it means to do history.

4

Method and Procedure: Ancient vs. Modern History

Having surveyed some complexities involved in the simple-seeming project of history, I would now like to examine two kinds of consequences. First, since we have been discussing the logic of history in general, we must consider the special case of ancient history. Second, I should draw these threads together by indicating the sort of procedure that a historical inquiry in our field might follow.

Method:
The Special Challenge of Ancient History

Historical method, in the sense of all history's logic and rationale, should be the same for any investigation, of an incident that occurred yesterday or during the Peloponnesian War. But we need to be careful about formulating universal principles from the work of those who study recent history, because they enjoy material conditions not available to historians investigating antiquity. If we measure our work against a wonderful guide such as Marc Bloch's, which draws examples from mediaeval documents, or Carr's research on the Soviet Union or Richard Evans' *In Defence of History* (2000), we may create impossible expectations.

As a historian of the twentieth century, for example, Evans does battle with post-modernist colleagues who emphasize the instability of all truth claims. He worries, with reason, that such persistent doubt, even where there is abundant evidence for an event or situation, can lead to Holocaust denial and other kinds of bad faith. Clinging to the proper principle of doubt, that is, historians can refuse to acknowledge anything at all as real.

Evans therefore insists on reckoning with truths established from plentiful independent evidence, supplemented in many cases by the personal memories of countless individuals.

If we simply applied Evans' principles to ancient history, we might conclude that skepticism about Josephus' description of Masada's end is a post-modern malady. Here I might respond to a basic misunderstanding of my work. Given how widespread the misreading seems to be (below), I must accept responsibility for it. From my first book onward I thought that I was working within an age-old Herodotean framework. Distinguishing stories and traditions from historical investigation, I argued that in our fields (re: Pharisees, Essenes, relations with Rome, the war) this distinction was often transgressed. Without venturing any sustained interpretation of Josephus, scholars tended to treat him either as a mine of data or as a collection of sources, either of which could be used without much reference to its narrative home, which seemed a nonexistent category for most interpreters.

In that first book, on the Pharisees, I was consciously joining a program, best outlined by Jacob Neusner, that called for a conceptual distinction between the interpretation of stories (e.g., Josephus, Mark, Luke–Acts, etc.) and hypothetical reconstruction of the lost realities behind them, the latter effort requiring understanding of the evidence: what it is, what it intends (for whom?), what it says.[1] Far from considering the real past uninteresting, I argued that a self-consciously methodical investigation requires such a distinction of object and method. Just as classicists were by then accustomed to distinguishing Tacitus' Rome from the real past, and biblical and New Testament scholars distinguished the Deuteronomistic History or Luke from Israel's real life or the historical Jesus, it was time for historians of Roman Judaea to catch up. Rather than trying to read the historical Pharisees from Josephus' texts as *data*, I tried to interpret them as components of his narratives, asking how they served those stories as wholes, and therefore why he talked about this group at all. This was intended to be, as I said then, preparatory work for more careful historical study of the group—earlier rounds of which had come to grief on implausible use of the sources—in the spirit of Neusner's project.[2]

Over the next decades the project of interpreting Josephus ballooned because that simple question opened up many possibilities. Volumes of collected essays and dissertations on "Josephus' portrait of X," a previously

---

1. Mason 1991: 1–17, esp. 10–17.

2. Mason 1991: 16–17, 44. Neusner laid out his program in the monograph of 1973. Neusner and Chilton 2007 realizes that program much more fully, with specialists focused on the Pharisees of Josephus, Mark, Matthew, rabbinic literature, etc., before the group is reconstructed.

invisible or uninteresting category, proliferated.³ So busy did I become with interpreting Josephus on various questions for which his work had been used (e.g., Essenes, the war, Judaean identity), and so complex did work on the Josephus commentary become, that colleagues apparently began to doubt my interest in history. My occasional published grumbles about taking shortcuts from Josephus' narrative to the real past were read as though they called for a moratorium on first-century history in general. Since doctoral-student days, when I was privileged to spend a year in Jerusalem, the most productive exchanges I have had on these matters have been with my friend Daniel Schwartz of the Hebrew University. His 2013 study of historical method is framed as a conversation with me and others. I respond briefly here to show how differently even friendly historians in regular conversation can see matters.

Schwartz's pointedly titled *Reading the First Century* opens by juxtaposing a quotation from me about the growing acceptance of the need to read *Josephus through*, and not "merely" read through his text to underlying sources and events, with one from the eminent historian Arnaldo Momigliano in 1974, stressing that the historian is not primarily an interpreter of texts but is concerned with the real past.⁴ A crucial move comes on the next page: "As our opening citation from Steve Mason indicates . . . , in Josephan studies today it is in fact very common to hold that we should, because of doubts pertaining to the move from any sources to history, or at least because of doubts pertaining to the move from ancient sources to ancient history, *stick to reading his writings in order to understand him and his works*."⁵ I have become a channel of Josephan solipsism, advocating that

---

3. The unprecedented crop of collected-essay volumes devoted to Josephus, usually stemming from conferences, began with Parente and Sievers 1994 and was still going strong with Edmondson, Mason, and Rives 2005. The Josephus Seminar of the Society of Biblical Literature began in 1999 and still thrives. Published and unpublished dissertations include Chapman 1998; Colautti 2002; Semenchenko 2002; Grünenfelder 2003; Landau 2006; Shenoy 2006; Gussmann 2008; Brighton 2009; Olson 2010; Siggelkow-Berner 2011; Tuval 2013; den Hollander 2014. Many are currently under supervision.

4. Schwartz 2013: vii.

5. Schwartz 2013: ix (my emphasis) and 94. He cites Rajak (citing me) for the idea that detective historians have "have had their day," but the latter phrase is not mine. I have observed that radical source criticism (the hope of recovering whole sources from Josephus) flourished in a bygone era (1870–1920), but the detective analogy is one I embrace (via Collingwood) as a helpful image of the historian's work. But just as good detectives must be relentless and figure out the angles of those making statements, so too the historian constantly questions and seeks confirmation.

only his text matters. Because others have formed a similar impression,[6] I take this opportunity to correct it.

Having myself cited Momigliano in justification of my first "composition-critical" study, I agree wholly with his elegant article on historical method, which Schwartz translates in an appendix.[7] We face the paradox that Schwartz understands his work as "footnotes exemplifying Momigliano's views," and I could say much the same of mine, though we apparently disagree. Schwartz makes a lively case, with much of which I agree and which readers should consult directly. Here I can only try to unpack the central issue of the relationship between reading texts and reconstructing the lost past.

I hope it is clear from this volume and *A History of the Jewish War* that curiosity about the real past drives my research. That past included the production of texts, however, which are among its most valuable survivals.[8] I have admittedly been stuck, so to speak, in interpreting this evidence, for example in editing and writing the first commentary on Josephus' thirty volumes, because there is so much original work to do and because of contractual commitments. But that is not because I have ever dreamed that historians must *stick to* the interpretation of texts and not concern themselves with lost contexts and events. From the first I have tried to say the opposite.

Asking that we interpret Josephus responsibly, in light of his narrative structures, purposes, and themes and the ambient culture—not saying that interpretation X is correct, but asking only that we recognize the need for interpretation—is no stranger than an archaeologist's resolve to understand a site or a numismatist's or epigrapher's taking years to publish a collection of coins or inscriptions. These are services to the community of historians. Interpreting survivals is particularly important in ancient history because the material is so alien, being in a foreign language and from a distant time. As all historians know from experience, if we make snap judgments about the meaning of evidence on first reading, we are likely to underestimate the possibilities and make a mistake.[9] It is important that some historians devote time to the patient auxiliary work of interpreting evidence contextually

---

6. So Klawans 2012: 8: "Some current writers—Mason prominent among them—are so taken with Josephus as a creative author that they practically give up on the possibility of discerning historical realities behind his writings." Cf. Bernett 2007: 20–21; Freyne 2009 passim.

7. Mason 1991: 12, 16 with Momigliano in (and trans.) Schwartz 2013: 181–89.

8. Schwartz 2013: ix n. 4.

9. Momigliano in Schwartz 2013: 185: If a nineteenth-century Italian text can present substantial difficulties of interpretation, "one may imagine the situation of someone who wants to understand Greek of 450 BC or Latin of AD 100."

without another kind of inquiry in mind. My commentary work and studies of Josephus on X are thus meant as a foundation for historical research, not to undermine it. To drive this home, when examining Josephus' Pharisees or Essenes I have concluded by trying to isolate features of the evidence that historical hypotheses about Pharisees or Essenes (involving also other evidence) will need to explain in Josephus,[10] an issue often overlooked because of impatient reading in the service of other hypotheses.

Returning to the main issue, then: Schwartz allies his view of history with Richard Evans' *Defence* and situates their shared concern with the real past against a group of scholars who are "overly pessimistic" about recovering "reasonable certainty"—from Josephus.[11] Those who doubt that one can be confident of the past from one literary account are grouped with postmodernists who doubt all historical knowledge irrespective of the abundance of evidence. It seems to me that this formulation conflates two quite separate questions. First: Should the historian pose problems and investigate evidence with the intention of recovering the *real past*, with whatever degree of confidence available evidence will permit? Yes! That is the point of history, and the question for which Evans is relevant. On this we agree.

The second, tacit question is not about our *desire* or our aims as historians, but about the actual limitations of our evidence. What do we do when we have only one literary source: Josephus' dramatic and reconfigurable narratives? Can we be *reasonably certain* about extracting intact sources and facts from that (or any) single text? As Schwartz partly concedes, this and not a general philosophy of history is the point of difference.[12] He argues in a number of publications that one *can* recover from Josephus the sources on his desktop, and shows a measure of confidence in doing this.[13] Detailed work on some of the same material has led me to think that source extraction and reconstructions built upon it are at least open to doubt, when all possible explanations of the same evidence are weighed.

My doubts about confidently recovering the ancient past from single literary sources therefore have nothing to do with post-modernism, Evans' concern, with which I do not identify. These doubts reflect the main stream of historical thinking from Herodotus through Voltaire to Bloch, Collingwood, and Momigliano.[14] Doubt is the governing principle. Josephus' ac-

---

10. Mason 1991: 372–75; 2011b: 243–51.

11. Schwartz 2013: ix n. 4: "Thus, this volume may be regarded as an instance and application of the type of position taken by R. J. Evans in his *In Defence of History*..."

12. Schwartz 2013: 7.

13. Schwartz 1983, 1990, 1992, 2013.

14. Herodotus and Collingwood above; Bloch 1992: 110–37 (110: "At the bottom of nearly all criticism there is a problem of comparison"). For Voltaire see "History" in

counts of Herod's murders or Cestius' ambush or *sicarii* actions in Cyrene are his accounts only, opaque about their origins (implying simply that Josephus knew). No amount of critical questioning or imagining of alternatives, which we should by all means do, will disgorge an alternative narrative in which we may place *confidence*. I agree with Evans and Schwartz in principle, but see the situation for ancient historians as materially (not philosophically) different from that of a modern historian such as Evans. Momigliano himself remarked that the amount of hypothesizing in ancient history, given the extreme scarcity of evidence, made it fertile ground for charlatans.[15]

Consider the Second World War, which has been the subject of intensive study and explanation since it began. Its many constituent events, which remain (as I write) in the living memory of a few senior citizens, produced veritable mountains of documentation: millions of personal testimonies, paper records, communication logs, film footage, and voice recordings. Now consider one tiny part of this whole. British Prime Minister Churchill held meetings with his War Cabinet and Chiefs of Staff, and with their American counterparts led by President Roosevelt. Most meetings were top-secret, but historians have tracked down sufficient independent evidence—participants' private journals, the official minutes, published memoirs—to construct a plausible picture of important moments, which is three-dimensional in that we can look from several angles. These reconstructions afford reasonable confidence, which can always be enhanced, in our understanding of the concerns, emotional states, and diplomatic/rhetorical ploys of the actors at various moments.[16] But when we turn to the ancient world no such possibilities exist. For most of the questions that might *interest* us, for example concerning the war and its background, we have either no direct evidence or only Josephus' literary account(s). For a precious few questions only we have material remains or fleeting indications in other texts.

In *HJW* I use the Allied bombing of the ancient Benedictene Abbey atop Monte Cassino, in February 1944, to help think about Titus' destruction of Jerusalem. The whole Mediterranean campaign, which was one small component of the war (1943–1944), illustrates the contrast I am

---

Voltaire 1901; cf. Momigliano trans. Schwartz 2013: 184: "If the documents turn out to be insufficient for that which he wants to know, the history will be insufficient... The historian's competence is seen in the extent to which he neither presents as certain that which is doubtful nor generalizes on the basis of an isolated case."

15. Momigliano 1974 in Schwartz 2013: 185.

16. E.g., Jonas 1975; Churchill and Gilbert 1966–1986; Gilbert 1991; Roberts 2008; Hastings 2009.

trying to make. A dozen years after the war's conclusion, in 1957, Fred Majdalany published a history of the Italian advance, which stalled for months outside the town of Cassino and put Churchill's indirect Mediterranean strategy in doubt. Defending the Allied decision to bomb the sanctuary in this context, Majdalany wrote: "It is pointless to consider any battle critically without relating it to the precise circumstances and conditions prevailing at the time and place . . . A commander's decisions can be properly appraised only if they are set against the background of *the exact and peculiar circumstances, atmosphere, climatic conditions, and pressures under which they were made.*"[17]

This is a sound historical (and historicist) position. In the absence of such detailed knowledge of all relevant factors, from high strategy to local weather and morale, we can say little with any confidence about why commanders made their decisions. Majdalany was anticipating John Keegan's famous book, *The Face of Battle* (1976). Keegan's investigation of conflicts from Agincourt to World War I moved beyond then-standard studies of military organization, weapons, armor, strategy, and tactics. He wanted to imaginatively reconstruct the gritty situations of battle, the real soldier's confusion amidst the blood and mud, because only those concrete particulars can explain why things unfolded as they did. A number of scholars have tried to apply the same kind of realism to ancient warfare.[18] This is all welcome.

It presents obvious problems, however, for ancient conflicts such as the war in Judaea. How *can* we come close to knowing such particular factors? Where can we find the strategic and tactical aims of the participants? Can we know who the key personnel were at any moment? What happened when they faced each other in the varied terrain of Galilee's flat valleys and lush hills, Palestine's coastal plain, the Jordan valley, or outside Judaea's fortress city of Jerusalem? How did the fighters on both sides feel in changing conditions each day and each hour? What was the condition of their physical health, fitness, and morale each day and week? What differences in experience and attitude marked the coalitions on each side? How serious were inter-unit tensions and personal animosities? What motivated individual fighters? How did the commanders' orders and speeches, which we do not have as such, match what they personally felt about the prospects?

17. Majdalany 1957: 108 (emphasis mine).
18. For Greek hoplite warfare see Pritchett 1974 and Hanson 1989; for Roman warfare, Goldsworthy 1996 and Daley 2002: x, 156. This realistic approach has influenced many studies of modern wars and warfare, which sometimes acknowledge Keegan (e.g., Ferguson 1998: x, 380; Evans and Ryan 2000: 3, 116, 204; Ellis 1984; Clark 2006).

Historians of the Italian campaigns can draw from an embarrassment of riches.[19] In addition to their own participant memories in some cases, which they realized gave them very *limited* understanding, copious comparative material had become available. They could revisit the site and retrace their own unit's movements. They could read official post-war histories of each participating force, of specific battalions, regiments, or divisions, as well as real-time war diaries. They could exploit the personal memoirs of commanders, Axis and Allied. They could interview hundreds of soldiers from both sides and such non-combatants as the Abbot's secretary, who remained during the bombing. They could use diaries and letters found on the enemy dead and prisoners of war, vividly recreating the private feelings of the ordinary soldier. Above all, masses of documentary material awaited scrutiny: dated memoranda, telephone logs, official correspondence, propaganda leaflets, press reports and newsreel footage from war reporters, and other such testimony to specific actions.[20] For the larger context of the war, historians have hundreds of thousands of transcript pages from unguarded P.O.W. conversations in Allied detention centers, which were bugged and translated by intelligence units.[21]

Such an array of evidence makes possible the thriving enterprise of World War II history, important new studies of which appear each year. Those who write about Cassino can proceed not only day by day, but often hour by hour, and shift from one vantage-point to another. They can elucidate individual motives, fears, and shortcomings, improbably poor weather, unexpected enemy reactions, interpersonal dynamics, the effects of casualty tolls on morale, missing and disobeyed orders, and failure of supply lines. They can describe all this with confidence *not* because they are "maximalists" or "minimalists" or realists, but because of the extensive surviving evidence. They may (and should) remain as skeptical as all other historians, but the wealth of evidence allows them to discount or relativize a general's self-serving memoir. Their fine-grained studies are possible because so much remains. Whereas ancient historians must imagine possibilities without being able to exclude most, the scholar who investigates the more recent past can exclude most imaginable scenarios because they would not explain the evidence.

This is far from our situation with the Judaean war with Rome, and so we should not pretend that we can reach similar levels of confidence.

---

19. Majdalany 1957; Ellis 1984; Colvin and Hodges 1994; Hapgood and Richardson 2002; Parker 2003; Pugsley 2004; Caddick-Adams 2013.

20. Cf. the fifteen pages of sources listed in Ellis 1984: 515–29.

21. See Neitzel and Welzer 2011.

Imagine that historians of Cassino after two millennia found only the highly readable memoir of U.S. General Mark W. Clark, who was commander of the Allied Fifth Army as it advanced along Italy's southwest coast. Although he was not only an eyewitness but also well-informed, as commander, about what lay beyond his direct observation, and he understood the highest-level context, we could not get very far with his account alone.[22] In fact, we would be required to doubt (*not* reject) every single thing he says, as a matter of historical principle. And no matter what ingenuity we brought to imagining the realities behind his story, there would be no way to tease out a picture in which we could place reasonable confidence. Turning a crafted narrative, with its plot and characters and coloring, into real life in all its complexity is a task for magic, not history.

Procedure of an Inquiry into the Ancient Past

On this foundation we turn finally to sketching a procedure for investigating first-century Judaea. The main thing to say is that all three of the diffuse trajectories I have sketched are valuable and there is no need to choose one. With a subject such as the Judaean War it is valuable to examine such *longue-durée* issues as imperial governance, Judaea's place in the provincial system, Judaean religious aspirations, Roman military organization, strategy and morale in times of conflict, and common political-social discourse. These issues come up in *HJW* Chapter 3 and partly elsewhere, and in the present volume. Most of *HJW* (Chapters 1–2 and 4–9) comprises investigations of particular events and the aims or thoughts of the individual actors and groups involved. Frequently, third, we came up against the shortfall between likely intention and outcome, even with Titus but most obviously with the rebel leaders trapped in Jerusalem, who surely did not plan on the city's destruction. The only requirement of history is that we investigate what is human from the past.

When it comes to re-imagining lost events, Collingwood's analogy of the police detective remains valuable. After all, detectives are called upon to conduct methodical inquiries into the human past, gather and understand evidence, imagine and weigh possible explanations, and finally, if they are able to do so with the available evidence, produce an account free of prejudicial investment.[23] The historian is not like a detective in all respects, of course. Modern judicial systems have many special rules of evidence and

22. Clark 2007 [1950].
23. Collingwood 1994: 266–82.

procedures unrelated to historical work. Collingwood's point was simply that a criminal investigation (in the early twentieth century) provided a kind of everyday laboratory for basic historical logic, and a valuable one because the stakes are so high. I agree, as long as we do not press the analogy too far. Let us, then, unpack some aspects of the detective-historian's work.

1. *The centrality of the question; ignorance as default position.* Like criminal investigations, history begins with a problem or a question. There is something we do not know that we wish to know, but cannot know without a successful inquiry. If the investigation proves inconclusive, we remain in the innocent state of not knowing.[24] The point may seem obvious, but it is ignored with surprising regularity. Scholars often claim that they are entitled to believe *something* unless someone else can either disprove it or produce a better explanation of the meager evidence—turning the logical tables.[25] A related trap is being tempted to believe some ancient story merely because it is the only one we happen to have.[26] All such errors assume that we need to *believe something*: if not this, then that. Scholarship abhors a vacuum.

The first principle of historical inquiry, however, is that we do not know the solutions to a given problem until someone has made a compelling case. Unless this condition is met, it would be irresponsible to claim knowledge. That is why detectives have so many unsolved cases: they could not make a case that would stick.

The table-turning is often done subtly, playing "pass the burden of proof." It should be clear that, if we can recover the historical past only by

---

24. Cf. the subtitle of J. Neusner's *Rabbinic Literature and the New Testament* (1993): "What we cannot show, we do not know."

25. E. Ullmann-Margalit notes the peculiarity of the Essene-Qumran debates in relation to standard views in the philosophy of science (2008: 65, my emphasis): "the Qumran-Essene theory is everyone's 'theory of choice'; it is *one's theory in the absence of good or conclusive reasons to switch to an alternative theory*. In other words, unless and until an alternative theory wins you over, you stick with the Qumran-Essene theory, regardless of whether you might consider it less than compelling and regardless of how many faults you may actually find with it." Contrast L. Goldstein's approach to the same issue (1976: 93–137).

26. Cf. Debevoise (1938: xxvii, my emphasis): "In any case we cannot profitably abandon all the traditional history of this early period as legendary merely because we are unable to check its accuracy in more than one source or because the sources themselves are much later in date. Such action, *though perhaps based on better historical method*, would leave the ancient historian *a small framework upon which to build* in future years." More recently Morgan (2006: 290, my emphasis): "But unless or until fresh evidence emerges, *we must make a choice* [among Plutarch, Suetonius, and Tacitus as sources for Otho]." Why must we make a choice and not admit that *we do not know*?

METHOD AND PROCEDURE: ANCIENT VS. MODERN HISTORY

means of inquiry, the burden rests exclusively on someone brave enough to make the case. If I propose that John the Baptist was an Essene, and colleagues point out evidence that would remain unexplained by that hypothesis, I may not object "But you cannot prove that he was *not* an Essene." Or "Well what do you believe happened then?" Of course they cannot prove that the Baptist was not an Essene, or a Martian. But that does not bring us a smidgeon closer to validating the hypothesis. History, understood as methodical inquiry into the human past, assumes that if we cannot successfully conclude an inquiry, we do not know. To suppose that historians must believe *something* is a category-mistake.[27] History is not religion. Not knowing is the whole foundation and prerequisite of history, the desire to find ways of knowing its motive. Since ignorance is our constant companion, we might as well make our peace with it.

We can remain clear about this, I think, as long as we remember that historical inquiry begins not with making yes-or-no decisions about what happened, but with a problem. Collingwood wrote:

> Francis Bacon, lawyer and philosopher, laid it down in one of his memorable phrases that the natural scientist must 'put Nature to the question' . . . Here, in a single brief epigram, Bacon laid down once for all the true theory of experimental science . . . It is also, though Bacon did not know this, the true theory of historical method.[28]

One simple way to formulate a problem is to put a question mark on received wisdom. If the textbooks assert that Judaea became a Roman province in A.D. 6, or that Great Revolt against Rome began in 66, or the Diaspora Revolt in 115, we may always ask again: "When and how did Judaea

---

27. The Qumran-Essene question is again the clearest example of routine transgression. There is nothing wrong with hypothesizing a residential site of Essenes at Qumran on the basis of undoubted parallels between the Qumran Scrolls and portraits of the Essenes in Philo, Pliny, and Josephus. Critics observe that the Essene descriptions make no mention of such a site, while hundreds of Qumran Scrolls do not clearly mention Essenes. Further, the images of Essenes and the Scrolls communities, considered separately, seem rather different. Why would elite men such as Philo and Josephus be keen on the sort of group(s) illustrated in the Scrolls, in praising the Essenes unreservedly? Some advocates believe so strongly, however, that they simply shift the burden of proof, as Beall (1988: 125): "The sheer number of parallels . . . puts the burden of proof upon those who would insist that the Qumran community was not Essene."

28. Collingwood 1994: 269. NB: he uses "scientific" in much the same way that Germans used *wissenschaftlich*, to indicate a discipline of thought. He rejects any obeisance to natural science as model. Cf. Momigliano (1977: 368–69): the historian "has to assess the value of his evidence not in terms of simple reliability, but of relevance to the problems he wants to solve."

become a province, and how do we know?" The stimulus can be anything at all: an oddity in a coin or inscription, a lacuna or strange vocabulary in a text, or our free imagination, fed by any number of other experiences.

Formulating one clear problem will often create a cascade. If I first think to ask about the Syrian legate Cestius Gallus' aims when he invaded Judaea in the autumn of 66, that question will quickly spin out several others: Who was Cestius Gallus? Who was in his social-political circle? What were his connections with Nero's court and the Senate? How were his relations with the Jerusalem leadership and the Herodian family? We rarely ask such questions, simple though they are, because our habit is not to ask free questions but instead to read Josephus and ask whether we consider his account "accurate," a procedure that severely limits our investigative horizon.

2. *Possibility and Probability*. Along with shifting the burden of proof, historians can speak of probability or "near certainty" with such freedom that it is hard to understand their meaning or justification.[29] Where the application of statistics to a database of some kind is not in view, probability is a tricky metaphor for the ancient historian. Its weighty sound comes from origins in reassuringly solid "frequentist" probability, where all possible outcomes are known and so we can calculate the likelihood of a particular one. The probability of rolling a 7 with a pair of dice, or drawing the Ace of Spades from a deck of 52 cards, is matter of simple calculation.[30] Probability in this root sense is the ratio of one outcome's frequency to the total number of possible outcomes.

The lost events of the distant past do not give us much opportunity to use frequentist probability, though it can come up in the stylometric analysis of texts or when tabulating ratios of Hebrew or Greek names in a corpus

---

29. Though the problem is familiar in scholarship, popular books provide the clearest examples. For Seward (2009), not only Josephus but also his father was "almost certainly" a Pharisee, which means that he had "never read the Greek classics" in Jerusalem (11, 15, 18). "Josephus *probably* looked very much the noble, in a silk tunic and wearing a gold ring ... *No doubt* he disguised himself in cheaper clothing" (53). Of the Zealots, "we can *assume with some certainty* that ... Simon and John were each hoping to establish a new Judean monarchy" (188). Josephus' Aramaic account of the war was *probably* no more than a pamphlet (244). The problem is not the use of probability language, but whether it is justified by anything more than a hunch.

30. On ancient (rhetorical and character-based) senses of probability, see Sprague 1972: 279–93; Kennedy 1994: 17, 24; Hoffman 2008: 1–29; on modern developments, Hacking 1975: 18–56. Positivistic attempts to apply statistical laws to history as prediction (Hempel 1942: 35–48; summary in Gilderhus 2010: 76–77) are discredited; cf. Pelz 1990: 767–69—though he treats realist vs. constructivist history somewhat simplistically.

of funerary inscriptions, for example.³¹ Nor does the distant past usually create space for Bayesian probability, which gives a formula for assessing confidence of judgment rather than specific outcomes, because that kind of judgment still requires knowing the values of key variables.³² The kind of probability most applicable to discussions of ancient history, probably, is the informal use explored by Stephen Toulmin. We use this when we say, "Now that is probably her finest painting"—without intending anything like precise calculation or quantitative reasoning. It is a qualitative judgment. But that does not let us off the hook, if we want to use the word meaningfully. Toulmin exhorts us to use such language with clear criteria in view.³³ It would be meaningless to say "That is probably her finest painting" if it is the only one I have seen. It is no more meaningful to say that Judaeans probably suffered more than others under Roman rule if we have not considered the others, or that Josephus as a Pharisee or a priest or *probably* knew or did X or Y, unless we have taken the trouble to establish some sort of comparative framework.

Remembering the frequentist roots of probability might help protect us from certain fallacies related to probability. One example is the "cumulative weight" argument, which goes: None of my arguments may be very strong, but taken together I find them compelling. In frequentist probability, however, cumulative weight dramatically reduces probability. That is, every additional proposition that I need to be true (i.e., certain), but is only probable, drags the argument down. Since probability is the ratio of that outcome I need to all possible outcomes, each new element brings a world of notional possibilities, which multiply uncertainty. Dissertation-writers in particular should be wary of building a case that depends on a number of merely possible interpretations of evidence, because the doubt about each (If A, if B, if C, and if D) infects the whole structure.

3. *Evidence and interpretation.* Once we have formulated a research problem, we identify and interpret the potential evidence. Since our questions are our own, we do not expect to find evidence pre-packaged and self-revealing, or even declaring itself to *be* evidence. It was not created for that purpose. Just as Euripides never imagined that his tragedies would become evidence for Athenian society, Virgil did not expect to be studied for Augustus' reign,

31. E.g., Williams 1992; 1994.

32. Carrier 2012 offers a friendly introduction to Bayesian logic, ambitiously applying it to the historical Jesus.

33. On Toulmin, see, e.g., Toulmin 2003 (1958): 83–85; assessment in Hitchcock and Verheij 2006.

and Galilean village families did not know their dishes would become evidence for cultural interaction, Josephus wrote from his own motives, not to provide heat-and-serve evidence for us. Artifacts *become* evidence only in the context of an investigation for which they are deemed relevant. That brings us back to the importance of beginning with a question.

Once we identify an item as relevant for our inquiry, we need to understand it. What *is* it, and what is it for? Often we become impatient here, and want to collapse interpretation and reconstruction of the past into a single exercise. Most often this involves the shortcut of finding a passage in Josephus and asking "Is this accurate? Is it what really happened?" We are not then trying to understand the thing in front of us for itself, but looking straight through it to the real past, as though it were transparent.

Collingwood illustrates the problem of doing this with the analogy of a murder investigation. A young woman comes forward and confesses, "I killed John Doe." But people confess to crimes for many reasons, their actual guilt being only one possibility: protecting a loved one, mental disorder, duress or threat, trying to lessen the punishment if police have signalled that you will be charged, situational false belief.[34] Scores or even hundreds of people have confessed to crimes involving celebrities. So the diligent investigator may not simply accept this woman's claim and declare the inquiry closed: "We have our killer: she confessed!" The first questions must be interpretative: Who is this person and *why is she saying* that she killed John Doe?[35] One explanation is that she did it, but detectives and historians cannot accept the word of a single source without collaboration, even if we can imagine no reason why she/he/it would lie. Outright distortion of the truth is a normal occurrence, but more importantly no one can ever tell the "whole truth and nothing but the truth" if they wish to do so. That is first because they do not know the whole truth, and second because any account of what they do know must convert the chaos of experience to a narrative with a shape, logic, plot, and characters.

When it comes to ancient history, Collingwood puts it like this:

> We no longer think that in reading Livy or Gibbon we are face to face with the early or late history of Rome; we realize that what we are reading is not history but only *material out of which, by thinking for ourselves, we may hope to construct history* . . . Livy

---

34. Cf. https://www.psychologytoday.com/blog/life-autopilot/201108/the-west-memphis-three-four-step-recipe-false-confessions; http://news.bbc.co.uk/2/hi/uk_news/magazine/7950613.stm.

35. Collingwood 1994: 275–76.

and Gibbon are no longer authorities, but sources merely: they are not to be followed, but to be interpreted.[36]

Michael Oakeshott elaborates: "[N]o object which has survived yields its authentic character to mere observation, and its worth in further historical enquiry depends upon an understanding of its authentic character."[37] The need to interpret even encyclopedic works such as Pliny's *Natural History* or Pausanias' *Description of Greece* is increasingly understood; even they are not simply collections of neutral data.[38] The case is no different with Josephus' narratives.

In stressing the need to interpret evidence, I am incidentally trying to displace the question I am most often asked after public lectures: How *reliable* (or accurate) is Josephus? It is an understandable question, if people assume that Josephus records data, but it cannot be meaningfully answered. We do not fret about whether Polybius, Livy, or Tacitus is accurate *as a whole*, because the category is inappropriate. Ancient history was a subset of literature and rhetoric, and judged for its insights and qualities of presentation. We do not ask whether a song or a painting is accurate. Although ancient historians were supposed to tell the truth, as we have seen the truth expected was much more moral than factual or forensically verifiable. Anyway, accuracy is a property of values that can in princple be checked against known quantities. So we properly speak about the accuracy of clocks, lenses, gauges, and music tuners. Josephus' main claims are not of this kind.

He does make occasional claims that are testable in principle, for example that Tiberias lies 30 *stadia* from Taricheae. If we know the locations of the places in question and what he meant by 30 *stadia*, we can check it.[39] He describes landscapes and built structures, which in some cases we can compare with existing topography (accounting for changes over time) and excavations. Other elements are also testable in principle, such as dates, though we usually have nothing for comparison.

But even if we could declare all such elements in Josephus accurate (or not), that would hardly touch the main content of his narratives. Above all he is interested in moral-political questions, and in the character of his various actors. Ancient history is qualitative in the extreme. Measurable bits are usually incidental. We cannot judge his character portraits and statements of motive, much less his claims about tragic scenes or temple pollution as

36. Collingwood 1994: 382–83. Emphasis added.
37. Oakeshott 1999: 56.
38. On Pliny: Murphy 2004. On Pausanias, a watershed was Habicht 1998 [1985]. See the exploratory essays in Alcock, Cherry, and Elsner 2001.
39. For Josephus' distances, see *HJW* Appendix A.

"reliable," any more than we could judge a musical score to be reliable. There is no logical link between the distance from Tiberias to Taricheae and the reliability of his claim that compatriot bloodshed polluted the temple.

Fortunately, it is not the historian's task to sit as a judge and pass verdicts on stories—"That one's accurate; no, not that one!"[40] Ours is the infinitely more interesting task of understanding and then explaining our evidence.

4. *Explanatory scenarios.* Goldstein aptly writes that the historian's work is "*not* one of inference—in any sense—at all. Rather, the historical occurrence is hypothesized in order to make sense of the evidence."[41] As we have seen, there is no water we can buy to reconstitute the bygone past from Josephus or other evidence. Rather, once we have provisionally interpreted each survival, we must creatively imagine scenarios, looking for the one with the greatest explanatory power, in much the same way as the detective imagines and tests hypotheses to see how well they explain the evidence.

Since the possibilities of human life are practically infinite, we need to imagine every scenario we can. One criterion is the principle of economy or simplicity, sometimes called the law of parsimony or "Occam's razor." This holds that we should favor hypotheses that require only what is common, familiar motives and responses, ahead of those that have many moving parts or posit extraordinary phenomena. When a patient with a headache visits a physician, although it is *possible* that she has a rare tropical disease or a brain tumor, the doctor looks first for common explanations. This does not mean that the more serious malady is excluded. Looking for simple and common explanations is merely a discipline of investigation, resting on the realization that to treat all possible explanations as equally likely would be irrational, when we know that some are far more common. So we work up a pyramid from the simple and common at the base. Only when these prove unsatisfactory do we advance up the pyramid, just as the physician rules out common causes of headache before testing for rarer conditions.

How does this apply to the ancient past? It could be that most first-century Jews were waiting for Messiah each day, or that they could not tolerate human or Roman government. But it is hard to imagine whole agrarian societies holding such views over centuries of foreign government. It is possible that when Simon bar Giora emerged from hiding dressed in purple and white (*War* 7.25–34), the act revealed his inner messianic

---

40. See Ginzburg 1991.
41. Goldstein 1976: 127.

consciousness. Given Josephus' remark that the massacres of auxiliary soldiers in Jerusalem and of Judaeans in Caesarea occurred on the same day (*War* 2.457), it is possible that the former happened early and an auxiliary rider covered the 120 km (72 mi) to Caesarea in record time, so that the second massacre occurred the same day. But simpler explanations of the evidence should be preferred.

Although economy is a valuable criterion for excluding possibilities, we usually reach confidence about a solution only with *corroborative evidence*. When two or more independent eyewitnesses agree that something happened, from different perspectives, it is difficult to explain their agreement without supposing that something like they imagined happened. Difficult, though not impossible.[42] Where we have only one literary source such as Josephus, given his literary creativity we might imagine a number of historical scenarios and still understand why he wrote as he did. The principle of corroboration is basic to historical (and legal) thinking for good reason. The problem in studying Roman Judaea is that we rarely have it.

Fortunately, the barriers to confidence about the ancient past do not create insuperable problems, as long as we accept our situation. If history is primarily a method for exploring the past, we may be happy with a rigorous investigation during which we relive possibilities and assess their value. We cannot be responsible for the *force majeure* that determined the nature, amount, and quality of surviving evidence, which may well prevent us in the end from deciding the matter.

5. I have expressed support for the view that history is ultimately concerned with humanity, with the thoughts behind the actions we are investigating.[43] Of course we want to get the dates and durations of events as right as possible, but the main reason to do that is to figure out what the actors thought they were doing.[44]

6. On concluding an inquiry, if there is anything to say, we write up our results. What form should this take? The ancient world bequeathed narrative

42. Crucial points about the limitations of eyewitness observation were made by Bloch (1992 [1949]: 40–50). For psychological research into eyewitness evidence and its problems see Wells and Loftus 1984; Chabris and Simons 2010. It remains possible for groups (or a series of independent witnesses) to be collectively deceived under certain conditions. But that error usually pertains to detail rather than to the occurrence of an event.

43. Collingwood 1994: 158, 162–64, 176–80, 214–16, 228–29, esp. 282–301.

44. Cf. Collingwood 1994: 213.

as history's proper form. Josephus' argumentative essay about the ancient past, *Against Apion*, was a rare exception.

The question of how best to represent the results of historical research was energetically debated in the nineteenth century. Thomas Babington Macaulay, in 1828 viewing the new scientific direction with alarm, stressed the need for literary skill in expressing human truths.[45] Yet he also exposed the problem with this demand when he expected of historians a perfect mixture of flowing, proportionate narrative with evidentiary support for every sentence:[46] "A historian, such as we have been attempting to describe, would indeed be an intellectual prodigy . . . We shall sooner see another Shakespeare or another Homer."[47] Macaulay's grand-nephew George M. Trevelyan would similarly require historians to have great literary talent. Emphasizing how little can actually be known of the past, he thought it merely honest not to suggest scientific pretensions, but to use obviously creative writing to express what were in large measure imaginative results.[48] In the year before Britain went to war with Germany, when there was a patriotic dimension to the suspicion of scientific history, Trevelyan wrote:

> It is because the historians of to-day were trained by the Germanising hierarchy to regard history not as an 'evangel' or even as a 'story,' but as a 'science,' that they have so much neglected what is after all the principal craft of the historian—the art of narrative . . . Yet history is, *in its unchangeable essence,* 'a tale.'[49]

It was a neat twist of fortune that E. H. Carr's social-scientific manifesto for history (above) came to life as the George M. Trevelyan lectures.[50]

From the other end of the spectrum, J. B. Bury's inaugural address in Cambridge on "The Science of History" (26 January, 1903) declared with scorn:

---

45. Macaulay 1898 [this essay 1828]: 167–68, 216–20.

46. The historian must attribute "no expression to his characters, which is not authenticated by sufficient testimony" (Macaulay 1898: 216).

47. Macaulay 1898: 220.

48. Trevelyan 1913: 9.

49. Trevelyan 1913: 14 (emphasis mine).

50. Equally amusing is that the idealist-historicist Isaiah Berlin should have been offered the first Auguste Comte Lecture at the LSE. Berlin felt the need of a tribute to Comte, and offered this (2002: 95): "His grotesque pedantry, the unreadable dullness of much of his writing, his vanity, his eccentricity, his solemnity, the pathos of his private life, his dogmatism, his authoritarianism, his philosophical fallacies, all that is bizarre and Utopian in his character and writings, need not blind us to his merits."

> I may remind you that history is *not a branch of literature*. The facts of history, like the facts of geology or astronomy, can *supply material* for literary art; ... but to clothe the story of a human society [note] in a literary dress is not more the part of a historian as a historian, than it is the part of an astronomer to present in an artistic shape the story of the stars.[51]

That was the old debate. Since about the 1960s, the assumption that historical writing must be a kind of narrative has led some scholars to emphasize its proximity to fictional narrative, given that all stories alike—whatever their aspirations in relation to truth—require plots and characters with beginnings, middles, and ends.[52]

Ancient historians wrote literary narratives, as we have seen, and were judged by literary standards.[53] I cannot see, however, why our own history-writing ought to take narrative form. If history is in the first instance methodical inquiry, an argumentative essay seems better suited to the presentation of its results, retracing the steps of the investigation.[54] This is not to suggest that argument is in any sense neutral, scientific, or rhetoric-free. It is after all the quintessential form of rhetoric.[55] Every choice we make about diction, phrasing, and sentence construction, or about what to include and exclude, reflects our bias and perspective. I do not recommend argument because it is objective, but because it allows us to convey most transparently the content of our inquiry to other historians. When we describe a problem, identify and interpret relevant evidence, and weigh solutions, we invite critical assessment at each point—more simply than when asking others to read a narrative we have produced with its necessary characterizations and plot devices. Systematic arguments enable us to isolate issues of rational judgment that all of us can engage, irrespective of the unique questions and biases that brought us to the problem. They are exercises in (limited) self-transcendence.

---

51. Bury 1930: 9 (emphasis added).

52. For these perspectives see, e.g., Jenkins 1991; 1997; Munslow 1997; Beeson 2007: 3–11. The most prominent name here is Hayden White (1973; 1978; 1987). For a sympathetic appraisal, beginning with a new essay by White reflecting on Primo Levi's *Survival in Auschwitz*, see Korhonen 2006. For critical responses to White see Momigliano 1981; Ginzburg 1991; Evans 2000: 100–102, 124–26; Iggers 1997: 118–47.

53. See e.g., Woodman 1988.

54. Goldstein (1976: 140–43) distinguishes helpfully between history's neglected *infrastructure*, of critical and open inquiry, and its *superstructure*, which may take various forms.

55. See Aristotle, *Rhet.* 1.1 [1354a–1355b].

Conclusion to Part I

I cannot deny that this first part of our study has an ulterior therapeutic motive. It may serve as a covert apology to friends and family members whose momentary delight at finding a "historian" on their quiz team quickly turned to regret, if nobly concealed, when they realized that I had little capacity for the recall of dates and names. Their perplexity was palpable, if unspoken: "But aren't you a historian?"

We have travelled a long road to reach a simple idea. I dared to invite readers on the journey because history seems to be burdened with many false expectations and with language that cannot stand scrutiny—in school, society, politics, historians' debates, or in the study of Roman Judaea. History is imagined as an authoritative record to be learned, or learned for its lessons, or as a social-scientific exercise that cares nothing for individuals, or as concerned only with important events or movements, or articulated thoughts. I hope to have helped the reader scrape off some of this encrustation, to return to the foundations. History is simply the methodical investigation of questions that we pose about the human past. Only by pursuing our questions in a systematic way—identifying, gathering, interpreting, and explaining evidence—can we liberate the past from authorities that would otherwise control and mediate it via the traditions that come to all of us unasked.

Recognizing the investigative nature of history creates more problems, to be sure, and the bulk of Part I has taken up some obvious ones. I should stress that contemplating our task as historians is an entirely different matter from understanding how writers of history in Graeco-Roman times viewed their task. We have not explored this question, though the second chapter of *HJW* takes up aspects of it, and Part II examines the shared values and conceptual world of ancient writers.

CONCLUSION TO PART I　　　　　　　　85

Our main conclusion, after establishing a view of history as inquiry, is that there is no need to narrow its remit to either social-scientific *or* humanistic modes. It is of course possible for someone to be a humanist, philosophically, and a social scientist in method. But the two trajectories in historical research that I have put under these labels have different interests, questions, and criteria. Social or social-scientific history tends toward the quantitative and statistical, especially for the modern period, where databases abound. This mode of history seeks to bring order to the potential chaos of the past by postulating transcultural models and types, at least as initial entry points, and to look for patterns, norms, and bases of prediction. Individuals matter chiefly as vivid examples, though rarely if ever as pure expressions of a notional type. A deep assumption is that large-scale social and economic drivers move events in ways no individual ever could. Philosophically, this way of exploring the past tends toward determinism and the marginalizing of individual thought and will alike.

It may be that humanistic history was in danger of extinction after Darwin, from its perceived lack of fitness in the university world. At least, one could gain the impression that after the massive human traumas in the 1910s, 1930s, and 1940s, when extreme forms of scientific history and applied science killed tens of millions,[1] humanistic history was not so readily dismissed as weak-minded. Perhaps the same impulses that gave rise to the Universal Declaration of Human Rights in the U.N. General Assembly in December 1948 also gave humanist historians a new lease on life. I cannot prove this, but it does seem that after World War II people were less sanguine about the scientification of all disciplines and more willing to give space to questions of individual human worth.

Humanists characteristically seek to explore the endless possibilities of human existence. This perspective tends to historicize the past and to care about the particular: specific texts, individuals, and their unique contexts. Individuals matter and may even be considered decisive, the irreplaceable movers of events (a Stalin, Hitler, Churchill, Mao, Saddam Hussein, George W. Bush, Tony Blair). Where social-scientific history looks for order, historicism embraces the chaos and even searches out the interestingly aberrant, the pattern-defying, and the disquieting, from a deeply rooted notion of individual freedom. This concern with situational difference tends toward moral relativism. If each case is different and we acknowledge that

---

1. Both the Third Reich and state communism rested on what they considered scientific principles and views of history, whether this was racial-nationalist or class- and economics-based. They shared the view that individual lives were of little concern in relation to the health of the nation-state, and that indeed a healthy state required constant purging and loss to remain vital (Burleigh 2008).

we cannot recover the many factors influencing individual thought, moral judgment goes out the window along with normativity and causation—though of course historians retain the right of all human beings to moral judgment on other grounds. But historicism throws a spanner in the works of large-scale syntheses by emphasizing the recalcitrance of the particular.

We need both kinds of history, though each of us may incline toward one side. It is hard to see how one could write a history of first-century Judaea or the war of 66 to 74, for example, without attention to both *longue-durée* conditions (e.g., Roman governance, military practice, village life in relation to *poleis*) and the predicaments, thoughts, and aspirations of crucial individuals. As the third "family" reminds us, with a wry smile, we had better remain open to surprise. Neither individual motives nor typical group behaviors will explain the evidence completely.

Maurice Mandelbaum captured the basic idea of history when he wrote: "We expect historians to engage in research, to weigh alternative possibilities, and to marshal evidence in favor of one rather than another of these possibilities."[2] My caveats are two, for ancient history. First, the "alternative possibilities" do not come out to greet us. We must imagine them and, since life is full of strange possibilities, try to imagine more. Second, in ancient history we often lack *evidence* that is of sufficient quality to favor one explanation decisively. In this field we need to make our peace with Herodotus' apparent view that the investigative journey is also a worthy destination.

---

2. See Mandelbaum 1967: 414; responses in Ely, Gruner, and Dray 1969: 275–94.

Part II

Mapping Peoples

To understand the truth about the Greeks and Romans, it is wise to study them without thinking of ourselves, as if they were entirely foreign to us; with the same disinterestedness, and with the mind as free, as if we were studying ancient India or Arabia.

—N. D. Fustel de Coulanges, *The Ancient City* (1864)

He who uses terms such as "transcendence," "capitalism," "superstition," "imperialism," "heresy," slavery," and "liberty" without asking what they meant in a given time and place (and whether it is indeed legitimate to use them with regard to certain times and places) is already for that reason a dangerous historian.

—A. Momigliano, "The Rules of the Game in the Study of Ancient History" (1974)[1]

Part I was a reflection on what it means to do (ancient) history. In working through those issues, however, I had to ignore the elephant in the room. In assuming that we *can* understand ancient survivals, that discussion sidelined the formidable problems presented by language and alien cultural scripts. Most of the survivals that interest us, whether literary texts, inscriptions, papyrus documents, or coins, use language—and never mod-

---

1. Momigliano 1974; this translation by Schwartz 2013: 189.

ern English. The obvious remedy is to learn the necessary languages. But what does it mean to learn a language? Anyone who has tried it realizes, painfully at times, that a wide chasm separates lexical-grammatical competence from deep, native-like knowledge of the way a language works: what its written and spoken codes signify in different contexts. We realize this even when faced with an English text, in a technical discipline or a register or genre (e.g., poetry), that we struggle to understand.

A text is after all an author's purposeful arrangement of signs (words and statements), which need to be decoded by competent readers or audiences with a comparable understanding of the symbol set. For the outsider looking in on Greek, Latin, or Hebrew texts after 2,000 years, decoding will be difficult even if we "know the language." Languages share a great lexical bank, which makes communication possible, and which is so important to life in society that we begin teaching it to toddlers at the earliest opportunity, with picture-identification books. The bank itself is invisible and inaccessible, living in the minds of community members, but it is incarnated in each new text they create.

Being humans and not robots, moreover, authors do not limit their creations to lexically permitted or conventional language, the sort of thing we deplore as bland bureaucratese. Writers usually want to compose in a stimulating way. They often challenge audiences by introducing a degree of tension with the bank of established meanings, using words in surprising ways and steadily enriching the bank in the process. This is by no means a matter of rational communication only. Authors try to affect the decoding audience through a range of rational and emotional levels, from simple indication ("See Spot the dog") to complex thoughts, allusion, contingency, subtle plays, irony, and the general subversion of expectation. A single writer may select an array of modes and registers for different occasions.

When we communicate in English, nevertheless, we assume the established bank as our point of reference and departure. We assume that remarks about *school, college, the supermarket, the office, police, a bar* ("A dog walks into a bar. . ."), *immigration, driver's license, income tax, legislature,* and *judicial system* will be intelligible to anyone in a modern western society. It is not that these words mean the same *particular* thing for Dutch, American, or Australian audiences. We expect such questions as: "What *kind* of school or college did you attend?" or "How does the legislature work in *your* country?" Everyone exposed to American film and TV knows that elected county sheriffs and U.S. Marshals, alongside FBI, state, and city police forces, are unique to that country. But we can still talk intelligibly, across jurisdictions, about the police or the courts or legislatures. These are shells awaiting specific content, but we understand them.

The Graeco-Roman world had its shared lexical bank, which obviously was different from ours. In the mid-second century A.D. Lucian could imagine a Scythian visitor to Athens, scarcely able to absorb the striking differences from his homeland but asking to be shown "their finest laws, their superior men, customs, festival assemblies, their life and constitution."[2] The categories were shared; the particulars were assumed to be different. Around the same time, Pausanias undertakes research among the Greek populations of the Balkan peninsula and Peloponnese, likewise assuming great variety even among "Greek" laws and customs. Although every place and populace has its own particular past, story, and institutions, they (and he) communicate by using the shared categories: *polis*, territory (*chōra*), constitution, citizenship, council, leading men, assembly, populace, priesthood, temple, festival calendar. We do not use these categories today, however, just as they lacked our school, supermarket, or penitentiaries. Since they cannot come to us, if we want to understand their discourse we must go to them, as it were. We must do the investigating.

Our interest is above all in the Greek lexical bank because that evolving treasury was the shared medium throughout our period, among writers as diverse as Herodotus, Polybius, Dionysius, Diodorus, Plutarch, Dio, the creators of post-biblical "apocryphal" texts, Philo, Josephus, and New Testament authors. Of course Phoenicians, Hebrews, Babylonians, and Persians had their own languages, dialects, and categories. By the first century A.D., however, literate elites throughout the eastern Mediterranean basin and the Near East, including the Parthian world of Iran and Iraq, had fully absorbed Greek and its ways of thinking. This was not purely for literary-creative purposes. Roman authorities and local eastern *polis* leaders drew from that bank to communicate, and their language both described and created realities on the ground. Roman provincial administration and imperial expectation rested on the success of such communication.

We shall occasionally note Latin, Hebrew, and Aramaic by way of comparison. But it is the *shared discourse*, rather than the private thoughts of a Celt, Pict, Judaean, or Arab, or the in-house conversations of North Africans or Phoenicians under Roman rule, that interests us here. Whatever they might have thought privately, we know prolific Judaean authors such as Philo and Josephus only through the Greek they composed. Their language is plainly not a superficial overlay on thoughts that do not fit. It is not translation-Greek. Their compositions show them thinking deeply with the categories, assumptions, and values they shared with literate elites around

---

2. Lucian, *Scyth*. 4: παραλαβὼν ξενάγησον καὶ δεῖξον τὰ κάλλιστα τῶν Ἀθήνησιν . . . νόμων τε τοὺς ἀρίστους καὶ ἀνδρῶν τοὺς βελτίστους καὶ ἤθη καὶ πανηγύρεις καὶ βίον αὐτῶν καὶ πολιτείαν.

the Mediterranean—whatever else they may have thought in different and unrecoverable recesses of their minds.

In his *Course in General Linguistics*, taught in Geneva between 1907 and 1911, Ferdinand de Saussure (1857–1913) distinguished *la langue* or (the) language, the invisibly shared social-linguistic reality in the minds of a community's members, from *parôle*, a specific effort at communication within the community of shared understanding.[3] We need not explore Saussure further to agree that understanding a culture's textual creations will require a grasp of its lexical bank or *langue*. That is the purpose of Part II in this book. Some readers may find affinities here with the "emic" side of social-scientific research,[4] others with analyses of rhetoric or discourses—a term owing much to Michel Foucault's *Archaeology of Knowledge* (1969). What we are going to examine resembles a Foucauldian "discursive practice" in some ways, though he would perhaps not support my interests in interpretation or intention.[5] I see no need to entangle ourselves in any technical vocabulary. In my view, our task flirts dangerously with common sense. When exploring other cultures we naturally want to learn the shared categories they use to order their knowledge of society.

John Richardson's 2008 study of Rome's language of empire illustrates the task. Countless historians before him had been interested in Rome's empire, and asked about the kind or type of empire it was in relation to all "empires," or about how the Romans built their empire, or why it declined—the category of empire itself being assumed. Richardson asked about the contextual meaning of the related terms in internal Roman-elite discourse. He traced the use of Latin *imperium* and *provincia* in authors from the third century B.C. to the second century A.D., to learn not what the Roman empire really or essentially *was* but how the Romans talked about it.[6] It was a productive exercise, for he found a development from an original focus on *imperium* as controlling power to derivative senses connected with territory.[7]

3. E.g., Saussure 1993: xvi–xxiv.
4. Pike 1954; Harris 1976.
5. Foucault 1972: 117: "it is a body of anonymous, historical rules, always determined in the time and space that have defined a given period, and for a given social, economic, geographical, or linguistic area, the conditions of operation of the enunciative function."

6. Richardson 2008: 5. He defines his research problem thus: "What did the Romans *think they were doing* as their power changed and expanded?" Remarkably, for 2008: "relatively little has been written on what the Romans *thought their empire was* as opposed to what they did to create it" (emphasis added).

7. The best review I know is Shatzman 2010, which appropriately works through Richardson's evidence and critiques it at points—rather than, for example, suggesting

An earlier example is worth mentioning because it shows the scope for misunderstanding even among specialists. It has long been common to speak of Roman social relations in terms of *patronage*: a system in which the wealthy supported their "clients" materially, in return for which the latter gave their patrons loyal support as needed. In a 1978 article, however, Peter White argued that viewing Roman society through the lens of patronage obfuscated the "Roman code of manners."[8] In their discourse a *patronus* was a master who freed a slave, the formal benefactor of a town or corporation, or a defense advocate, not someone who supported poets.[9] When we use the term for the social relationships of writers we are borrowing from the very different early modern world, where wealthy men enabled artists to pursue artistic careers by maintaining them. But these conditions did not hold for the Latin poets—White's case study—and he offers a brief account via the Middle Ages of how patronage in the modern sense came to be. His interest is in understanding the ancients according to their own categories and values.

The Latin poets, he pointed out, were relatively wealthy men. They usually belonged to the equestrian order, which required property of 400,000 sesterces' value, and would have been able to live comfortably from the income that generated. They were hardly worried about their next meal. Nor were they career artists in the way of modern clients. Moreover, they typically express their gratitude to several friends, rather than to a single benefactor of the patron type. What the powerful friends offered the poet was not basic maintenance, but benefits associated with the code of friendship: pleasant accommodation in the city, help with legal problems (e.g., if forged writings began circulating under his name), and most importantly the wealthier man's social network. Poets needed audiences, in a world without publishers, and the nature of the Roman social code was such that a man of senatorial status, for example, could best provide that. He could furnish a venue for recitations and round up audiences. Friendship also brought the expectation of gifts, in most cases small tokens but with the possibility of bequests or property.

White's crucial point is about anachronism.[10] If our concern is to understand how the Romans thought and spoke, then we must recognize that they did not cast the relationship between poets and rich friends in the terms of a modern patron-client code. They did not *call* the parties patrons

---

that he should not have asked the question.

8. White 1978: 74; cf. already White 1975 on poets' "friends."
9. White 1978: 79.
10. White 1978: 74–82.

and clients because that would have violated their code of manners, but rather placed all these relationships under the code of friendship (*amicitia*). That they were dramatically lopsided was obvious, but "patron-client" labeling would have made things charmless—and too restrictive. Supposing a patron-client code can lead to further misconceptions, for example in imagining a state program of cultural support for artists under Augustus via his friend C. Clinius Maecenas.

White's essay was in the spirit of what follows in this chapter, which asks in a broader way how Greek (and Latin) authors communicated about basic sources of identity. The student of Roman Judaea should note a parallel issue with the language of "client kingship," the term we often use for King Herod. The Romans themselves raised what we call clients to the dignity of "friends and allies of the Roman people," and this may be important for understanding how the kings actually viewed themselves, notwithstanding the massive gap in power between the two parties.[11] There is a further parallel today, as American leaders call foreign leaders who look like their satellites or clients "our friends."

Disagreements with this approach[12] were encapsulated in the sharp response that White's article elicited from Richard Saller, a renowned expert in the Roman economy and patronage. Using the Flavian poet Martial as his main example, Saller argued that this man was a client by any definition. Although he enjoyed equestrian status, a country farm with slaves, and a small townhouse in Rome, he felt in regular need of support from wealthier people. Martial received money in addition to expensive gifts that were convertible to cash. Finally, Saller noted, the Latin word *patronus* does turn up occasionally in inscriptions, though indeed not in literature concerning these social relationships.

Saller's methodological point is most important for us. He bluntly declared White's concern with ancient usage a "red herring," which should be "eliminated from the discussion."[13] The Romans may have favored friendship language, he conceded, but so what? "But it would be wrong to conclude that the modern scholar must therefore restrict himself to the vocabulary of friendship in his analysis and avoid the word 'patronage'. *The historian never confines himself to the language and categories of the subjects of his study,*

---

11. Braund 1984; and the general spirit of the essays with introduction in Jacobson and Kokkinos 2009.
12. E.g., Schwartz 2011.
13. Saller 1983: 255.

PART II: MAPPING PEOPLES   93

though they must be taken into account; he always organizes and analyses his material in terms of his own questions, interests, and categories."[14]

Notice here a curious reversal of motives. White had not written to exclude, restrict, or confine. The whole spirit of his piece is about opening up new angles of vision on Roman social realities by shedding anachronisms. He does not address the interests of social scientists, but writes in the humanistic philological stream of history. Saller appears to the one who would restrict things, rejecting White's question out of hand and scheduling it for *elimination*. There may be a parallel with issues we shall discuss below. A deeply entrenched scholarly model is challenged on the basis of actual ancient usage. Respondents perceive this as an aggressive move toward domination of scholarly discourse, even as *they* convert the discussion to one of binary choices and *they* dismiss the new insights out of hand.

In Saller's view, the relationships found in ancient Rome qualify as "patronage, as we define it today" (viz., "a continuing reciprocal but asymmetrical exchange relationship")[15] and so we should use the term without hesitation. When he justifies his view further by citing a study of "cause and meaning in the social sciences"[16] we see the real source of the conflict. The humanist White tries to read himself into the language and concepts of Roman authors while the social-scientist historian Saller understands himself to be an external analyst. Much like the physician who compares my sore elbow with all sore elbows and diagnoses bursitis, without asking me what I think about my elbow, the social scientist of this persuasion need not bother with internal perceptions. That is fine and understandable, but why should it be exclusive?

Similar conflicts and misunderstandings can arise with the material of this chapter, experience suggests,[17] on ancient terminology connected with Roman Judaea. I hope that the following two points are clear by now, and enough for us to proceed. First, historians must indeed ask their own investigative questions, as Saller observes, and not try to turn ancient texts into transparent data for what happened. In Chapter 1 I have argued that investigation of our research problems is the only indispensable part of history. *One* important question about the Graeco-Roman world, however, which we need to address if we are interested in interpreting the texts that provide much of our evidence, concerns their way of ordering their social-

14. Saller 1983: 256; emphasis added.
15. Saller 1983: 256.
16. Gellner 1973.
17. Two responses of many (to Mason 2007) are Schwartz 2011: e.g., 210, 221, 229; Reinhartz 2014.

political-religious world. This question need not interest everyone, but there is also nothing wrong with it.

Second, if this kind of study is not about the trans-temporal models of the social scientist, it is equally not about essential inner realities, another source of confusion we shall encounter below. In discussing ancient discourse categories we are not asking about genetics or real identities, but simply about the common language people used to communicate with each other. The changes in such discourse from one era to another, as White showed with the evolution of patronage conceptions through the Middle Ages, confirms that these discourses are *constructed*—and potentially reconstructed in dialogue with large-scale political and social change. They are no less important or consequential for being socially constructed, however, just as our constructed world of countries, passports, courts, and borders is not something we lightly ignore. People act on the basis of the shared lexicon, because those are the terms in which they think. In antiquity, shared categories and value sets fostered the creation of *poleis* with civic squares, consecrated council houses, temples, altars, and *gymnasia*. Rome's provincial governors made a point of visiting the *poleis* (only) in their province and knew to seek out the "best men" in each one for political cultivation. The discourse and the reality were mutually confirming, but both could have been different.

So we are not examining eternal Platonic truths, and we are free to understand ancient motives and actions otherwise, for example in terms of social-scientific models and analogues if they will help. But there is nothing wrong with trying to understand that constructed world, and we must do it *if* our interest is in the communicative efforts produced from the shared lexical bank by a Diodorus, Philo, Plutarch, or Josephus.

Two final cautions anticipate what is coming. First, to speak of ancient categories is not to suggest that these constituted anything resembling a coherent *system* comparable to the biologist's phylum, class, order family, genus, and species. Observing how people talk, and which words go with which, is not a matter of defining each in exclusionary terms: *ethnos* means this and not that. On the contrary, all the terms we shall consider turn out to have been impressively elastic—not unlike our modern categories. We have no qualms in using "state," even quite formally, for polities as different as the Vatican (pop. 1,000 and 0% birth rate) and China (pop. 1.4 billion), the fifty constituents of the United States, and the twenty-eight member-states of the European Union.[18] All such categories must be flexible. Here we are explor-

---

18. *CIA World Factbook* (https://www.cia.gov/library/publications/resources/the-world-factbook/).

ing ancient categories, which were of course very different from those of our post-Enlightenment, post-revolution, and post-industrial world.

Second, exploring the discourse of elite Greek-speaking authors does not assume that any constituent group's internal values, or grievances, were readily expressible in Greek. The idea is not that because Philo or Josephus could communicate Judaean values in the common coin, those values as first constructed in Hebrew and Aramaic had *essentially* changed to become generic. Scholars have long been fascinated by the Greek Bible's rendering of Hebrew-biblical key terms (beginning third century B.C.).[19] Recasting *Torah* ([divine] instruction) as convention (*nomos*), ṣedeq (righteousness) as *dikē* (justice), and *ḥatta'* (sin) as *hamartia* (shortcoming, failure) required a stretch on both sides of the transfer.

Likewise in the first century A.D., Hebrew conceptions of "freedom" (e.g., *ḥerut*) likely had different connotations from the nearest Greek equivalents, whether *eleutheria* referred to *polis* qualities or internal philosophical dispositions. When Josephus identifies a group called Zēlōtai (we commonly transliterate as Zealots), and makes fun of the way their name works in Greek (only), we are left to imagine what they actually called themselves in Hebrew or Aramaic and the connotations of those terms.[20] Nevertheless, the Judaean aristocrat, who was at home in both worlds, could express confidence that he was able to explain Judaean matters in Greek terms (*Ant.* 1.5–26; *Apion* 1.51). It is that shared communicative medium, the way people talked with each other, and not essential realities of Judaism, Jews, or Idumaeans, that interests us here.

I have chosen four clusters of basic terms related to social-political-religious (shorthand "cultural") identity, on the simple criteria of prominence, commonality, and durability. That is: they persevere in a wide range of authors throughout the classical period. I treat them in a sequence on the spectrum from givenness to voluntary choice. That is to say, everyone was unavoidably born into an *ethnos* or extended family group, which provided the customs and traditions with which they grew up. Only some, though certainly those who wrote elite literature, lived in a *polis* (including its territory or *chōra*). One could change *polis* residency, by moving, much more easily than one could change one's *ethnos*-belonging. Both *ethnos* and *polis*, third, came with the expectation of worship by means of animal and other sacrifice (*ta hiera*). But one's identity as a worshiper was more flexible in that most people could join cults voluntarily in addition. At the elective end of the group-identity spectrum were various kinds of voluntary association

---

19. Dodd 1935 deals with basic questions.
20. *HJW* 444–50.

(e.g., *thiasos*, *synodos*), including philosophical communities (*philosophiai*, *haireseis*). These were by definition optional, though social pressure to join an ethnic or guild group might have been considerable. In any case, they could potentially shape one's identity in more profound ways than given *ethnos-polis*-cult expectations. This last category is important for understanding the place of both Judaeans and Christ-followers in Roman society.

5a

The Classical Paradigm: *Ethnos* and *Polis*

Ethnos and Associates

The Greek Bible only occasionally uses *ethnos* for the Hebrew/Judaean people, when translating *goy* in the singular, a term more familiar from its plural *goyim*—nations (*ethnē*) or gentiles—a use found also in the New Testament.[1] The translators render Hebrew *'am* as Greek *laos*, or people. Philo and Josephus, by contrast, both thinking and composing in Greek, speak most readily of the Judaeans as an *ethnos*. In doing so they range them alongside other *ethnē*. Josephus uses *ethnos*-forms nearly 450 times, making this noun-group one of the dozen most frequent in his corpus, and Philo more than 300 times even though he has many interests other than comparative description.[2] When we see many other writers and material remains labeling the Judaeans an *ethnos*, we must conclude that this seemed the most obvious category in the shared lexical bank. Why? What sorts of associations did the word-group suggest? What terms went with it?

Before we proceed, I must stress that we are not now talking about the social-scientific category *ethnicity*, much less trying to define *that* or decide how a model did or did not fit various groups. Ethnicity is a modern term, first attested in 1920 and coming into common use only from the

---

1. For the singular (in God's promise to make his people a *goy gadol*, great nation), see Gen 12:2. Hebrew *'am* becomes the special *laos* or people of the covenant.

2. See the statistical tool at www.tlg.uci.edu. The main noun *ethnos* alone ranks 83 among all words (including much, all, be, day, year, only, different), with "person" (*anthrōpos*) at 77 and just behind "two."

1950s.³ Most discussions of ancient *ethnos* language known to me, in scholarship and in conferences on antiquity, shift quickly if not always clearly to sometimes anguished discussions of ethnicity. Scholars appear to want to find some reality or essence, even while everyone insists that the one thing ethnicity does not indicate is something "essentialist."

The meaning of any new coinage lies in the gift of the one who coins it. If it catches on and more people use it, dictionaries will take note and try to convey the growing range of meanings. Those who prefer to discuss trans-temporal models of ethnicity may define the term as they wish. But this has nothing necessarily to do with ancient discourse.⁴ Discussing the ancient world through the lens of ethnicity is comparable to asking about terrorists, separatists, or socialists in antiquity. Spending our time debating the meaning of these words, so that we know whom to include, has a kind of circularity to it. Our question here is not about ethnicity. We are simply trying to observe and understand how the ancients used *ethnos* and the words that went with it.

Through the millennium from Hecataeus of Miletus (ca. 500 B.C.) to Stephanus of Byzantium (early 500s A.D.) we find Greek writers fascinated with other peoples (plural *ethnē*) and their peculiar habits, laws, worship, and customs. Descriptions of the barbarian Other helped to reinforce Greek identity and cultural confidence or superiority, in a way that looks familiar to modern western treatment of the foreigner.⁵ But there seems to have been also a real fascination with the possibilities of human exis-

---

3. On the complexities of defining ethnicity see Barth 1969: 9–37; S. Jones 1997: 56–83; applying this to ancient history, Hall 1997: 18–20; 2002: 9–29 on emic/etic; 1997: with 1–33 on fundamental problems. Hall pursues a mainly etic approach focused on (real and fictive) kinship. Ulf (2009) contrasts an etic analysis with the claims of internal categories. Morgan 2009a: 11–36 surveys various possibilities for etic criteria in connection with antiquity. According to the editors of the volume containing her essay (1–9), "ethnicity is a form of *self*-ascription that may vary across time and space" (4), but in these discussions even the insider view is configured by social-scientific criteria: looking for universally applicable signs of "we-feeling," exclusion, inclusion, etc. That is not yet a study of ancient terminology as such. Konstan (1997), unusually, takes ancient usage as the central issue, as do Cohen 2000 and many essays in Malkin 2001. McInerney 2014, comprising essays by thirty-eight ancient historians vividly illustrates the concern with ethnicity. Vlassopoulos 2015 is a splendidly concise summary of often overlooked problems.

4. Rives 1999: 10–11 makes a clear distinction between discussion of the ancient Germani as "a single ethnic group" in terms of the criteria for ethnicity, and "Graeco-Roman ethnography," which "drastically simplified this complexity" and viewed the Germans as "a single discrete people."

5. For trenchant analysis of the Greek/other contrast in Herodotus' treatment of the Scythians, see Hartog 1988. More generally on binary oppositions, see Cartledge 2002a: 8–166, and the essays in Harrison 2002.

tence in remote places.[6] This ethnographic interest comes to our view, from surviving texts, in the late sixth century B.C. As we saw in Chapter 1, the Persian empire then extended its reach to western Asia Minor, including Hecataeus' Miletus. Fragments of his work, though lost in their original context, were preserved in the *Ethnica* of Stephanus, which provides a neat terminus for our constructed classical millennium (i.e., outside the special Christian lexicon).

Already in the generation following Hecataeus, Herodotus (Chapter 1) drew inspiration from his Milesian neighbor. To judge from Herodotus' extended portraits of Egyptians (2.2–182) and Scythians (4.5–82), it seems that a pattern for describing foreigners was already in place. One should examine the *origins* (indigenous, from time immemorial, or migrants), *geographical situation* (natural environment including strange phenomena), *laws, customs,* and *traditions* (social structure, cult, institutions, everyday practices), and *defining past* (great rulers and achievements) of the *ethnos*.[7] This pattern roughly matched the categories that rhetorical education taught for the assessment of individuals (see Clearchus' Aristotle below).

An enduring strain of ethnographic analysis appears in the text *Airs, Waters, Places*, attributed to the medical writer Hippocrates and composed in the late 400s B.C. This attributed the supposed physical characteristics of entire populations—their physical build, reproductive and digestive capacity, psychological temperament—to their distinctive environmental conditions, such as temperatures or qualities of wind and water (*Airs* 24):

> All those who inhabit a mountainous, rough, elevated, and amply watered land, and where the seasonal changes are very great, for this reason are likely to have a variety of forms and be nurtured for coping with hardship and for manliness... But all those who inhabit hollows and meadows and closed-off places, and experience a greater share of hot than cold winds, and use hot waters, these are not likely to be of large size or well proportioned...; manliness of soul and coping with hardship are not in them by nature (*physis*), though custom (*nomos*) might inculcate them.

This "environmental determinism"—you are what you breathe and eat—would have a long afterlife. Even in this ancient text, however, the author opens a gap between nature (*physis*) and custom (*nomos*—custom,

---

6. A forceful corrective to reductive assumptions about ancient views of the Other is Gruen 2011. Romm 2011 admits many of Gruen's points while insisting that otherness remained part of ancient self-definition.

7. See Bar-Kochva 1992: 10–13, 192–219.

shading into law). Although it would remain a default assumption that nature and nurture collaborated in producing ethnic variety, some Sophists argued for the radical (somewhat post-modern) view that custom had no natural foundation, but was wholly constructed. Herodotus could challenge the link between nature (*physis*) or environment and the regional peculiarities of Europeans, Asians, and Africans (e.g., 4.41–45),[8] but some of his descriptions assume a link between ethnic character and environment, as when he writes of the Egyptians (2.53.3–4):

> Along with this atmosphere that is unique to themselves, and a river [Nile] that is different from all other rivers, so also they have established customs and also laws that are backwards to those of the rest of humanity. Among them the women go to the market and conduct business, whereas the men, remaining at home, do the weaving! And whereas others weave the nap upwards, Egyptians weave it downwards . . . Their women urinate standing, the men sitting . . .

His portrayal of Scythian customs as inversions of Greek ways (4.59–82) is likewise framed by a discussion of Scythian geography (4.46–58, esp. 4.46–47).[9] Alongside more nuanced explorations of other peoples' ways, which might include admiration for pure noble-savage virtue over against the decayed habits of civilization,[10] the mirror-image style of ethnography would also remain a staple. Poseidonius, Diodorus (below), and the Roman Tacitus presented the Judaeans in such terms:

> Moses, wanting to strengthen his grip on the nation for the future [note the trope of Oriental tyranny], gave them new rituals contrary to those of other people. What is sacred among us is unholy for them; on the contrary, things impure for us are permitted among them.[11]

A typical element in the assessment of nations (*ethnē, gentes*), which may be hinted at in Tacitus' reference to Moses' grip on the people (as tyrant?), was foreigners' perceived capacity for either freedom or slavery.[12] Plato had argued that each people's customs and laws reflected its corporate nature or character, a point that would be developed by neo-Platonists

---

8. See Thomas 2000: 75–134.

9. See Hartog 1988: 34–60; Marincola 2001: 52–53.

10. See Rives 1999: 16–20, 51.

11. Tacitus, *Hist.* 5.4. See Bloch 2002 for detailed analysis of the passage, differing from my emphasis here.

12. See Rives 1999: 51; Cartledge 2002a: 133–66.

(below).¹³ Aristotle agreed, adding that the barbarian (or non-Greek-speaking) world was slavish *by nature*. Although they possessed souls, barbarians' reasoning capacity was defective and that is why they did not produce a natural ruling class (*Pol.* 1252b.1-8).

Aristotle used a version of his *golden mean* principle to argue that, because Greek cities were located away from the world's extreme climactic zones, they did not suffer either from either the (hot) Middle-Easterners' lack of spirit, which caused them to be perpetual slaves, or from the (cold) northern Europeans' lack of intelligence, which led to their failure of political organization—in spite of abundant spirit. The Greeks, blessed with a moderate geographical situation, enjoyed an optimal balance of spirit and intelligence. Consequently they both enjoyed freedom and had the natural capacity to rule others—if only they could fashion a political unity (*Pol.* 1327b). Aristotle's qualification here is one example of the many cracks that ancient writers incidentally noted in their schemes of classification, though they seldom explored the cracks.

In the second century B.C., Polybius was working from the same ethnographic assumptions when he characterized entire peoples as angry, treacherous, or freedom-loving.¹⁴ A few decades later, the Roman Cicero expected to be understood when he made offhand comments about Syrians' and Judaeans' being "nations born for slavery" (*Prov. cons.* 5).

Offensive though this kind of thinking is to our sensibilities, we should recognize that our sensibilities are quite recent in relation to the human past, dating from about the two World Wars—and that also in our societies the stereotyping of others is hardly absent. Ancient stereotyping itself, often imagined to be justified by environmental conditions, endured from late antiquity to the most respectable circles of modern times. Among the neo-Platonists of the third and fourth centuries A.D., regional ethnic diversity was enhanced by a sort of management chart, according to which local protective or tutelary deities presided over the various *ethnē* and nurtured their distinctive characters and constitutions.¹⁵ The emperor Julian (361–363), a neo-Platonist, held that the codes of discipline promulgated by various lawgivers reflected the innate dispositions of their *ethnē*. Germans were fierce lovers of liberty, though undisciplined; Syrians, Persians, and other easterners were docile and ready to accept despotic regimes.¹⁶

13. Plato, *Resp.* 544d–591; cf. Xenophon, *Vect.* 1.1.
14. Polybius 1.13.12; 3.3.3 7.1; 4.1.1–8, 53.5; 5.106.
15. Cf. Celsus in Origen, *C. Cels.* 5.25.
16. Julian, *C. Gal.* 131c, 138b.

Especially after the recovery of ancient culture in the Renaissance, this kind of outlook seemed dignified. In the mid-eighteenth century the French writer Montesquieu, whose work on *The Spirit of Laws* exercised much influence on American and French political thought, devoted Book 14 to the influence of climate on laws:

> If we travel towards the north, we meet with people who have few vices, many virtues, and a great share of frankness and sincerity. If we draw near the south, we fancy ourselves entirely removed from the verge of morality; here the strongest passions are productive of all manner of crimes ... In temperate climates we find the inhabitants inconstant in their manners, as well as in their vices and virtues: the climate has not a quality determinate enough to fix them.[17]

His contemporary David Hume debunked in detail the idea that *climate* accounted for national characters, but he also accepted the premise that there were national characters.[18] His effort to sever the environmental foundation was futile, as we see in Hegel, who prefaced his study of nations and their spirits (*Geiste*) by emphasizing "the geographical basis of history."[19] In 1790 Edmund Burke opposed both the French Revolution and its British sympathizers—provoking Thomas Paine's *The Rights of Man*—on the premise that each European nation had an ancient character and constitution, which evolved institutions that could not suddenly be eradicated.[20] In 1832 the future British Prime Minister Benjamin Disraeli based his deep Euroskepticism, as we would call it, on that principle. If we supplied *ethnos* and dropped "religious" from the list, we would be close to ancient usage, which these classically educated authors consciously preserved:

> There is in all countries a healthy fund of legitimate spirit, springing out of the national character; that national character is formed by the influence of particular modes of religious belief, ancient institutions, peculiar manners, venerable customs, and intelligible interests. The government that does not respect these the hallowed offspring of reverend Antiquity and sage Experience, can never stand.[21]

17. Montesquieu 2001 (1848), 248–49.

18. Hume, *Essays* 116–27.

19. Hegel 1900: 79–102. Though holding back from outright determinism, Hegel found in varied natural contexts "the special possibilities from which the Spirit of the people in question germinates" (79).

20. Burke 1790 passim.

21. Disraeli 1832: 50.

On similar principles, sociology's founder Auguste Comte (Chapter 1) found ideal conditions for a priest-led caste system among "the yellow races," given "a fine climate with a fertile soil . . . ; a territory admitting naturally of internal communication; and a country so isolated as to be secure from invasion . . ."[22] And Lord Acton, soon to become Regius Professor of Modern History at Cambridge University (1895), said of the Irish:

> The Celts are not among the progressive, initiative races, but among those which supply the materials rather than the impulse of history, and are either stationary or retrogressive. The Persians, the Greeks, the Romans, and the Teutons are the only makers of history, the only authors of advancement. Other races possessing a highly developed language, a copious literature, a speculative religion, enjoying luxury and art, attain to a certain pitch of cultivation which they are unable either to communicate or to increase . . . The Chinese are a people of this kind . . . So the Hindoos . . . So the Huns . . . So the Slavonians . . . To this class of nations also belong the Celts of Gaul.[23]

It is hard to see much difference from Aristotle's time, except that the modern statements fatefully fused ancient *ethnos*-conceptions with notions of Darwinian competition and racial biology, as we saw in Chapter 1.

Having detoured to sketch the impact of a potent idea, let us return to ancient *ethnos*. Alexander the Great's fourth-century B.C. advance into Persia brought a renewed impetus to understand the distinctive ways of non-Greek peoples. Hecataeus of Abdera, attached to the court of the successor-king Ptolemy I (ca. 300 B.C.), was one of several writers to explore Egyptian—and Judaean—customs from his base in Alexandria, Egypt.[24] In the same context, elite members of some newly subjugated peoples, such as Manetho in Egypt and Berosus in Persia, tried to balance Greek ethnographers' impressions by writing their own self-portraits. Familiar with Greek language and culture, they adopted the standard *ethnos* categories, but as authentic insiders explaining the truth of their cultures.[25]

An anonymous work from about this time, called the *Voyage* and falsely attributed to an earlier writer named Scylax, is illuminating for its terse use of *ethnos* and *polis* as crucial descriptive categories. The fragmentary text follows a clockwise tour of the Mediterranean littoral (*Per.* 85–86):

---

22. Comte 1896: 3.62.
23. Dalberg 1922: 240–41.
24. See Bar-Kochva 1992: 1–43.
25. Sterling 1992 places Josephus in this long tradition of "apologetic historiography."

After the Becheires are the Long-heads, an *ethnos*, and Itch Harbor, then Trapezous, a Greek *polis*. After the Long-heads are the Hut-dwellers, an *ethnos*, with West-Wind Harbor, Choirades, a Greek *polis*, Ares' Island. They live in mountains.

For this author, foreign peoples are *ethnē* linked with particular locations, and the greatest interest attaches to their physical and social traits. When he comes to the eastern Mediterranean, he offers (*Per.* 104–106):

After Cilicia comes an *ethnos*: the Syrians. In Syria the Phoenicians, an *ethnos*, live along the sea ... A *polis* of the Tyrians is Sarapta; another *polis* is Tyre, having a harbor within its walls. This is the royal island of the Tyrians ... And Akē [Acco], a *polis* ... Carmel, a mountain sacred to Zeus. Arados, a *polis* of the Sidonians. Ioppē [Jaffa/Yafo], a *polis*—they claim that Andromeda was put here for the sea-monster [i.e., in Greek myth]. Ascalon, a *polis*—and a royal one, of the Tyrians. This is the limit of Coele-Syria ... After Syria [i.e., further east] are the Arabs, an *ethnos*, horse-riding nomads who have pastures for all kinds of animals—sheep, goats, camels ...

This kind of travelogue would remain standard for centuries. King Herod's aide and biographer, Nicolaus of Damascus (d. ca. A.D. 5), who became a main source for Josephus, wrote up his own collection of ethnic character traits: an Illyrian tribe called Dardanes were supposedly washed only at birth, marriage, and death. A Scythian *ethnos* called the Dairy-Eaters had no homes, but wandered around drinking horse-milk and eating cheese from it, sharing their wives and children.[26] Writers such as Strabo, Pliny, and Solinus populated this kind of human zoo with entertaining stories of bizarre customs and weird body types associated with each *ethnos*.[27]

In the late first century B.C., Diodorus of Sicily showed the same interest when he retailed stories about the Judaeans, from their origins to their subjugation by the Roman general Pompey (63 B.C.). Having been driven out of Egypt for impiety and leprosy, he claimed, the refugees "occupied the places around Jerusalem, got together *and formed the ethnos of the Judaeans*, and made the hatred of humanity their tradition; for the same reason, they introduced completely outrageous laws," which isolated them from fellowship with every other *ethnos* (34/35.1.2; cf. 40.3.8). Notice Diodorus'

---

26. Dindorf 1870: 145 lines 3–15.

27. Namely: Strabo, *Geography*; Pliny, *Natural History* (cf. 1.7); and Solinus, *Gallery of Remarkable Things*—drawn largely from Pliny. On Pliny's use of ethnic wonders to define the normal world, by contrast, see Murphy 2004: 18–22.

THE CLASSICAL PARADIGM: *ETHNOS* AND *POLIS* 105

untroubled assumption that a new *ethnos* could be constructed from an existing one, a point to which we shall return.

Strabo of Amaseia was born in the same year as the emperor Augustus, which happened to be the year that Pompey captured Jerusalem for the Romans. He lived to be nearly 90 in the reign of Tiberius (ca. 64/63 B.C. to ca. A.D. 25). Identifying the whole area from the Euphrates River to Egypt as Syria (16.2.1), Strabo described its constituent populations as follows (*Geog.* 16.2.2):

> Some divide up Syria as a whole into Coele-Syrians, Syrians, and Phoenicians, and claim that four *ethnē* are mixed in with these: Judaeans, Idumaeans, Gazaeans, and Azotians.

Strabo makes the same point as Pseudo-Scylax about Joppa's connection with Andromeda in the Greek myth concerning Cepheus, king of Ethiopia, his daughter Andromeda, and Perseus' rescue of her from a sea-monster (16.2.28; cf. Ovid, *Met.* 4.663–803). He pauses to note remarkable events and geographical features of the region. When he turns to the inland part of southern Syria, after remarking that Idumaeans are originally Nabataeans who joined with the Judaeans, Strabo comments (16.2.34):

> In general and also in particular cases, it [the area] is settled by mixed tribes [*phylai*] from the Egyptian, Arab, and Phoenician nations [*ethnē*]. . . . But in this general mish-mash, the prevailing opinion, of the credible ones, concerning the temple in Jerusalem declares the ancestors of those now called Judaeans to be Egyptians.

In keeping with standard ethnography and rhetoric, Strabo then moves from origins to a potted history of notable Judaean leaders and events.

Writing later but independently in the same century, Pliny the Elder (A.D. 23–79) likewise emphasizes the complex ethnic composition of southern Syria. For entertainment and local color, he singles out a most peculiar *gens* (nation, tribe). These are the Essenes of Judaea, who are astonishing because they somehow perpetuate their remote, anti-*polis* way of life without women (*Nat.* 5.73). From his terminology, and given the variety of *gentes* in the area, it is not clear that he considers the Essenes Judaeans.

Particularly interesting is a forty-four-volume universal history in Latin by Pompeius Trogus, a writer from Augustus' time who treated affairs in the eastern empire and the Parthian world. Although the work was once considered to be on a par with the admired Sallust, Livy, and Tacitus, it has survived only in a selective and rewritten précis by a certain Justin (perhaps M. Iunianius Iustinus), nearly two centuries after its composition. Both

Trogus and Justin were committed to a Roman, moralizing approach to history, which minimized Greek speechifying and emphasized the distinctive characters of the world's *ethnē*.[28] In spite of the interval between the original author and his abbreviator, who writes long after Jerusalem's destruction in A.D. 70, both writers include the Judaeans (*Iudaei*) as one of the world's well known peoples and nations (*gentium nationumque*, 1.1).

Like the others, this text offers a creative account of Judaean origins, history, and culture (36.2.1–3.9). A certain Israhel was supposedly king of Damascus after Abraham. Having ten strong sons, Israhel created an equivalent number of kingdoms, but nevertheless named all his subjects *Judae-ans* in honor of his deceased son Juda. His youngest son Joseph became a master of science, both general and occult. When Joseph's equally remarkable son Moses (in that story) was expelled from Egypt, so as not to contract an outbreak of disease, he took with him the sacred instruments of the Egyptians. Moses made his son Aruas (cf. Aaron) priest over his Egyptian-derived cult in the new place. According to this story, the Judaeans were heading back to their ancestral Damascus, but decided instead to settle in in the region that naturally became *Judaea*, on account of their group name. They celebrated weekly sabbaths in memory of finding food after a long search. But they kept themselves aloof from the region's other inhabitants: originally because they were afraid of spreading the contagion from Egypt, but later because the segregation from others became a fixed trait of their *ethnos* character (36.2).

This little survey will suffice to show that people around the ancient Mediterranean who considered themselves well enough informed to write their views knew of the Judaeans as an *ethnos*. Like all others it had distinctive customs, which could be traced to a particular origin, ancestry, location, and national story. Judaean peculiarities—every *ethnos* had some—included a refusal to make anthropomorphic images of their god, though this was common among peoples of the Near East.[29] They practiced male circumcision, as did some Arabians and Egyptian priests.[30] They kept the weekly day of rest, often misunderstood as a fast day. And they were known to abstain from pork, considered delicious food by Greeks and Romans. This too was a custom shared with some others (Herodotus 4.63). They were famous for

28. See Yardley and Develin 1994: 1–10.

29. Herodotus 1.131. See Bickerman 1979: 70; Millar 1993: 12–15; Mettinger 1995; Gaifman 2008 (challenging either-or schemes that would pit Graeco-Roman iconic representations of a deity in the East over against allegedly indigenous, aniconic/litholatrous conceptions).

30. E.g., Herodotus 2.36.3; 37.4 (alleged uniqueness of Egyptian circumcision); cf. Josephus, *Apion* 1.168–170; Barclay 2006 n. 500.

their region's balsam trees, dates, and mysterious Dead Sea (Lake Asphaltites) with its buoyancy and bitumen.[31]

Although many ancient peoples were curious about their neighbors and sought to understand how the world came to be as it was—the Bible includes a table of nations tracing all of humanity to the sons of Noah (Gen 10:1–32)—the Greeks pursued the subject most energetically and developed the most enduring, albeit far from precise or scientific, language for this kind of study.[32] The basic categories by which they and later the Romans understood the inhabited earth (*oikoumenē*) included these: the people or nation (*ethnos*), the tribe (*phylē*), and the kind, class, or ancestral line (*genos*).[33] Each *ethnos* was assumed to have ancestral customs, conventions, laws, rituals, and stories of origins (*nomoi, ethē, patria, nomima, hiera, mythoi*), often connected with a founding lawgiver. An *ethnos* typically had some kind of mother-city (*mētropolis*), which was the most concentrated expression of the national ethos, expressed in a distinctive calendar, festivals, citizenship, civic structure, and citizenship laws. Underlying the whole was worship of one or more deities by means of animal sacrifice (below).

Here I need to stress or restate three points that follow from our project of examining the way the ancients used *ethnos* language. First, *ethnos* was a highly malleable term, not one that meant something specific and definable. From its early sense of any body, company, or flock—of persons or animals—it came to denote the whole range of population types and sizes. One may distinguish four general levels here: inhabitants of a *polis* and its territory, such as the Athenians, Messenians, or Lacedaemonians (Spartans and their subjects); larger regional populations such as Boeotians, Phocians, Argives, Arcadians, Calchidians, and Thessalians; the main trans-regional *ethnē* (Dorians, Ionians, Achaeans, and Aeolians); and such large national groups as Persians, Egyptians, Syrians, and Hellenes.[34]

---

31. Pliny, *Nat.* 12.111–113; 13.26–49; cf. Strabo 16.2.41–44; 17.1.15; Horace, *Ep.* 2.2; Josephus, *War* 3.517; *Ant.* 4.100; 9.7; Pausanias 9.19; Galen, *Simpl. med. temp.* 7.245; 12.171, 375; *Comp. med.* 13.536, 560; *Pis. ther.* 14.260; *Antid.* 1.4; 14.60–62; Justin, *Epit.* 3.1–7.

32. Josephus reinterprets the biblical table of nations along Greek ethnographical lines in *Ant.* 1.122–129.

33. See Jones 1996.

34. See, e.g., Herodotus 1.56 (Greek *ethnos*); 7.85 (Persian *ethnos*); 2.32.4 on the *ethnē* among the Libyans; Thucydides 6.1–6 on *ethnē* connected with Sicily and Syracuse; Aeschines, *Fals. leg.* 116 on the various Greek *ethnē*; Polybius 2.49.6; Diodorus 11.6.3 (Medes); 15.26 (Boeotians and Spartans among Greek *ethnē*); Dionysius, *Ant. Rom.* 3.10.3 on the Greek *ethnos*; Plutarch, *Mor.* 761d; Or. Sib. 8.127 (Syrian vs. Greek vs. barbarian *ethnos*). Ps-Scylax 45 with Pausanias 4.1.3 show the Messenians as an *ethnos* only, without a *polis*, before Messene was created. For Athenians (to Attikon

A passage from the composite and anonymous *Art of Rhetoric*, perhaps written in the second century A.D., reflects the ambiguity of *ethnos* language. Advising readers about the way to assess texts, the author cites the commonplace that speech must suit the character of the speaker.[35] But unusually, he approaches this issue in ethnic terms, specifying that term *ethnos* has both a general and a specific sense (*Ars rhet.* 11.3). First, "one must distinguish the *ethnos*: whether the character is Greek or barbarian" (11.5). But that is not enough, for under each of these *ethnos* tents lives a variety of *ethnē*, each with its distinctive character. So it is not enough to say that *a barbarian* is speaking. One must clarify whether it is a bloodthirsty Thracian or a curt Scythian, for example, for that will properly shape audience expectations. If a Greek, similarly: "Which *ethnos* of the Greeks?" A sharp, loquacious, and wise Athenian is, after all, hardly the same as a simple Boeotian or a treacherous and slippery Thessalian, though they are all Greeks. The passage continues to explore *ethnē* and their varied characters.

Second, although the simple-seeming ethnic taxonomy would endure throughout antiquity, according to which each person belonged to an *ethnos* with a given character and set of customs, even within their own discussion of *ethnē* in other contexts it was nowhere so simple, let alone in lived reality. They did not consider boundaries among *ethnē* impermeable (cf. Strabo 8.1.2), and they assumed that periodic migrations created new *ethnē*, somehow derivative of older ones while absorbing new influences. The Spartans, though renowned for uniquely disciplined laws and customs, were transplanted Dorians (Thucydides 1.107.2; Pausanias 10.8.2), hence connected by ancestry with Corinthians and Cretans. But Spartans were distinctive of course. The Judaean Hasmoneans were not the only ones to assert common ancestry with this admired *ethnos*—in their version because of common ancestry from Abraham (1 Macc. 12.21). Again, Polybius ponders why the Cynaethians are so savage, given that they originate from the placid Arcadian *ethnos*, and decides that the Cynaethians' neglect of music is to blame (4.20–21).

The perception that Judaeans derived from Egyptians, which is evidently a sketchy version of the biblical story rather than independent history, turns up often. Two of the less familiar passages are these. Eusebius preserves a fragment of Julius Africanus, who preserves a fragment of a Greek historian named Polemon, which claims that a part of the Egyptian army had been expelled in antiquity, and "settled in the part of Syria called

---

ethnos) see Herodotus 1.57.3 with Cohen 2000; Funke and Luraghi 2009 and in that volume Morgan 2009b: 148–82; Ulf 2009 on the constructed nature of "Dorian" and other ethnicities; Vlassopoulos 2015 for an overview.

35. For context see Heath 2003.

Palestine not far from Arabia." This is enough for the two Christian authors to find an independent proof of the biblical Exodus (*Praep. ev.* 10.10). Second, Herodotus engages in a fascinating example of ethnic cladogenesis (evolutionary splitting), involving Judaea without naming it.[36] He writes: "It is obvious that the Colchians [though on the Black Sea] are actually Egyptians." He guessed this because of their physical similarities, he explains, and his inquiry among members of both nations confirmed their connections. But what sealed the matter was that "they are the only nations that from the start have practiced circumcision." Everyone else who practices circumcision—he mentions a variety of Syrians, including those of Palestine—trace it to either Egyptians or Colchians. QED: Egyptians are the source of all the others (2.104–105).

In support of his view of Egypt's boundaries, Herodotus tells a story that highlights both potential flexibility and a concern for fixity in *ethnos* categorizations. Some Egyptians living near the (ancient) Libyan frontier considered themselves Libyans and not Egyptians, apparently because they did not like the Egyptian prohibition of beef as food. But the authoritative Oracle of Ammon put them straight: they *were* Egyptians and therefore bound by Egypt's customary law—and Herodotus could claim divine support for his impression of Egypt's reach (2.18).

Also illustrating flexibility and migration, Diodorus unabashedly explains that the Romans adopted many of their most famous traits, including purple-striped togas, ivory chairs, lictors, houses with peristyles, the alphabet, understanding of Nature and the Gods, and divination, from the Etruscans (5.40.1–2). And in a passage that traces Greek wisdom to the Egyptians, he claims that the Persian king Darius I (6th cent. B.C.), seeking to follow a life of virtue and piety,[37] studied Egyptian holy books under the tutelage of Egypt's hereditary priests and tried to imitate (*mimeō*) their great kings (1.95.4–5).

The general assumption of derivation and fluidity makes Diodorus' claim about the Judaeans' Egyptian origins or Strabo's identification of Idumaeans as Arabs who adopted Judaean ways unsurprising. They were a normal part of the game of *ethnos* mapping.

Third, however, such linkages and derivations only came up because writers understood each *ethnos* to have a clear enough identity that they *could* puzzle out how it came to be that way, and where it came from. They could not have done this if everything was a chaos of indistinct peoples. The complexities did not lead them to abandon the simple, deceptively clear

---

36. Josephus did not miss the reference: *Apion* 1.168–169.
37. The verb here is *zēloō*, on which see *HJW* 444–50.

ethnographical model, or to create a supplementary lexicon for all the variations. The basic idea that everyone belonged to an *ethnos* persisted without visible challenge.

That the Judaeans were considered one *ethnos* alongside others is clear, for example from ancient lists of *ethnē* such as we have seen in Strabo. In Pompey's eastern conquests from 66 to 63 B.C., Judaeans appear with the other conquered peoples. The reverses of silver coins issued by A. Plautius in Rome (55 B.C.), showing "Bacchius the Judaean" kneeling in surrender beside his camel with olive branch extended are indistinguishable in type from the images on silver coins issued by Plautius' colleague M. Aemilius Scaurus, who had been Pompey's lieutenant in the East, showing King Aretas (of the Arabs) in the same posture.[38]

As far as Pompey and his associates were concerned, Judaeans and Arabs were two species of the same genus: *ethnē* with distinctive customs and territory conquered by Rome. His triumphal procession (Sept. 28–29, 61 B.C.) was preceded by inscriptions naming these subjugated peoples (Plutarch: *ta genē*): "Pontus, Armenia, Cappadocia, Paphlagonia, Media, Colchis, Iberia, Albania, Syria, Cilicia, Mesopotamia, Phoenicia and Palestine, Judaea, Arabia," along with the pirates who had first provoked his campaign (Plutarch, *Pomp.* 45.1–2).[39] When Diodorus names the kings of some of the same peoples—Darius of the Medes, Artōlē of the Iberians, Aristobulus of the Judaeans, and Aretas of Arabia—along with their territories (40.4), he makes the same comparison.[40]

More than a century later, early in Nero's reign (A.D. 54–68), the citizens of Aphrodisias, a special protectorate from Augustus' time in western Anatolia (Turkey) named for Aphrodite, erected a temple (Sebasteion) in honor of the goddess and the Julio-Claudian emperors—she (as Venus) being the matriarch of that dynasty.[41] Leading to the sanctuary was a promenade about the length of a football field but narrower (about 14 m or 45 ft). Its two sides were formed by the colonnaded fronts of facing porticoes, with rooms behind each façade. This façade was decorated, on the second

---

38. For Scaurus and King Aretas see Josephus, *Ant.* 14.29–32, 81. For coins of the otherwise unknown Judaean Bacchius and King Aretas, see in the British Museum (http://www.britishmuseum.org/research/collection_online/search.aspx), refs. 1946,1004.78 and R.8739.

39. On Pompey's third and greatest triumph see Beard 2007: 7–41.

40. This section of Diodorus is preserved only in the 10th-century *Constantinian Excerpts*, though it is generally considered part of the original text. Appian gives a full account of the triumph, first including Judaeans unnamed among the peoples of Syria conquered by Pompey then singling out the Judaean king Aristobulus among the other defeated royals (*Mith.* 116–117).

41. See http://www.aphrodisias.org.uk/a-brief-history.html.

and third stories above street level, in the spaces between the columns. The south façade hosted reliefs of gods, emperors, and mythical scenes, whereas the northern recesses hosted female statues representing subject *ethnē*.[42] This museum-of-conquest part of the complex appears to have imitated galleries in Rome and elsewhere, although they are now lost.[43] In Aphrodisias a seventh-century earthquake and various invasions since have badly dislocated the marble figures, though some have been recovered near where they fell.

The remains suggest that the *ethnos* gallery along the northern façade once hosted perhaps fifty statues, making vivid Rome's domination of the world. Each statue base featured a garlanded male head surmounted by a large-letter inscription of the *ethnos* in question, with a draped woman standing atop this base and representing the nation.[44] Thirteen inscribed *ethnē* names have survived, plus those of the largest islands of the Mediterranean given as places (Sicily, Crete, Cyprus). The main interest for us is that this gallery, presumably like lost counterparts, has "Of the *ethnos* of Judaeans" on a surviving statue base.[45] Again the Judaeans were known as one *ethnos* among others, whether these were large and well known such as Egyptians, Arabs, and Dacians or obscure like the Andizeti, Bessi, Iapodes, and Trumpilini.[46] These monuments confirm both the inclusion of Judaeans and the great elasticity of the category.

In the early second century A.D. we continue to see the new Flavian province of Judaea—no longer merely an *ethnos* or its region—personified and ranged alongside other ethnic provinces. The coins of Hadrian (A.D. 117–138) show this Judaea in the same posture as Gaul and Arabia, loyally offering sacrifice.[47]

To summarize thus far: Although the two centuries from Pompey to Hadrian witnessed massive political change, the ingrained ethnic discourse

42. Smith 1988: 51.

43. For the now lost Augustan models, especially that emperor's Portico of the Nations in Rome, see Smith (previous note) with Pliny, *Nat.* 36.39 and Servius, *Ad Aen.* 7.281.

44. The Oxford Aphrodisias Project page at http://www.arch.ox.ac.uk/APH1.html includes an image of one full example (the *ethnos* of the Dacians).

45. One image is at https://www.flickr.com/photos/ibexes/3903393337/in/photostream.

46. Smith 1988: 58: "The various peoples and places are of rather heterogeneous character and status."

47. For copper-alloy *sestertii* showing the personified province greeting Hadrian over a sacrificial altar see in the British Museum collection (http://www.britishmuseum.org/research/collection_online/search.aspx) the coins with ref. BM 1872,0709.583, 1872,0709.581, 1872,0709.587, 1934,1018.15.

remained much the same, as it would until Christian writers began to reshape the lexicon (Chapter 6). That is the foundation for understanding ancient expectations about *ethnos* identity and loyalty, differentiation, realignment, and much else.

We have seen that Judaeans had a place in this constructed discourse as a large and famous eastern *ethnos*. Although they had large migrant minorities throughout the Mediterranean, they were permanently connected by ethnographic and philosophical (hence rhetorical) principle with their defining place of origin: the renowned mother-*polis* and homeland in southern Syria. Some of their traditions were admired by others, especially their sublime view of the invisible deity and the comprehensiveness of their legal system, though others were ridiculed as barbaric, especially male circumcision. But other barbarian nations were thought to follow customs even more peculiar, such as milk diets, human sacrifice, or even cannibalism. Egyptians and Celts were objects of Roman ridicule for their peculiar piety and customs alike. In spite of occasional ridicule and cultural chauvinism, by the first century the Judaeans had an established place among the subject peoples. Their ancient heritage commanded a measure of respect, even if they were thought to be an Egyptian offshoot.

Polis and Associates

If *ethnos* (cf. Latin *gens*) language was fundamental to discourse, *polis* and its cognates (e.g., *politēs, politeia*) jump out even more frequently from the pages of ancient texts. In the New Testament Acts, when Paul in Jerusalem needs to impress a military tribune who has arrested him, he says: "Yes I'm Judaean as a person, but I am a Tarsian from Cilicia—a citizen of a rather important *polis*!" (21:39).[48] In Strabo, *polis* is the most frequently occurring substantive (1,434 times). The same holds more or less for Diodorus (2,597), Dionysius of Halicarnassus (2,282), Plutarch ([after *logos*] 2,482), Dio Chrysostom ([after *anthrōpos*] 680), and Pausanias (778).[49] When we see *polis* also at the top of Josephus' word-frequency table (1,764 times, 2,275 including cognates, above *Ioudaios*), we conclude that he shares fully in the common discourse. Even in Philo's corpus, thought it is largely biblical and philosophical in content, *polis* ranks high alongside "law" and "Moses" in frequency.[50]

---

48. The same narrative has Paul announce his Roman citizenship rather coyly, only after he has been beaten (16:22-39) or been bound for a beating (22:25-29).

49. These word-frequency counts are from the statistical tool at www.tlg.uci.edu.

50. The TLG tool ranks *polis* at 60 for Philo, Moses at 61, law at 54, among all

The statistics tell us nothing about the meaning or value of the term, of course, only that it was of great importance. Jörg Rüpke explains why, speaking of the Roman period:

> Membership in a *polis* was for people in the ancient Mediterranean basin . . . the most important focus of geo-social identity, the strongest political tie. For it was being born into a *polis* that always remained the principal means of acquiring legal status, privileges and thus appreciable social and economic life-chances.[51]

Louise Revell adds, from a Roman-Latin perspective:

> A person's allegiance was defined by the place in which they were born (their *origo*), and if they moved they became an *incola* [foreign resident]: subject to the laws of, and with certain responsibilities toward, their adopted town, but with few privileges and only limited political rights.[52]

The importance of one's home *polis* to identity is suggested by the phenomenon of naming people by their *polis* of origin, on the assumption that it said something basic about them. Even if it served mainly to distinguish one Ptolemy from another, it confirmed the importance of the *polis* (rather than a modern country, say) to one's identity. Polybius of Megalopolis, Poseidonius of Apamaea, Nicolaus of Damascus, Apion of Alexandria, Demetrius and Menippus of Gadara, Lucian of Samosata, Ptolemy of Ascalon, Nicomachus of Gerasa, and Josephus of Jerusalem (cf. *War* 1.1-3; *Life* 1-6) all remained in significant ways defined by their home *polis*' culture, while they lived much of their lives abroad. And in cases such as Acts' Paul above or Josephus' enemy Apion (Josephus, *Apion* 2.135-136), pride in a certain *polis* identity and the desire to keep that identity clear emerge clearly.

Social-scientific theorizing of the city[53] has not overwhelmed inductive assessment of the ancient *polis* in the way that ethnicity research has with *ethnos*. Numa Denis Fustel de Coulanges' magisterial 1864 study of the ancient *polis*, which stressed how uncongenial it was to modern sensibilities—framed, he insisted, by the values of the primitive-religious

---

words. Although "God" and "mind/soul" are at 2 and 4, most of the intervening words are not substantives: "say, all, none, only, other, be," etc.

51. Rüpke 2007: 18.
52. Revell 2009: 53.
53. E.g., Weber 1958 [1921].

mind[54]—anticipated less pejorative research of a century later, focused on the ancient *polis* as such.[55]

We should beware of two possible distractions, nonetheless. One is a concern about whether a given ancient settlement was a real or true *polis*, where "true" is defined by criteria other than ancient usage in the scholar's mind. A real *polis* is thought to have certain essential institutions or structures (a charter, a council, gymnasium, defined citizen body), and a place lacking these cannot be a *polis* no matter what the ancients said. Scholars have thus debated whether Jerusalem or other sites in the region were true or formal *poleis*. For Galilee, scholars are willing to admit Tiberias, because we hear something of its administration, but perhaps not rival Sepphoris (of comparable size and status).[56]

Second, the ideal of the Greek *polis* as a notionally autonomous entity with a citizen army is so clear in classical Greek texts of the fifth and fourth centuries B.C. that it has cast doubt on the value of the value of the category after Alexander the Great, the successor kings, and the arrival of Rome, all of which removed the scope for independent action (below).

Both kinds of qualification stem from modern definitions, which are understandable as efforts to classify and distinguish. But we have insufficient evidence about the internal structures and activities of many eastern *poleis*. In any case, again, our interest is simply in what ancient writers labeled *poleis*, a generous category indeed.

What was a *polis* for them? Edward Cohen's description of Herodotus' usage holds for many later authors: "*polis* seems to be used indiscriminately to denote towns, states, countries, territories, political communities, central urban areas, municipalities, and villages."[57] Josephus initially sounds more thoughtful in his distinction of *poleis* from villages (*kōmai*), and his description of Galilee assumes a distinction between "Galilean" rural folk and inhabitants of the *poleis*.[58] But he can label the same place a *polis* and a village

---

54. Fustel de Coulanges 1877 (third English edition): 9–14.

55. Stambaugh 1988 (Roman); Hansen 1993a, 1993b, 2006; Hansen and Nielsen 2004 (Greek). M. H. Hansen's Copenhagen Polis Centre, which finished its work with his retirement, took a comprehensively inductive approach. See http://www.teachtext.net/bn/cpc/cpc_95theses.html for "95 Theses" on the *polis*, especially nos. 19 and 21. Hansen's coverage ended in 323 B.C., as our period was about to dawn. I would never suggest that we *assume* correspondences between the classical and the Hellenistic-Roman *polis*. Simply, writers of our period were still focused on the *polis*, and that is our interest.

56. Tcherikover 1964; Jones 1971: 80 (Tiberias "a genuine city").

57. Cohen 2000: ix.

58. See *Life* 30 and following for "Galileans" as non-urban.

when it suits his purposes.[59] And when he claims that the smallest Galilean village had more than 15,000 inhabitants (*War* 3.43)—possibly approaching the population of Jerusalem and larger than either Sepphoris or Tiberias—we must give up trying to infer technical distinctions from his work.

The most important point to bring over from the preceding section is that *ethnos* and *polis* were not mutually exclusive categories.[60] Whatever size of settlement one came from, as with John "of Gischala" in Upper Galilee, that was one's *patris* or place of origin. When speaking of the defining features of an *ethnos*, especially of such famed *ethnē* as Athenians, Spartans, or Judaeans, it seemed natural for the ancients to view their epicentral *polis*' history and customs as crystallizing the ethnic character. Just as Attic and Athenian can be used interchangeably, so too the Lacedaemonians and Judaeans are inseparable from their famous homelands and home *poleis*. Virtually all writers on the Judaeans, whether Philo and Josephus on the Judaean side or Poseidonius, Diodorus, Strabo, Pliny, or Tacitus among outsiders, intimately link the supposed Judaean character and its world-wide laws and customs with the story of the mother-*polis* Jerusalem.[61]

In Pseudo-Scylax, a few of the *ethnē* he mentions live without any sort of *polis*, but these are cave-dwellers, hut-dwellers, and nomads grazing herds. Greek regions such as Phocis or Messenia were also rural districts of small settlements before the development of *poleis*. But most *ethnē* came to have *poleis* in their territory, and by the first century B.C. in the eastern Mediterranean these were sources of identity and prestige. One center might naturally be called, or several might vie for the status of, the *ethnos*' mother- or *mētro-polis*. Although our English word metropolis has completely lost its original sense—our "Metro" hardly suggests the warmth of motherhood—the ancient term signified the mother-*polis* of an *ethnos*.

---

59. *Life* 188 distinguishes three *poleis* in Galilee from its many villages, and *Life* 235 counts 204 *poleis* and villages in total. But Iotapata and Iapha are villages at 188 (cf. 230), elsewhere *poleis* (*Life* 332; *War* 2.289). Gabara is a *polis* at *Life* 123, 235 but a village at 229. Gischala is a *polis* at *War* 2.629; 4.1, 92, but a weak town (*polichnē*) at *War* 4.84, 123, and *Life* 271 seems to contrast it with a *polis*.

60. See Morgan 2009b: 148.

61. This is obvious in Josephus' works, written to explain his people in Rome: *War* (about the rise and fall of a great *polis*: 1.9–12), *Antiquities* (structured around the two temple eras of Jerusalem, its rulers and high priests), and *Apion* (reprising the latter). It is equally true of Diodorus, whether using Poseidonius (34/35.1.1–5) or Hecataeus of Abdera (40.3; cf. Stern 1974: 1.20–44), and Tacitus (*Hist.* 5.1–13, esp. 5.2–5). Josephus' opponents in *Against Apion* were not antiquarians but, in their hostility to present-day Judaeans in Alexandria (chiefly), devoted much of their interest—even if Josephus has over-stressed this—to the origins of Jerusalem and Judaea. The *Letter of Aristaeas* makes the same intimate connection, as did apparently the lost work of Alexander Polyhistor *On the Judaeans* (Stern 1974: 1. 157–64).

It was called this because it gave birth to colonies and/or because it was the principal *polis* and notional sustainer of regional dependents. In either case, it was the place where the laws and customs of the *ethnos* were fully realized.[62]

Strabo and Josephus had no trouble rattling off the mother-*poleis* of famous *ethnē*, which must have been part of common elite knowledge.[63] Strabo marvels that two of these, Tarsus and Alexandria, continue to flourish even as they mother colonies elsewhere and export citizens (14.5.13, 15). Both writers understand Jerusalem to be the *mētropolis* of all Judaeans in the world.[64] Both assume that a mother-*polis*' colonies (*apoikiai*), which we problematically call the Diaspora for Judaea, strive to remain loyal to the laws and traditions of the *mētropolis*. Strabo notes that this intention is complicated by necessary accommodation to conditions where the colonists settle.[65]

Long before our period, Homer's epics had portrayed the Trojan War as a conflict over Helen, from the *polis* of Sparta, fought between an alliance of mainland-Greek *poleis* and the eastern-Aegean *polis* of Troy. In those stories, set in the Mycenaean age, each *polis*' military contribution is led by a strongman-king (*basileus*): Agamemnon of Mycenae, the Aiases (Ajaxes) of Salamis and Locris, Nestor of Pylos, Odysseus of Ithaca, Achilles of Phthia, and Menelaus of Sparta, against Troy's leading men Hector, Priam, and Paris. Although a great deal had changed by the classical Greek period (sixth to fourth centuries B.C.), and much more by the Hellenistic-Roman world of our interest, Homer's epics remained basic cultural and

---

62. See Cohen 2000 on Athenians as an *ethnos*.

63. E.g,. Strabo 1.2.33 (Phoenician Sidon—or Tyre, 16.2.22, noting their rivalry for status of Phoenician *mētropolis*); 7.4.4 (Bosporian Panticapaeus); 9.31, 4.1 (Opountian Opus); 10.4.6 (a writer is derided for thinking the Dorian *mētropolis* Doris a colony of the Thessalians), 4.7 (Cretan Cnossus); 11.11.1–3 (Bactrian Bactra); 12.2.7 (the Cappadocian Cilicians' Mazaka: τὰ Μάζακα ἡ μητρόπολις τοῦ ἔθνους); 16.2.10 (Macedonia's Pella, honorary *mētropolis*), 2.28 (Judaea's Jerusalem), 4.21 (Nabataean Petra). Cf. Josephus, *Ant*. 1.127 (Cilician Tarsus); 4.82 (Arabian Petra); 6.71 (Galadene Jabesh); 7.123 (Ammonite Rabbat); 10.269, 11.159 (Persian Susa); 11.160 (Judaea's Jerusalem), 340 (Samarian Shechem); 12.119 and *War* 3.29 (Seleucid and Syrian Antioch); *Life* 372 (Tyrian Tyre). Latin did not have such an elegant word as *mētropolis*. Workarounds such as *urbs urbium* eventually yielded to transliteration of the Greek.

64. Strabo 16.2.28; Josephus, *War* 2.400, 421, 517, 554, 626; 4.123, 181, 228, 234–288 (also the Idumaeans' *mētropolis*), 346f., 407; 7.375 (ἡ τοῦ παντὸς 'Ιουδαίων γένους μητρόπολις); *Ant*. 11.160.

65. Strabo 4.1.4 (re: Massilia's colonies); 10.4.17 (challenging the assumption that customs were most fully realized in the mother-*polis* and preserved less perfectly in colonies).

educational resources. Their simple *polis* model continued to make sense, even though the structures and functions of the *polis* had evolved a great deal.[66]

The centrality of the *polis* meant that the ancient counterpart of what we call *politics*, in our large nation-states, was conceived of quite differently: as related to governing a *polis*. That this remained the case through the Roman period is illustrated by Dio Chrysostom's speeches, given before *polis* assemblies, and an essay such as Plutarch's *Advice to the Politician* (or *Statesman*), which is about *polis* governance. Herodotus had described the Persians' Greek-like discussion of governance, though the Persians lacked the same *polis* discourse.[67] Similarly, for Plato and Aristotle constitutional discussions had to do with governing the *polis*. Plato's *Republic* was thus called by him *The Politeia*, or *Polis*-ness, a term with various applications. It could refer to the structure of a *polis*, law and hence legal constitution, and/ or to the human constituency of the *polis*, including criteria of *citizenship*.[68] The ideal "state" for Plato was a *polis*.

I shall leave *polis* untranslated as we take on board its various meanings without needless baggage. The most common rendering is *city*, though an ancient *polis* was unlike a modern city in that it was not one population center among many in a larger state—not like Birmingham, Boise, or Bordeaux. Though considerably smaller than a modern city, a *polis* enjoyed (and aspired to) a much higher level of relative autonomy. Many scholars prefer *state*, *city-state*, or *citizen-state* as a translation.[69] For its members, in any case, the *polis* was the main locus of identity, with some measure of self-determination and self-regulation (*autonomia*), self-sufficiency (*autarkeia*), and in a word freedom (*eleutheria*)—a crucial Greek concept, which they clung to in spite of all contrary reality.

The core of an ancient *polis* (the *asty* or city proper, often called the *polis*) was a usually walled area containing the central institutions and structures. Where possible it was built next to an acropolis (hill-*polis*), with a temple or two (as in Athens, Corinth, Pergamum, Philippi, Scythopolis, Gerasa). The walled structure below rarely extended more than a kilometer (0.6 mi) or two in each direction. The smaller the *polis* (broad definition), research has shown, the greater the share of its population living within the

---

66. See Hansen 2006: 39–47.

67. Herodotus 3.80–88 (esp. 80–82). See 3.80.1: "words were spoken that [seem] unbelievable to some Greeks, but they *were* spoken."

68. Cf. Plutarch (or Pseudo-Plutarch), *Mor.* 826c–827a.

69. See Hansen 1993b.

walled area (as much as 80%); the larger the *polis*, the greater the percentage (60–70%) that was housed in the surrounding countryside.[70]

Aristotle discusses optimal size of a *polis*, vaguely but with characteristic moderation: not too small to field a competent army, not too big to maintain effective law, order, and good government (*Pol.* 1326a–b). The criterion is not a certain size, but effectiveness (*dynamis*) as a unified and self-determining structure. One cannot count the "large numbers of slaves, resident aliens, and [visiting] foreigners" (he might have added women), but only "as many as are a part of the *polis* and from which distinctive parts the *polis* holds together" (1326a). Aristotle is talking notionally about male citizens.[71]

This distinction between those who truly belong and the rest is especially clear in classical Sparta, high on Aristotle's list of admirably potent *poleis*. There the large Helot and "around-dwelling" population, which made Spartan life possible, greatly outnumbered the 8,000 or so Spartiates—males who had passed through the traditional education (*agōgē*) and been admitted to a communal citizen-mess.[72] Athens had perhaps 50,000 male citizens in the fifth century B.C., a total citizen-family population of about 100,000, plus perhaps 25,000 resident aliens and 100,000 slaves, well over half of these living outside the walls. All of these numbers dropped dramatically by the late fourth century.[73] Colin McEvedy made a case for 35–36,000, and not more than 50,000, residents of the walled city in about 431 B.C.[74] More ordinary *poleis* ranged considerably in size, from under 4 ha (10 acres) to more than 150 ha (0.6 mi2; 1.5 km2), and citizen populations from 2,000 to 25,000 were fairly common.[75] Jerusalem, likely the largest *polis* of southern Syria-Palestine, may have had 60–75,000, but more likely fewer than 20,000 within its walls in the mid-first century A.D.[76]

To understand *polis* pride and asserted independence, we need to put aside modern assumptions about *countries*, national and international norms, universal conventions, and all such notions. Not only did the classical *polis* (before about 330 B.C.) field a citizen army, with men called from normal business during the summer fighting season—the Spartans were different in living for war-readiness. It even observed a distinctive calendar.

70. Hansen 2006: 67–72.
71. Cohen 2000 explores, however, the complexities of real social life.
72. Cartledge 2002b: 27, 125.
73. Joint Association of Classical Teachers (JACT) 1984: 155–57.
74. McEvedy 2011: 51.
75. Hansen 2006: 74 (Table 2).
76. Geva 2014.

THE CLASSICAL PARADIGM: *ETHNOS* AND *POLIS*   119

Shocking though it is to us, even in the Hellenistic-Roman period each *polis* had retained its own system for such basic life-ordering tasks as numbering and naming years (e.g., under the presidency or consulship of X), which were counted from the *polis*' uniquely chosen "Year One," the number and names of its months, the season in which the civic year started (different years might operate simultaneously for various purposes), methods for keeping the lunar months and festivals aligned with solar seasons (intercalation), internal divisions within the months, names for days and means of counting them, and the unique festivals and other holidays of this community.[77] One scholar has analyzed ninety-six calendars from ancient Greek *poleis*.[78]

Even our assumptions about seven-day weeks and weekends were far from obvious. Some *poleis* used three periods of ten days to constitute a month, with festivals distributed throughout. The Romans favored "eight days a week," though in the late first century B.C. they came to adopt the sabbatical—that is, astrological (and Babylonian/Judaean)—weekly unit.[79] It was a specific *polis* festival in classical Athens, running over five days in mid-Elaphebolion (roughly March) and devoted to the God Dionysus, that hosted the tragedies and comedies we study in school as much more universalized "Greek drama."

When coinage first came into use (ca. sixth century B.C.), the individual *polis* quickly became the issuing authority.[80] That token of independence continued to an extent, as a privilege granted to certain *poleis*, throughout the Roman period. Tyre, Ascalon, Gadara, and others remained fiercely proud of their *polis* coins, and this is an issue that must be considered in relation to Jerusalem's production of silver coins during the conflict with Rome of 66 to 70.[81]

In short, the *polis* was the center of Greek political life and the prism through which Greeks viewed human society. Before Alexander there was no larger political *system*, but only shifting alliances or leagues led by one or another *polis*—or under the foreign power Persia. After Alexander, the *poleis* were under the kings of his successor dynasties, though they retained much of their identity. Many new *poleis* named Alexandreia, Seleuceia,

---

77. For ancient cross-cultural perspectives (including the Near East) see James 1963; for Athens, Pickard-Cambridge 1988; Parker 2005: 136–217.

78. Samuel 1972: 57–138. Cf. Meimaris 1992; Clarke 2008: esp. 7–26; Feeney 2007: 7–23.

79. See Rüpke 2007: 198–200.

80. Carradice and Price 1988: 20–47.

81. See HJW 468–87.

Ptolemais, and Antiocheia in honor of Alexander or his successors turn up across the eastern Mediterranean and Middle East.

The proliferation of *poleis* under Alexander and his successors brought increasingly elaborate reflection on their nature. The opening paragraphs of Aristotle's *Politics* argue that the *polis* is the natural form of human community (*koinōnia*), where independence is best asserted and justice optimally achieved. A solitary human, being neither a god nor an animal, is not self-sufficient: the *polis* is a requirement for normal human beings (*Pol.* 1252a–1253a). Although scholars have often spoken about "the decline of the *polis*," focusing on its loss of independence after Alexander and his successors,[82] one could easily make the contrary case, for massive expansion and growing importance. Literary and epigraphic evidence alike shows that Roman-period *poleis* multiplied, flourished, competed with one another for honors, cherished even a constrained freedom, and looked back on former glories as though in a continuous line to the present.[83] Polybius' *Histories* trace interactions between the newly powerful *polis* of Rome and the old *poleis* of Carthage, Greece, Asia Minor, and Syria. The individual sites remain his focus even though they have long since become parts of Hellenistic kingdoms.

Although Roman domination brought an integrated superstructure to the Mediterranean, Augustus and his successors continued to support the creation or re-foundation of *poleis*[84], which now frequently bore such names as Caesarea, Sebastē, Augusta, Livias, or Iulias in honor of the imperial family. This was no mere generosity. The Romans used *polis* structures as the most efficient way of managing their interests, sparing the need for large investment and legionary sandals on the ground. Documents from the Flavian period allow us to see *poleis* coming into being, their leaders facing the momentous challenge of calendar choices, including the nature and sequence of festivals, which they know will endure long into the future.[85] Alignment of distinctive *polis* calendars with those of a greater power, Macedonian or Roman, remained imperfect at best.[86] The speeches of Dio from the late first and early second centuries A.D. show the vitality of these communities—and their abiding concern with status.[87]

82. See Hansen 1993: 7–29; Vlassopoulos 2007: 56–60; Harland 2006: 21–49.

83. E.g., Jones 1940; 1971; Bowie 1970: 3–41; Swain 1996: 65–100; Boatwright 2000; Alcock 2002; Krause and Witschel 2006; Grieb 2008; Carlsson 2010.

84. Lomas 1998.

85. Revell 2009: 40–79.

86. Samuel 1972: 138–88.

87. Dio Chrysostom, *Or.* 38.3–7; 48.7; 39.4.

One reason for the proliferation of *poleis* is that Roman administrators relied on them.[88] A governor's duties in his province depended on his success in cultivating productive relationships with *polis* leaders, whose trusted friend he strove to become, and they usually reciprocated. In return for his provision of resources for the building of public works and enhancing their prestige, they would give him loyalty, information, and support in everything from tax collection to maintenance of law and order. A governor in post spent much of his time visiting at least the main *poleis* to maintain these relationships and judge cases presented to him by local officials. Villages were considered part of the respective *poleis*' territories (below).[89] Louise Revell speaks appropriately of an "ideology of urbanism," according to which Roman authorities depended upon the ambitions of wealthy, public-spirited citizens.[90]

In the second century, Hadrian founded a large number of *poleis* and, as an aficionado of things Greek, encouraged existing ones to celebrate their ancient heritage.[91] Pausanias' tour through Greece's regions and ethnē, describing their origins, achievements, customs, is preoccupied with the region's *poleis*, a word he employs nearly 800 times. On entering each district he moves quickly to its main *polis* and describes it in light of its past from ancient times—dwelling on events before 300 B.C.[92]

Where old *poleis* existed, as throughout the East, the Romans consolidated a pecking order and established a hierarchy of favor: ordinary *poleis*, which paid full taxes and were expected to govern themselves by their laws as far as possible but with no assurance of internal freedom; "free" *poleis*, which were flattered with concessions to a level of autonomy, including an explicit recognition of their internal law and possibly the right to mint coins; and at the top of the pyramid, allied *poleis*, which enjoyed a treaty with Rome guaranteeing their freedom from taxation and a general gold-plan status, something that Jerusalem enjoyed under Herod and his grandson Agrippa I. Alongside these three were fully Roman cities created around the empire, whether as colonies for army veterans (*coloniae*) or *poleis* granted Roman citizenship corporately (*municipia*).[93] Both of these types

---

88. Braund 1998.
89. For tax collection in Judaea, see Josephus, *War* 2.405–407.
90. Revell 2009: 44–54; cf. Millar 1967: 81–103; Ando 2000; Meyer-Zwiffelhoffer 2002: e.g., 224–25.
91. Cf. Boatwright 2000: 8–15.
92. Habicht 1998 (1985): 19–20, 23.
93. Richardson 1976: 49–52.

in principle followed Roman law and used Latin as the official language, though as always things were more complicated on the ground.[94]

Discussions of *polis* governance returned to the three basic alternatives discussed by Herodotus (above): rule by one person (monarchy), by all *polis* citizens (democracy), or by a subset (oligarchy / aristocracy). Plato had championed one-person rule on the proviso that the monarch be wise, but many writers professed to favor a sort of democracy. The widespread abhorrence of "mob rule" meant, however, that this word evolved in meaning from Athens-style government by lot-chosen citizens to a *de facto* aristocracy, construed as "for the people's best interests."[95]

A *polis* was assumed, therefore, to comprise two clearly distinguishable groups: the wealthy, first, leading, best, prominent, well-born, or powerful men (*prōtoi, aristoi, gnōrimoi, dynatoi, eugenai*), and the rest of the populace, citizenry, masses, mob, or rabble (*ho laos, dēmos, ochlos, to plēthos*). The wealthy tended to see this as a natural division between a small male elite raised for a life of public leadership, of which the masses were simply not capable. Women and children were more or less appendages of the male citizens, sharing a reflected status. Slaves, which may have constituted a quarter or more of a *polis'* population, were the property of the citizens. Josephus shares this general perspective. He champions Judaea's hereditary aristocracy and the constitution (laws of Moses) that gives them peerless leaders, yet characterizes the leading aristocrats as "lovers of democracy."[96]

Others preferred a mixed constitution with elements of monarchy, aristocracy, and democracy keeping each other in balance—a principle borrowed by the framers of the American constitution.[97] In Hellenistic-Roman thinking generally, kingship was abhorrent. It belonged to an unfortunate stage of the primitive past, and continued only among eastern barbarians accustomed to slavery. Even über-Greek Sparta's dual kingship (later matched by Rome's two consuls) appears in Herodotus as more barbarian than Greek (6.58.1-2), and Sparta's lavish funeral rites for its kings suspiciously suggested superhuman honors for mortals.[98] Nevertheless, under the emperors many writers found it prudent to praise virtuous modes of monarchy.[99]

94. Concannon 2014: 47-74.

95. See Swain 1996: 26-27, 173 (democracy *means* "an aristocratic constitution based on the rule of law"), 276-83.

96. E.g., Josephus, *Ant.* 4.184-187, 223; 6.36, 84, 268; 11.111; 19.178; 20.251. Aristocrats as democrats: *War* 4.319, 358; possibly *Ant.* 20.234.

97. See the sixth book of Polybius' *Histories* and Cicero's *Republic* (e.g., 2.9.15).

98. Cf. Cartledge 2002a: 175-76.

99. Seneca, *On Clemency*; Pliny, *Panegyric*; Dio, *Kingship Orations*; Aelius Aristides, *To Rome*.

By the first century A.D., standard features of a *polis* were readily observable, in spite of the many differences, from Athens, Corinth, and Philippi to Ephesus, Pergamum, and Lydia, to coastal Caesarea, Sebastē, Jerusalem, Scythopolis, and Gerasa (Jarash). Built structures included an open-air marketplace (*agora*) surrounded by shops, covered porches lined with monumental columns, statues evocative of the *polis*' founding myths, law-courts, and magistrates' quarters. Of vital importance were the educational, cultural, and recreational facilities: the *gymnasium* with its gardens, porches, *palaestra* (open exercise area), statuary, baths, and meeting rooms; theatres cut into hillsides or (under Roman influence) as separate structures; colonnaded and stone-paved streets; amphitheaters or hippodromes (big enough for chariot races); and/or multi-function entertainment facilities. Whereas the Greek *gymnasium* had included a modest bath area, the Romans developed independent facilities for elaborate bath complexes (*thermae*). These were effectively public or private health clubs, as well as meeting places for the governing classes.[100] Each *polis* also had a range of housing areas and types, from the villas of the wealthy with their internal courtyards and water services to the precariously stacked and plumbing-free apartments of the poor in crowded parts of town. Finally, each *polis* had one or more temples for its god(s), on the acropolis or in the main city or both, along with altars for the sacrifice of the god's preferred animals.

In spite of the common features, each *polis* was assumed to be quite distinctive. At opposite ends of the spectrum from classical times were democratic Athens, with a vigorous voting assembly comprising all male citizens, ten tribes, village demes, five-hundred strong council, and nine annual *archons*, and aristocratic Sparta, with its thirty-member senate (*gerousia*), dual kingship of limited authority (the kings also being part of the *gerousia*), committee of five annually elected *ephors*, and a citizen assembly that was limited to voting up or down on the senate's proposals. Rome's government was complex already in the Republican period, with distinct social orders, tribes, voting assemblies, senate, and progression of magistracies up to the two annual consuls and censor. With the emergence of the supreme *princeps* ("emperor") under Augustus and his successors, it became simpler, because the top man essentially ran everything, but more complicated because of the fictions required to preserve the illusion of traditional Republican institutions.

Amidst all this local variety, the common discourse with its generic categories facilitated comparison. Every *polis* was expected to have a citizen

100. In general see Sear 1982 and Stambaugh 1988. For Roman baths, Yegül 1992: 40–79, on the relation between Roman *thermae* and Greek gymnasium; Yegül 2010; Fagan 1999.

assembly (*ecclēsia, dēmos*), whatever its exact roles and make-up, some sort of tribal constituencies, a deliberative council (*boulē*) of hundreds, which might overlap with or be separate from a council of elders (*gerousia* or senate), a smaller executive board and/or an individual with provisional authority (*archōn[s], decaprōtoi* or decurions, Judaean chief priests), various magistrates, and priests for supervising the civic cult—normally elected in the Greek world but a hereditary caste in the east. Because of these familiar categories, comparing *poleis* presented no great problem.

Examples are Dionysius' description of Rome's distinctive practices (*Ant. rom.* 2.5–17) or Pausanias' comparison of Sparta with Athens (3.11.2):

> Now the Lacedaemonians in Sparta, they have an *agora* worth seeing, and the council-chamber of their senate and the offices of the *ephors*, law-guardians, and those called Bidaeans are all at the *agora*. The senate is the council with authority over their constitution, whereas the rest constitute the leaders (*archontes*) ... The *ephors* manage the particularly important matters of concern, and they furnish the *epōnymos* [after whom the year is named], *just as in Athens* the *epōnymos* is an *archōn* from the designated nine.

I have emphasized the small size of even famous *poleis*. The walls of Athens enclosed an area no larger than about 220 ha (0.85 mi2), Rome's (Servian) walls about 50% more—though these were only partly visible by the first century. Rome's total population is often estimated at 1 million but may have been only 250,000.[101] For population density, contrast the 75,000-strong population of Peterborough in Ontario, Canada, which sprawls over about 60 km2 (23 mi2). But each *polis* was assumed to anchor a dependent territory known as its *chōra* or countryside (Latin *territorium*), which is where many citizens lived on their land.

Like the other terms we have been considering, *chōra* was a hugely flexible category (Aristotle, *Oec.* 1343a), and all territories were subject to enlargement or shrinkage through war or conquest. Classical Sparta held bragging rights for the size of its *chōra* after it came to dominate the southern Peloponnese. That ca. 8,000 km2 (3,100 mi2), in Laconia and Messenia across the mountains, was nearly matched by Syracuse in Sicily, whereas Athens had a more modest 2,500 km2 (965 mi2) in Attica.[102] Jerusalem's territory of Judaea, before it was divided among various *poleis* after Pompey, was about 3,300 km2 (1,274 mi2)—bigger than modern Liechtenstein and even Luxembourg, and larger than the territories of prestigious Tyre and

---

101. McEvedy 2011: 318–20.
102. Cf. Cartledge 2002b: 23.

Sidon (modern Lebanon). Most *poleis* had *chōrai* of perhaps only 100 km2 or less.

Polis and *chōra* lived in a symbiotic relationship. The *chōra* provided living space, villas for the wealthy, a labor supply, and natural resources, including the produce regularly brought in to the *polis* market as well as quarried stone, grain, wood, wool, milk, and meat—especially for sacrificial animals. There might even be mines, as the silver mines of Laureion (Lavrion) in Athens' *chōra*. In return the *polis* gave the *chōra* its identity, leadership, courts, calendar, a festival and entertainment center, and possibly currency in the Roman period. It furnished opportunities for social prestige, as citizens could seek office and boost their status by paying for civic works as public benefactor (*euergetēs*).

An inland *polis* would try hard to secure a harbor on the sea or any large lake—as Athens' Peiraeus, the ports of Azotus and Iamneia in southern Syria, eventually Joppa on the Mediterranean for Jerusalem, and inland Gadara's harbor on the Sea of Galilee. The Mediterranean was the western world's main interface, by far the most efficient route for communication and the gateway to trade in everything from luxury goods to slaves.[103] Because of Athens' large port, Attic vases were distributed across the Mediterranean and the city's *drachma* and weight units were standards, even into the Roman period—there being no "international standards" as such.[104]

Dynamics between a *polis* and its *chōra* varied. Two of the *chōrai* we know best, Athens' Attica and Sparta's Laconia, were very different cases. Attica was occupied and controlled by Athenian citizens engaged in all manner of enterprise, and was often synonymous with Athens. But it included independently famous towns such as the mystery-cult center of Eleusis, which welcomed initiates from all over Greece and later Romans including emperors—before its destruction in A.D. 395 under the new Christian order.[105] Athens' *chōra* had partly independent traditions, such as rural Dionysia festivals, which staged dramas before their famous counterpart in Athens.[106] In contrast, classical Sparta's Laconia and Messenia (before the latter's liberation in 371 B.C.) hosted subject populations that served the needs of the male Spartan citizens. Graeco-Roman Judaea, Jerusalem's *chōra*, hosted no temples, games, or slave populations. But priests of the central sanctuary often lived in countryside estates—most famously the

---

103. See Hansen 2006: 34.
104. On the vases see Marconi 2004.
105. Parker 2005: 327–68.
106. Parker 2005: 51–78, 192–217.

Hasmoneans of rural Modein[107]—and came to the mother-*polis* when it was the turn of their priestly section, or course, to serve for a couple of weeks.[108]

I have dwelt on this basic ordering language partly because of its importance for understanding the outbreak of the Judaean War. One of the two leaders of the revolt in its final phase, John of Gischala, lived just 10 km (6 mi) from Kedesh, a village that was part of coastal Tyre's large *chōra*. Tyre's old conflicts with Jerusalem were mirrored in tensions between Gischala and Kedesh. Likewise, the Judaean *polis* of Tiberias had a *chōra* abutting those of Scythopolis 45 km (25 mi) to the south and Hippos across the lake, and leading figures in Tiberias (such as Justus) appear to become embroiled in the local tensions (*Life* 42). Those problems had nothing directly to do with Rome, however.[109] Considering villages part of a *polis*' *chōra*, enemies could attack their enemy by attacking these without the greater risks of assaulting the walled and elevated *asty*.

As with *ethnos*, assuming *polis*-affiliation as a simple identity-marker masked a world of complexity. Under Roman rule, a *polis* could rapidly change its identity if it became a veterans' colony or was declared a *municipium* subject to Latin law. But the most routine complication was that, from Hellenistic times onward, many people lived in a *polis* unrelated to their *ethnos*. Whereas the simple discourse assumed an Athens for Athenians (more or less), Sparta for Spartans, and Jerusalem for Judaeans, *poleis* had come to include sizeable contingents of foreigners. Their families may have been there for generations, and they might identify with the *polis* in many ways, but it was no simple matter to gain full citizenship (*politeia* or *polis*-belonging), if that was their aspiration.

Such problems may have been uniquely troublesome for Judaeans. They could neither (in fidelity to ancestral law) set up another temple or altar outside Jerusalem, as other *ethnē* could in principle with the support of the host populace—temples of Isis were found throughout Italy and elsewhere—nor join in the worship of the host *polis*' gods; nor could they join in worshiping many translocal deities. Many Judaeans might hold back even from the main public festivals of the *polis*, since these involved sacrifice to the local gods, along with games and dramatic theatre. If they were going to eat meat and follow their ancestral laws, they would need butchers to provide meat slaughtered according to biblical prescriptions. And if they were expected to work or be available for court or other civic duties on the

---

107. See Schwartz 1993.

108. On priestly courses: 1 Chr 24.1–9; Josephus, *Ant.* 7.365–367; Luke 1:5–8.

109. Josephus, *War* 2.458–460; 4.105; cf. *Life* 44–45, 341–342, 410. Cf. *HJW* chapters 3 to 5.

terms of the *polis* calendar, which disregarded sabbaths and Judaean holidays, practical life could be difficult.

Josephus has preserved, albeit in mangled and sometimes misdated form, decrees by Roman authorities and city councils throughout Asia Minor that granted their Judaean minorities specific exemptions, so that they could follow their traditions in these *poleis*. Some were privileges of indeterminate origin and long standing. Some were catalyzed by Julius Caesar's immense gratitude for Judaean assistance, or by the friendship of King Herod's family and Hyrcanus II with Marc Antony and Augustus.[110]

Even still, in Antioch the long-settled Judaean community faced repeated attempts at expulsion around the time of the war with Rome. In Scythopolis the Judaean minority reportedly joined the citizens in fighting off Judaean attackers, only to be massacred as an untrustworthy fifth column. In coastal Caesarea, the Judaean minority made a bold effort to have this conspicuously Greek-Roman *polis* redefined as Judaean, which only exacerbated the hostility of the majority, leading to removal of the Judaeans' existing privileges, expulsion, or massacre. In Alexandria, the struggle between the large Judaean colony and the citizen majority was reportedly age-old.[111] Josephus permits Eleazar at Masada to summarize: "Perhaps [one might say], those [Judaeans] found themselves no match for their enemies, on land that *belonged to others*, and so faced death."[112]

This discussion of status both in one's own mother-*polis* and away from it accords, though colleagues will dispute parts, with the general view. The general pattern of exclusivity in Greek citizenship, the difficulty of imagining *polis*-membership for a large population that could not participate fully in *polis* life,[113] the exemptions granted Judaeans corporately in Asian *poleis*, the vulnerability of Judaean expatriates everywhere in times of crisis, and Claudius' letter (below) are among the indications that Judaeans abroad were not usually citizens of their *poleis*, though prominent individual families might be. Before we take a closer look at the case of Alexandria, I should mention a 2015 study that constructs a rather different picture.

---

110. So *Ant.* 14.188–267. For discussion see ben Zeev 1998: 25–232; Eilers 2004.

111. Antioch: Josephus, *War* 7.100–103, 108–11; *Ant.* 12.121; Scythopolis, *War* 2.466–476; Caesarea, *War* 2.266–270, 284–292; Alexandria, *War* 2.490–498.

112. *War* 7.361–69, quotation from 369: κἀκεῖνοι μὲν ἴσως ἐπ' ἀλλοτρίας γῆς οὐδὲν ἀντίπαλον εὑράμενοι τοῖς πολεμίοις οὕτως ἀπέθανον.

113. Ritter (2015: 297) acknowledges the problem: "It was not Josephus's or Philo's intention to propose even partial answers as to how Judeans could reconcile their observance of ancestral customs and their status as citizens, and it remains a deeply conflicted position in their work."

Bradley Ritter stresses a point easily lost in scholarly discussion: that Philo and Josephus both unmistakably describe Judaeans generally as citizens of Alexandria, Antioch, and other *poleis*. They call Judaeans *politai* (citizens) and refer to their *politeia* (citizenship) or even equal citizenship (*isopoliteia*).[114] Scholars who share the common view, which comes in many flavors,[115] do not ignore these texts but find conflicting indications even within them. They suppose that literary authors tend to misunderstand and/or misrepresent matters for rhetorical reasons, and that statements about citizenship are explainable this way. Ritter asks in challenge: "But what if Philo and Josephus knew what they were talking about?" Finding implausible the reasons proposed by scholars for Philo's and Josephus' alleged misrepresentations, he works through the evidence again on this alternative hypothesis. Closely scrutinizing specific terminology in our sources, he argues that even incidental words confirm that most Judaeans were indeed citizens of their eastern *poleis* of residence.

Ritter may be right. If he is, some of my interpretations and specific interpretations will be off (and vice versa), though it seems that the general framework proposed here would be unaffected. We would shift from the view that most Judaeans abroad were not citizens, though some were, to the view that most were but some were not. My book was completed in draft before I saw Ritter, and I lack the time to reconsider each piece of evidence. While I welcome this bold re-opening of all such questions, my hesitations come from what strikes me as in some cases a too-mechanical or static reading of authors, situations, and terms, with perhaps insufficient appreciation of the elasticity of *polis*-related or administrative language—and of the disconcerting freedom of ancient authors to change their story according to context. We shall see an example of this in the case of Antioch.[116] Available

114. Ritter 2015: 1–2, 10, 279–82, and passim.

115. Ritter 2015: 1–11.

116. Situations: Ritter's arguments (also for Acts: 2015: 48) depend partly on his assessments of Philo's and Josephus' aims and audiences, which seem too facile. He proposes that each work has apologetic aims and that anything contradicting these has a claim to historical reality (42–44). But it is doubtful that multi-volume histories can sustain agendas lucid enough to identify contradictions. Thus he finds Josephus wanting to present the war in a manner "favorable to Vespasian and especially Titus" (20), though Josephus frames the work in opposition to such partiality (1.1–10). He thinks it "fairly obvious" that *War* minimizes the involvement of Josephus' class in the recent conflict (43), though Josephus opens the work by celebrating his status as captured enemy general (1.1–3) and offers plentiful evidence of priestly militants. He asks (21) us not discount Josephus' "own comments" about writing for the whole Roman world (not for an audience in Rome particularly), but does not seem to notice *War*'s opening emphasis on the provocations *in Rome* that spurred him to write (1.1–6, 13–16)—and slips in the suggestion that "he aimed some of the *Bellum*" at Judaeans, a difficult

time does not permit more thorough interaction with this bracing study, but I hope that I have given sufficient warrant to explain my readings.

Excursus: Conflicted and Competing Identities in Alexandria

It is worth pausing to consider Alexandria because it offers perhaps the best-documented case of the fusion of *ethnos-* and *polis*-identity issues we are discussing, at least for a period in the mid-first century. The eyewitness Philo's elaborate narratives may be compared with slight information in Josephus, an imperial letter, versions of texts by the Alexandrians themselves, and various tangentially related material finds from ancient Alexandria.

On the ancient soil of Egypt, which Herodotus had made famous to the Greek world,[117] Greek traders had been present from the 630s or so B.C., especially at the river port of Naucratis and its outlets to the sea. But after Alexander the Great established the port city of Alexandria in 331 B.C. with its man-made harbor, it quickly became world-famous. For nearly three

---

communicative conception.

Authorial freedom: Ritter blends episodes from Josephus' *War* and *Antiquities* without observing how completely the latter work often changes episodes. Josephus' descriptions of political and provincial life are particularly malleable: *War* 2.117–118 make Judaea a province in A.D. 6 whereas *Ant.* 18.1–2 annex it to Syria. On the Caesarea stories, contrast Ritter 241–59 with Mason 2009: 25–36.

Mechanical terminology: *katoikos* (96–99), which Ritter says *must* mean resident and not metic, though the usual "settled resident" or "colonist" works well; *isopoliteia* (34, 148, 251) *must* be "synonymous" with *politeia*, though elsewhere the former implies a special arrangement of some kind, such as reciprocal citizenship or Rome's extension of citizenship to Italians (Strabo 5.1.1)—like but not the same as citizenship of Rome; *eparchoi* (241–242 with notes) *must* refer to provincial prefects from A.D. 6, though both context and Josephus' usage make that—and Ritter's restriction of *eparchia* to a Roman province—unlikely (Mason 2008: 220–21); *stasis* (e.g., 34, 293–94) refers to conflict as in a Greek *polis* among *citizens*.

On p. 256, concerning Josephus' claim that the massacre of the Jerusalem garrison and of Caesarea's Judaeans occurred on the same day (*War* 2.457): "certainly what must have happened" is that a rider brought news of the auxiliary massacre to Caesarea (covering the "nearly" 90 km in a "short day's travel"), which then massacred its Judaeans. By placing the two events on the very same day, however, in *poleis* 120 km away, by his reckoning (*War* 1.79; *Ant.* 13.312) and in reality—two days on horseback—Josephus can safely attribute the Caesarean episode *on the same day* to "other-worldly provision," which is to say divine retribution for the heinous crime in Jerusalem. He deliberately excludes the possibility of natural consequence. If we prefer to imagine that Jerusalem caused Caesarea, in spite of Josephus, I see no reason to keep his "same day" assertion.

117. According to Herodotus (2.2.2–5), the Egyptians believed they were the oldest people on earth until King Psammetichus discovered that the Phrygians alone were more ancient.

centuries it served as the capital of the Ptolemaic dynasty, which succeeded him. This Graeco-Macedonian creation included all Egypt, in one sense, as its *chōra*, though it also had a *chōra* proper.[118] This presumption did not sit well with the Egyptian population or especially with the priestly caste. Its exotic lore from millennia past, which had brought the world so much knowledge, its custody of proud ancient languages, and its traditional status markers in Egyptian society were all bumped from their perch in the new orbit of the implanted *polis* Alexandria.

Predictably, Alexandrian citizenship (*politeia*) became a restricted and carefully guarded privilege. There must have been opportunities for numbers of Egyptians to become citizens during the lost early years. For all its vaunted Greekness, Alexandria did not impress Polybius a century and a half later, when he visited. He grumbled that local Egyptians and uncouth mercenaries still dominated this so-called *polis*. The "Greek" citizen-class was wholly uncivil and of mixed ethnicity.[119] But opportunities for Egyptians to blend with the citizenry apparently evaporated as the new citizen body, now matter how imitation-Greek they may have been, took shape and began to insist on the demarcation typical of *poleis* to protect their privilege.[120] For a couple of decades (ca. 207–185 B.C.), disaffected Egyptians in the interior seceded from Alexandria's reach, aspiring to live again under traditional Pharaonic-priestly leadership.

To judge from the second-century B.C. *Oracle of the Lamb* and *Oracle of the Potter*, which are apocalyptic anti-Greek texts, some Egyptian leaders yearned for the restoration of their ancient capital Memphis—and hence of their class. Given their education and social standing, priests had relatively good chances of social and economic advancement outside and perhaps inside Alexandria. But they still faced the challenge of balancing cherished old and new identities.[121] Robert Ritner remarks of the late Ptolemaic period:

> Mixed marriages between Egyptians and Greeks were increasingly common, particularly in the countryside, and the resulting families maintained conscious connections to both ethnicities, often expressed in the form of double names (one Greek, one Egyptian) accorded their children.[122]

118. Capponi 2004.

119. Polybius 34.14, preserved by Strabo 17.1.12.

120. For an illuminating effort to explore that early development see Scheidel 2004.

121. See Fraser 1972: 1.38–92; Green 1990: 187, 323–26; Thompson 2001: 73–79; Baines 2004: 33–62; Honigman 2003: 61–102. The critical Greek edition of the *Potter's Oracle* is Koenen (1968: 178–209). For concrete details concerning the population of Hellenistic Egypt, see Clarysse and Thompson 2006.

122. Ritner 1998: 5.

People need to get along with whatever political situation they find themselves in, and in spite of any enduring resentment, many Egyptians adapted well.

Once again we find the simple categories of *ethnos* and *polis* cracking along their seams, as they probably always had. Nevertheless the categories endured, and they are our interest.

When the Romans annexed Egypt in 30 B.C. they effectively did to the Alexandrians what Alexandrians had done to the Egyptian elite. They pushed them off the top rung and exacerbated tensions between natives and the long-stay foreigners. The pyramid of social status now heightened with the addition of upper stories.[123] On top now were Roman citizens, including legionary soldiers stationed near Alexandria and their retirees or veterans. They enjoyed freedom from personal taxes among other privileges, though they remained subject to land taxes and compulsory civic service ("liturgies"). Only Roman citizens—chosen also from among the wealthiest Alexandrian citizens—were eligible for the province's highest civic offices.[124]

Below the Roman citizens came citizens of Alexandria, whom the Romans regarded as their closest peers and a recruiting pool for future Romans. Alexandrian citizens also enjoyed generous exemptions, especially from the burdensome head tax imposed by Augustus (*laographia*) and compulsory civic duties, and they faced much-reduced property taxes. Certain official positions under Roman governance were reserved for Alexandrian citizens,[125] including the office of priest in the imperial cult.

The next rung of privilege included Egyptian priests and residents of the smaller *poleis* in each district (*nomē*), throughout Egypt, who paid taxes at substantially reduced rates (ca. 30–50%).

At the bottom of the pyramid were millions of native Egyptians. Although the poorest in the land, they were the only ones compelled to pay the full *laographia*, all land taxes, and countless other imposts; they were subject without appeal to periods of forced labor and ad hoc requisition.[126]

123. See Lewis 1983: 18–19; Capponi 2005: 5–64 *et passim*.

124. Capponi 2005: 51–63.

125. Keyes 1931: 263–69, providing evidence for a combined poll-tax of 44–45 drachmas annually in that highly productive region. Those further south paid only 16 drachmas. Cf. Delia 1991: 30–34; Ritner 1998: 1.10–11. Capponi (2005: 138–55) analyses the evidence for each kind of tax. The status of citizens in the smaller Greek cities of Naucratis and Ptolemais with respect to taxes is uncertain, though scholars assume an exemption comparable to the Alexandrians'.

126. Cf. Capponi 2005: 65–81. Diodorus (1.31.6–8) gives a widely accepted figure of 7 million for the entire population of Pharaonic Egypt but then, depending on the manuscript one follows, either drops the figure to 3 million for the late first century B.C. or leaves it the same. Josephus in *War* 2.385 has 7.5 million outside of Alexandria.

Slaves were not part of the pyramid at all, being considered property with no civic status.

Although Roman rule brought unprecedented opportunities for some, then, its imposed social structures in Egypt had the potential to alienate many. The Romans' instinct for finding allies in urban centers led them to sharpen the distinction between Egypt as a whole and the *polis* Alexandria. They designated their governor "Prefect of Alexandria *and* Egypt" and spoke of "Alexandria by [rather than *in*] Egypt." The resentment of native Egyptians continued unabated, perhaps intensifying. The Judaean Philo, supported by a papyrus from A.D. 34/35, relates that the governor Flaccus had to disarm the Egyptian population because "they had often revolted." In a thorough search of homes, the governors' agents turned up hoards of weapons (*Flacc.* 92–93).[127] Egyptian resentment of both Alexandria and Rome helps to explain the nation's reputation for banditry and withdrawal to the countryside, to avoid taxes, something of an Egyptian specialty.[128] In A.D. 172, eventually, came the violent uprising of the Boucoloi ("herdsmen") near Alexandria, led by the Egyptian priest Isodorus. His traditional and yet Greek name means "Gift of Isis" (Dio 71/72.4.1–2).[129]

Those who imagine Judaea as oppressed by Roman imperial rule might note that Rome's impact was more vivid and pervasive in Egypt. This province had to supply a large share of Rome's grain requirements along with head and land taxes, high import and export duties, and the rest.[130] Not to be underestimated for psychological effect was the permanent presence of two (sometimes more) Roman legions near Alexandria, whose maintenance costs were borne by the people. Complemented by dozens of auxiliary cohorts in the province and settlements of tough and privileged veterans, the Roman forces had the constant potential to humiliate and offend locals, sometimes in chilling ways.[131] In parts of Egypt they truly were an *occupying* army, something unknown in Judaea before the war. Though they might be invited to settle local disputes as third parties, and might be welcomed by elements of the host population, Rome's citizen-soldiers enjoyed a *de facto* immunity for sometimes terrible behavior.[132]

127. For the papyrus see Capponi 2005: 185–86.
128. See Alston 1995: 83–86.
129. They had been restive for many years before the uprising: see Bowersock 1994: 51–53.
130. See Strabo 17.1.13; Josephus, *War* 2.386.
131. See Alston 1995: 163–91, for a list of units and evidence.
132. Campbell 1984: 243–314. Alston (1995: 53–68) seeks to modify Campbell's argument that the emperors' need to keep the army happy resulted in the military's steadily growing and unchecked power. Neither scholar doubts, however, that the

Many symbols of Egyptian national self-respect were sidelined by Rome. From A.D. 19 Tiberius imposed a weak form of currency in the local *tetradrachm*, which began at less than 33% silver content (compare Tyre's 98%) and declined steadily from there. This would have inhibited independent trade with the rest of the empire.[133] Instead of holding a value equivalent to four Roman *denarii* as elsewhere, this ostensible four-*drachma* piece was worth just one *denarius*. In stark contrast to the proud symbols and legends on the coins of many nearby Syrian cities (Tyre, Sidon, and Antioch, even Ascalon and Dora), Alexandrian coins mainly advertise— aside from the occasional exotic crocodile or hippopotamus—the imperial family, dominating them from afar. Not only Egyptian priests but sometimes privileged Alexandrians became embittered.

An ongoing irritant was the Romans' refusal to allow these proud citizens the council (*boulē*) that was normal for *polis* life (above).[134] It is not difficult to imagine Rome's reasons. This fertile province, which enjoyed outstanding natural defenses, had been the base for Queen Cleopatra and Marc Antony in their conflict with Octavian's Rome. The same considerations that led the emperors to forbid senatorial colleagues from entering Egypt without special permission inclined them to avoid enhancing any sense of Alexandria's autonomy. Encouraging a degree of mutual resentment among Egyptians, Alexandrians, and Judaeans might indeed serve Rome's famous "divide-and-rule" approach.

The so-called *Boulē Papyrus* from the time of Augustus, which may be a real submission to the emperor or a draft of talking points, respectfully proposes four reasons why a council is needed.[135] The first two are the need for a watchdog body to keep the citizen body pure of "incorrigible and uncouth men," by closing the ephebate loophole (below), and to ensure that non-citizens paid their taxes, which Rome should welcome. The papyrus also argues that a council would speak up for Alexandrian citizens if their land was unjustly assigned to the imperial Special Account (*Idios Logos*),[136] and would ensure that men chosen for embassies to Rome were of the very best sort.

In response to the feeling of oppression under Rome, especially to the upheavals of A.D. 38–41 (below), a substantial Alexandrian literature

---

occupying army often abused its power or that redress for locals could be practically impossible.

133. Burnett 1992: 688–713. Cf. Capponi 2005: 157–68, and Bagnall 2009: 189–90.
134. In Tcherikover and Fuks 1957–1963: 2.25–29 (no. 150).
135. On the council and the interpretation of this papyrus see Delia 1991: 115–24.
136. See Swarney 1970; Capponi 2005: 32–34.

began to circulate among eager audiences. Because no one had a motive to preserve it in later centuries, we know it only from papyrus fragments. Called by earlier scholars *The Acts of the Pagan Martyrs*, but now usually the *Acts of the Alexandrians* (*Acta Alexandrinorum*), these texts provide clear evidence of Alexandrian alienation from Rome, among some important players at least, for about two centuries.[137] The authors saw themselves as victims of Roman rule: champions of a Hellenic culture trodden down by the great military power, which gave undue favor to Alexandria's foreign Judaean minority.

When in the 70s or 80s the orator Dio Chrysostom gave an address in Alexandria's great theatre, the scene of earlier violent struggles with the Judaeans (Dio does not mention this), he cautioned the citizens to control their rioting or risk facing Rome's medicine. Although the speech writes off the troublesome behavior as drunken frivolity, he alludes to a specific incident that risked Roman retaliation, warning them of the consequences: "Would *you*, then, revolt from anyone? Would *you* wage war for a single day?"[138] Early in Hadrian's reign (from A.D. 117), that emperor would need to quell rioting in Alexandria (Dio 69.8.1a). And a century after him, Alexandrian boldness in ridiculing the emperor Caracalla provoked his personal visit, to superintend the slaughter of thousands and the widespread destruction of property (Dio 78.22).

Diana Delia estimates that Roman Alexandria housed a maximum of 600,000 persons, of which free citizens (both genders and all ages) accounted for no more than half, and Judaeans numbered as many as 180,000. According to Philo, two of the city's five districts were predominantly Judaean in population and character (*Flacc.* 55).[139] The other resident groups were Egyptians, slaves, and assorted foreigners. This *polis* thus had a very large Judaean minority—much larger than Jerusalem's native population.

---

137. Musurillo 2000 (1954). Harker (2008: 178) thinks that *Alexandrian Stories* would be a more accurate name.

138. *Or.* 32.71; cf. 1, 4, 7, 17–20.

139. Because Philo also says that the districts were named for the Greek alphabet's first five letters (A, B, Γ, Δ, E)—NB: this was the same as numbering them from 1 to 5, since there were no separate numbers—and Josephus remarks (*War* 2.495) that during the riots of 66 the Alexandrians rushed into "what is called the Delta," where Judaeans "had been joined to the city," scholars generally assume that "the Δ quarter" was Judaean. That may be, but: (a) it would not fit easily with Philo's description of *two* Judaean quarters plus wider distribution; (b) other evidence suggests that the Δ zone was in the west, whereas Josephus locates Judaeans in the east; and (c) Josephus' language does not necessarily refer to a district of the city (or if it does so, that may be an understandable mistake); see Mason 2008: 355 n. 3055.

With Roman citizenship only a remote possibility, for the majority unable to undertake a legionary career, Alexandrian citizenship was the most attainable prize. But the only sure way to be a citizen of the *polis* was to win the gene lottery and be born to citizen parents. At age 14, when males became liable to the personal tax unless exempted, their parentage was assessed by *polis* officials. Those who passed the inspection of ancestry were enrolled as citizens. (Women, again, held a derivative status by their connection with fathers and husbands.) Certain others *could* notionally become citizens, but as in the *poleis* of old Greece this was a rare privilege, normally requiring a nomination procedure and vote of the whole citizen assembly, in Alexandria also the consent of the Roman prefect. That process is best attested for star athletes from other Greek *poleis*, hardly ever for local Egyptians.[140] As in other areas of life, the emperor could step in to facilitate the creation of citizens, by ordering his prefect to make it so, but emperors were loath to intervene so heavy-handedly.[141] Native Egyptians and even longstanding foreign residents who wished to become Alexandrian citizens faced a stone wall with few cracks in it.

The non-citizen and free (non-slave) residents of Alexandria were likely to prize the Greek culture of the *polis*, for itself and as an index of social status. Those who could afford it would enroll their boys in Alexandria's *gymnasium*, or in the gymnasium of a smaller *polis*, for the prestigious year of citizen training known as the *ephebate* (students were called *ephebes*). This was the standard means of acculturating male citizens for a life of service to the *polis*, but the Alexandrian ephebate appears to have admitted others who could make a case for entry—and above all, could pay.[142] This loophole created opportunities for non-citizens to become as fluent in the *polis* culture as citizens, even as it fuelled the resentment of those who jealously guarded citizenship. With Roman encouragement, they were keen to protect that exclusive status. Those who were being kept out, we may guess, found it difficult to grasp why, as residents of the same *polis* for generations and sharing the same cultural values, they should be forever relegated to a lower civic status, and high taxation.

140. Delia 1991: 53–56.

141. On the emperor's freedom and restraint in this area (citing imperial precedent), see Pliny's correspondence with Trajan concerning his Egyptian physician (*Ep.* 10.6–7). Pliny committed a *faux pas* in imagining that because the man had been manumitted from slave status he was eligible for Roman citizenship; he had not known to recommend only an Alexandrian citizen for the Roman franchise—a deficiency that Trajan remedies quickly.

142. Delia 1991: 71–88, esp. 76–79.

Alexandrian citizenship shared with its Roman counterpart the problem that it was easy to assert but not always easy to document. An appeal could require investigation of one's ancestry, with affidavits from guarantors. Papyri show the Romans' concern for the careful vetting (*epikrisis*) of those claiming either Roman or Alexandrian citizenship status. Complications arose in particular from the complex personal lives of legionaries, who had to be Roman citizens by the time of their recruitment, or of auxiliary soldiers, who became citizens on discharge. Both frequently had sexual partners and therefore produced children, whose status became an issue once they left active duty.[143]

In the early first century, Strabo marveled at Alexandria's unique generosity in welcoming foreign visitors (14.5.13). This general atmosphere may explain why a large Judaean community had flourished there for so long. But when push came to shove, the potential for exclusion became clear.

The problem seems to become visible in a papyrus fragment from 5/4 B.C. A Judaean with the Greek name of Helenos son of Tryphon, who is nearing or just past the age of 60, is appealing to the Roman governor against the ruling of a lower official that he has to pay the *laographia*.[144] The aggrieved Helenos has not been used to paying it, he insists, but his arguments are telling. He introduces himself as both an Alexandrian and the son of an Alexandrian. But someone, perhaps the scribe who wrote up his dictated petition, has stricken out "Alexandrian" and substituted "*a Judaean of Alexandria*"—whether because Helenos himself realized the need for precision, on second thought, or because the clerk simply corrected him. Whatever else it may signify, this correction appears to confirm the ambiguity of "Alexandrian," and the need for clarification in context of legal status, taxes, and exemptions.

Helenos claims to have lived his life in the *polis* and to have received as good an education as his father's means allowed, a curiously indirect statement that may suggest the *ephebeia* without raising the question of why he was permitted entry. Finally, he invokes "the remaining time of the *laographia*," which expires on his upcoming sixtieth birthday, and so the whole business is pointless in any case. Taken as a whole, the somewhat contradictory arguments (I have not paid the tax because I am not required to, and if I am required to the age of liability is nearly finished) appear to suggest that Helenos is not an Alexandrian citizen. But he has managed to avoid the tax thus far, if we may take him at his word in such an official

---

143. See examples in Grenfell and Hunt 1916: 12.148–49 (no. 1451); cf. Campbell 1984: 154–56; Alston 1995: 57–68, 216–17.

144. In Tcherikover and Fuks 1957–1963: 2.29–33 (no. 151).

THE CLASSICAL PARADIGM: *ETHNOS* AND *POLIS* 137

document, and this exemption has had something to do with his inclination to consider himself an Alexandrian and feel fully a part of *polis* culture since the time of his education. In his senior years he is rudely confronted with a bill by a zealous bureaucrat, and marshals all the arguments he can think of for a continuing exemption, to get him past sixty.[145] Although some scholars have proposed that all Alexandrian Judaeans as such were exempt from the *laographia*, it is telling that Helenos cannot appeal to his Judaean identity, which is not in dispute, as the basis for exemption.[146]

The issue of embassies from Alexandria to Rome, mentioned by the *Boulē Papyrus* as one justification for a council, became particularly relevant in the years A.D. 38 to 41. In a puzzle of events that continues to stimulate investigation and debate,[147] Alexandrians and their Judaean minority came into deadly conflict at that time. Judaeans lived throughout Egypt, but Alexandria hosted their largest community by far (above).[148] When Gaius Caligula came to power (March 16, A.D. 37), he appointed his friend Agrippa I, grandson of Herod the Great, to a kingdom northeast of Judaea. The proud new king's decision to stop in Alexandria en route to his kingdom prompted a wave of anti-Judaean demonstration, in which the long-serving governor Avillius Flaccus was either complicit or impotent (Philo, *Flacc.* 25-38). Flaccus allegedly permitted the ransacking and burning of Judaean homes, the desecration of synagogues by the placing of statues in them, the corralling of Judaeans into a small part of one district (*Flacc.* 55), and unbridled violence against their families (*Flacc.* 39-72). He even supervised the public flogging of Judaean elders, some of whom died from their wounds, and ordered a (fruitless) house-to-house search for Judaean weapons (*Flacc.* 73-96).

For failing to fulfill his main task of maintaining peace in his province, Flaccus was quickly removed by Gaius and exiled to a remote island, where he was soon executed (*Flacc.* 103-91). His replacement, who arrived in October of 38, permitted Alexandrians and Judaeans both to send embassies to Rome, to state their cases before the emperor.[149] But after a perfunctory

---

145. For an attempt to reconstruct the context of Helenos' plea and a case that the Judaean community enjoyed privileges nearly equal to those of Alexandrian citizens, including tax-exemption, see Gambetti 2009: 57-76, esp. 63-67.

146. So Harker 2008: 217-18; Gambetti (2009: 59-62; n. 23) gives earlier dissenting views.

147. E.g., Smallwood 2001 (1981): 201-55; Kasher 1985: 233-357; Modrzejewski 1995: 161-84; Barclay 1996: 48-81; Gruen 2002: 54-83; van der Horst 2003: 18-37 *et passim*; Pearce 2007: 1-16; Gambetti 2009: passim.

148. Kasher 1985: 106-67; Cowey and Maresch 2001; Clarysse and Thompson 2006: 92, 321-22; Gambetti 2009: 43-47.

149. See Philo, *Embassy to Gaius.*

hearing Gaius abandoned them for about a year, going off to visit Rome's armies in Germany. He heard their cases only after returning late in A.D. 40. But before he could reach a decision he was assassinated (January 24, 41). When news of Gaius' death reached Alexandria, the delighted Judaeans reportedly rioted, for a period long enough to reach the ears of the new emperor Claudius, who ordered his new governor to clamp down on them (Josephus, *Ant.* 19.278). Claudius also received two new delegations from the antagonistic communities. His response to their petitions was published in Egypt, in October A.D. 41. According to the *Acts of the Alexandrians* mentioned above, however, he executed two prominent delegates from the prior Alexandrian embassy, Isidorus and Lampon.[150]

For our discussion of *polis* identity we must be content with a few observations on this intricate series of events, which I can only sketch. First, the precise status of Alexandria's resident groups was not objectively clear. Many Judaeans could see themselves as long-established residents and fully *Alexandrian* in important ways. The well-connected Philo seems to have felt quite at home in the city's cultural facilities.[151] His brother was a Roman citizen, as Philo may have been; that brother's first son had married the daughter of Agrippa I; the second son (Tiberius Iulius Alexander) would rise to the highest levels of Roman administration open to a man of his (equestrian) rank, including the governorship of Egypt. Tiberius Alexander would become important in the rise of Vespasian to power, as Agrippa I had been in Claudius' accession, and would serve as Titus' second-in-command in the siege of Jerusalem.[152]

Second, although prominent members of each ethnic group were well known in the *polis*, and might have attained citizenship, many others fell in grey areas with regard to self-perception, outsider perception, and documentable status. Note Philo's remark (*Flacc.* 96) that many non-Judaean women were assaulted in 38 on the false assumption that they were Judaeans. One could not tell, in many cases, by looking.

Third, legal status within a *polis* did not necessarily determine people's perceptions of each other or create permanent alliances. Because our only literary accounts of this situation come from the Judaean Philo, scholarly tradition has seen Alexandria's Judaeans as victims of an anti-Semitic *pogrom*, history's first, driven by powerful Greek and Roman gentiles acting in concert against the Jews. But although he claims that Flaccus was

150. For this sequence see Harker 2008: 10–15. On the execution of the emissaries, see Harker 2008: 39–45 with Tcherikover and Fuks 1957–63: 2.66–81 (no. 156a–d).

151. E.g., Philo, *Ebr.* 177, on his many visits to theatre performances (cf. *Flacc.* 19; *Legat.* 79, 359, 368). On the familiar accouterments of the city see *Opif.* 17, 78

152. See Turner 1954 for a contextual discussion of Tiberius Alexander's career.

temporarily in league with some of Alexandria's prominent men, *because they had manipulated him* for their purposes, Philo also claims that the same men had been the Roman governor's vociferous critics, and that soon they would become accusers again, eventually bringing about his execution (*Flacc.* 125-135). This fits with the underlying resentment of Rome (above) and illustrates how alliances could shift tactically, as elsewhere. Judaeans had lived in Alexandria for centuries, and must have had decent relations with non-Judaeans most of the time.[153] Although we would expect there to be tensions and resentments in any such situation, a simple or static picture of gentile-Jewish conflict could not make sense of the evidence.

At any rate it seems that the Alexandrian citizens did not consider the Judaean minority generally to be citizens, no matter how long the community had lived there. Like Strabo and Josephus, Philo routinely speaks of Jerusalem as the Judaean mother-*polis* (μητρόπολις). Putting Judaeans on the same level as Romans or early Greek monarchies, he sees Jerusalem as a source of *colonization*: its colonies (*apoikiai*) in Alexandria and other prosperous lands carefully preserve the customs of the mother-*polis*.[154]

The definitive statement about Judaean status comes in Claudius' letter of A.D. 41, which responds to Greek and the Judaean embassies that were dispatched to him, perhaps to congratulate him on his accession while also pressing their cases. Our best version of this document is a generous excerpt by a Hellenized Egyptian (not an Alexandrian) named Nemesion, a tax official from the secondary *polis* of Philadelphia.[155] Even in Nemesion's rather partisan summary (e.g., he includes Greek delegates' names, not the Judaeans'), Claudius comes across as even-handed. Nemesion includes Claudius' observation that the Alexandrians have unfairly blamed Judaeans for all the disturbances, and the emperor's fury at them: this was no mere "disturbance" or mutual civil strife, but virtual "a war against the Judaeans." He is also outraged at those who have revived the conflict, whoever they may be. He demands that Alexandrians treat their Judaeans, who are after all long-term residents of the *polis* (he does not say citizens), with kindness and gentleness—and not disturb *their* ancestral worship or other customs.

All the same, Claudius is clear about the basic structure of things. The Alexandrian citizenry, to whom the *polis* belongs, does not include Judaeans as a group, and the latter must not agitate for more than they have. They

---

153. Gruen 2002 emphasizes this aspect of "diaspora" life, giving perspective to the few incidents of conflict we hear about.

154. *Legat.* 203, 281; *Flacc.* 46. Cf. Strabo 4.1.4; 10.4.17.

155. Harker (2008: 25-26), gives cogent reasons for regarding the papyrus (P. Lond. 1912; Tcherikover and Fuks 1957-63: 2.36-60 (no. 153) as Nemesion's personal crib of Claudius' originally fuller directive.

enjoy freedom to follow their customs, *in a polis that after all belongs to others* (ἐν ἀλλοτρίᾳ πόλει), and an abundance of good things. They must neither intrude themselves into Alexandrian citizen institutions, such as gymnasium events, nor think they are entitled to bring in Judaeans from Egypt or neighboring Syria. (Note that no province of Judaea appears.[156])

Glossing over all the complications, then, Claudius affirms the simple model in Alexandria: this *polis* and its *politeia* (citizenship) belong to an *ethnos*, the Greeks long settled in Egypt. Foreigners may reside in the *polis* but it is not theirs. They have their own *poleis* elsewhere, and the Judaeans' mother-*polis* Jerusalem is the famous home of their laws and customs.

That simple model turns up elsewhere, in various authors. According to Josephus' *War*, Judaeans had gravitated toward residence in Antioch, the capital of Seleucid and Roman Syria, from Seleucid times. Although King Antiochus IV harassed them badly, his successors (a) permitted Judaeans to live in the capital without fear (7.43) and (b) restored their synagogue, permitting them "to share the *polis* on equal terms with the Greeks" (7.44). It is far from clear that this refers to citizenship, because in the next sentence Josephus mentions the continual renewal of such favors by subsequent monarchs, which would not seem necessary if Judaeans had citizenship (7.45). He adds that many Greeks joined the Judaeans in their distinctive worship, and so were "made part of them [the Judaean community] in some way" (7.45).

Everything changed dramatically in 67, however, when Vespasian arrived in Syria, taking over the governor's responsibility to suppress the violence in the south (massacre of the Jerusalem garrison, raids against *poleis*, ambush of Cestius' legion), and particularly to silence Judaean militants. Animosity toward Judaeans now rose rapidly in Antioch. Remarkably, it was fuelled by a Judaean, the son of the distinguished "president of the Judaeans in Antioch" (ἄρχων τῶν ἐπ' Ἀντιοχείας Ἰουδαίων). He came before the "Antiochian citizen-body meeting in assembly in the theatre" (τοῦ δήμου τῶν Ἀντιοχέων ἐκκλησιάζοντος εἰς τὸ θέατρον, 7.47) to allege that his own father and certain other Judaeans, including some from elsewhere, were planning to burn down their great *polis* (7.46–49). The man's name (Antiochus) and his ability to make a speech before the citizen assembly suggest that his family enjoyed citizenship, whereas the Judaean community as a whole is clearly not present and also has its own institutions.[157] After calling for the arrest of

---

156. In Tcherikover and Fuks 1957–63: 2.36–55 (no. 153), lines 88–100; translation on 42–43.

157. E.g., two inscriptions from the *polis* Berenice in Cyrenaica (*IBerenike* 17, 18). In the former, likely from A.D. 24, a group of distinguished Judaean leaders praise the Roman governor for his generosity and humanity. He not only gives a hearing to

the alleged Judaean instigators, the enraged citizen-body (ὁ δῆμος) burned them in the theatre, and then pursued the Judaean masses (τὸ πλῆθος . . . τῶν Ἰουδαίων). They had come to believe that a swift reaction was necessary "to save their ancestral home" (τὴν αὐτῶν πατρίδα σώζειν νομίζοντες, 7.49).

In the story it turns out that the Judaean Antiochus does all this mischievously, to secure himself in Antioch's febrile atmosphere by seeking to prove his own loyalty as the tide of opinion turns. He makes a show of having severed all ties with other Judaeans and despising their customs, sacrificing according to Greek custom, and advising the Antiochians to compel all Judaeans to do as he has done—proving their loyalty to their *polis* of residence—or to kill them (7.50–53). He somehow secures military support to enforce the suspension of sabbaths and "harshly lorded it over his *polis*-fellows" (7.52: τοῖς αὐτοῦ πολίταις). In *War's* concentric or ring-compositional patterning, this Antiochus in Book 7 sounds suspiciously like King Antiochus IV, whose attempt to eradicate Judaean law and custom opens the work (1.34–35). Josephus' explicit mention of that king in this episode (7.44) makes the connection unmistakable.

Josephus explains this as background to a further disturbance in late 70 or 71, after Jerusalem's fall. A serious fire erupted then, he says, destroying much of the central *polis*. Antiochus naturally "accused the Judaeans," and the charge sounded plausible because of the earlier alleged plot. So "the Antiochians" (οἱ Ἀντιοχεῖς) went after the Judaeans with a fury (7.56), though the acting legate proved that Judaeans were not responsible (7.58–62). Thus far, although Josephus' language is fuzzy in relation to technical status, the picture is of a minority in Antioch, separate from the citizen body (*dēmos*) and its institutions, including the regular assembly in the theatre. The Judaeans are long-time residents protected by royal decrees and custom, but they remain extremely vulnerable in a time of crisis if the *dēmos* think that their homeland (*patris*) might be in peril from these residents, whose ultimate loyalties lie elsewhere.

This is the setting for Titus' visit to the region (7.100), which inspires "the citizen-body of the Antiochians" (ὁ δὲ τῶν Ἀντιοχέων δῆμος) to rush out several miles with the urgent request that he "expel the Judaeans from the *polis*" (ἐκβαλεῖν τῆς πόλεως τοὺς Ἰουδαίους, 7.103). To this urgent request

---

"citizens individually" (τοῖς κατ' ἰδίαν ἐντυγχάνουσι τῶν πολιτῶν), they say, but he also shows his care for our Judaean *politeuma*, both corporately and individually (τοῖς ἐκ τοῦ πολιτεύματος ἡμῶν Ἰουδαίοις καὶ κοινῇ καὶ κατ' ἰδίαν). This makes a clear distinction between Judaean community and citizenry, though it makes the best sense if the notable donors belong in both groups. Text at http://philipharland.com/greco-roman-associations/306-honors-by-a-corporate-body-of-judeans-for-a-roman-provincial-official-2.

Titus gives an explained refusal, before leaving for a short time. On his return, "When the council and the citizen-body of the Antiochians kept expecting him, having sent many petitions that he would come to their theatre, in which the entire body/number had gathered, he graciously consented" (7.107). Now they will have the chance to press their plea that "he drive the Judaeans out of the *polis*" (7.107).

The realistic reason that Josephus gives Titus for flatly refusing is revealing of the categories were are exploring, all the more because here he emphasizes the Roman's fairness and probity. Titus does not say that these Judaeans are citizens of Antioch and therefore should be left alone, or that they belong here as much as anyone. Rather, with some sympathy for the Antiochian protest, he replies: "But *their* ancestral homeland, to which it would make sense to expel them, since they are Judaeans, lies destroyed, and there is no other place that would take them now" (ἀλλ' ἥ γε πατρὶς αὐτῶν, εἰς ἣν ἐκβαλεῖν ἐχρῆν ὄντας Ἰουδαίους, ἀνῄρηται, καὶ δέξαιτ' ἂν οὐδεὶς αὐτοὺς ἔτι τόπος, 7.109).

Seeing that their main request, for which they have elaborately prepared, is going nowhere, the Antiochians turn to Plan B. They ask Titus at least "to remove the bronze tablets on which are inscribed the Judaeans' legal provisions" (τὰς γὰρ χαλκᾶς ἠξίουν δέλτους ἀνελεῖν αὐτόν, ἐν αἷς γέγραπται τὰ δικαιώματα τῶν Ἰουδαίων, 7.110). Again Titus refuses, and for understandable reasons. If he is going to confirm the Judaeans' permission to remain, he cannot leave them to the tender mercies of a fiercely hostile Antiochian citizen-body, which has already massacred some. So he "left in place everything that the Judaeans of Antioch formerly had" (ἐάσας πάντα κατὰ χώραν τοῖς ἐπ' Ἀντιοχείας Ἰουδαίοις ὡς πρότερον εἶχον, 7.111). This again sounds like protected-minority status at the corporate level, rather than normal citizenship of the *polis*. The Romans are aware of the human tendency to mistreat ethnic minorities merely for being different in law and custom, and suspected of disloyalty to *polis* values for that reason. As a pragmatic matter they will continue to protect this foreign minority, leaving inscribed in a central and visible location the rights to which Judaeans can appeal before the imperial legate.

Even in this relatively clear passage we have noted vague terminology: Antiochus IV's successors let the Judaeans share the *polis* "equally" with the Greek, and Antiochus harasses "his *politai*." In his later works, which lack such stories, Josephus is much more direct. *Ant.* 12.119 reports that the Judaeans, after military service for the "kings of Asia," were granted honors, among which Seleucus Nicator (Alexander's successor and founder of the Seleucids) granted them citizenship (*politeia*) in all his new *poleis*, including Antioch. He gave them the same honors he accorded Greeks and

THE CLASSICAL PARADIGM: *ETHNOS* AND *POLIS*   143

Macedonians, and "this citizenship" survives until Josephus' time. Shortly thereafter (12.121–23), Josephus appears to refer to the episodes we have just considered in *War* 7 when he says that Alexandrians and Antiochians both begged Vespasian and Titus that "the rights of the citizenship" should no longer apply to the Judaeans. But the emperors did not consent, in spite of having motives to act against Judaeans after the war. They took away nothing that belonged with the citizenship (*politeia*). Similarly at *Apion* 2.39 Josephus incidentally cites Judaeans who were called Antiochians because the founder of Antioch gave them *politeia* at the beginning. I suggested earlier that this kind of difference between *War* and the later narratives—a clear citizenship for all Judaeans from the founding of the *polis* would make no sense of *War*'s account—may be comparable to the different treatment of Judaea's provincial status or the Caesarean conflict in the same works.

We seem to find the same pattern in Antioch, then, as in Alexandria, Scythopolis, and elsewhere. Like every other *ethnos*, Judaeans living outside their famous ancestral home are foreigners with restricted rights. They may enjoy protections in foreign *poleis*, acquired by various means over decades and centuries, which may not be trifled with. But those places are not *theirs* and the Judaeans can quickly become vulnerable in times of turbulence.

Both the simple model and some of its complexities appear in Josephus' *Against Apion*. He cites the late Apion, a proud son of Alexandria and one of the *polis*' delegates to Gaius in A.D. 39, as ridiculing the notion that Judaeans should claim to be Alexandrians, given the incompatible traditions of that *ethnos* with that *polis*. Josephus has a devastating response, however, to which his dead opponent cannot reply. Although Apion was world-famous as an *Alexandrian* intellectual, Josephus addresses him posthumously as *an Egyptian* who has somehow wangled citizenship in the great *polis*—but who never shed his *Egyptian* prejudices or base instincts (*Apion* 2.65–73, 81). Josephus will not take instruction on the worship of the deity from an *Egyptian*! (Egyptians attracted much bemusement in the Roman world for their reverence of reptiles.) Whereas Judaeans agree with the cultured nations of the world, Apion's Egyptian compatriots have bizarre customs, revering crocodiles and the like (2.85–88, 132–133, 137–39).[158] Apion prided himself on his Alexandrian culture, but in reality he was the lowest Egyptian (2.32, 135–136), and "one might fairly pity Alexandria if she prides herself on the likes of him" (2.136).

The abstract view according to which everyone is loyal to their *ethnos* and the *polis* that embodies its laws and customs was not up to the challenges of real-life migration and re-attachment. The learned Claudius intervened

158. See Barclay 2006 on this passage.

decisively to affirm Alexandria's traditional structure, even though Rome's approach to citizenship was entirely different. In the late first century B.C., Dionysius of Halicarnassus contrasts it with the Greek models that still obtain in most places. Because Athens, Thebes, and Sparta both destroyed their enemies and "guarded their own privileged ancestry, sharing their citizenship with none but a very few," he observes, a single military defeat could effectively wipe out their citizen base.[159] The Romans went about things in a smarter way. They preserved the nations they conquered, wherever possible, established colonies among them, and offered their citizenship to worthy foreigners. Already under Rome's founder Romulus, he wrongly imagines, this enlightened self-interest gave Rome supremacy and unconquerable freedom, for it could absorb even large military defeats with such a vast pool of potential recruits (*Ant. rom.* 2.16–17).

Two centuries later Aelius Aristides likewise criticizes the Greek model of citizenship while enthusing over Rome's innovation (*To Rome* 59–63):

> But this is what really deserves more attention and wonder than everything else. I mean your handling of membership in the *polis*, and the magnificence of its conception, because there is nothing similar anywhere else. Dividing all those in the empire (I say this meaning the whole world) into two parts, to the most gifted, noble, and prominent of them you have everywhere extended not only citizenship but even kinship, while the remaining part is obedient and ruled. Neither a sea nor an intervening landmass creates a barrier to citizenship ... No one worthy of leadership or trust is considered a foreigner (ξένος) ... Being 'great in a great way' you have measured out your citizenship. It was not by being reserved and haughty that you made a wonder of this [citizenship], or by refusing to share it with anyone different from you; but you saw the value in its expansion.[160]

Arthur M. Eckstein agrees with ancient writers that Rome's diplomatic innovations, more than its famous militarism (which it shared with all ancient states), was its distinctive advantage. Faced with the challenge of dealing with the Greek East after 200 B.C., the Romans fastened on this idea of defining Romanness in a new way, "by gradually divorcing citizenship at least somewhat from either ethnicity or location, and thus leading to a unique inclusiveness."[161] Even ordinary free men of good background in the provinces might be offered citizenship to qualify them for a career

---

159. On the classical Athenian view of citizenship, see now Lape 2010.
160. Oliver 1953: 926–29.
161. Eckstein 2006: 312–13.

in the legion. Within Rome itself, freed slaves normally became citizens and assumed the names of their former owners, something not at all normal in a Greek *polis*.[162] And the freedmen of the emperor, much to the chagrin of the senatorial class, could acquire enormous power—up to the governorship of Egypt.[163]

Writing in Rome, in the work he devoted to ridiculing Alexandrian portrayals of the Judaeans, without mentioning Rome's innovation Josephus contrasted the nervously guarded citizenship of the typical *polis* with the open welcome offered by his own *ethnos* and its mother-*polis*:

> All those who want to come over and live under our laws he [Moses] welcomes heartily, reckoning that *the kinship bond exists not only through ancestry but also by virtue of the deliberate choice of life*, though he did not want those who came by in a casual way to be integrated in our close society. (*Apion* 2.210; cf. 2.123)

Even though this model of citizenship (contrasted with that of Athens and Sparta, 2.257–69) exposed the inadequacy of a simple *ethnos-polis* model, it was the only language available and Josephus exploited it for his purposes. We shall return to this issue.

Of course human identities do not—outside the fantasies of racial mythologists—sit there as objective, static realities waiting to be studied. Everyone has a sea of conscious and unconscious memories, instincts, and feelings about who they are, beneath any documentable identities. The need to articulate one's identity arises normally in response to a stimulus, and each articulation will be somewhat different. Catherine Morgan aptly reflects: "[I]ndividuals' social identities consisted of a palimpsest of inherited and ascribed traits which were more or less important under different

---

162. These three grave reliefs from the first century B.C. show former slaves, with Greek given names, celebrating their freedom and status as Roman citizens. In the first (ca. 80 B.C.), Aurelius Hermia and his wife Aurelia Philmatium appear in citizen clothing and legal marriage (not possible for slaves). In the second (early first cent. A.D.), former slaves Philonicus and Demetrius, surrounded by tools and implements of debated significance, proudly bear the Latin forenames Publius Licinius. See Ashmole 1956: 71–73; Manning 1964: 25–28. In the third example (same date), L. Antistius Sarculo, a Roman citizen and Master of a lower priestly college, appears with his wife, the former slave Antistia Plutia in matching shell niches and surrounded by wreaths of immortality. Two of the couple's former slaves paid for the monument, according to the inscription, in gratitude to their patrons. See Strong 1914: 147–56 These images may be studied in the British Museum's research collection (http://www.britishmuseum.org) under refs. 1867,0508.55, 1954,1214.1, 1858,0819.2.

163. See Capponi 2004: 184–85, concerning Hiberus, apparently Prefect in A.D. 26–28 (Dio's *Kaisareios* 57.19.6).

circumstances, and the political identity of individual communities was constructed from a complex of associations, *including relationship to a polis, an ethnos or variously constituted groups within these*, which could be differently weighted to the perceived advantage of that community."[164]

Even today, objective-seeming citizenship can be complicated by our holding of multiple passports, none of which may really say much about how we actually think of ourselves. It is during civil conflicts, such as wars in the former Yugoslavia, Iraq, or Sudan, that questions of identity may suddenly be forced on people and sharpened to crisis point. Something like that seems to have happened in southern Syria, where large Judaean minorities had lived untroubled for decades before the war.

But ancient *ethnos-polis* terminology in the shared discourse was never meant to be a vehicle for individuals' internal explorations of their identity—a preoccupation of our therapeutic age. It was a helpfully vague and logical-seeming means of classifying populations in a world that lacked our refined but still vague political states, policed borders, immigration bureaucracies, and passports. *Ethnos* and *polis* were malleable terms, but this is what made them readily intelligible and universally useful.

164. Morgan 2009a: 23; emphasis mine.

5b

The Classical Paradigm: Sacrificial Cult and Voluntary Association

Ta Hiera / *Ritus*: Cultic Ritual, Sacrifice, Priests, and Divination

We turn now to a set of connected terms that do not leave such a clear impact (as *ethnos* and *polis*) on ancient literature, but which turn up in various configurations everywhere in antiquity, especially in the material remains unearthed by archaeology. The whole sphere of worship, sacrificial cult, and purification ritual shifts us farther along the spectrum from what is given at birth toward voluntary association.

Paul Cartledge has written: "[I]f there was one religious ritual that made a Greek conventionally and normatively 'Greek', it was eligibility to participate in a bloody animal sacrifice, which constituted an act of communion in the strict sense. Thus for the full (adult male) citizen of a *polis* it was the very cornerstone of the city, defining precisely what it was to constitute and participate in that peculiar mode of political and social organization [i.e., the *polis*]."[1]

As we read surviving ancient works and recognize their authors as fellow human beings, we too easily ignore the centrality of animal sacrifice to *polis* life.[2] The problem is disguised or mitigated by the fact that many fine studies of Greek and Roman *religion* use that comfortable word in their titles. The reader soon discovers, however, that their contents have little to

1. Cartledge 2002a: 176.
2. For comparative ancient perspectives see Baumgarten 2002; Knust and Varhelyi 2011.

do with what we would recognize as religious practice in our synagogues, temples, churches, and mosques.³ Academic authors are usually quick to explain that they are writing about a rather different and particular kind of "religious" expression, one centered in the ritualized offering of animal and other sacrifices to a deity.⁴

Whether we are thinking of the place of religion in western society or the internal functions of what we call religions, we must conclude that the ancients had no conception of anything similar, and hence no language that corresponds well to our *religion*. They could neither have asked nor have answered such standard modern questions as: "Are you religious? What is your religion? Has your religion changed from that of your parents?"

The Latin word *religio*, from which English "religion" ultimately derives, is an ancient word certainly. But its meaning has evolved, much in the way that the Greek terms *ecclēsia* and *leitourgia*, which once had to do with features of *polis* life, came to mean "church" and "liturgy" in a Christian environment. Only in Christian usage did *religio* come to mean "a system of religious belief, a religion." The etymology of the word was already disputed by the ancients, but in practical use its basic sense was of some solemn obligation or commitment, which might refer to *a superstition*, an oath in wartime, or a particular *sacred object* (or the sacredness of the object). It could indicate the sacrificial *ritual* in honor of a particular god or a *mentality of awe* or devoted scrupulousness.⁵ A person described as *religiosus* was remarkably scrupulous, whether in life generally or in relation to rituals, though some grammarians thought that it was the suffix *-osus* and not the root that implied excess. Things described as *religiosus* were essentially *taboo*, or separate from ordinary life, in good or bad senses (Aulus Gellius 4.9).

In the ancient world, further, *priests* were nothing like modern clergy, who are trained in the exposition of sacred texts, theology, religious history, foreign languages, pastoral counseling, and the orders of service for

---

3. E.g., Burkert 1985; Beard, North, and Price 1998; Klauck 2003; Scheid 2003; Rüpke 2007; Rives 2007.

4. So Burkert 1985: 8: "ritual and myth are the two forms in which Greek religion presents itself to the historian of religion." On pp. 55–60 he emphasizes the centrality of animal sacrifice in that ritual. Scheid (2003: 18–29) carefully qualifies the meaning of religion in his study—focused on sacrificial ritual—to avoid anachronism. The central part of his book then explores ancient sacrifice with examples and insightful analysis (79–110). Rives (2007: esp. 13–53) takes care to separate out many spheres of Roman life in which "religious" phenomena were to be found. Particularly clear, if less inviting for modern readers, are such books as Turcan 1996; Larson 2007; and Dignas and Trampedach 2008, which signal this interest in the title.

5. See the range of meanings even in Julius Caesar, *Bell. alex.* 74.3; *Bell. gal.* 6.16.1, 37.8; *Bell. civ.* 1.11.2, 76.5; 2.32.10; 3.28.4; generally, Lewis and Short 1945 *s.v.*

regular worship, and who assist their congregants at birth, marriage, and death. An ancient priest, in addition to being a *polis* official, was a specialist in the sacrificial rituals customary for that *ethnos* and *polis*. He knew the prescriptions for selecting, inspecting, preparing, slaughtering, sacrificing or immolating the animals, and separating their parts for consumption, as well as the appropriate offerings of wine, cakes, and incense. These items often accompanied animal sacrifice, or they might be made on their own where an animal sacrifice was too elaborate.

The priest was responsible for supervising all such activities, which might physically be carried out by attendants and slaves, to ensure that they conformed to ancestral custom or law. He was also expert in the movements, gestures, music, and incantations that accompanied such sacrifices—the music serving partly to keep away evil spirits. The presence of priests was by no means necessary for every kind of Greek and Roman sacrifice, but they oversaw the major civic cults and preserved traditional knowledge of sacrificial etiquette.[6]

Sacrificial ritual was integral to nearly every facet of ancient public life: politics, entertainment, sport, and military campaigning. In Athens, the civic center was a sacred space, barred to those facing disgrace and marked off by the same water basins for purification that were located outside temples. Meetings of the *polis* council or the political assembly would be preceded by the carrying of a sacrificed pig around the circumference. This sanctified the proceedings as well as the participants.[7] Dramatic festivals and athletic competitions in Athens were devoted to some *polis* Gods and accordingly were also marked by sacrifices and related rituals. Still in the Roman period, actors were not members of modern-style guilds but belonged to associations devoted to the God Dionysus.

Likewise the Roman Senate could meet only in a consecrated building, each meeting of its members ("Conscript Fathers") being preceded by a sacrifice of incense. Rome itself and Roman colonies were defined by a sacred boundary (*pomerium*) marked out by the *augurs*, a boundary that had nothing necessarily to do with the city's defensive walls. From the area within this line, death and other forms of pollution were in principle excluded, the dead being buried outside it—at least before the inevitable growth of the city put some tombs inside. The powers granted to military commanders and provincial governors lapsed when they crossed this ritual boundary in Rome. In Republican times, armed soldiers were banned with few

---

6. We do not have many literary accounts of sacrifice because it was such a common feature of daily life. But there are a few. Scheid (2003) gives narrative examples of both public (86–89) and private (92) sacrifice.

7. Parker 1983: 19.

exceptions, a principle respected as far as possible (e.g., except the imperial bodyguard) well into the later Empire.[8] The entire city of Rome was thus a *templum*: a sacred space and one marked out for authoritative divination.

Roman military life from camp routines to preparation for a military campaign or the solemn ceremonies marking the demobilization of long-service comrades, was also shot through with rituals of divination and sacrifice—both the traditionally Roman rituals and those suited to the ethnic make-up of particular units.[9] In this the Romans were continuing a much older tradition among all armies. The Spartans were scrupulously observant of divine rites, and would sacrifice a goat before engaging in battle.[10] The triumphal-memorial columns of Trajan (ca. A.D. 113–117) and Marcus Aurelius (ca. A.D. 192) feature scenes of sacrifice in their frieze panels, as does the Arch of Trajan at Beneventum.[11] In some of these, the emperor in his priestly function supervises the traditional sacrifice of a pig (*sus*), sheep (*ovis*), and bull (*taurus*)—the so-called *suovetaurilia*—outside the fort, to purify the army before a campaign. In his work *On Agriculture* (142), Cato the Elder had prescribed the ritual (including prayers to Mars) for the *suovetaurilia* in the non-military context of purifying land. This fundamental ritual had several functions in addition to the army's purification for combat.[12]

Pompey the Great, a candidate for the status of Rome's greatest general ever, illustrates well the integration of attendance on the Gods with military life. When he had been granted unprecedented power over the entire Mediterranean and its contiguous lands, to deal with maritime threats, defeat King Mithradates VI of Pontus, and settle eastern lands for Rome, he reportedly first made a point of offering public sacrifice, as generals customarily did (Plutarch, *Pomp*. 26.1). Most telling are the coins issued following Pompey's three subsequent triumphs. Surprisingly to modern observers, perhaps, they feature the implements of Pompey's *priestly office* of augur: a jug and a crooked staff—a symbol preserved by Christian bishops. Some

---

8. Essentials are in Platner 1911: 34–37, 43–48; Oliver 1932: 145–82. For issues of purity and pollution see Hope and Marshall 2000: 85–173—essays by John R. Patterson, Hope, John Bodel, and Hugh Lindsay. For a pithy summary see Patterson's essay there, 85–103 (88–97).

9. See Webster 1985: 275–81; Le Bohec 1994: 236–54; Herz 2002: 81–100 (with a valuable effort to recover concrete procedures); Stoll 2007: 451–76.

10. E.g., Burkert 1985: 59–60.

11. On the Beneventum arch see Beard 2007: 126–28.

12. See the sketch of a Roman relief by an anonymous Italian artist in the mid-16th century in the British Museum (http://www.britishmuseum.org, ref. 1947,0319.26.154). It resembles scenes depicted on the two columns and elsewhere: e.g., scene 53 from Trajan's Column, spiral/panel 8b on drum 6–7 in the *McMaster Trajan Project* (http://cheiron.mcmaster.ca/~trajan); cf. Ferris 2009: 67–69.

SACRIFICIAL CULT AND VOLUNTARY ASSOCIATION   151

highlight the close connection between Pompey and these priestly implements, by arranging the jug and stuff around Pompey's image.¹³

If we imagine any modern general, from Napoleon to Rommel, Montgomery or Patton, from Westmoreland to Schwarzkopf or Petraeus, choosing to be photographed for posterity in clerical garb, framing his battlefield maneuvers in elaborate religious rituals, or thinking it important to dedicate a religious building after a conflict, we immediately see the differences between "religion" in our world and the ways in which sacrificial cult, priests, and rituals were embedded in most aspects of ancient life.

Rome, the best-documented *polis* for our period, is a good example of diversity within the standard categories. By the first century B.C. a complex collection of state priesthoods had developed there, both colleges (*collegia*) of high officials and individual posts open only to the senatorial class or the small elite subset of patricians (families of ancient nobility). These included the "king and queen of sacrifices" (*rex* and *regina sacrorum*) as well as the *flamines* or individual priests of the leading Gods: Jupiter, Mars, and Romulus (*Dialis, Martialis*, and *Quirinalis*). As with Jerusalem's high priest, the prestige enjoyed by Jupiter's priest (the *flamen Dialis*) came with serious constraints. Appointed from the small circle of patrician families, he was more or less confined to the city of Rome. He was not permitted to touch a corpse or look on an arrayed army, and hence was personally disqualified from warfare. He could not touch bread made with yeast. His clothing could contain no knots. He lived each and every day in the high state of holiness required of others only when they visited sacred sites.¹⁴

Among the highest honors that the emperor and military conqueror Augustus could claim for himself, in the autobiographical *Res gestae* that he published near the end of his life (A.D. 14), was membership in Rome's seven leading priestly colleges (*Res gestae* 7.2): "I have been *pontifex maximus, augur*, in the Commission of Fifteen Supervising the Sacred Activities, in the Commission of Seven Supervising Sacred Banquets, an Arval Brother, a *sodalis Titius*, and a *fetial* priest." These priestly bodies oversaw Rome's attention to the gods (*cura deorum*) and the interpretation of the divine will through omens. The named colleges were the preserve of the senatorial class and, since they were life-long positions in contrast to year-long

---

13. In the British Museum (http://www.britishmuseum.org) see the gold coin from Pompey's first triumph (71 B.C.) as ref. 1867,0101.584 and the silver issues from in 44–42 B.C. and A.D. 112–114 (refs. 1860,0328.155, 1862,0415.8).

14. So Aulus Gellius 10.15, summarizing in the mid-2nd century A.D. what he had read in Fabius Pictor, who wrote nearly four centuries earlier. For the priestly colleges see also the 1st-cent. B.C. Dionysius of Halicarnassus, *Ant. rom.* 2.64–76.

magistracies, avidly sought honors.[15] Augury was in its origins a form of divination by *auspicia* (from *aves* [birds] + *specto* [observe]): observing the flight patterns and noises of specified birds in a prescribed area and from a consecrated vantage point.

Auspicia (auspices) had a long tradition in Rome. They were taken before various public undertakings, including the election of magistrates. But the great orator-statesman Cicero, a member of the senatorial College of Augurs, sounds rather like a modern liberal Protestant when, in a dialogue with his brother ridiculing the superstition involved in seeking the divine will through animal movements, he writes (my emphasis):

> 'It is hard for an augur to speak against auspices!' [you say]. For a Marsian,[16] sure; but for a Roman it is no problem. We are certainly not augurs who speak about the future by observing birds and the various other signs! I do believe that Romulus, who founded the city on the basis of auspices, held the view that knowledge of coming things lay in augury—for antiquity often went astray in these matters. But we can see that *things have changed*, whether you ascribe this to experience, to education, or to the great age [of the practice]. Still, with a view to both *the imaginations of the rabble and expediency for the state*, we maintain custom, superstition, discipline, the law of augury, and the authority of the [augural] College. (*Div.* 2.33 [70])

Cicero's emphasis on the social utility of the ancient rites, including the perpetuation of superstition among the masses, was shared by many of his class.[17] In the twenty-first century we stand at the end of a much longer progression, and yet we still speak of *inaugurating* officials and *auspicious* days—without necessarily knowing about the practices behind these terms.

By Cicero's time in the mid-first century B.C., the College of Augurs had become an elite group of enormous prestige. A century and a half later it was likewise political honor and fortune, not the opportunity to exercise a spiritual function, that delighted Pliny the Younger when he was appointed to the same college:[18]

---

15. Beard, North, and Price 1998: 55.

16. The Marsi were one of Rome's old neighboring tribes, to the northeast of Latium.

17. Cf. Polybius 6.56.7–12, admiring the Romans' exploitation of superstition; similarly Diodorus 1.2.2; 34/35.2.47. Josephus hints at the same principle when he allows that popular Greek beliefs about judgement after death (which he does not believe) are valuable in promoting virtuous behavior among the masses (*War* 2.158).

18. *Ep.* 4.8 (emphasis mine). Cf. *Ep.* 10.13, where Pliny requests the honor.

You [Maturus Arrianus] may congratulate me on having been received among the Augurs, and you may congratulate me with justice: first because it's a fine thing to follow the judgments of such a great *princeps* as ours [i.e., Trajan was also an *Augur*] even in smaller matters; second, because this priesthood itself is old and sacred, and indeed has a clear and marked sanctity to it, *which is not taken away from a living incumbent*. Surely other positions of roughly comparable authority are granted, but they are also taken away. In this case the element of luck is limited to the giving of it.

In other words, one need only wait on fortune for elevation to Augur status. Once you have it, even bad luck in other areas cannot take it away from you. Whereas a senator such as Pliny might aspire to one such college membership, the emperor dominated any possible rival for prestige by holding *all* the important priesthoods at the same time. He was also in the unique position of securing memberships for the others as new positions opened up.

Like the other senatorial colleges, that of the Augurs preserved a body of secret ancient lore for advising the state. Every nation presumably had some such experts in its traditions. Josephus mentions a sub-group of "priests who were experts in the ancestral traditions," who were brought forward to convince their revolution-minded colleagues that excluding sacrifices from foreigners, as they were planning, would be both untraditional and dangerous (*War* 2.417). In Jerusalem as elsewhere around the Mediterranean, priests were an integral part of *polis* leadership.

Augustus' self-representation provides ample evidence of the value he placed on public cult and its priesthoods. Even when describing his consulships (*RG* 8), which could sound to us purely secular and political, he mentions that he conducted the traditional expiatory sacrifices of a pig, a sheep, and a bull (the *lustrum*) upon completion of each population census, something unimaginable for a modern government Census Office. He is frequently pictured on coins and reliefs offering sacrifice, his toga raised over his head in reverence to the divine.[19]

The importance that the emperor attached to his membership in priestly colleges reflected both the centrality of the gods to Roman life and his practical concern for controlling every avenue of upper-class influence and prestige. Particularly noteworthy is his title *pontifex maximus*. In its narrow sense the term designated the leader of the sixteen or twenty men

19. See the gold coins in the British Museum (http://www.britishmuseum.org), ref. 1932,0408.2 (16 B.C. Rome), 1871,1203.6 (16 B.C. Spain), 1864,1128.22 (13 B.C. Rome).

known as *pontifices*, who were charged with overseeing ritual correctness and advising the Senate as well as leading citizens. The *pontifices* constituted the most prestigious of Rome's priestly colleges.[20] But Julius Caesar's assumption of the position, which Augustus and his imperial successors followed, gave the title the effective meaning of "high priest of the Roman state."[21] This sublime office was often mentioned first by emperors on their coins, inscriptions, and military diplomas (for auxiliary soldiers becoming citizens).[22]

When Augustus' autobiographical record was published (August 19, A.D. 14), Latin *pontifex maximus* was rendered in Greek as *archiereus* (*RG* 7.2)—the same word used for the Judaean "high priest," the head of Jerusalem's cultic-sacrificial regime who also had important roles in *polis* life.[23] Similarly, the "High priest of Alexandria and all Egypt," who supervised all of provincial Egypt's temples and its imperial cult, held the highest civic office to which a wealthy Alexandrian citizen could aspire.[24] *Pontifex Maximus* has survived to modern times as one of the Pope's unofficial titles.

Although the senatorial priestly colleges were the most visible and important, at least half a dozen other such colleges were available for Romans of equestrian rank, and a very few were open to ordinary Roman citizens. Of the last group, the most famous was the college of *haurspices*, which comprised sixty Etruscans of noble ancestry.[25] They are a good example of Rome's unique traditions because their functions arose from Rome's history of conquest and debts to the older civilization of Etruria to the north (see above). Roman public ritual required these Etruscan specialists at crucial points to read the internal organs, especially the liver, of a sacrificed animal. These organs were the parts of the sacrifice burned on the altar—for the

20. See Dionysius, *Ant. rom.* 2.73.
21. See Beard, North, and Price 1998: 191–92.
22. See in the British Museum collection (www.britishmuseum.org): 1843,0116.522 (coin of Caesar depicting him as *augur* and *pontifex*); R.3594, R.5033, R.6440, R.6441, R.6458, 1901,0601.150 (coins of Gaius Caligula, *pon. m.* or *p.m.*); 1912,0607.59, R.6583, R1874,0715.11 (coins of Galba *p.m.*); 1872,0709.465 (coin of Vitellius *p.m.*), 1894,1105.1 (inscription for new bridge built by Domitian, *pontf. maximus*), 1813,1211.1, 1813,1211.2 (diplomas from Trajan, *pontifex maximus*). Compare these examples from the reigns of Gaius Caligula (copper *as* of A.D. 37–38, 1853,0105.131) and Aulus Vitellius (denarius of April to December, A.D. 69, R.10252); both advertise their status as *pontifex maximus* and feature the Goddess Vesta with sacrificial bowl (*patera*) on the reverse. They are © Trustees of the British Museum.
23. This development was of course different and driven by local conditions. Cf. Bickerman 1988: 140–44.
24. Cf. Capponi 2005: 41–42.
25. Rüpke 2007: 40, 223–28.

SACRIFICIAL CULT AND VOLUNTARY ASSOCIATION   155

god—whereas the rest of the roasted meat would be eaten. They were examined partly to determine whether the sacrifice was accepted and partly, according to a tradition of divination, to read significance from the condition of various sections of the organ. The secret knowledge required to undertake this divination could, however, be viewed as a threat to rulers.[26]

Just as the integration of cult with public and military life was a common feature of ancient life, so also notions of pollution (*miasma*), taboo, and purification were widely shared, if differently handled from place to place.[27] Pollution seems to have been understood essentially as contamination: the mixing of things that ought to be kept separate, each in its proper place. Purification therefore meant restoring things to the pure or unmixed state. In cultic contexts, proper separation meant above all keeping the immortal gods and the spaces consecrated to them free from exposure to the phenomena of mortality—the human processes associated with child-bearing and death, and sometimes including such bodily discharges as blood and semen. We see here the basic difference from modern conceptions of *hygiene*, on the one hand, and from theological notions of *sin* on the other—though pollution could certainly overlap with both. Serious violations of the moral order such as murder were particularly troublesome, but even naturally and unavoidably appearing bodily fluids associated with life and death, like death itself, had to be kept away from sacred areas.

Many kinds of pollution were considered communicable, contagious through contact, or even inherently communal. Consider the pollution of Thebes by Oedipus' unwitting outrages against the natural order in *Oedipus Tyrannus*, or the growing atmosphere of doom that Josephus portrays as he describes wartime Jerusalem and the pollution of its sacred spaces.

Purification involved the restoration of a polluted person, group, or space to its whole condition. Those who wished to enter consecrated spaces needed to undergo a symbolic purification by washing with water. This was not for hygienic purposes, as bacteria were still unknown, though obvious dirt or blood would have needed to be removed as a blemish. If people had contracted specific kinds of impurity, more elaborate rituals involving sacrifice and restitution might be needed to complete the process of restoration. Very serious cases, involving kin bloodshed or temple robbery, might place the perpetrators under a curse that only their suffering or death could resolve.

26. Rüpke 2007: 149–50, 252–53.

27. For cross-cultural perspectives compare Parker 1983: e.g., 18–31, with Milgrom 2004, and both of these with anthropologist Douglas 2002; also Baumgarten 2002. An accessible summary, though it emphasizes Israelite-Judaean conceptions, is Attridge 2004: 71–83.

Such common notions were shared, at least in broad terms, from one *ethnos* and *polis* to another. But as with the the other categories we have been discussing, beneath such broadly shared notions of *piety, sacred matters, cult, worship,* and *rites* lay a wide range of local cultic practices. Herodotus transmits stories about Persian and Scythian sacrifices, for example, highlighting their differences from Greek parallels. Yet still he recognizes them *as* the established customs (*nomoi, nomaia*) of those peoples. The Persians thus do not use temples, altars, or statues (as they do not think of their gods in human form), he says. They take their sacrificial victims out to open spaces, cut them up, boil the meat, lay it out on the grass, receive the consecrating chant of a priest (*magus*), and finally take away the whole lot to use as they wish (1.130-32). He contrasts the Greek norm: a fixed altar for roasting the animal to accompanying music, ancillary offerings of wine and barley, and division of the victim so that part of it is burned up for the god, part goes to the priest(s), and part goes to the sacrificers (1.132.1).[28]

The Scythians, again, offer animals—mainly horses (not pigs, as the Greeks)—to various gods, with Greek-equivalent names, boiling the meat in a cauldron (no Greek-style roasting). They build a kind of altar, but only to honor their version of Ares, god of war, to whom they also barbarically sacrifice one *man* from every hundred they take prisoner (4.59-63).

The apparatus for worshipping and appeasing the deity thus varied with each *polis* and its local traditions. Although the same divine names turned up across the Hellenized world (Roman Jupiter, Syrian Baal-Shemim, and the Judaean Yahweh might all be identified with Zeus), their characteristics in each place varied considerably. Traditional cultic prescriptions and systems for choosing priests and other officials were quite different, even in Greek Athens, Sparta, and Corinth. A distinction was commonly made, however, between the central cults of each *polis* and those that functioned either below or above *polis* level. The latter were less definitive of distinct peoples and *poleis*.

Our focus must be on those public cults and festivals at the *polis* level, but we should acknowledge other related activities. First, throughout the Greek world (as also in Egypt, Judaea, and elsewhere) individuals and heads of households were free to bring sacrifices in fulfillment of vows, to accompany petitions (e.g., for a good harvest or health), and to express thanks to the deity.[29] Second, in the Hellenistic-Roman period male citizens and sometimes women and slaves could be initiated into a local group devoted to the worship of Demeter and Korē, Isis and Osiris, Serapis, the Great

---

28. See the discussion in Cartledge 2002a: 176.

29. Parker 2005: 9-49.

Mother Cybele, or Mithras. Or they might join a club or guild that, as part of its corporate life, worshiped a patron deity with regular sacrifices (see below on Voluntary Associations). Finally, there were various kinds of trans-local cultic activities: inter-*polis* festivals with athletic games every four years at Greece's pan-Hellenic sites (e.g., Delphi, Delos, and Olympia), which were deliberately sited at some distance from the powerful *poleis* and managed by committees; prestigious cults (such as that of Demeter and Korē at Eleusis in Attica) in which people from other *poleis* were welcome to participate; and Jerusalem's cult, which both served Judaeans everywhere and welcomed gifts and visits from non-Judaean visitors.

Judaeans throughout both the Roman and the Parthian worlds looked to their sole temple in the *mētropolis* of Jerusalem. They sent funds annually for its upkeep, and undertook pilgrimages to it if they had the means and inclination.[30] The exclusivity of Jerusalem as home of the Judaean cult is confirmed by these donations and pilgrimages, by the comments or complaints of outside observers about them (e.g., Tacitus, Hist. 5.4), and by biblical laws that developed out of earlier cultic variety and specified Jerusalem as the sole center of cultic activity (Deut. 12: 5–14). Nevertheless, there was a Judaean temple in Lower Egypt until the mid-70s A.D., and some important sacrifices *may* have been offered elsewhere under some circumstances. We know very little about either of these complications.[31]

No matter what his personal beliefs may have been, then, a citizen of either a Graeco-Roman or a Near-Eastern *polis*, including Jerusalem, would have had a constant awareness of the local god(s) and the traditional precautions for maintaining purity near spaces consecrated to that god. Ancient Hebrew, Aramaic, Greek, and Latin all had numerous words for laws, customs, observances, piety, ritual, sacrifice, pollution, purity, and so forth. They needed no word for a separate sphere of life comparable to *religion* in our world, and they had none.

When I describe religion today as separable from the rest of life, I recognize that for many individuals this distinction may not sound right. They may feel that their religious outlook grounds and informs everything else they do: business and leisure activities, charity, diet, and dealings with

---

30. See Lee 2012.

31. The slight but intriguing literary and material evidence for sacrificial cult outside Jerusalem in the Graeco-Roman period is gathered in Runesson, Binder, and Olsson 2008: 274–94. Cf. the suggestive remark of Josephus and *Ant.* 2.313 with Colautti 2002: 7, 24–32, 231–35. On earlier temples in Egypt (at Elephantine), see Bickerman (1988): 44–45, 239). On the temple in Leontopolis, Egypt, see Josephus, *War* 1.33; 7.421–436; *Ant.* 12.388; 13.70, 285; 20.336, with critical analysis and reconstruction (exploiting relevant inscriptions) by Capponi 2007.

others. But we are discussing societies, not personal outlooks, and the way in which *public life* is ordered. In modern western societies, religion *is* a voluntary sphere of activity involving worship, prayer, the study and exposition of texts, moral exhortation, a certain life discipline, possibly with dietary implications, and special rites of passage marking at least birth, marriage, and death. My point is simply that there was no such unified but separate sphere in ancient life. The categories to which Graeco-Roman and Judaean writers resorted (*ethnos*, nature or character, ancestral custom, and law; *polis*, citizenship, and constitution [*politeia*]; and sacrifice-centered rituals for attending to the Gods of the *ethnos* and *polis*) grew from different assumptions.

The zone or sphere of life that we recognize as *religion* would emerge in the first instance from gradual Christian changes to the ancient-social lexicon, in which process elements of ethnic, political, ritual, and philosophical life were fused to produce *systems of belief and practice*. This new amalgam of religion stripped and reconfigured what it needed from *ethnos*, *polis*, and cult, leaving the rest to wither as empty shells. After centuries of a new kind of faith-based integration of state and society, which followed in the medieval period, the transition to religious –isms was renewed with a vengeance in the Enlightenment as in the American and French Revolutions, where religion (though usually remaining welcome) was isolated in principle, as a voluntary pursuit of mind and spirit, from governance and the essential operations of society.

This section has obvious consequences for thinking about Judaean life under Roman rule and for the revolt against Rome. In scholarship and in film (e.g., *Ben-Hur*) alike, the relationship is usually cast in religious terms: the Jews were a uniquely religious people, whom hard-headed, practical Romans could not understand. The war against Rome was largely motivated by such religious concerns. In this chapter I am not at all suggesting that "religious factors" were irrelevant. They were part and parcel of all Mediterranean society: among Greeks, Syrians, Romans, and Judaeans. But the ancients had no language for separating out such philosophical, ritual-cultic, and ancestral-legal matters from their various embedded places in life and creating one package called *religion*. If they could have done so, it would not resemble our modern religious practices. The difference is that we make a separate issue of religion. Concerns with ancestral law, custom, piety, and cult were paramount for all peoples.

Thiasos–Hetairia–Collegium: Voluntary Associations and *Philosophiai*

The categories of belonging and identity that we have been considering were basic to the classical paradigm because they were universal. Every person unavoidably belonged to an *ethnos*, with its ancestral traditions connected with a place, and participated in sacrificial worship. For most, the *polis* or its village territory focalized these identity markers, whether one lived at home or away. These are precisely the features of ancient life that the emperor Julian would strive to restore against the tide of the Christian paradigm, which was rapidly closing temples and marginalizing both *ethnos* and *polis* identity.[32] But our survey of crucial belonging-groups in antiquity would not be complete, especially if we seek to understand real-life conditions for Judaeans and Christians, without some attention to the voluntary associations, clubs, or guilds (*thiasoi, hetairiai, synodoi, collegia*) that were found in every *polis*.

These associations were many and varied. Because their membership was largely non-elite, their internal goings-on left little trace in literature. We are learning much more about them through the collation and examination of relevant inscriptions, a project in which Canadian scholars figure prominently.[33] When they do appear in literary texts or in laws, we are often witnessing outsiders' fears of their potentially subversive character as subgroups with exclusive membership and rituals (below). The more we learn, the more hazardous it becomes to generalize about their various reasons for being, nomenclature, structures, activities, legal standing, or relations

---

32. The tendencies are clear in the earliest Christian texts, with the itinerant Paul ("our *politeuma* is in heaven, and from there we await a savior," Phil 3:20). Cf. Acts 19:23–40 and Pliny *Ep.* 10.96 on early damage to local economies, sacrificial meat sales, cultic tourism, and *polis* pride. On the fourth-century Christian initiatives see, e.g., Libanius, *Or.* 30 (*For the Temples*); Julian, *Ep.* 89b (= 288b), *Fragment of a Letter to a Priest*; for Julian's responses, Ammianus Marcellinus 25.4.15; Theodoret, *Hist. eccl.* 3.2–4, 15–22; Julian, *C. Gal.* 116a–b, 131b–d, 141c–d, 143a–b, 176a–c, 168b–c, 171a, d–e, 176a–c, 184b–c, 198b; 99e (Loeb numbering), with Bowersock 1978; Belayche 2002; Finkelstein 2011.

33. Cf. Kloppenborg and Wilson 1996; Arnaoutoglou 2002, 2005; Harland 2003, 2009; Liu 2008; Verboven 2011; Kloppenborg, Ascough, and Harland 2011; Ascough, Harland, and Kloppenborg 2012. Various websites host databases of Greek and Latin inscriptions, e.g.: http://epigraphy.packhum.org/inscriptions, http://www.bbaw.de/forschung/ig/index.html, http://www.csad.ox.ac.uk, http://www.uni-heidelberg.de/institute/sonst/adw/edh/index.html. Philip Harland maintains one, maintaining a high level of scholarship in a user-friendly format, that is devoted to voluntary associations: http://philipharland.com/greco-roman-associations. Last access to all websites: 2 August 2016.

with the *polis* in which they existed.³⁴ They could be groups linked by trade (silver-smiths, bakers, dye-makers, barbers), ethnic affiliation, worship of a deity, or some other unifying purpose. We are not speaking here of ad hoc gatherings, but of defined groups with initiation procedures, fees levied to a common fund, rules of behavior, and regular meetings that would typically include special dinners.³⁵ They might have undertaken to care for members in distress or illness, in societies lacking welfare systems, and for funeral arrangements. Some welcomed slaves, women, and foreigners, and so offered alternatives to the social hierarchies of *polis* life.

Two inscriptions of many will give a flavor of their diversity and possible relevance. The first, from mid-first century A.D. Ephesus, is a funerary inscription that is intriguing on many levels: the connection of a trade guild with burial, women's control of wealth and possible affiliation with the group, the possibility of mischief in finding burial places, and not least mention of the very same tradespeople who appear in Acts:

> The grave, the area around it, and the underground tomb belong to M. Antonius Hermeias, silversmith (*argyrokopos*) and temple-keeper (*neopoios*), and to his wife Claudia Erotis. No one may be buried in this grave except those written above. But if anyone dares to bury a body or to erase the inscription, that one will pay 1000 *denarii*³⁶ to the silversmiths in Ephesos. The association (*synedrion*) of silversmiths takes care of this grave. Erotis dedicated 500 *denarii* and the distribution was done on the eighth day of the sixth month.³⁷

Whereas Acts' Paul finds accommodation in his travels among practitioners of his trade (Acts 18:1-3), when he comes to Ephesus he runs afoul of the association of silversmiths, whose business of making silver statues for the goddess he damages (Acts 19:24-28). The other inscription is much longer, found in sixty-five fragments in 1816 and perhaps originally forming the wall of a bath. Coming from an important town (Lanuvium) in the southern outskirts of Rome and dating to A.D. 136, it spells out terms of membership and some activities of an association (founded in 133) devoted to Dionysus and Hadrian's deceased lover Antinous. Notice the seeming

---

34. Kloppenborg and Ascough 2011: vi, 1-13.

35. A famous example, the provisions of which should not be universalized, is the detailed club charter from Lanuvium in A.D. 133 (*CIL* 14.2112).

36. This very large fine represented three or four years' wages for a soldier or laborer.

37. *IEph* 2212, translated by P. Harland at http://philipharland.com/greco-roman-associations/161-grave-with-fines-payable-to-the-silversmiths.

preoccupation with death (even in the few provisions I include) and financial responsibility, as well as rules for conduct that recall those of the Qumran Community Rule (1QS 6–7):[38]

[1] It was voted unanimously that whoever wishes to enter this association shall pay an initiation fee of 100 sesterces and an amphora of good wine, and shall pay monthly dues of 5 asses (1.25 sesterces).

[2] It was voted further that if anyone has not paid his dues for six consecutive months and the common lot of humankind befalls him, his claim to burial shall not be considered, even if he has provided for it in his will . . .

(line 30) But if a member dies farther than 20 miles from town and notification is impossible, then he who has carried out the funeral shall claim his funeral expenses (*funeraticium*) from the association . . .

[5] It was voted further that if a slave member of this association dies and his master or mistress unreasonably refuses to relinquish the body for burial, and he has not left written instruction, a funeral with an image of him will be held.

[6] It was further voted that if any member takes his own life for any reason whatever, his claim to burial shall not be considered.

(line 40) [7] It was voted further that if any slave becomes free, he must give an amphora of good wine.

[8] It was voted further that if any master (*magister*), in the year when it is his turn in the membership list to provide dinner, fails to comply and provide a dinner, he shall pay 30 sesterces into the treasury. The man next in line shall be required to give the dinner, and the delinquent shall be required to reciprocate when it is the latter's turn.

[9] Roster (*ordo*) of dinners: 8 days before the Ides of March (Mar. 8), on the birthday of Caesennius . . . the father; 5 days before the Kalends of December (Nov. 27), on birthday of Antinoüs; on the Ides of August (Aug. 13), the birthday of Diana and of the association (*collegium*); 13 days before the Kalends of September (Aug. 20), on the birthday of Caesennius Silvanus, his brother; the day before the Nones of (Sept. 12 [?]), the birthday of Cornelia Procula, his mother; 19 days before the Kalends of January (Dec. 14), the birthday of Caesennius Rufus, patron of the municipality.

38. *CIL* XIV 2112 = *ILS* 7212, translated by J. S. Kloppenborg at http://philipharland.com/greco-roman-associations/310-regulations-of-the-worshippers-of-diana-and-antinous.

[10] Masters (*magistri*) of the dinners in the order of the membership list (*album*), appointed four at a time in turn, shall be required to provide an amphora of good wine each, and for as many members as the association has, bread costing 2 asses, four sardines, the setting, and warm water with service . . .

[14] It was voted further that if any member wishes to lodge any complaint or discuss business, he is to bring it up at a business meeting, so that we may have the banquet in peace and good cheer on festive days.

[15] It was further voted that any member who moves from one seat to another so as to cause a disturbance shall be fined 4 sesterces. (line 60) Any member, moreover, who speaks abusively of another or causes an uproar shall be fined 12 sesterces. Any member who uses any abusive or insolent language to a president at a banquet shall be fined 20 sesterces.

I mentioned that literary and legal texts tend to see danger in at least some provincial associations, although the epigraphic evidence shows many of them thriving in symbiosis with their *polis*. More secretive associations (e.g., Freemasons or fraternities in elite universities) always attract suspicion and possibly fear from outsiders. Speculation abounds concerning their real motives, activities behind the scenes, and hidden influence. In the Roman world, suspicion could be intense enough to result in harsh measures, though these were locally conditioned. A quick review of these measures will incidentally shows how associations flourished, for they could only be prohibited at certain times and places if they were otherwise active.

During the civil war that brought Rome's Republic to an end, the men contending for power did not shrink from using gladiators or men's associations as their muscle, and even under Augustus, Suetonius talks about armed gangs giving themselves a respectable *collegium* name. So the Senate in 56 B.C., Julius Caesar as dictator in 45, and Augustus ordered associations, companies, and clubs closed, the last two exempting "those of ancient foundation."[39] In Alexandria ca. A.D. 35, Philo says that clubs were a nuisance, giving dignified names to their anti-social and politically dangerous activity, and so the governor closed them.[40] The emperor Claudius was reportedly a traditionalist. He executed anyone falsely claiming Roman citizenship, forbade the use of Roman clan names to foreign-born citizens, and shut down the clubs that Caligula had permitted; the attached sentence claims that he forbade the large Judaean community from gathering.[41] Pliny

39. Cicero, *Q.F.* 2.3.5; Suetonius, *Caes.* 42.3; *Aug.* 32.1.
40. Philo, *Flacc.* 4, 136.
41. Cassius Dio 60.6.6. Dio stresses that he permitted Judaeans to follow their

the Younger's correspondence with the emperor Trajan in about 110, from his assigned province Pontus-Bithynia, reveals that the emperor ordered all clubs shut, except in the free *polis* of Amisus, and that this ban prevented Christian meetings.[42]

The Christian Tertullian (ca. 200) knows that Christians are a voluntary association or school (*secta*) dating only from the time of emperor Tiberius, but he complains at their unfair treatment on this basis. Although their behavior is entirely virtuous, in contrast to the dangerous or carousing clubs (*factiones*) that were once banned but have been reinstated, Christians remain banned with the most disreputable.[43] Finally, Justinian's sixth-century *Digest* preserves edicts from the jurist Marcianus, writing shortly after Tertullian's time, who reports that (recent?) emperors have ordered provincial governors to prohibit the creation of new associations, with some qualifications: poor soldiers may do so, if meeting no more than once per month, and meeting for some solemn obligation (*religio*) may be permitted. Even in the case of recognized associations, a person may belong to one only.[44] In short, voluntary associations of all kinds thrived in *poleis* through early Roman period. In times of political upset, however, in Rome or the provinces, officials periodically forbade most new associations from forming.

Recent fascination with *collegia* stems in part, one must suspect in view of its research home in departments of religious studies, from the fading of "religion" as a useful term for the study of antiquity. In the past "Judaism and Christianity" were considered two *religions*. But an ever-growing concern for historical precision and the recognition that religion was not a current category in the Roman period has helped direct attention to associations. This category has the advantage of currency among the ancients, but it also invites more fine-grained and particular (historicist) analysis. Instead of seeking awkward "Judaisms and Christianities," we may look (in principle, where evidence exists) at *this* association of Judaeans or Christ-followers in Rome or Ephesus at this time, and *that* one in Alexandria or Antioch. Judaeans living outside Judaea and Christ-followers (some also Judaeans) met in such groups.[45] But as we have seen the Judaeans were known first as an *ethnos* with a corporate presence in the *polis* and a famous cult in Jerusalem,

---

"ancestral way of life," without meeting, and did not try to expel them from Rome because of their numbers. Suetonius (*Claud.* 25.4) and Acts (18.2) agree that he did expel some or all Judaeans, perhaps later in his reign.

42. Pliny, *Ep.* 10.33–34, 92–93, 96–97.
43. Tertullian, *Apol.* 5.2; 21.1 (a *secta* dating from Tiberius); 6.7–8; 39.1, 20.
44. Justinian, *Dig.* 47.22 (from Marcianus, *Institutes*, 220s–230s).
45. On Judaean associations see Ritter 2015: 54–75.

whereas Christians had only the local association. Unlike guilds of bakers, metalworkers, or stevedores in a given *polis*, they had chapters around the Mediterranean, where travelling members could feel at home—as long as they shared the same kind of Christ-worship.

Paradoxically, the closest ancient parallels to what usually takes place in churches, mosques, and synagogues today occurred not in bloody sacrifices near temples, which we usually call "ancient religion," but in these associations and especially in the subset devoted to the pursuit of philosophy. The reading and exposition of texts, discussion of the soul and afterlife, moral exhortation, and some kinds of personal conversion in modern religion look similar to what occurred in schools of Stoics, Pythagoreans, or others committed to the discipline of a sometimes counter-cultural philosophical life. Since philosophers were known to carp at society's superficial values and norms, a loose association with philosophy gave Judaeans and Christ-followers a certain latitude for social criticism and oddness.[46]

Likewise, the closest ancient counterparts to self-help books by modern clergy[47] were essays on the good life by Cicero, Seneca, Epictetus, Plutarch, and Marcus Aurelius—philosophers, even if they also served as priests. It was to philosophy that one looked for advice about a healthy lifestyle, limiting food and drink, dealing with anger and other destructive emotions, and facing suffering and death, whether one's own or that of loved ones. And people who felt that they had yielded too much to the world's temptations, pleasure, and acquisitiveness, who wanted to "sober up" and start living right—or "get religion" we might say—were most likely to find that evangelical sort of appeal in philosophy. Although one could certainly shape up to become pure enough for sacrifice and worship, to effect a lasting change in this comprehensive way one would look not to a temple, altar, or priest but to philosophy.[48] Lucian's *Wisdom of Nigrinus* describes, though satirically, the experience of just such a born-again convert to philosophy.

In contrast to the common prescriptions of our more comforting culture, however, the philosophers' version of self-help did not focus on

46. One of the most potent Judaean attacks on the general culture, though apparently written for other Judaeans tempted by it, is the so-called Wisdom of Solomon, which may come from Alexandria in the first century B.C. Christian critiques of Roman society become increasingly sophisticated, from Pau's modest sallies (cf. Rom 1:17–32, borrowing from *Wisdom of Solomon*, with 13:1–7 and the non-Pauline 1 Pet 2:13–17) to the frontal assaults of apologists in the late second century and the sustained sarcasm of Clement of Alexandria (*Protreptikos*) and Tertullian (e.g., *Apol.* 35.2–3) around 200.

47. E.g., (Pastor) Rick Warren 2007 and (Rabbi) Harold S. Kushner 1981; 1986.

48. See Nock 1933: 164–86. Cf. Seneca's moral essays, the lectures and handbook by Epictetus; Lucian, Wisdom of *Nigrinus, Hermotimus*; Marcus Aurelius' *Meditations*; Boethius, *Consolation of Philosophy*.

learning to love oneself or discovering one's "passions." These mostly male constituencies often wished to learn instead how to toughen themselves and *avoid* the fluctuating impulses of passion, pleasure, lust, greed, fear, and pain. They wanted to face sickness, injury, pain, loss, and death itself with equanimity. Seneca's mentor Attalus reportedly prescribed harsh regimens for his students in connection with diet and sex, requiring them to sit on hard seats, for example (Seneca, *Ep.* 108.14). Lucian may have been exaggerating when he claimed that philosophical initiates often passed out from their exertions, and that they were subjected to whips, knives, and cold baths (*Nigr.* 27-28), but Josephus expressed his pride in having come through a three-year regimen of twice-daily frigid baths and scavenging for natural food, studying with the toughest local philosopher (*Life* 11).

Josephus has often been criticized for presenting his teacher Bannus as well as the Pharisees, Sadducees, and Essenes as *philosophical schools*,[49] because of a modern assumption that they were obviously *religious* groups. But there was no such terminology available to Josephus. He could say that these groups or individuals were concerned with piety, simple living, contempt for suffering and death, and expectation of a certain afterlife, and he does. But these were the province of philosophical schools, and so he calls them philosophies. There was no *genus* religion, of which any of these could be a *species*.

A close relationship was thus assumed between philosophical and military ideals. Soldiers (as needed) and philosophers were both supposed to live in highly disciplined ways, expect little from life, adapt to harsh circumstances without complaint, and face death unflinchingly. The connection between virtue and masculinity is clear in the tendency of philosophers to make Sparta—a disciplined warrior society, contemptuous of the pleasures and fears that motivate normal people—a kind of Utopia, if discounting Sparta's preoccupation with actual war-fighting.[50] The fourth-century B.C. adventurer Xenophon describes the Spartan warrior-king Agesilaus II and the philosopher Socrates in remarkably similar terms.[51] The king, he says, was a model for those wishing to train in manly excellence because he made a fortress of his soul and became a master of endurance (*karteria*). Socrates receives the same praise for his tough regimen (*diaita*).[52] Both trained

49. *War* 2.119-166; *Ant.* 13.171-173; 18.12-25; *Life* 10-12.

50. Tigerstedt 1974: 1.228-309; cf. Plato, *Leg.* 626c-d; Aristotle, *Pol.* 1270a-b, 1333b; Plutarch, *Lyc.* 31.1-2.

51. *Ages.* 8.8; 9.5; 10.1-2; cf. *Mem.* 1.2.1-4, 2.5-15; cf. 2.1.20; 3.1.6.

52. Somewhat like its English heir "diet" (everyone has some kind of diet), Greek *diaita* can refer to any way of life. But the choice to use this word usually suggested a *particularly disciplined or strict* way of life. So it was often used in discussions of

themselves to be impervious to changes in weather, hardships, pleasures, and things feared by other men. Philosophers, whether Platonist, Cynic, Stoic, or Epicurean, found models in Spartan toughness, their preservation of honor at all costs, and calm in the face of pain and death.[53] That is how the beard and rough cloak (*tribōn*, Lat. *pallium*) of the Spartans came to be adopted by philosophers.[54]

They did so from very different perspectives, however, and philosophers viewed Christians not as allies but as another example of what was wrong with the world: in this case, irrational exuberance. Philosophers had no taste for what seemed to be just another superstition: worship of a crucified man and hope for a physical resurrection.[55] Many Christians devoted their energies to their secretive, other-worldly society, in which normal citizenship (*politeia*) counted for nothing, and in which men, women, and slaves mingled freely after hours.[56] Paul, whose expressed orientation was very much away from the present world,[57] had declared that "our political organization (*politeuma*) is in heaven, from where we are awaiting a savior" (Phil 3:20). The letter to the Hebrews had likewise insisted that the Christians' temple was in heaven (8.1–2). Many Christian writers were redefining standard *polis* language in spiritual terms.[58]

Conclusions

In the two parts of this chapter I have attempted a rough survey and synthesis of the most prominent elements of ancient discourse concerning society,

---

Spartan practice. Josephus used it often of the Judeans and of their admirable Essenes. Of about 72 occurrences in his work, see, e.g., *War* 2.137–138, 151, 155, 160; *Apion* 1.182; 2.173–174, 235, 240.

53. Tigerstedt 1974: 1.228—2.30–48.

54. Demosthenes, *Con.* 34; Plato, *Symp.* 219b; *Prot.* 335d; Arrian, *Diatr.* 3.1.34; Diogenes Laertius 6.13; cf. Tertullian, *On the Pallium*. Sherman 2005, by a professor in the U.S. Naval Academy, Annapolis, is an effort to recover Stoicism for modern military conditioning.

55. See Wilken 1984 for a contextual treatment of the philosophers Celsus, Porphyry, and Julian on Christianity.

56. See MacMullen 1966: 46–94, 128–62; Benko 1984; Sordi 1986.

57. He evidently expected Christ's return from heaven, and the evacuation of Christ's followers from coming wrath, in the very near future (1 Thess 1.9–10; 4.13–18; 5.1–23; 1 Cor 7.25–31; 15.35–51).

58. Obvious cases are *ekklēsia* (citizen assembly [becomes "church"], 1 Cor 1.2; 4:17; 7:17; 14:4; Rom 16.1–16), *leitourgia* (public service, 2 Cor 9.12; Phil 2.25, 30), *thysia* (sacrifice spiritualized, Phil 2.17), *spendō* (pour a libation, Phil 2.17), *euergesia* (benefaction, Luke 2.25–27; Acts 10.38).

politics, and what we call religion. The frequency of the terms considered and the shared understanding make it reasonable to call this a paradigm. I have argued for a pyramid of identity-markers, the foundation of which was one's given *ethnos* and its presumed character (*ēthos*, associated with region, *genos, phylē, nomoi, ethē*). Whereas everyone born belonged to an *ethnos*, only the civilized beneficiaries of Greek culture in the eastern Mediterranean or beyond belonged to a *polis*, associated with *politeia, chōra*, time-ordering festivals, notable figures, and defining institutions. That was the place where most truly belonged, the ancestral home (*patris*) where their customs and laws held sway. Various ancient terms related to the sphere of life that involved attention to the gods (piety, worship, attendance on the gods, temples, altars, purity, pollution), whether as part of *polis* life, by affiliation with translocal groups, or in the privacy of one's home. This category of cultic piety comes higher on the pyramid because the language was so varied and because it was possible to hold back in some measure[59] or to be an enthusiast of cults also outside the *polis*. At the top of the pyramid were wholly voluntary activities, which might turn out to be of paramount importance for a given individual, as with devotion to Isis or to the philosophical life, but which did not erase the more basic, given social categories. One should still be loyal to one's *ethnos, polis*, laws, and ancestral customs.

In view of the discussion in Chapter 1, I would like to stress the historical motive and frame of this inquiry, though it is neither a history of events nor the exploration of a social-scientific problem. Most importantly, here as elsewhere the evidence does not speak for itself. That is why most academic discussion remains rooted in the language of "Judaism(s) and Christianity" as religions, though these terms are not part of the ancient paradigm. What I have tried to tease out of ancient texts in some kind of order is far from self-explanatory, and it may be wrong in significant ways. It is an effort to recover *what lies beneath* the particular texts and other remains from the past, the shared but now hidden discourse that makes these efforts at communication possible. In keeping with the method of Chapter 1, I have argued that everything depends on our question and line of inquiry. This kind of inquiry, more common in classics than religious studies, is by no means the only kind worth pursuing, but it is legitimate and possibly even interesting. At all events, it is not a matter of merely observing and reporting, but of questioning and imagining: What best explains the language that we find coming to the surface in our texts? What did they expect audiences to understand? How to group these key terms and map their affiliations? I

59. See Whitmarsh 2016, who makes many valuable observations about the scope for atheism in antiquity, though it seems to me that he minimizes the embeddedness of sacred or consecrated spaces and activities in virtually aspects of public life.

have tried to show that the paradigm tentatively constructed here can help to explain what we read in specific texts. But it cannot simply be inferred from the texts, which rarely explain what they assume.

Because no ancient handbook lays out such categories, others would put things together differently. For example, some would extrude *myth* in all of its manifestations—statuary and other sculpture, relief, mosaic floor, fresco painting, literary education, and dramatic re-enactment—as another top-level category, different from *ethnos* or *polis* affiliation and arguably basic to identity.[60] That would be perfectly understandable. If I prefer to treat myth along with calendar and festivals under the umbrella of one's *ethnos* and *polis* baggage, it is partly because Judaea was famously reticent about the figural representation that was so important to the expression of myth in various *poleis*. Although Judaeans had myths too, in the Bible's charter stories of divine-human interaction, the laws and customs of Jerusalem were famously different from typical Greek *poleis* in lacking statues and paintings of human figures. Still, the category was within the broad range of *ethnos*-diversity, and shared to a large extent by other Near-Eastern peoples.[61]

I have also emphasized that none of the categories we are discussing was defined with any precision in antiquity. On the contrary, it was their versatility that made them useful. Here I would stress that even the spheres of life I have isolated for discussion were not actually isolable from one other, much less hermetically sealed: they were part of an integrated whole of ancient life. *Ethnos* usually found expression in a *polis*, where ancestral laws and customs prevailed, and the sacrificial cults that were part of ethnos life found expression both there and elsewhere, in colonies or on military campaigns, and in entertainment. En route to assuming leadership roles in a *polis*, which might expect service as a priest overseeing the rituals of the *ethnos* (whether one believed them or not), the elite male would often become acquainted with philosophical teachings by a period of devoted study or absorption from the atmosphere.

Dionysius of Halicarnassus (late first century B.C.) illustrates this integration in his portrait of Rome's King Numa. This legendary successor to Romulus, he says, gave that *polis* its basic structure by addressing equally matters of *piety* toward the Gods (*eusebeia*), which included the sacrificial-cultic and priestly apparatus, and *justice* toward fellow-citizens (*dikaiosynē*), which involved the establishment of durable laws (*Ant. rom.* 2.62.5). The piety-justice tandem, which had turned up occasionally in

60. Beard, North, and Price 1998: 1.1–11; Graf 2004; Rives 2007: 28–37; Rüpke 2007: 109, 126–30.

61. See Ehrenkrook 2011: 19–59.

earlier Greek writers, was a natural way of summarizing the whole of human obligation. Josephus happens to use it more than any known writer in his descriptions of Judaean law and tradition.[62] It was not, after all, far from the classic biblical statement of human duty: to behave justly, love mercy, and walk humbly with God (Micah 6:8). But he communicated in the terms of the shared elite paradigm.

Finally I must reiterate that we have been discussing universally understood categories, rather than creative individual or small-group language. Josephus, for example, favors a noun that suggests "divine worship, ritual, cult, and piety" (*thrēskeia*) along with its cognate verb *thrēskeuō*: usually, "to worship." Though rarely found in non-Judaean writers,[63] this group had some currency among Judaeans before he picked it up.[64] He apparently found it convenient for his repeated claims about the unique Judaean disposition toward piety (*eusebeia*), a word group he uses even more often (146 times). So he often pairs *thrēsk-* and *euseb-* words as close in meaning.[65] The difference from modern religion is immediately clear from the fact that, in more than half of its occurrences Josephus includes God in the phrase: *thrēskeia* of God, to God, or concerning God; and the verb has God as object.[66] But one could not speak of God's religion or of religioning God. In most cases, moreover the word has to do with the temple environment, sacrificial worship of God (and no other), and Judaean festivals anchored in sacrifice. Josephus' audiences understood both words, of course, even if they did not share Josephus' investment in them. Christians would later develop *thrēskeia* in the direction of *religio*.[67] In our world, much as *religio* (solemn obligation, taboo, pious commitment) has evolved into *religion* in Romance languages (compare Hebrew *dat*, originally law), so *thrēskeia* is the modern Greek term for religion.

62. Josephus, *War* 2.139; *Ant.* 1.21; 2.196; 6.160, 275; 7.269, 338, 341, 356, 374, 384; 8.121, 208, 280, 300, 314, 394; 9.16, 236, 260; 10.50; 12.43, 56; 14.283, 315; 15.182, 375–376; 16.42, 172; 18.117; 20.13; *Apion* 2.125–146, 170, 291, 293.

63. Herodotus 2.18, 37; Dionysius, *Ant. rom.* 2.63.2; Strabo 10.3.23.

64. 4 Macc 5:7, 13; Wis 14:27; Philo, *Leg.* 232, 298; *Det.* 21; *Fug.* 41; *Spec.* 1.315.

65. Everything in Judaean life under *eusebeia*: *Apion* 1.60; 1.212, 146, esp. 170–171. Pairing and near synonymity or epexegetical relationship: *Ant.* 3.49; 6.90, 148; 7.341; 9.260; 11.120; 13.244; 16.115; 20.113.

66. *War* 6.100; *Ant.* 1.222–224; 4.61, 306; 6.19; 7.78, 341; 8.225, 251, 395; 9.95, 133, 157; 10.53; 12.253, 271; 13.199; 15.248; 16.174; 17.214; 18.349; 19.284, 297; *Apion* 1.261. The verb with God as object: *Ant.* 3.49; 6.148; 8.127, 192 (also other gods); 9.260; 289–290; 10.63.

67. In contrast to the authors mentioned in the preceding notes, Josephus has the noun 91 times and the verb 23 times.

Against my case, which was far from original in the study of religion (above), that the classical world knew no *category* of religion, Daniel Schwartz has recently argued that Josephus' investment in *thrēskeia* sometimes intersects with our religion, and this shows that there *was* religion in the first century. He includes a passage from 4 Maccabees, a couple from Acts, and several from Josephus to conclude that, although the word most often means worship, cult, and sacrificial ritual, in some cases those definitions are too narrow, and "by Josephus' day, it had come to be used in a broader sense, 'religion,' which includes worship . . . but also much more."[68] But what sort of *more*?

After sympathetically noting the principle I explained for the Brill commentary, of trying to keep Greek and English semantic ranges aligned where *possible* (Schwartz's reading: the project "strives . . . to employ the same English word *to render all occurrences* of the same Greek word"),[69] he presents *thrēskeia* as evidence at odds with my argument about the common discourse. He also thinks that I miss the continuing use of the "sacrifice" metaphor in modern churches, and so understate the link between ancient cult and modern religion.[70]

If such a careful and genial scholar as Schwartz considers this case detrimental to mine, I need to restate mine briefly, at the risk of exasperating the reader. To begin with, his severe interpretation of our Brill translation principles does not reflect the spirit of the Series Preface (above), which said: "Our goal has been to render individual Greek words with *as much consistency as the context will allow*."[71] As I have explained, this meant that rather than readily changing each translation for the sake of English variety, *where possible* we use consistent translations. Consistency is often not possible, of course, and so even with the nine occurrences of *thrēsk-* words in the *War* 2 volume I had to vary the translation.[72] Thus far, Schwartz and I agree, and the Brill translation principles are beside that point.

68. Schwartz 2014: 91–100 (94).
69. Schwartz 2014: 92 (emphasis added).
70. Schwartz 2014: 99.
71. Mason 2008: x (emphasis added).
72. *War* 2.10 (at Passover, visitors head to Jerusalem "for *the* [act of] *worship*"), 42 (at Shavuot/Pentecost "it was not the *customary worship* that brought the populace together, but. . .") 198 (Petronius is amazed at the "insuperable devotion" of the Judaeans, as Pilate had been at the purity of their *deisidamonia*, 2.174), 391 (Agrippa II cautions against war: "Consider how the purity of your *cultic practice* [will be] hard to manage"), 414 (Jerusalem's leaders complain that closing the temple to foreigners was courting war and also "grafting in a strange [form of] worship" contrary to temple tradition), 425 (Eleazar's faction, on the feast of wood-carrying to the altar, "shut out their [Judaean] foes from worship" in the temple), 456 (Josephus is scandalized at the slaughter of the

But when Schwartz proposes that sometimes Josephus' *thrēskeia* is best translated by "religion," I would suggest that this begs the question.[73] That is, since we have the category *religion*, it is not surprising that this word comes to mind when we see Greek words relating to the obligations of piety. The *euseb-* group is often translated as *religion*-esque, and that would presumably be as good as a candidate for asserting the presence of ancient religion. But such translations do not answer the question whether the ancients knew a category of life comparable to modern religion. Since *religion* would not work as a translation, also according to Schwartz, for most cases of *thrēskeia*, the word could not have stood for something like the modern category. His proposal thus throws us back on the question: Did those broader connotations occasionally found in *thrēskeia*, beyond divine service or worship, approximate our *religion*? A rough and very imperfect analogy might help to explain my negative answer.

We are all familiar with registration forms requiring at least our name, date of birth, and nationality (irrespective of complexities). Many include a box with the heading *Sex*. It does not expect "yes" or "good" as responses, but rather M or F, which are often printed as the only choices. Even though sex and gender are now understood to be highly complex matters for individuals, the category itself is entirely familiar and no more problematic than "nationality," which is to say: quite problematic if we think about it, but we know what they are after.

Although a box for *Religion* is not as commonplace as it once was, in my adult life it has still been common for new inmates of hospitals, prisons, the military, or some school systems to declare their *religion* upon entry—if for no other reason than assignment to the appropriate chaplain.[74] It did not

---

Jerusalem garrison on a sabbath, "on which, *for the sake of worship*, they observe a moratorium even on holy activities"), 517 (as Cestius' troops come near, during the Feast of Booths, Jerusalemites go out to confront them, ignoring both the festival, "though the sabbath was certainly their paramount *devotional commitment*": ἦν γὰρ δὴ τὸ μάλιστα παρ' αὐτοῖς θρησκευόμενον σάββατον), 560 (many women of Damascus had been attracted by "the *Judean worship*"). Nearly all of these have to do with activities in the temple area. With 2.414 compare 4.275, which complains about the temple being walled off to "foreigners, who used to come for worship (εἰς θρησκείαν)." Schwartz is probably right that my effort to keep *worship* for this group where possible—though by not as stubbornly as he suggests—does not always capture the nuances. But (a) the translation is there to introduce the commentary, which explores meanings, and (b) substituting *religion* in most cases would not help much. One does not come to the *polis* or temple for religion, and the sabbath is not the most important religion.

73. For a different view of *thrēskeia* see Barton and Boyarin 2016: 123–52.

74. When my son was born in Germany it was still an important issue, partly for taxation (and state church support). When we lived in Newfoundland there were only religious schools and one had to choose.

matter how complicated one's own views of religion were. The form simply wanted to know your religion, and everyone understood the *category*. In spite of the complexities of secularization and new religions with unusual structures, the main religions are understood to be systems of belief and practice with voluntarily joined communal structures and trained, vetted, and authorized representatives. In many jurisdictions these religious officials are permitted to certify government-recognized marriages and funerals, and in most places have privileged access to the institutions mentioned above for spiritual care.

Religion's place as a top-level organizing category, alongside and separate from politics, business, and entertainment, became clearest when Enlightenment thinkers such as Voltaire, David Hume, and Thomas Paine made an issue of it, isolating special claims to knowledge from those of univeral reason, and when leaders of the American and French Revolutions enforced that separation constitutionally. That was by no means the end of the discussion, and religion continues to have a central place in most western societies, but its place in western social-political discourse as a voluntary pursuit detached from others was set. People could have no religion, be deeply committed to one, change religions, or blend them. This place of religion in the shared discourse, I stress, has nothing to do with either individual feeling that one's religious identity shapes all aspects of one's own life (e.g., my principles as a physician are undergirded by my faith) or the doubts of whole communities (Hindus, Jews, Sikhs) that the label religion is anywhere near being adequate.

Departments in universities have been established for "the study of religion"—alongside economics, politics, literature, sport, business, and other familiar categories of modern life. We all understand the street questions: "Do you think that religion is a force for good or harm?" "What are your views on science and religion?" "What's your [or your parents'] religion?" "Are you religious?" A phrase such as "freedom of religion" has evident meaning.

Religion has, in other words, a well-established place in the modern western lexical bank. This does not make it unproblematic, but it is a primary ordering category for us, if one that periodically fades in importance. I am referring to the discourse with which we communicate, which none of us can change, in which religion is a genus with many species: Christianity, Judaism, Islam, Hinduism, Buddhism, Jainism, and so on. High schools and universities offer classes on such "religion(s)." If asked what typically happens in religious groups, a modern westerner might list something like: worship, prayer, rituals, chant or song, God-talk, reading and exposition of sacred texts, with sermons of consolation and exhortation to faithfulness and/or the communal virtues. It is a voluntary sphere of life, localized in what phone directories call "houses of worship" divided by religion, in which one may participate or not.

I hope that the drift of this chapter is clear enough. My simple and unoriginal argument is that our modern frames of reference were not available in antiquity. To put it in culinary terms, we have created a dish called religion, which like the hamburger or pizza part of a menu is easily recognizable today, in spite of its countless forms. The ingredients for pizzas and hamburgers have always existed, but the categories or concepts themselves are post-industrial. So too, if the reader will indulge such a crude analogy, elements of our "religion," something we immediately recognize in spite of all varieties and complexities, were in antiquity distributed in *ethnos* law and custom, ancestral practices, *polis* leadership and festivals, stage drama, sport, medicine, military life, physical sacrifices of animals, grains, and wine, philosophical schools, and other voluntary activities.

Schwartz's observations that Josephus (a) likes the *thrēsk-* word-group and (b) uses it in a wide range of connected senses, though entirely correct, therefore seem part of a different inquiry. Josephus' usage, no matter how elastic, could not change the fact that *thrēskeia* was not a category comparable, with respect to internal content or place in social-political discourse, to our religion.[75] Josephus could not have anticipated the modern (or late-antique) conditions under which religion became "a thing"—a dish if you will.

A more widely discussed effort to integrate various religion-relevant elements of ancient life under one umbrella came in a treatise of forty-one volumes on *Ancient Origins of Divine and Human Affairs* by the Roman soldier and polymath scholar M. Terrentius Varro (116–27 B.C.). Varro loved to classify every aspect of knowledge, as his encyclopedic *Nine Books of Disciplines* and famous work on the Roman calendar showed. In the work on divine-human affairs, now lost with nearly all his writings, Varro posited three varieties of the genus *theologia* (or god-talk): that of the poets and writers of myths, which casts the gods in human-like forms and comes to expression in the theatre; the rather different discourse of philosophers about the divine, which one can find in their schools; and the language used of the gods in *polis* (*urbs/civitas*) life, which comes to expression in public ritual and sacrifice. Although Varro brings these three dimensions under one umbrella, this is a creative intellectual exercise on his part, and

---

75. When Schwartz wonders why I did not feature *thrēskeia* in my 2007 article, but included it along with other ancient terms related to cult, worship, and ritual (2014: 94), our different questions are clear. It *was* a minor term in general discourse, and closely though not exhaustively related (as in Josephus) to cultic worship and ritual.

again his *theologia* does not resemble, in purpose or content, the modern category *religion*. His grouping of *polis* with cult, bypassing of *ethnos* (*gens*), and elevation of theatre and philosophy all show that he was innovating, proposing this abstract *theologia* as a way of bringing order to what were normally quite different areas of life—difference being as much the point as his unifying term.[76]

In A.D. 197 the Christian Tertullian would find Varro's scheme valuable for his critique of Graeco-Roman society. Varro had actually exposed, Tertullian charged, the *invented* nature of the gods—given that these three perceptions were wholly incompatible (*Ad nat.* 2.1). Tertullian makes it clear that this is Varro's proposal, not a unified concept of common discourse. It was the fifth-century Christian intellectual Augustine who preserved this piece from Varro, for much the same reason as Tertullian but expanding considerably. He wanted to show his Christian audience how this most learned Roman, the best conceivable spokesman of their world,[77] tried in vain to bring coherence and plausibility to something that was entirely unlike the true and unified Christian way (religion).[78] He was referring most pejoratively to the real-life complexities of classical civilization and its now-vanished paradigm of *ethnos*, *polis*, sacrificial cult, and voluntary association.

---

76. Augustine, *Civ. dei* 6.5–7.
77. Augustine, *Civ. dei* 6.1.
78. Augustine, *Civ. dei* 6.4.

6

The End of the Classical Paradigm

The preceding chapter surveyed core components of the ancient lexical bank. Readers will have noticed the absence of such staple terms in scholarship as religion, Judaism, Diaspora, or Christianity. In this chapter we ask how these terms came to enter the lexicon, connecting the changes with other aspects of ancient mapping of the inhabited earth (*oikoumenē*). Central questions here are: the degree to which Judaeans were exceptional in relation to standard discourse, the capacity of that discourse to accommodate well-known features of Judaean life (e.g., exclusive temple, majority population far from Jerusalem, "conversion," and the destruction of Jerusalem in 70 and prohibition of Judaean access from the 130s). I propose that the classical paradigm accommodated all of these without becoming bent out of shape. Changes came only with Christian social-political dominance, for it was the Christians who had powerful motives to change the lexicon and social structures with it.

The Demise of the Classical Paradigm —and Rise of the Christians

Let us begin with the seemingly uncontroversial term Judaism. There is no more basic, assumed category in our field. After long decades or centuries in which a legalistic "late Judaism" (*Spätjudentum*) was imagined by theologians to be the antithesis of Christian salvation, the gradual creation of religious and Jewish studies programs in universities became a major catalyst to scholarly dialogue on sounder bases, which began to generate paradigm changes from the 1960s through the 1980s. The explosion of research on the gradually appearing Dead Sea Scrolls in roughly the same years demanded a rethinking of the nature of Judaism, and the fateful Jewish-Christian relationship was re-examined from many angles. Jacob Neusner's characteristic insistence on understanding particulars in context led to the popularity of "Judaisms" for a while.[1] I should add that, outside of the specialized tasks of ancient history (translation, interpretation, and reconstruction) I have no qualms about saying that my research is in ancient Judaism. I do not boycott the Hellenistic Judaism group in the Society of Biblical Literature because of its name.

Remarkably, however, we do not find the term itself or anything formally comparable to it in ancient discourse. Nor can we imagine a *genus* of Greek-isms of which Juda-ism could have been a *species*. As we shall see, the use of Greek *Ioudaismos* to mean a system of practice and belief called "Judaism" was a Christian innovation. This may sound like mere quibbling over terminology: So what if the term was not used? Surely the *thing itself* was present. Although names may not matter much if one takes a suprahistorical view of the past, they matter a great deal *if* we are interested in how the ancients called things. There was nothing just like Judaism under a different name, and use of such a term implicitly shapes our thinking in ways that may be inappropriate to the time.

If there were such a system of belief and practice, it would be natural to ask as we do about its shape and limits, at what point one should speak of *Judaisms*, how one entered or left Judaism (e.g., with Paul or Tiberius Julius Alexander), whether Judaism was legalistic or missionary-minded, and what the alternatives to Judaism were. If no Judaism or anything like it was yet conceivable, however, all such questions lose their point, with no criteria available for assessing them. What exactly would we be investigating—our own thoughts and categories? When we assume the existence of *Judaism* in the first centuries B.C. and A.D. we further overlook the changes to the lexical bank that ascendant Christianity would bring, blurring the lines between different periods and ignoring the extent to which our categories may be profoundly Christian.

As we have seen, the *polis*-endowed *ethnos* of the Judaeans was considered already in the Hellenistic-Roman period an ancient and complex civilization comparable to others. Having used the word civilization, and planning to use it along with culture without embarrassment in what follows, I should pause to anticipate the criticism: Why are you so comfortable using *these* non-ancient terms and yet so pedantic about "religion" or

---

1. See Kraft and Nickelsburg 1986 for developments to that point; Neusner in (e.g.) Frerichs, Green; and Neusner 1987; Neusner 1991; Chilton and Neusner 2004; and for recent perspectives on Christianity and Judaism, Nanos and Zetterholm 2015.

"Judaism"?[2] In case it is not obvious, the answer is as follows. Whereas my concern with religion and Judaism is that they were not known by the ancients, I am not suggesting for a moment that culture and civilization were known to them. These words have quite different functions in my presentation; I am not smuggling in some baggage unscreened.

We are communicating in English. My proposal in English is that— among the countless questions one might ask about the Graeco-Roman past—it is not uninteresting to explore their use basic ways of communicating about their world, their categories. In order to facilitate that refocus of our attention from our own time and our habits of thought, I need an English term or two for "their way of life back then." Culture is the best little word that comes to mind, for this heuristic or mediating purpose: In *our* culture we say X, whereas in theirs they said Y. Of course they themselves did not know the English word *culture*.

They used a wide variety of overlapping terms for laws and customs, ancestral practices, constitutions, natures, characters, and so on (*nomoi, ethē, patria, politeia, physis, ēthē*). I am asking that we pay attention to *that* language, the language of *their* culture. Similarly with "civilization": making a case in English, I look for a resonant term to capture this impression of an ancient and well-known mētropolis-based *ethnos*, something comparable to what we would readily call Athenian or Spartan civilization. I would not use "religion" for such an invitation to explore ancient terminology, because it has nothing like the same scope or sense.

The *Ioudaioi* were understood, by insiders and outsiders, to be part of the mental map of the world's *ethnē*. They were an *ethnos* with a mother-*polis*, where their distinctive laws held sway, a lawgiver whose name was well known,[3] a legal code, famous customs, a hereditary priesthood, a world-renowned temple, and sacrificial system. But just as there was no Egyptism, Romism, Ascalonism, or Idumaeism, and such terms would sound very odd to us, ancient discourse could not and did not produce Juda-ism, which will sound equally odd if we try to think in terms of ancient categories. No one talked about such a thing before the Christians began to tinker with the common discourse.

I cannot repeat here the arguments of my 2007 article on this question in *Journal for the Study of Judaism*, but I can update the five most important considerations.

2. Cf. Schwartz 2011: 229, "In Mason's case, rejection of religion causes him to use with insufficient precision such equally loaded terms as nation, culture . . . , and ethnicity." Ethnicity is a telling slide, because that is not my term. "Nation" is only the standard translation of ancient *ethnos*, used for variety.

3. Gager 1972.

First, Greek *-ismos* nouns did not indicate corporate belief systems as English Marxism, Catholicism, or Republicanism do. Rather, without exception as far as I know, they represented the action of the corresponding verb in *-izō*: *seismos* (shaking), *hoplismos* (arming for war), *mychthismos* (jeering), *galēnismos* (calming), *ostrakismos* (ostracizing), *analogismos* (reckoning). An ancient reader would therefore naturally understand *Ioudaismos* as the nominal form of the action *Ioudaizō*, Judaizing—whatever exactly that should entail.

Second, this *ethnos*-affiliated form *Ioudaismos*, though obviously different from the mundane actions just mentioned, would not have seemed frightening because there was a well-known subset of such *-ismos* nouns having to do with *ethnē*. These were *Mēdismos*, *Persismos*, *Athēnismos*, and *Lakōnismos*. The first two meant *Persia-izing*, the other two *Athenizing* and *Spartizing*. They came from the storied past of the Persian and Peloponnesian wars, when entire *poleis* but sometimes prominent individuals found it prudent to align themselves with one of the powers. Even if this was understandable in the circumstances, such shifts were lamentable in view of the ideal of *polis* autonomy and self-determination.

Reasons other than perceived failures of virtue in political crisis extended the unsavory connotations of *ethnos* verbs in *-izō* and their *-ismos* nouns. Lucian punctures the pretensions of those who Egyptize—putting on airs that they have acquired esoteric knowledge of the spirit world and some Egyptian language—and Suetonius' book *On Insults* included a group for use against slaves that were drawn from *ethnē* and *poleis*. To accuse someone of Cilicizing (after Cilicia) is to say that they deceive, of Egyptizing that they behave disgracefully, of Cretizing that they lie.[4] Some of these verbs also generated *-ismos* nouns (*Cilcismos*, *Crētismos*) with precisely the same insulting senses.[5]

Third, the verbal sense and negative tinge of such words presumably help to explain why *Ioudaismos* is nearly invisible in non-Christian texts, whether by Judaeans or by outside observers—though they talk a great deal about Judaea-Jerusalem, its laws, customs, people, and expatriate communities. *Ioudaismos* was clearly not the word for that sort of thing—not

4. Lucian, *Symp.* 18; *Philops.* 31; Suetonius, *On Slanders*, in Taillardat 1967: section 9 (under insults *eis doulous*). Plutarch's *Table Talk* includes an indulgently patronizing section on why Judaeans abstain from pork, and one possibility raised with respect to their related avoidance of rabbit, is that these putative barbarians from Egyptian stock also Egyptize their view of animals (*Mor.* 670e).

5. Photius and the *Suda* both have entries for *Cilicismos*, attributing it to the 4th-cent. B.C. with the meaning of either drunken or lawless murder. Plutarch, *Aem.* 26.3 says that Perseus the Macedonian "used *Crētismos*" in dealing with Cretans, which has the same sense as the verb *Crētizō* shortly before (23.10).

"Judaism"—and so it does not appear in Philo, Josephus, or most other Judaean writers. Nor does it make even one appearance in Menachem Stern's magnificently thorough two-volume collection of texts concerning "Jews and Judaism" in Greek and Latin authors.[6]

Fourth, given the word's near invisibility, we should think carefully about why *Ioudaismos* first (and nearly last) should appear four times in the second-century B.C. text we call 2 Maccabees (2.21; 8.1; 14.38 twice).[7] The later 4 Maccabees, which borrows extensively from it, also has the word once (4.26). As we ponder the word's meaning, it cannot escape our attention that the same text coins two other *-ismos* nouns: *Hellēnismos* and *allophylismos*. And the author could not be clearer about their significance, for they provide the foundation of the book. It is a classic case of ethnic disloyalty, viewed from the inside and described in the familiar terms of Greek discourse.

An impious priest with the Greek name Jason offers Antiochus IV huge sums of money to become high priest, and more still if he will grant him authority to establish a Greek-style gymnasium in Jerusalem, to enroll young men in the Greek institution of the ephebate, and to make Jerusalem's populations citizens of Greek-style Antioch (2 Macc 4:9). When Antiochus agrees, Jason seizes power and immediately "turned his compatriots to the Greek type [of life]" (4:10). Doing away with the Seleucid royal concessions that had protected Judaea's distinctive laws, "while dissolving the customary political forms, he introduced new customs contrary to the laws" (4:11: τὰς μὲν νομίμους καταλύων πολιτείας παρανόμους ἐθισμοὺς ἐκαίνιζεν). He not only built the coveted gymnasium but was soon leading the city's noblest young (priestly) men in ephebate training, "under a *petasos*" or Greek hat—and not much else, since Greeks exercised naked (4:12). The author is scandalized that the priests were neglecting their core sacrificial duties, being so keen to engage in the "unlawful goings-on of the wrestling floor," and in general that they "deemed the ancestral honors of no account and had regard only for the finest *Greek opinions*" (4:15). This was a mass defection from the *ethnos*' defining character by those who should have been its most vigorous champions.

The dynamic-verbal sense of *Hellēnismos* and *allophylismos* is clear when the author puts them together in a programmatic sentence encapsulating everything he has been describing: "Thus there was a high water mark of hellenizing and a push in foreignizing" (2 Macc 4:13: ἦν δ' οὕτως

6. Stern 1974.

7. Pasto 2002 anticipated crucial points here and in my 2007 article concerning 2 Maccabees. I regret that I did not know this essay when I was writing in 2005–2006, and failed to reference it.

ἀκμή τις Ἑλληνισμοῦ καὶ πρόσβασις ἀλλοφυλισμοῦ).[8] *Allophylismos* appears again at 6.24 with a resonant example, when the virtuous old Eleazar refuses to participate in foreignizing (*allophylismos*) by eating pork—or even pretending to, as his compassionate enforcer suggests (6.18). Even this man, incidentally, who embodies a Judaizing against foreignizing and Graecizing to preserve ancestral tradition, is praised in the standard terms of the Greek lexicon:

> After taking up this reasoning—urbane [*asteios*: *asty*-ish] and worthy of his years, the dignity of his age, his achievement, his conspicuous grey hair, and his fine constancy since childhood (ἐκ παιδὸς καλλίστης ἀναστροφῆς) . . .—he made an abrupt declaration, saying they should dispatch him to Hades. (6:23)

The noun *anastrophē* ("constancy") here will return with Paul below.

Allophylismos is here no *system*, like Catholicism or Marxism. It is an *activity* that in the author's view threatens the survival of the *ethnos*. The extreme nature of the threat seems to explain why *Ioudaismos* should also be introduced and repeated in this work: precisely because Judaizing is the right and proper response to the foreignizing or Hellenizing of Judaeans. In this moment of extraordinary danger there is no risk of the usual negative tinge to Judaizing/*Ioudaismos* because, paradoxically, the people to be Judaized are not foreigners. It is the Judaean priests and leaders who must be called back to their own laws and customs, before it is too late. The crisis facing the *ethnos* makes Judaizing honorable, in keeping with the entrenched (Greek) value of loyalty to one's *ethnos*, *polis*, and ancestral traditions.

It seems to me that in all four occurrences in 2 Maccabees, *Ioudaismos* is easiest to understand as the potentially violent *activism* of Judah and a small band of others, who harass the enemy and intimidate their compatriots into "Judaizing" Judaea again, a paradoxical task necessitated by the crisis (8:1). Their *Ioudaismos* is thus described as an expression of masculine courage (2:21). It is also something of which they can be accused of *having done*, and entailing physical hazards, when Judaean law and custom have been outlawed (14:38). It is not, evidently, Judaism as a general way of life.

This is not to deny that one or two of these references (and especially 4 Macc 4:26) could *also* make sense if something like later Judaism were in view, as translators have universally assumed. But the contexts in 2 Maccabees

---

8. In literature, though *Hellēnismos* will appear in grammatical-rhetorical contexts in the much narrower sense of (usually) a non-Greek or low-class or dialect-afflicted person using good Greek.

appear to require something active and dynamic, some sort of dangerous activity at this moment.[9]

I have offered reasons to doubt that ancient readers could have conjured a static or systemic sense from the form *Ioudaismos*. And if *Judaism* had been the clear meaning of *Ioudaismos*, one would have expected it to have caught on from this widely read work, rather than disappearing completely from all the elaborate discussions of Judaean law, custom, and life in both Judaean authors and outside observers that followed in the coming centuries.

The clever coinage "foreignizing" (*allophylismos*) found no use in later Greek literature, a fate that might have befallen *Ioudaismos* also if a sequence of Christian writers had not found the world useful. This is the fifth and final point I wanted to make about the word. It is undeniable that, in marked contrast to the extreme reticence of Judaean writers or their contemporaries, later Christian writers loved *Ioudaismos* and indeed eventually created *Judaism* from it. Word frequency goes off the charts with these writers: 31 uses of *Ioudaismos* in Origen alone, 19 in Eusebius, 43 in Epiphanius, 36 in John Chrysostom. A telltale sign of their new lease of the term is Latin *Iudaismus*, which is exclusively Christian and frequent, although Latin did not make *-ismus* words.[10] But what they came to mean by *Ioudaismos* was a stale and reduced system of laws, which could be placed on the shelf with other not-Christ *-isms* of Christian invention.

It seems that we can even watch roughly how this development occurred among the Christians. Like other writers, Paul nowhere uses

---

9. Boyarin (2004: 8) notes the limited use of *Ioudaismos* to (mainly) 2 Maccabees, and its lack of correspondence to "Judaism," but takes it to mean there "the entire complex of loyalties and practices that mark off the people of Israel" (i.e., not the religion of Judaism. I do not understand Seth Schwartz's criticism of my 2007 article (Schwartz 2011: 225): "*Ioudaismos* ... still presupposes the disembedded existence of such a body of stuff, whether or not that body is defined as specifically religious, as opposed to 'national' or 'cultural.' . . . 'Judaizing' presupposes disembedded *something*, even if we decide not to call it religion." Why Judaizing should require more than a Judaean place, law, and people eludes me: Athenizing, Spartizing, Egyptizing, and Persizing did not require a disembedded essence that could be called Athenism, Spartism, Egyptism, or Persism.

10 Classical Roman authors have no use for Latin *Iudaismus*, though they often discuss Judaeans and Judaea (cf. Stern 1974). It is attested only in Christian texts: before A.D. 500 119 times. In four of these it renders Greek *Ioudaismos*, in the 4th-cent. Christian Vulgate translation of 2 Macc 8:1; 14:38; Gal 1:13-14. It is revealing that the Christians did not translate the word; they could simply transliterate it because they had nativized it in Latin for the system called Judaism. The other occurrences are in Tertullian (21), who must be considered the innovator here, Marius Victorinus (37), Filastrius (4), Ambrosiaster (17), Augustine (20), Possidius (1), John Cassian (2), and Jerome (13). Several use the word far more often than even 2 Maccabees, in this new generalized sense.

Ioudaismos when he is speaking of Judaean life or law, for example in Romans or the heart of Galatians. He does use the word, however, at the beginning of Galatians, where he faces a problem of Jerusalem-inspired Judaizing among gentile Christ-followers (cf. Gal 2:14). Near the beginning of the letter he needs to establish his own (former) Judaean bona fides, and he does so in language strongly evocative of 2 Maccabees (Gal 1:13–14):

> You have heard of my former constancy / commitment in the *Ioudaismos* (τὴν ἐμὴν ἀναστροφήν ποτε ἐν τῷ Ἰουδαϊσμῷ), namely: that I kept harassing the assembly of God and trying to destroy it. I was advancing [or cutting a swathe] in the *Ioudaismos* beyond many of my age and peer group, being an extreme devotee of my ancestral traditions (προέκοπτον ἐν τῷ Ἰουδαϊσμῷ ὑπὲρ πολλοὺς συνηλικιώτας ἐν τῷ γένει μου, περισσοτέρως ζηλωτὴς ὑπάρχων τῶν πατρικῶν μου παραδόσεων).

Connections with 2 Maccabees are striking. An all-consuming commitment to his Judaean ancestral traditions led Paul to extreme actions, by his own description, against Judaeans he perceived as straying from the ancestral traditions, a movement he tried to destroy. Such activity, with 2 Maccabees, he calls *Ioudaismos*. He uses the definite article perhaps because Judaizing is the obvious issue here (cf. 2:14), which he now vehemently opposes, having been called by God to abandon the Judaizing in a complete about-face (1:15–17 with 2:15–21). He also reuses *anastrophē* from 2 Maccabees' description of aged Eleazar, archetype of combat against alien ways.

Anastrophē is bleached, in translations of Jewish and Christian texts, as though it meant simply one's "way of life." Here it would indicate Paul's former "way of life in [the] Judaism," preserving traditional categories at the expense of the dynamic context. But *anastrophē* does not refer to a settled "way of life." Granted that etymology does not decide meaning-in-use, it is still worth asking how a word built from *strophē* (turn, twist, maneuver) and *ana* (back, again)—hence turn(ing) again or back—came to be linked with behavior at all. The word's erratic distribution shows that is a synonym neither for communal *ethnos* custom (*ethos*) nor for personal way-of-life terms such as *bios* (*biōsis, bioteia*), *zōē, diatribē,* or *diaita* (*diaitēsis*). More than a third of the attested occurrences before the New Testament are in Polybius, Diodorus, and Dionysius. The word had limited usefulness, an observation confirmed by Josephus. Among his thirty volumes, all five occurrences fall in the linguistically peculiar *Antiquities* 17–19, which Thackeray attributed to a "hack" literary assistant.[11] The few authors who like *anastrophē* exploit

---

11. See Thackeray 1929: 99–115 on the "Thucydidean hack" blamed for this section.

a spectrum of connected meanings, from the literal "turn again/back" to several secondary senses:

- physical turning back / return, surge;[12]
- a turn or twist of fortune;[13]
- one's turn—that is, chance, opportunity, occasion, period of delay;[14]
- the place to which one constantly returns, or home;[15]
- activity to which one returns, habitual action, preoccupation.[16]

The verb *anastrephō* is favored by some Jewish and Christian authors because it conveys disciplined striving, a constantly cultivated way of virtuous or righteous living—by repeatedly choosing to associate with good people, for example.[17] This sense of *striving* creates a possible overlap with "way of life," no doubt, but they are not interchangeable terms. *Anastrophē* has a dynamic quality of turning and returning, a demonstrated *constancy* of effort or commitment.

It was thus a suitable word for old Eleazar, who ever since childhood had not ceased *exerting himself* for Judaean tradition. It is not simply that he *was a Jew* or living *in Judaism*. Paul's one-time choice of the same word for his former exertions in "the Judaizing" that is the subject of Galatians, which he illustrates by citing his tireless efforts to destroy the Christ community, seems a knowing allusion to 2 Maccabees.

A couple of generations after his letter, Bishop Ignatius of Antioch borrowed from Paul and likely 2 Maccabees in his letters. He too was faced with widespread Judaizing (*Ioudaismos*) among his gentile Christians. Vehement denunciation of this inspired him to coin *Christianismos* as counter-term. Whereas 2 Maccabees had offered the noble "Judaizing" (*Ioudaismos*) of Judaeans as paradoxical remedy to their *foreignizing* and *Graecizing*,

---

12. Polybius 3.115.3; 4.54.4.

13. Josephus, *Ant.* 18.359 ("in case some reversal for the worse should happen to them").

14. Polybius 1.66.3; 70.4; 2.33.3, 51.4; 4.61.4, 65.1; Tobit 4.14 ("Be attentive in all your deeds, my child, and be cultured/disciplined in your every turn/action/commitment").

15. Aeschylus, *Eum.* 23; Plutarch, *Apophth. Lac.* 216a (= 5.14 *Agis*).

16. *Ep. Arist.* 130, 216; Josephus, *Ant.* 17.345 ("the seers, whose activities were about dreams"); 19.28 ("[Chaerea] had been a soldier for a long time, and could not bear the behavior [just described] of Gaius").

17. 2 Cor 1:12; Eph 2:3; 1 Tim 3:15; 1 Pet 1:17; *1 Clem.* 63:3; *Did.* 3:9; *Barn.* 19:6; *Shep.* 43:12; 59:6; 104:2, though Acts uses it with the simple meaning "return" (5:22; 15:16).

Ignatius deployed the same irony to call for the Christianizing (*Christianismos*) of Christians, to combat Judaizing (*Ioudaismos*): "It is weird to talk Jesus Christ and to Judaize [*Ioudaizein*], for Christianizing [*Christianismos*] did not put faith in Judaizing [*Ioudaismos*], but rather Judaizing [turned to] Christianizing" (*Magn.* 10.3). He has just explained his meaning (*Magn.* 9.1-2): "those who had devoted their energies (*anastrephō*) to ancient practices came into a new hope, and were no longer keeping the sabbath, but living by the Lord's day . . ." This sounds like a précis of Gal 1:13-17: Paul *formerly* exerted himself in Judaizing, but was called by God to stop that and Christianize. For both writers, plainly, the time of Judaizing is finished.[18]

Once *Christianismos* was on the table, it became more generally serviceable for Christians who were in need of a vocabulary because they had no obvious place, other than as a voluntary association, in the *ethnos-polis* paradigm.[19] Tertullian reified the Greek word when he brought it into Latin to mean the whole Christian system of belief and practice: *Christianismus*. The dramatic rise in the use of *-ismos* words thereafter is most simply explained on the premise that *Ioudaismos*—in the static sense of a *Juda-ism*— is as much of a Christian polemical creation as *Christianismos*.[20]

In my first year of university, when I took a year-long introduction to Indian religious traditions, after a few weeks I began to feel uncomfortable. It seemed to be a course in Indian history, from Indus Valley civilization to British rule. That was fine, but not what I expected in religious studies. Coming from a Christian background, I naively assumed that everyone had a creed, which could be neatly lined up for comparison with others. Christians believe X; what do Hindus believe? After one class I asked the

---

18. So also *Phil.* 6.1: "If someone interprets [scripture] in a Judaizing way, don't listen to him! It's better to hear Christianizing from a man who has the circumcision than Judaizing from one with a foreskin." Also *Magn.* 8.1, where *Ioudaismos* is introduced as strange opinions connected with useless ancient stories.

19. Tertullian, *Marc.* 4.6, 33; 5.4, 6. A number of recent studies have argued that Christian authors of various periods engaged in more or less subtle ethnic reasoning, or by implication saw their communities as incipient *ethnē* (e.g., Buell 2005; Hodge 2007; Sechrest 2009; Concannon 2014; Horrell 2016). The plausibility of the readings in question, which in some cases I find most insightful, is obviously a separate issue from our discussion of *shared* categories and common discourse. Whereas everyone understood *Ioudaioi* to be an *ethnos*, Christians were not considered an *ethnos* by outsiders or, arguably, by very many insiders (even if by some, possibly, by implication and argument) through their first three centuries.

20. Two inscriptions of the late third or fourth century, well after our period and *possibly* influenced by Christian terminology, use *Ioudaismos*. Being inscriptions, they provide insufficient real-life context for clear interpretation. From the clues present and by analogy, one can easily imagine scenarios in which *Ioudaismos* refers to a (gentile or formerly gentile) life devoted to Judaeans. See Mason 2007: 476-80.

professor—this recollection brings no pride—"When are we going to study what Hindus believe?" He smiled, or I took it as a smile, and advised patience. I had no awareness then of my *Orientalist* outlook.[21] That course, and a companion on Chinese traditions without –isms,[22] turned out to be illuminating journeys. I admit to being influenced by the thinking they sparked over the following decades, as I sometimes had to teach world religions, in reflecting on the ancient Mediterranean world. But in the end we are required to explain evidence, and the evidence in this case comes together best, it seems to me, if we do not assume that anyone knew of, or could have articulated, a "Judaism" before later Christians began adjusting the language to their advantage.

This brings us to the recently much debated translation of *Ioudaios*.[23] Some work of mine has become a reference point in this debate, unfortunately imagined by some colleagues as an effort to impose "Judaean" on everyone as the only acceptable translation.[24] We take up the question both for its intrinsic interest and, self-servingly on my part, to correct misunderstanding. I wrote about the issue in a 2007 article because a large component of my research agenda is the Brill publication project *Flavius Josephus: Translation and Commentary*. An international team is working on sections of the thirty-volume corpus. I have assigned myself three volumes, and as editor I also work through each draft in conversation with the colleague in question.

Now everyone understands that translation is a creative activity. There is therefore no default or right translation, which we work from—no authorized version, which we accept or reject as we go along. Our task is a new one each

---

21. The classic study is Said 1978: e.g., 236–40. See also Sardar 1999: esp. 116; Macfie 2002; Kalmar and Penslar 2005.

22. Cf. Smith 1963: 61: "I have not found any formulation of a named religion earlier than the nineteenth century" and "the people involved could have had no use for a term or concept 'Hindu' or 'Hinduism'" (63–64). Fung Yu-Lan (1948: 1–6) insisted that what westerners call *Chinese religion* was the product of writers better considered philosophers.

23. See Miller 2010, 2012, 2014, a designed trilogy with the aim of deciding how *Ioudaios* should best be translated, which mentions most contributions. This avidly researched and well written series has surprisingly little bearing on our question. In trying to include many scholars' questions and contexts, the first article lacks a clear problem to be solved (e.g., not the problem we are exploring). The second and third explore ethnicity and modern issues—all interesting but not very illuminating in relation to ancient discourse. For a variety of perspectives, of varying relevance to our question, see "Jew and Judean: A Forum on Politics and Historiography in the Translation of Ancient Texts" (26 August 2014: http://marginalia.lareviewofbooks.org/jew-judean-forum/?"). The fullest statement by a prominent participant is Schwartz 2014 (cf. Schwartz 2007).

24. Reinhartz 2014.

time: to try to understand the text as well as possible and "bring it over" into readable English, the particular way of doing so being dependent on many factors on both sides. Although we are constrained by the source text and not freely composing, we must still decide how to render each word, phrase, and sentence. Even the equivalents of "but" and "and," as in the routine Greek *men . . . de* construction, offer numerous possibilities. There are thousands of such decisions to be made, and *Ioudaios* is just one challenge.

As a historian who researches and teaches, I consider all my work "translation" or cross-cultural communication: trying to understand an alien world and helping students to do so. Thus when Tom Robinson and I prepared a sourcebook-textbook on Christian origins, one of my former teaching areas, I used much of the Introduction to stress the strangeness of these seemingly familiar texts. I suggested to students that traditional Christian terminology in the NRSV translation used in our volume might obscure the sense of some Greek terms, and so proposed: *the* (singular and uniquely Pauline) *special announcement* rather than a blandified and shared *gospel* for *to euaggelion*; *assembly* rather than *church* for *ecclēsia*; *student* rather than *disciple* for *mathētēs*; *brothers* rather than the happier *brothers and sisters* for *adelphoi*; a rude word for feces rather than *garbage* for *skybala*.[25] These alternatives implied no criticism of the NRSV, which was prepared for purposes other than historical investigation, including recitation in churches. Seeking out ancient ways of talking and thinking is simply a different project. Whether we are translating Strabo, Josephus, a Christian text, or Cassius Dio, historians often want to immerse themselves and their readers, though this is possible only in tastes and glances, in that alien world.

The Brill Josephus Project had precisely such a historical focus. We first considered providing only a commentary on the Greek with no translation: printing Greek phrases and then commenting on them by exploring the ancient context. When we finally decided to include a translation, it was because we felt the reader needed an anchor for the commentary, rather than keeping two books open. Since there were many problems with printing a Greek text (the state of the text being quite uncertain), and many potential readers were not likely to work from a Greek text directly, we decided on an English reference-translation. This function implied that it should try to mirror the diction, devices, and structures of the Greek as vividly and transparently as possible, even if this meant leaving ambiguities—to be discussed in the notes. It also meant that we would try to be consistent in our choice of semantically related English words as counterparts for Greek cognates,

---

25. Mason and Robinson 2013 [1994].

where this was possible (below). English elegance or familiarity were not priorities because this was not to be a standalone translation. Its purpose was to lead the reader into the Greek text and commentary, to think about the ancient realities.

Here is a concrete example of what I mean about the effort at consistency. The word *genos* has a vast number of possible translations: class, kind, type, pedigree, ancestry, family, roots, bloodline, etc. When he introduces his autobiography at the end of the *Antiquities*, Josephus emphasizes that the work will take up his *genos* (*Ant.* 20.266). And sure enough, the first six sections of *Life* host six occurrences of *genos*—two in the first sentence—before he gives a Mafia kiss to those who impugn his (*Life* 6). Now there is obviously no right translation of this word, but one's choices will be determined by one's aims. Creating a standalone translation for the Loeb series, and valuing variety, Henry St. John Thackeray used several English words for the same Greek word in this brief section: family, line, ancestors, blood, line, pedigree. He was not wrong. His translation reads beautifully, and he made his choices in light of his aims and audiences. For our commentary on the Greek text, however, it made no sense to translate the same key word differently. Both for the practical task of tagging the main note to the first appearance of a Greek word and for conveying the importance of this term, it was better to find a single English translation if possible. "Ancestry" worked for all six cases. It is repetitive, but it shows the reader more clearly Josephus' emphasis on this word. That is what I mean about trying for consistency where possible, but it is not always possible. The 359 occurrences of this utility term in Josephus could certainly not be translated "ancestry" in most cases.

When the first printed volume went into production, Louis Feldman's *Antiquities* 1–4 (2000), I had to decide on English titles for Josephus' two main works. These were known all but universally as *Jewish War* and *Jewish Antiquities*. After working and teaching with classicists for a decade, however, I had personally come to prefer *Judaean*, as a term that stimulated students to think about ancient values and categories. Simply, it seemed to fit better with all the other ethnographical *-aios* labels one found alongside *Ioudaios*. The original team discussed this issue among many others, as we hammered out working principles from our beginning in 1996–1997, and it was plain that we had different preferences. That was to only to be expected. So in the Series Preface that accompanies each volume I used *Ioudaios* as a good example of diversity among the contributors, notwithstanding our general effort at consistency where possible: it would not come at all costs. Sometimes the same words have quite different senses and require different translations. In other cases, experts differ in their sense of the best English rendering. *Ioudaios* and cognates were one example of this, which I used to alert the reader to expect difference on some matters. That took care of the internal content, but what about the title?

As it happened, Feldman (2000) opted to use *Judean* in that first volume, which would introduce the series and its title. The agreement of the inaugural volume's author and the series editor counted for something. Another consideration was that some colleagues who preferred *Jew(ish)* in general, our discussions had shown, thought *The Judaean War* was apt because the conflict involved the homeland alone.[26] But the *War* volumes would not appear for some time and, if we used *Judean* there, it might seem odd to switch to *Jewish* for *Antiquities*. We could not ground our choice in one scholarly hypothesis. Choosing *Judean Antiquities* would not be as familiar to readers, obviously, although Heinrich Graetz had used German *Judäer, judäisch* (rather than *Juden, jüdisch*) for the ancient part of his great *History of the Jews*, which came through in the English translation as *Judaean*.[27] So there was precedent, but this option would seem strange to many. Finally, I considered our expected audience and decided that, given the technical material and immersive aim of the commentary, they would understand either choice.[28] So *Judean Antiquities* (in U.S. spelling) went to press, and I gave only the same sort of brief footnote to "Judean" in the Introduction that would accompany thousands of other translation decisions throughout the project.

That choice, understandably, attracted a level of attention that would not have attended a *Jewish Antiquities*.[29] One anonymous e-mailer was indignant on Josephus' behalf because we had messed with his plain English: "Josephus didn't write the Judean Antiquities. He wrote the Jewish Antiquities!" After receiving more serious criticisms in conversation, some tinged

---

26. Cf. now Schwartz (part of the current team, not in those discussions) 2014: 48–61.

27. Graetz 1862 (second edition of 11-volume original), 1914 (5th edition of 3-volume popular version from 1888), and 1956 (English translation in 5 vols.). The translation tries to preserve Graetz's German and, in the two volumes dealing with antiquity, *Judaean* appears 1,009 times. *Juden / Jews / Jewish* appear a few dozen times (precise counting is difficult because Jews is in metadata and page headers), for the post-Mishnaic period and when mentioning ongoing themes (the Jewish race, the Jews of today, Jewish history). Independently I discovered the careful treatment in Schwartz 2014: 62–82.

28. I called HJW *A History of the Jewish War* because I imagined the readership to be rather broader.

29. The eminent classicist Louis Feldman opted for *Judean* in his translation of the first volume of the series (Feldman 2000), the volume for which I had to make the decision.

with moral concern for having potentially driven a wedge between ancient Judaeans and Jews, I thought that it might be useful if I could integrate an explanation of this choice in an article on the larger problems that ancient historians in our field face—or do not face. Hence the broad subtitle of that 2007 article: "Problems of Categorization in Ancient History" and the structure, in which the *Ioudaios* question arose only after two basic categorical explorations: ancient "Judaism" and "religion". As a point of departure, because I very much wanted to remain focused on the historical question and avoid polemics, I mentioned only the most open-ended criticism, which had come in a published review.[30]

My concern, then, was not to demand or impose a translation of *Ioudaios*, or even to say how it *should* be translated. I was trying to open a space for this alternative on standard philological principles, to help redirect our language from the familiar categories to the surprises and discomforts of ancient discourse. One's choice in translating *Ioudaios* as a single word hardly matters to me. Those who prefer *Jew*, for any reason but even if they think that this better captures ancient realities, will meet no objection from me. They are not required to defend their preference, since it has the weight of tradition.

Since each of us must make our own choices, there being no "correct" default, I tried to explain why I preferred *Judaean*. Those who publish new proposals are expected to situate them in existing scholarship, showing how they agree with or differ from other positions. One may not simply ignore everyone else. So I engaged the most important contributions: citing notable examples of standard usage and the principles that others had offered for using religion or not, for claiming that *Ioudaismos* represented a religious-cultural system, or for supporting a change from *Judaean* to *Jew*. There was no polemical intent, much less a prescriptive one. It was not about what was "appropriate," certainly not for others. Mine was a defensive case for tolerating *Judaean* as a reasonable alternative to the familiar *Jew* in ancient-historical work.

Why, then, did *Judaean* commend itself to me, for the sort of work I do most days? The basic point may be simply put. It is not possible to conceive of an inhabited place without its people: America without Americans, Egypt without Egyptians, Syria without Syrians, Samaria without Samarians, Idumaea without Idumaeans, or Judaea without Judaeans. But there was a well-known Judaea (*Ioudaia*) in antiquity, the *chōra* of mother-*polis* Jerusalem. So there *were* Judaeans (*Ioudaioi*). In modern English, when there is no familiar place called Judaea, Judaean has no such obvious meaning, just as

---

30. Pearce 2004; cf. Mason 2007: 457–58 (opening sentences).

we must now stop and think about *Dacians* and *Thracians*. But all of these ethnonyms were immediately understood in antiquity because the places and their peoples were famous.[31]

This is, incidentally, the problem with invoking English dictionary definitions when translating ancient texts. Dictionaries are certainly useful when, as is normal, phenomena expressed in the source culture—Dutch- French- or German—correspond closely to something in Anglophone societies. In that case we may easily "bring over" (trans-late) what is basically the same thing (school, courts, police, legislature) from one to the other. English dictionaries then help us to find the *mot juste*. When translating ancient texts, however, we cannot assume such correspondences. We cannot assume that an English dictionary has a good word for *princeps*, *imperator*, *archē*, *genos*, or *ethnos*, because these are not categories. *If* our primary aim in translating is to challenge our readers to think imaginatively about a truly foreign and alien ancient past, then translating with familiar English terms may not be the most helpful route.

I emphasize again that translators have no single purpose, and their preferences also vary widely. Many fine translations of classical texts, especially those meant to stand by themselves, are extremely friendly to modern readers. They work hard to remove the cultural divide by pulling ancient terms over the bridge in our direction. Sometimes they convert ancient proverbs or expressions (Owls to Athens, I care not a fig), divine names (*Tychē*, *Artemis*), dates, distances (*stadia*, paces), and units of measurement (obols, *drachmae*) into familiar equivalents (Coals to Newcastle, couldn't care less, Fortune, Diana, yards, etc.). Virtually all forms of Zeus or Jupiter end up as the happy Jove in some translations.

There is nothing wrong with that, if it supports the translation's aims. But a translator with the more single-minded purpose of encouraging readers to go and cross that bridge to visit the strange past might prefer less familiar terms. Such a scholar might not shrink even from odd coinages, as translators of the comic playwright Aristophanes do when trying to capture his humor, if these will stimulate curiosity. Again, there is no single right or appropriate choice in translation for all purposes and contexts. And even if we claim to have found a principle to cling to, we all eventually make our compromises with common sense.

Let us bring this down from high principle to the realities that face the translator in the case of *Ioudaios*. Consider three passages. First, in his final known writing Josephus claims to quote a story from a digression in a book

31. The phrase "Judaea and Samaria" is used in Israel today for what is often called the West Bank (formerly of Jordan). Ancient *Judaea* was universally known and meant something different: the territory anchored in Jerusalem.

by Aristotle's student Clearchus about the great philosopher's encounter with a remarkable *Ioudaios* he met in Asia. When Aristotle's interlocutor responds with eager impatience, Aristotle reminds him of the rhetorical principle that a man's origin or ancestry (*genos*) is crucial to understanding his character. So he first explains (*Apion* 1.179):

> That fellow was by origin a *Ioudaios*, from Coele-Syria. These [*Ioudaioi*] are descended from the philosophers in India, and they are called, as the philosophers from India say, Calani. But among the Syrians the *Ioudaioi* have received their name from the place. For the place they inhabit is styled *Ioudaia*. The name of their *polis* is altogether trickier: that they call *Hierousalēmē*.

Although Thackeray rendered *Ioudaioi* as "Jews" in both cases, and that was not wrong, Aristotle/Clearchus' pointed connection between place and people means that if our translation aims to draw attention to the Greek devices, *Judaeans* would obviously commend itself: "The *Judaeans* have received their name from the place . . . *Judaea*."

Here we come upon a second problem with casting the question as "how we should translate" *Ioudaios*—in addition to the problem with "should," that is. If we understand this as a problem of translation, we already skew the discussion. That is because there is a difference between translation proper, or finding the best term in the target language, and *transliteration*. As a general rule translators are expected to translate in the proper sense, to avoid transliteration unless exceptional circumstances require it. For if we leave a large number of foreign words in their original language, merely using readable characters, we are not doing our job.

Even when there is a similar word in English, and using it would not be mere transliteration, it is usually safest to avoid the related English term because its evolved meanings will likely differ from those of the ancient Greek. For example, our word *character* comes from Greek *charaktēr* (engraver, tool, imprint, image, type, form), but it would nearly always be misleading to translate the Greek as English character. A subtler case is Greek *zēlōtēs*, the ultimate source of English *zealot*. The Greek word is routinely rendered Zealot in Josephus translations, though it has none of the negative connotations that attach to the English—because of Josephus' famous description of this group. It was as admirable to be a *zēlōtēs* (disciple—of something or someone good) as it is now objectionable to be a zealot. To translate Josephus, and try to capture what his first audiences heard in his Greek, with an English term decisively shaped by the impact of his own work seems rather circular. To understand his points about the

zēlōtai, perhaps we ought rather to use something like *disciple* or *devotee*.³²
In general, then, translation requires the translator to find the English terms that are closest in sense, not in appearance, to the original. That is why, in bilingual countries, parallel advertisements or government notices in the two languages often look very different.³³

Names of places and peoples (ethnonyms) are, however, a universal exception. It would be absurd to translate them in the proper sense, to an "equivalent" in the target language. If a place is named after a great leader, such as Washington, or after phrases in a native population's language (as Canada's Ontario, Quebec), it would be comical for people of other countries to give them their own names—for the French to call Washington "Napoleon." Place names and their ethnonyms are not translated, but transliterated, even if the result looks a little different in each language. This is obvious in the modern world: America / Americans, Australia / Australians, Italy / Italians, Germany / Germans, Israel / Israelis. What the words might mean is completely irrelevant. The same principle is clear in ancient writers, from Homer, Herodotus, and Pseudo-Scylax through Julius Caesar, Strabo, Pliny, and many others: there are places and peoples with related names, which the competent author must struggle to get right. Italy, Galilee, Gaza, Ascalon, Galilee, and Idumaea and their related ethnonyms are not translations, but simply the given names, which authors represent in the as best they can. Philo and Josephus may try to take the strangeness out of Judaean place names by discussing etymologies, true or false, but they must still use those original names.

As soon as we frame the *Ioudaios* question as a debate about the "best translation," then, we already remove it from the standard treatment of place names and ethnonyms and begin debating the inner content of terms. What comes to mind for you or me when we hear *Jew* and *Judaean*? What is the *real* meaning of these words? Suspicions of ulterior motives easily arise. Although I have also used "translate" in the broad sense of the translator's task, my practice has been simply to transliterate this place name and its ethnonym as we normally do. As Judaea is the transliteration of Greek *Ioudaia* via Latin *Iudaea*, so Judaeans transliterates *Ioudaioi* / *Iudaei*. Consistency is the simple basis for my preference, which has nothing to do with the true inner content of either *Jew* or *Judaean*.

32. Cf. *HJW* 444–50.
33. In a Dutch government office, a sign in English said that all documents would be scrutinized *for their authenticity*. The Dutch version agreed word for word, whereas the German and French versions declared that the authenticity (not the documents) would be scrutinized.

To return to our passage, Josephus' Clearchus juxtaposes *Ioudaia* and all *Ioudaioi*, stressing the semantic connection. How shall I handle that textual fact? If the issue is not how one should *translate* but, more simply, whether to transliterate both, then my preference is clear. It is true that English *Jews* also derives ultimately from *Ioudaioi* (via Latin *Iudaei* through old French *juiu*), but it is not a transliteration obviously matching Judaea.

So there is no right way to render *Ioudaioi* in Greek texts. More than one option exists, and everything depends on one's question and aims. I understand and respect colleagues who argue that their understanding of *Jews* (or restrictive view of *Judaeans*) recommends the former. But we are asking and answering different questions. When it comes to place and people names, it is hard to see the point in debating what terms *really mean* or what the best translation equivalent might be. I have no view on what it truly means to be Jewish or Christian, American, Japanese, Canadian, or Australian.[34] My interest is in capturing the sense of the ancient text, which uses place and people names as given, fixed terms requiring no translation—even if an explanation of etymology can display the author's learning. In Josephus' quotation from Clearchus, transliterating both place and ethnonym so that the bond is preserved in English seems to me the best way to capture the author's point. This is not the only option, but it is a legitimate one.

Our second example of a close *ethnos-patris* link is from Cassius Dio in the early third century A.D. After describing Pompey's entry into "Syria-Palestine" in 64 B.C. (the name of the province at Dio's time), Pompey's removal of Aristobulus II and recognition of Hyrcanus II, Dio continues:

> So this is what happened in Palaestina—for that is what the whole *ethnos* that lies beside the Internal [Mediterranean] Sea, from Phoenicia as far as Egypt, has been called from of old. They have also a different, acquired name: the territory is styled *Ioudaia* and they themselves *Ioudaioi*.[35]

---

34. Regrettably I have been read (from Mason 2007) as though I considered "Jews" a religious term (e.g., Reinhartz 2014). That would run counter to my central arguments and my words. I actually said: (a) that the arguments of *other* scholars that *Ioudaios* becomes religious in antiquity, which leads *them* to propose the translation *Jews* (*because they* associate this name more with religion), were difficult, given that the purported change left no marks in ancient discourse itself, in which *religion was not* an available category; and (b) that modern discourse, which I cannot change, plainly has a genus-category "religion," which subsumes the species Judaism along with Christianity, Islam, Hinduism, etc.—even though (I stressed) members of each community vehemently reject that homogenizing, quasi-Orientalizing umbrella term. My observations were about universal discourses in different periods, not about what it means to be a Jew.

35. Dio 37.16.5: ταῦτα μὲν τότε ἐν τῇ Παλαιστίνῃ ἐγένετο· οὕτω γὰρ τὸ σύμπαν

If Dio had described a region called *Aigyptos* or *Syria* and said that its people were *Aigyptioi* or *Syroi*, we would transliterate *Egyptians* or *Syrians* without hesitation. Even if there were a notional alternative, such as Levantines for Syrians, the lexical connection recommends transliterating both in English—unless the translator's priorities were otherwise, for example in telling the story of *Levantines* through the ages. Since Dio's point is in fact to explain *Ioudaia* and *Ioudaioi* in relation to each other, transliterating the former while translating *Jews* would not be as clear. For my purposes, the issue is much the same as when the first-century naturalist Discorides mentions the curative properties of "the Judaean stone . . . produced naturally in Judaea."[36] No one would presumably translate "Jewish stone." This is not to say, I repeat, that *Jews* would be wrong or inappropriate in Dio. E. Cary, translating Dio for the prestigious Loeb edition, rendered: "the country has been named Judaea, and the people themselves Jews." That is fine, but must every translator follow suit? If my aim is different from that of the Loeb series, in wishing to draw attention to the Greek text on which the attached commentary is based, the transliterated ethnonym *Judaeans* better serves these purposes.

In our final passage, the third-century Christian Origen is criticizing the second-century philosopher Celsus for disparaging Judaean laws, in some places, while elsewhere respecting Judaeans as an *ethnos* that has a place in the world and an "overseer" god, over against the Christians, who lack all this. It is noteworthy, incidentally, as an index of the classical paradigm's vitality, that neo-Platonists *could* build their system on the ethnographic model, so clear and entrenched was it. They not only understood *ethnē* in terms of their home environments but introduced this notion of a protective deity (overseer) assigned to each *ethnos* and homeland, who nurtured the *ethnos* with its unique character and customs (*C. Cels.* 5.25). The emperor Julian will express the same balance of a generic respect for Judaeans, as an ancient ethnos with *patris* and god, and disparagement of them over against superior Greek ways. In arguing that Celsus' respect and disdain for Judaeans are contradictory, Origen draws out the philosopher's ideas for challenge:

ἔθνος, ὅσον ἀπὸ τῆς Φοινίκης μέχρι τῆς Αἰγύπτου παρὰ τὴν θάλασσαν τὴν ἔσω παρήκει, ἀπὸ παλαιοῦ κέκληται. ἔχουσι δὲ καὶ ἕτερον ὄνομα ἐπίκτητον· ἥ τε γὰρ χώρα Ἰουδαία καὶ αὐτοὶ Ἰουδαῖοι ὠνομάδαται· For Syria-Palestine as ancient see Herodotus 1.105.2; 2.104.12, 106.3; 3.91.6; 4.39.9; 7.89.3. For Palestine, Aristotle, *Met.* 359a; Polybius 16.40.2.

36. Dioscorides Pedianus, *Materia Medica* 5.137: ὁ δὲ Ἰουδαικὸς λίθος γεννᾶται μὲν ἐν τῇ Ἰουδαίᾳ.

THE END OF THE CLASSICAL PARADIGM 195

I would like to ask him . . . who it could be, then, who distributed the different parts of the earth to different overseers . . . and in particular allotted the *chōra* of the *Ioudaioi* and the *Ioudaioi* themselves to its receiver or receivers. Was it Zeus, as Celsus would call him, who assigned the *ethnos* of the *Ioudaioi* and their *chōra* to some power or powers, and who wanted the one receiving *Ioudaia* to establish such laws among the *Ioudaioi*?

If one is interested in the contours and emphases of the text, again, transliterating *Ioudaioi* as Judaeans would seem to best capture this close and explanatory link among *ethnos*, *chōra*, and ethnonym. The bond is as strong in this third-century text, long after Jerusalem's fall, as it ever was.

Now if I render *Ioudaioi* as Judaeans in such places as these, how could I justify not doing so elsewhere where the same discourse is in use? What shall I do when *Ioudaioi* are ranged alongside all the other *-aioi ethnē* in a passage, and I translate the others as *-eans*? The bond between an *ethnos* and its land is ingrained in the classical paradigm. It works through the whole library of surviving texts by both outside observers (Hecataeus of Abdera, Poseidonius, Diodorus, Strabo, Pliny, Tacitus)[37] and Judaean authors: the *Letter of Aristaeas* or the corpus of Philo and Josephus. As with all other *ethnos-polis* groupings, this link does not say much by itself; it leaves open or even creates questions about status-ambiguity. What about such individuals as Tiberius Alexander of Alexandria, Antiochus of Antioch, or Paul of Tarsus, among millions of other *Ioudaioi* outside Judaea? How should we understand their various affiliations?

But the common categories did not evolve to settle cases, any more than our conceptions of citizenship, religion, nationality, or state can explain personal situations. They were meant to facilitate general communication. With due regard for the individual complications and fascinating figures whose lives complicated matters, we also need to understand the shared lexical bank. Only then can we probe its possibilities, uses, and limits, and only then can we interpret specific communicative efforts that use this paradigm.

A number of scholars have independently opted for *Judaean* when translating ancient texts, for reasons that are not necessarily mine,[38] and many now consider it an option. Most interesting is that some eminent scholars who ultimately prefer *Jew* nevertheless recommend—or insist upon—*Judae-*

---

37. Collected and superbly annotated in Stern 1974.

38. E.g., Esler 2003: 70–72; Barclay 2004: 90–127; Chapman 2006: esp. 132; Elliott 2007: 119–154 (whose main argument is for *Israel[ite]* as the proper emic term); Hanson and Oakman 2008: 11.

an in some periods. According to Shaye Cohen, "all occurrences of the term *Ioudaios* before the middle or end of the second century B.C.E. should be translated not as 'Jew,' a religious term, but as 'Judaean,' an ethnic-geographic term."³⁹ The question then is only whether something happened in classical antiquity to disrupt or dismantle the classical paradigm, so that we should change our translation of the same Greek terms at some specified point.

Cohen finds such a turning point in the late second century B.C., as we just saw, after which what seems to him the restrictively "ethnic-geographic" translation Judaean no longer captures the sense of *Ioudaios*. Incidentally I am not sure why, if *Judaeans* signifies the people whose ancestral *ethnospolis* home (*patris*) is Judaea, it should be more geographically restrictive than other ethnonyms, but we may leave that aside. Cohen proposes that the Hasmonean expansion, which saw large numbers of people of other *ethnē* accept Judaean law and customs, severed the *ethnos*-place bond. Although *Ioudaios* did not lose its ethnic root altogether, the phenomenon of mass conversion gave the word newly *religious* connotations, which he thinks are better captured by *Jew*.

Daniel Schwartz likewise hears something geographically restrictive in *Judaean*, though he too accepts that this was the original sense of *Ioudaios*.⁴⁰ He has argued that a series of changes, beginning with the Babylonian Exile (sixth century B.C.) and concluding with the fall of the second temple in A.D. 70, created an ever-widening gap between that original valence and later, ever-more *religious* and geographically detached senses of *Ioudaios*.⁴¹ In recent studies he has located the decisive change in the immediate aftermath of A.D. 70, discerning a shift in Josephus' use of *Ioudaios* between the *Judaean War* (in the 70s) and *Jewish Antiquities* (in the 90s).⁴² Or more precisely, in these later terms, *Judaean* remains a valid designation for people resident in Judaea, and it seems their literary products pertaining to Judaea written abroad (so: *Judaean War* of Josephus), but when they are in the Diaspora they are really *Jews*, and writings reflecting diasporic values are Jewish (so: *Jewish Antiquities*).⁴³

Our questions thus appear to be quite different, an impression confirmed by Schwartz's case that both *religion* and *Judaism* were present in the

39. Cohen 1999: 70, 125–29, 134, 137.

40. This geographical-religious dichotomy underlies Schwartz 2014, which sees 1 Maccabees as a Judaean work, diasporic 2 Maccabees as Jewish (11–20).

41. Schwartz 1992: 5–15.

42. Schwartz 2005: 68–78; 2007: 10, 18–20; 2014: 48–61. His student Michael Tuval amplifies the case in his published dissertation (2013). Mason 2014a is a review responding to Tuval.

43. Schwartz 2014: 83–90.

first century (above).⁴⁴ They may have been, in unstated and amorphous but real ways (how would we know?), but my simple observation has been that they were not discussed *as such*. The advantage of asking what people were talking about, as distinct from what really was or what people thought, is that we can read their surviving exchanges. I am interested in that shared discourse, enabling communication, which Josephus used in addressing the same sorts of groups in Rome in both his major works. His *Antiquities* everywhere assumes the audience's knowledge of *War* and builds directly on it (e.g., *Ant.* 1.1-7) to explore the earlier history of the people and its constitution and governance in its land.

The proposal that *War* and *Antiquities* "mean" different things with the same words may not be implausible, if one is asking about Josephus' inner world. We all change. But if our interest is in Josephus' overt language and the shared underlying discourse (*la langue*), we have a problem because the two works were written for similar audiences in the same location. Leaving aside debates about the interpretation of specific passages, can we find evidence that people living from, say 200 B.C. to A.D. 300, let alone between 77 and 93 in Rome (the time of Plutarch, Tacitus, Pliny, Josephus), made distinctions between *Ioudaioi* who were in *Ioudaia*, thereby sharing its local values, and *Ioudaioi* who lived abroad and thought diasporically, and that when Josephus' Roman audiences heard *Ioudaioi* in the two works they distinguished *Judaeans* from *Jews*? Given the great difficulty of arguing such a scenario, I must conclude that Schwartz and I are asking different questions—and he may be right about his.

These studies by giants in the field are full of insight, and I have no quarrel with anyone who prefers *Jews* as a translation term. If they will permit me to use *Judaeans*, there is no "debate," any more than there is about the thousands of other terms some of us are translating every day. In a strange twist, what began for me as a defensive case, as others were chagrined at my departure from ubiquitous translation tradition, has come to seem prescriptive and domineering, as though I were demanding that everyone change or defend themselves.⁴⁵ But I have never had a problem with other people's translation choices, and hope they can tolerate mine.

44. Schwartz 2014: 91-112.

45. E.g., Reinhartz 2014. Schwartz titles an appendix responding to my 2007 piece, "*May* We Speak of "Religion" and "Judaism" in the Second Temple Period?" (my emphasis, 2014: 91-111). Of course we *may*. I happily teach "ancient Judaism." Although Schwartz refreshingly clarifies both the context and the main content of my article, he still portrays it as though it were about how one *should* translate, and what is *appropriate* (91: "Mason argued ... the appropriate translation ... it is not appropriate [or useful] for us to translate *Ioudaios* as Jew"). But I did not write in such language, and used "appropriate" not for my arguments but only for questions and claims of ancient

In sum, since the division of the ancient Greek lexical bank dealing with peoples and places did not noticeably change, outside Christian circles, from Hecataeus' *ethnos* analyses in the fifth century B.C. to Stephanus' preservation of them a thousand years later, it is hard to find criteria to argue for a dramatic shift in meaning. Whose or which meaning(s) are we discussing? I have tried to make my criteria clear: the contextual cues given by an author to guide interpretation and the evidence of the larger communicative palette. The mutually exclusive proposals given above for the date of a decisive change, ranging over centuries, or for concurrent differences in meaning in complex relationship with one's location and related outlook, appear to confirm that *the shared discourse* left no traces of this changed understanding.

Writing a century and a half after Jerusalem's destruction, Cassius Dio still assumes the *ethnos-patris* bond when he tries to explain *Ioudaios* identity (37.17.2–3):

> They stand apart from the rest of humanity in more or less everything that relates to one's way of life, and particularly in that they show no honor at all to other gods but strenuously revere a certain one only. They never had any statue, even among themselves in Jerusalem, but supposing that he could not be represented in word or in image, they offer worship (*thrēskuousi*) in the most excessive way among humanity. They built him a sanctuary that was extremely large and exceedingly beautiful, except in that it was both huge and uncovered . . .[46]

The same *ethnos-polis* language remains, with all the old people-homeland assumptions, in Judaean and non-Judaean texts alike (granted a paucity of the latter after 100) through the time of Vespasian, Trajan, and Hadrian, from Diodorus through Strabo, Philo, Pliny, Josephus, Dio, and on to Julian in the fourth century.

Only Christian writers, it seems clear, from their ascendance in the fourth century, had the motive, means, and opportunity to change the general shared discourse. And they demonstrably effected this change.

---

writers or modern scholars together. The article had a specific purpose, which was to challenge ancient historians to think in terms of ancient values, categories, and configurations (Mason 2007: 2, emphasis added: "The following essay is my effort to *explore the problem* [raised by my reviewer] more adequately. This is not for the sake of the commentary alone. I offer it *also as a contribution to a fundamental question* in historical research: the *problem of appropriate categories* [NB: not translations of words, but how we approach the ancient world]." The case could be mistaken in whole or in parts, but it was not about *prescribing* what others may say.

46. This may refer to the large enclosed court of Herod's outer temple, as distinct from the roofed shrine (Holy Place), which was not very Greek or Roman. Dio may be worried that so many people would be left exposed to blazing sun in its precincts.

Gradually, over two centuries or more, they had created new terms that sidelined traditional *ethnos, polis,* and cult identities and tried to replace them with new reference points, assumptions, values, and social structures, connected with religions and -isms. They were able to do this because their originally sectarian, burn-the-house-down lexicon, which began with the apocalyptically-minded Paul and took decisive shape in the Greek apologists of the late second century and Tertullian's Latin, gradually became normative with Constantine and his successors. The black-sheep emperor Julian was the most influential figure who tried to reverse this flow, but his effort died prematurely with him, and his passing sapped the drive of likeminded but less powerful figures to stem the Christian tide.

In the modern west we are unavoidably heirs of this Christian reconfiguration, which shaped western society through the modern period, notwithstanding adjustments in the Enlightenment and revolutions. As ancient historians, however, we are permitted to investigate conditions before the Christianizing of society, thought, and language. As academics and historians, we naturally ask different questions and prefer different language. I have tried to explain mine.

Did Conversion Rupture the *Ethnos-Polis* Paradigm?

The prospect that religious conversion brought something new to classical discourse, which required a new understanding of *Ioudaios*, even if this left no evident changes in actual vocabulary, is intriguing and merits further probing. In Cohen's view, the new phenomenon could not be accommodated by *Judaean* language: "The Hasmonean period attests for the first time the idea of religious conversion: by believing in the God of the Jews and following his laws, a gentile can become a Jew."[47] The tacit premise here appears to be that it would make no sense in the classical paradgim (my term) to speak of becoming a Judaean. But why not?

The examples that Cohen and Schwartz find most telling seem to be: King Antiochus IV's deathbed effort to convert (2 Macc 9:17), the conversions of Idumaeans and Ituraeans under John Hyrcanus and Aristobulus, and the conversion of the Adiabenian royal house towards the middle of the first century A.D. I would suggest that the language used in these accounts is not about religious conversion at all, but depends for its sense on the ingrained assumptions of classical discourse. The stories are all the more surprising and interesting for that reason.

47. Cohen 1999: 137.

Again we need to clarify what our question is. Mine is not whether we find the ancients' terminology logical, serviceable, or readily translatable. I simply want to know how ancient writers communicated: to try to understand better the conceptions and values they express. If *they* had felt that standard language could not accommodate the incidents in question, we might expect to see new word coinages or strenuous efforts to show that something new was afoot. But ethnic re-alignment was routinely spoken of, when new *ethnē* derived from older ones (Judaeans from Egyptians, Idumaeans from Phoenicians or Arabs), when Egyptians or Judaeans became Alexandrians or Romans, when whole towns were re-founded as Roman colonies, or when individuals were seen as defecting from their traditional customs or *poleis*. Whether such things ought to have strained the categories *ethnos* and *polis* we cannot say, but their actual use did not noticeably change.

How, then, did ancient writers describe the adoption of Judaean laws by others in these cases?[48]

1. *King Antiochus IV.* The first example comes in 2 Macc 9:11–29, which relates the death of the Seleucid king who had provoked the Hasmonean Revolt with an intense and bloody persecution in Jerusalem and its *chōra*. Mortally ill and finally admitting the sovereignty of the true God, the king desperately asserts a change of heart, which he hopes will save him. His deathbed repentance is too late, however, for God or the author.

In the narrative of 2 Maccabees, this episode recalls the story of Heliodorus' deathbed repentance in Chapter 3. Heliodorus was an aide to Antiochus' predecessor, Seleucus IV, who dispatched him to bring treasure from the Jerusalem temple at the suggestion of a mischievous temple official. When Heliodorus tried to complete his mission, however, a supernatural horse and two angels blocked his path. They brought him to death's door with kicks and relentless blows. In this case, perhaps because Heliodorus had only been carrying out orders, the prayers and sacrifices of the high priest Onias effected his complete recovery and restoration. He offered sacrifice and returned to tell King Seleucus about "the supreme God" of the Judaeans (2 Macc 3.1–39).

The prospects of repentance for King Antiochus IV, who had persecuted and killed Judaeans on his own authority, are not nearly so clear. But in hopes of restoration, Antiochus lays out four concrete commitments (9:14–17). (i) There and then he declares the holy *polis* Jerusalem free, in

---

48. *Polis* frequently but note 2 Macc 3:1, 14; 4:39, 48 (with dependent villages); *chōra*, e.g., 2:21; 9:24.

the Greek sense (τὴν μὲν ἁγίαν πόλιν . . . ἐλευθέραν ἀναδεῖξαι), suggesting internal autonomy and permission for Jerusalem's council and notables to arrange their own affairs—the most privileged status possible in his kingdom. (ii) Similarly and in confirmation he elevates *all* Judaeans (presumably those of his large kingdom) as notional equals of the citizens of the most prestigious Hellenic *polis*, Athens (πάντας αὐτοὺς ἴσους Ἀθηναίοις ποιήσειν), which is not in his kingdom. (iii) He will magnificently adorn the mother-*polis* Jerusalem's temple and cover the costs of its traditional sacrifices from his own resources (τὰς δὲ ἐπιβαλλούσας πρὸς τὰς θυσίας συντάξεις ἐκ τῶν ἰδίων προσόδων χορηγήσειν). (iv) Finally, in the most dramatic about-face, this recent persecutor and hellenizer will *become* a *Ioudaios* (καὶ Ἰουδαῖον ἔσεσθαι). Visiting every place in the world, he will declare the sovereignty of their God (καὶ πάντα τόπον οἰκητὸν ἐπελεύσεσθαι καταγγέλλοντα τὸ τοῦ θεοῦ κράτος).

We may leave aside the question whether the author means us to understand this as a genuine effort or merely the horrid man's final ploy. The general scenario of repentance echoes biblical models, not to mention the universal and cinematic plotline of the brutal oppressor who gets his comeuppance and begs pathetically for mercy.[49] But the reader will have noticed (I am not making this up) that Antiochus' first three provisions happen to check off, rather precisely, the boxes of the classical paradigm: *polis*, *ethnos*, and sacrificial cult. The mother-*polis* and *ethnos* along with their temple and its ancient sacrificial system will receive great honors. The use of Athenians as analogue makes the classical framework clear.

But what of Antiochus' final promise? Suppose he had been a king of old Macedonia who had tried to destroy Athenians or Corinthians, and now urgently repented as he faced death. Could he not have likewise promised to honor Athens, its citizens, and its temple of Athena, finally undertaking to share their very identity and *become* an Athenian? Cohen and Schwartz, surmising that Antiochus must have planned to keep his Macedonian identity, conclude that he would become only a "Jew by religion."[50] I do not know what it would mean to be either a Macedonian king *without religion* or a Judaean/Jew *in religion only*—or how these are suggested by the text. The category seems to beg the question. At any rate, the thoroughly conventional

---

49. Cf. Haman in Est 7:1–10; Nebuchadnezzar and Darius in Daniel (Dan 4:34–37; 6:26). Both the latter potentates harshly oppress the "exiles from Judah" until they are terrified by divine power, submit to the sovereignty of the Judaean God, and begin to declare God's greatness everywhere. Daniel dates to about 165 B.C., but some stories in it are older; cf. Collins and Flint 2001–2002. It would be hard to extract a purely *religious* action from any of these stories, which are set in royal courts.

50. Cohen 1999: 92–93, 129–30; Schwartz 2008: 360–61.

language does not seem to suggest such a conceptual-linguistic innovation, in that short phrase about becoming a *Ioudaios*.

2. *Idumaean Forced Conversion*. The Idumaeans who accepted Judaean laws during the Hasmonean expansion are undoubtedly an intriguing example of *ethnos* redefinition. And that is precisely how a range of ancient observers describe them: matter-of-factly and without awareness that they somehow broke the lexical bank. Strabo has no trouble saying of Idumaeans, within a single passage: (a) they are considered one of four distinct *ethnē* in southern Syria alongside Judaeans, Gazans, and Azotians (16.2.2); (b) they *are* Nabataean Arabs (Ναβαταῖοι δ' εἰσὶν οἱ Ἰδουμαῖοι); but, (c) after being expelled from Nabataea, they "went over to the Judaeans and began to share in *their ordinances/customs*" (προσεχώρησαν τοῖς Ἰουδαίοις καὶ τῶν νομίμων τῶν αὐτῶν ἐκείνοις ἐκοινώνησαν, 16.2.34). He gives no hint that the Idumaean experience requires a new social-linguistic model, or a category such as religion, to accommodate their fortunes.

Centuries after the Idumaean conquest, an evolving series of dictionaries of near-synonym or homonym pairs would include the pair "*Ioudaios* and *Idoumaios*." The two names were sometimes confused, perhaps partly because of the famous Judaean-Idumaean King Herod.[51] Philo of Byblos in the late first century A.D. seems to have been the first to compile one of these dictionaries, but the most complete example, with 522 pairs of names, is attributed to a certain Ammonius and may come from the late fourth century.[52]

In spite of its transmission puzzles the passage merits consideration. Ammonius' version begins:

> Judaeans and Idumaeans differ, as Ptolemy affirms in the first [book] of *On Herod the King*, for whereas *Judaeans* are such by origin and naturally, *Idoumaioi* are not such [or not *Ioudaioi*?] by origin, but rather Phoenicians and Syrians. But having been overpowered by them, and having been forced to undergo circumcision and to pay taxes into the *ethnos*, and to follow the same laws/customs, they were called Judaeans [variant: Idumaeans].[53]

51. Aelian, *Nat. anim.* 6.17 tells a cock-and-bull story from "the land of those called Judaeans, or Idumaeans, at the time of King Herod."
52. Nickau 1966 is the Teubner text. See Nickau 2000 and Geiger 2012 for discussion of the complex textual history, which seems to include Ptolemy of Ascalon, cited by Ammonius a few times.
53. Ammonius' Greek: Ἰουδαῖοι καὶ Ἰδουμαῖοι διαφέρουσιν, ὥς φησι Πτολεμαῖος ἐν πρώτῳ Περὶ Ἡρώδου τοῦ βασιλέως. Ἰουδαῖοι μὲν γάρ εἰσιν οἱ ἐξ ἀρχῆς φυσικοί· Ἰδουμαῖοι

However we reconstruct the variants, the lexicographers are discussing the matter with no evident astonishment, but by way of explaining *ethnos* relations in familiar terms. Whether the point of the original was to contrast the origins of Idumaeans among Phoenicians and Syrians with the claim that Judaeans were always such (contrast the Judaeans' generally assumed derivation from Egypt), or to speak of Idumaeans changing yet again to become Judaeans, all such shifts were possible in the normal framework without resort to religion, which does not appear. The Idumaeans' adoption of Judaean identity is clearly marked by their circumcision, submission of taxes to the Judaean *ethnos* (presumably to Jerusalem), and acceptance of their long-time neighbor's laws.

Josephus' description of the Idumaean conquest, written for Greek-speaking audiences in late first-century Rome, and in the later work characterized by Schwartz as Diaspora-Jewish, depends on the same *ethnos-polis* framework (*Ant.* 13.257–258):

> Hyrcanus also captures the [Idumaean] *poleis* of Adora and Marisa, and when he had taken all the Idumaeans in hand, he let them stay in the *chōra* if they circumcised their genitals and if they were willing to live with the Judaeans' laws (τοῖς Ἰουδαίων νόμοις χρήσασθαι θέλοιεν). In their yearning for their *ancestral land* (πόθῳ τῆς πατρίου γῆς), they patiently submitted to circumcision and to practicing the very same regimen of life in other respects as the Judaeans. Given what happened to them then, from that time onward *they were Judaeans* (ὥστε εἶναι τὸ λοιπὸν Ἰουδαίους).

Although we know that much more was going on—that some Idumaeans fled to Egypt rather than accept Judaean law, while others nursed a grudge and desire for revolt, and Idumaeans would remain recognizably distinct in the following centuries[54]—Josephus like Ammonius describes the conquest and shift of corporate identity in the terms of classical discourse.

Before we discuss the final example of a conversion that has seemed to require a new religious turn, let us recall some relevant classical models, which do not come up in these discussions but which might throw valuable light on the possibilities of the classical paradigm, especially in Josephus' featured Adiabenian story.

δὲ τὸ μὲν ἀρχῆθεν οὐκ ['Ιδουμαῖοι] ἀλλὰ Φοίνικες καὶ Σύροι, κρατηθέντες δὲ ὑπ' αὐτῶν καὶ ἀναγκασθέντες περιτέμνεσθαι καὶ συντελεῖν εἰς τὸ ἔθνος καὶ τὰ αὐτὰ νόμιμα ἡγεῖσθαι ἐκλήθησαν Ἰδουμαῖοι. The Teubner edition reads *Idumaeans* at the end, following the logic we saw above: Idumaeans did not begin as such, unlike the Judaeans, who did (Nickau 1966).

54. See *HJW* 233, 263, 461–63.

Whereas the Idumaeans were forced either to adopt Judaean ways or to leave their territory, in the passage from Cassius Dio that opened this section he describes others who voluntary emulate Judaean law. He continues to use the customary language. Having remarked that (Syria-) *Palaestina* also acquired the name *Judaea* as its people were *Judaeans* (above), he continues immediately (37.17.1):

> Just when this [Judaean] designation came into use I do not know, but it holds also for other persons, all those *who emulate* (*zēloō*) *their legal precepts, though being of another ethnos* (καίπερ ἀλλοεθνεῖς ὄντες). This kind [or class, τὸ γένος τοῦτο] is found even among the Romans. Although suppressed many times it has grown still larger, such that they have pushed their way through to the open expression of those customs (ἐς παρρησίαν τῆς νομίσεως ἐκνικῆσαι).[55]

Members of other *ethnē* who adopt foreign ways can thus be considered members of the new *ethnos*, though perhaps also remaining bad examples of their native group. Dio's verb "emulate" (*zēloō*) and cognates, characteristically used of students' desire to be like their professors (a uniquely ancient phenomenon), turn up in various texts where members of one *ethnos* or *polis* fancy the laws and customs of another.[56] The Seven Sages mentioned by Plato's Socrates furnished a model. Hailing from various *poleis* and *ethnē*, they were nevertheless "all emulators (*zēlōtai*), lovers, and students of the Spartan culture."[57] Plato distinguishes their philosophical interest in Sparta, however, from that of the general mob, who are merely impressed by Spartan muscles and athletic training.

Josephus uses the verb *zēloō* several times in describing the desire of foreigners to embrace Judaean laws.[58] In *Apion* 2.261-275 he gives a list of *poleis* and *ethnē* that have punished those who show disloyalty to their own laws and/or follow those of others, while insisting that Judaeans themselves (a) do not emulate (*zēloō*) the ways of others but (b) magnanimously welcome those who wish to share theirs, unlike other famously exclusivist *poleis* and *ethnē* (2.261). Dio will later claim, according to his abridger, that

---

55. Or "opinion, belief." LSJ gives only these definitions with a note that νόμισις is cognate to νομίζω. But Dio otherwise consistently uses use the word for "custom, usage" (8.36.21; 38.13.5; 53.18.1; 59.9.2), and the same translation works better here.

56. Cf. Ptolemy, *Diff. voc.* "ζῆλος": ζῆλος μίμησις καλοῦ, οἷον ζηλοῖ τὸν καθηγητὴν ὁ παῖς.

57. Plato, *Prot.* 343a: ζηλωταὶ καὶ ἐρασταὶ καὶ μαθηταὶ . . . τῆς Λακεδαιμονίων παιδείας.

58. *War* 7.357; *Ant.* 20.41; *Apion* 1.166, 225; 2.261, 273, 280, 282, 285-286.

because Judaeans in Rome were "bringing over large numbers of the locals to their own customs" in A.D. 19, Tiberius drove most of them out of that city (57.18.5a).

Narrating events of the same year, Suetonius describes Tiberius' ban of foreign (*externa*) cults and rites. This targeted Judaeans and Egyptians together, because both *foreign groups* were enticing Romans to neglect their own ancestral traditions.[59] Josephus pairs Judaeans and Egyptians in a different way, describing one as committing cultic and the other ethno-political offences, and suffering different punishments as a result (*Ant.* 18.65). An elite Roman woman who has become a devotee of Egypt's Isis (θεραπείᾳ τῆς Ἴσιδος σφόδρα ὑπηγμένην, 18.70) is violated by a lusting and scheming equestrian, who enlists money-grubbing Roman priests of Isis for his deception. This provokes Tiberius to destroy that temple of Isis and crucify its priests (18.66-80).

The other woman "had come over to the Judaean laws/customs" (νομίμοις προσεληλυθυῖαν τοῖς Ἰουδαϊκοῖς, 18.82). Taking advantage of her sincere effort to support the Judaean homeland financially, four unscrupulous Judaeans residing in Rome defraud the woman (18.81-84). Their crimes cause the whole expatriate community to be expelled, 4,000 of the men being sentenced to hard labor. Josephus continues immediately by saying that the Samarian *ethnos* (τὸ Σαμαρέων ἔθνος) did not escape calamities at this time either (18.85). His whole story depends on the classical ethnographic model, according to which each *ethnos* has its own defining place of origin (*metropolis, patris*), where they truly belong; as minority communities elsewhere they remain vulnerable. The Judaean sympathizer or convert wants to support the foreign homeland (itself permitted by special exemption), and the Judaean community is expelled as a foreign problem.

By Claudius' time, according to Dio's epitome, Rome's Judaean population had grown too numerous to be expelled and could only be prohibited from assembling (60.6.6). Later in his narrative, elite Romans are accused by Domitian and his agents of "drifting into Judaean customs," an activity deemed punishable by death because it is construed as treason against Rome (67.14.2; cf. 68.1.2). These are not distinctively *religious* matters; they have to do with *polis*- and *ethnos*-loyalty.

As we have seen, Graeco-Roman authors were scandalized by the prospect of abandoning one's own laws and customs for those of another people, though attraction to old Sparta was a forgivable exception. To forsake one's

---

59. Suetonius, *Tib.* 36.1: *Externas caerimonias, Aegyptios Iudaicosque ritus compescuit.*

most basic loyalties was a betrayal of kin and clan, a deep insult to the community. Herodotus observes (3.38):

> If someone could somehow design an experiment, directing all humans to choose the finest customs from all [known] customs, even after making a careful examination each would choose their own. To such a degree do they consider their own customs to be the finest.

He makes these observations while claiming that the Persian Cambyses was mad. For that king showed contempt for the sacred customs of *both* Persians and their allies: opening graves in Egypt, mocking the cult statue of a god, and entering spaces permitted only to priests (3.37).

Herodotus also tells the story of eminent Scythians who were murdered by compatriots for adopting foreign ways (4.76–80). Anacharsis was of royal blood, though an exotic noble savage in lifestyle. He wandered off to Greece in search of wisdom and the best legal system. His story became paradigmatic, as we see in Josephus' mention of it in the list mentioned above (*Apion* 2.269) and the Syrian Lucian's fascination with it, centuries after Herodotus.[60] After becoming a close friend of the lawgiver Solon, Anacharsis attained citizenship in the *polis* of Athens as well as induction into Attica's cult of Demeter (Lucian, *Scyth.* 8). He had been anticipated by another Scythian named Toxaris, a physician, whom Athens' leading men had warmly received among them (*Scyth.* 4). The king thus declares himself the student and disciple (μαθητής ... καὶ ζηλωτής) of the physician, from his longing to learn Athenian laws and culture.

On his return home, however, Anacharsis is shot down by an arrow, possibly by his royal brother in an honor killing. Here are shades of the Bible's Phineas, who shot the Israelite Zimri along with his Midianite wife for violations of native law (Num 25:6–13). Anacharsis' crime, for which his name would thereafter be banished from Scythia, was that "he deserted his people for Greece and *took up with foreign customs*" (Lucian: ξεινικοῖσι ἔθεσι διεχρήσατο; cf. Herodotus 4.76, 78: διὰ ξεινικά τε νόμαια). The story of Anarchasis was well known through the following millennium, and cited often.[61] Josephus' use of Anacharsis as someone executed for having seemed fully infected by the customs of the Greeks (*Apion* 2.269), where he is comparing attitudes toward foreigners among various *ethnē*—Spartans and Athenians

---

60. Lucian wrote one piece on *The Scythian*, cited here, and named others on cultural interaction after *Anacharsis* and *Toxaris*.

61. Other accounts of Anacharsis include Plutarch, *Banquet of the Seven Sages*; Lucian, *Anacharsis* (a sharp dialogue between Anacharsis and Solon) and *The Scythian*; Diogenes Laertius 1.101–105.

in relation to Socrates or Anaxagoras—confirms that he is communicating within the shared discourse.

Anacharsis' fate was similar to that of the Scythian king Scylēs. According to Herodotus, whenever Scylēs was safely out of the view of his own people he would put on Greek dress and follow the Greek way of life (ἐχρᾶτο διαίτῃ Ἑλληνικῇ; Herodotus 4.78). One time he let his guard down, however. After being seen reveling among a local group of Bacchants, he lost his head as punishment. Herodotus recognizes a universal demand for *ethnos*-loyalty but considers the Scythians extreme: "This is how the Scythians protect their own customs, and the kind of retribution they visit on those who bring in foreign laws" (4.80).

Ethnē and *poleis* were expected to be justifiably displeased at defection or disloyalty. The Spartan general Pausanias was condemned for his "contempt for the laws [of his native Sparta] and emulation (*zēlōsis*) of the barbarians [Persians], . . . all the occasions on which he had in any way *departed from the prevailing customs*" (Thucydides 1.132.1-2). When Tacitus complains that Judaeans of his time owe their strength to the fact that the worst of other peoples, having abandoned *their ancestral devotions*, bring gifts and contributions to the foreigners, he seems to be operating in the same social-political field. Those who go over to Judaean customs (*transgressi in morem euroum*) learn quickly to despise the gods, he scorns, to disown their own homeland, and to devalue their own parents, children, and brothers (*Hist.* 5.5). It is a comprehensive abandonment of one's natural and organic bonds. Tacitus' description is rightly described as an *ethnographical* excursus.[62] Its comparison of Judaeans with Egyptians confirms that such movements across *poleis* and *ethnē*, even if scandalous, could be accommodated by the paradigm. Scandal arose precisely from the established discourse of loyalty to *ethnos* and *polis*.

Perhaps the sharpest statement on the subject comes a few decades after Tacitus in fragments of the philosopher Celsus' *On the True Word/Teaching* that are preserved by the prolific Christian writer Origen. Celsus considers the laws and customs of various Greek *ethnē* superior to those of the Judaeans, but fully respects the Judaean laws for being ancient and grounded in a famous place (*C. Cels.* 5.25, further below). He is offended, however, at the adoption of Judaean laws by others (5.41):

> Certainly if the Judaeans protect their own law, in accord with these principles, they have no blame. It lies rather with those who have abandoned their own ways, professing those of the Judaeans. If, as though they now prided themselves on

62. Bloch 2002.

wiser understanding, they reject the fellowship of their peers as though they were not as pure . . . [they will find comparable piety among other *ethnē*: there is no need to join the Judaeans] . . . Nor is it the least bit probable that they [Judaeans] are in favor with God or are loved more than these other [*ethnē*], or that messengers are sent to them alone, or that they had received some *chōra* [i.e., Judaea] of the blessed. For we can see very well who they are, and what sort of *chōra* they were thought worthy of [i.e., post-70 and post-135]. Let this chorus [of Judaizers] vanish, then, after paying the penalty of their boasting. For they do not know the great God [i.e., the Ultimate behind all local expressions], but have been lured and cheated by Moses' deceptiveness, and become its student for no good end.

For Celsus there is no point devoting oneself to foreign ways, and abandoning one's own for that purpose, because all regional laws and traditions are locally conditioned, by the *ethnos*' place and experience, and far from the ultimate truth that a philosopher seeks behind any such tradition.

Judaean authors use the same categories and make the same basic assumptions, advocating steadfast loyalty to one's own customs and respect for others (Josephus, *Ant.* 16.176–178). They lament or excoriate compatriots who have abandoned their ancestral traditions.[63] Josephus' Joshua thus gives a speech to his army, admonishing them to remain observant of the laws that will maintain God's alliance, for "if you turn aside to emulation of the laws of different *ethnē* he will turn away from your *genos*."[64] The crucial difference is that Judaeans do not see their laws as merely another local instance, but as closely reflecting the law of nature itself and ultimate truth. That is why, to Celsus' chagrin, they welcome foreigners willing to risk the enormous hazards required to embrace their laws and customs. For Philo, the Judeans are a new *ethnos* whose lawgiver Moses gave them a constitution (*Mos.* 1.34):[65] "The Judaeans were foreigners (*xenoi*), as I said before, the founders of the *ethnos*—on account of famine, through lack of food— having migrated to Egypt from Babylon and the upper satrapies." Precisely

---

63. E.g., *War* 7.47–53 (Antiochus of Antioch); *Ant.* 20.100 (Tiberius Alexander of Alexandria), 143 (Drusilla, sister of Agrippa II), 146 (Polemon, who briefly married Berenice—though she is blamed for the contrivance and dirty motives).

64. Josephus, *Ant.* 5.98: ἐκτραπέντων δὲ εἰς ἑτέρων ἐθνῶν μίμησιν ἀποστραφησομένου τὸ γένος ὑμῶν.

65. E.g., Philo, *Mos.* 1.1, 7, 34; *Decal.* 97; *Spec.* 2.163, 166; 4.179, 224; *Virt.* 108, 212, 226; *Prob.* 43, 57, 68, 75. Cf. in general support see Birnbaum 1996: 50–58, though she speaks of Judaism and Jews.

as an *ethnos*, the *Judaeans* of Alexandria are in constant tension with other residents of the *polis* over civic status (Chapter 2).⁶⁶

Philo's treatment of what we call *religious conversion* operates within the same *ethnos-polis* framework (*Virt.* 102–103):

> Having *legislated* for fellow-members of the *ethnos*, he [Moses] holds that newcomers must be deemed worthy of every privilege, because they have left behind *blood-affiliation, homeland, customs, sacred rites and temples of the gods, the gifts and honors too*, having undertaken *a noble transfer* (γενεὰν μὲν τὴν ἀφ' αἵματος καὶ πατρίδα καὶ ἔθη καὶ ἱερὰ καὶ ἀφιδρύματα θεῶν γέρα τε καὶ τιμὰς ἀπολελοιπότας καλὴν δ' ἀποικίαν στειλαμένους) ... He directs those of the [Judaean] *ethnos* to love the newcomers, not only as friends and relatives, but as themselves in body and soul.⁶⁷

3. *The Adiabenians.* With this background in view, we return finally to Josephus' detailed account of how the royal family of Adiabene (in modern Kurdistan, Iraq) came to embrace Judaean law and life, the moral high point of *Antiquities*' final volume (*Ant.* 20.17–96). James Dunn agrees with Cohen and Schwartz that only the "shift to a more religious significance made it possible for the idea of non-Judaeans becoming Jews, as in the famous case of Izates, king of Adiabene."⁶⁸ But it is difficult to see much difference between Josephus' story and the famous accounts of the Scythians mentioned above, or the other mentions of attraction to and emulation of (*zēloō*) the laws of another polity. In all of these cases we are dealing with elites of one *ethnos* becoming so enamored of another that they identify with it, endangering their lives under a cloud of perceived betrayal.

Some readers may have had the privilege I have had of exploring the tomb complex of the Adiabenian royal family in Jerusalem. These tombs are not in northern Iraq, as one might expect if the Adiabenians had undergone a mere change of outlook or values (or "religion"), but a few hundred yards northeast of Jerusalem's Old City. The family fully joined the Judaean *ethnos* and identified with them in their mother-*polis*.

Izates reportedly adopted Judaean law when he saw his mother Queen Helena "taking utter joy in the customs of the Judaeans" (τοῖς 'Ιουδαίων

---

66. Cf. Philo, *Flacc.* 1, 21, 43, 191; *Leg.* 117, 170, 178, 194, 210.

67. I cannot follow Cohen here (1999: 130): "Philo clearly describes conversion in theological terms."

68. Dušek 2003: 263; cf. Cohen 1999: 78–81; Schwartz (2007: 14): "a long account of King Izates of Adiabene who converted—to what? ... Given the way we use English, could we possibly say he wanted to become fully, stably, a Judaean?"

ἔθεσιν; *Ant.* 20.38). When he resolved to undergo circumcision, the famous Judaean-male ethnic marker (Gen. 17:10-14), his mother tried to prevent him—on the ground that the Adiabenian people would not accept a king who embraced *foreign and alien customs* (ξένων . . . καὶ ἀλλοτρίων αὐτοῖς ἐθῶν; 20.39; 20.47). Izates' Judaean advisor also saw the danger and counseled that, given the danger to his life, the prince could avoid circumcision "if indeed he resolved to emulate (*zēloō*) completely the *ancestral ways* of the Judaeans (τὸ θεῖον σέβειν εἴγε πάντως κέκρικε ζηλοῦν τὰ πάτρια τῶν Ἰουδαίων)." All this is described in the standard language of inter-ethnic attraction—and defection (20.41-42).

Izates persevered. Rather than merely emulating the foreign customs, he actually became a Judaean by undergoing circumcision. There is nothing new or religious about Josephus' language here. Izates' older brother Monobazus II, who would be king at the time of the Judaean War a generation later, joined his relatives and together they "abandoned their *ancestral traditions* to embrace the *customs of the Judaeans*" (τὰ πάτρια καταλιπόντες, ἔθεσι χρῆσθαι τοῖς Ἰουδαίων; 20.75). In keeping with their new affiliation, both princes sent their sons to be educated in Jerusalem (20.71). Some of them would assume leading roles in the war, demonstrating their complete identification with Jerusalem. Queen Helena herself visited the Judaean *mētropolis*, constructed a beautiful palace there, and donated money to alleviate famine. Indeed she would be buried in Jerusalem with other members of the family (20.49-53, 95).[69] Still another royal Adiabenian, named Graptē, also maintained a palace in Jerusalem (*War* 4.567). These activities all have to do with concrete *ethnos-polis* affiliation.

The Adiabenians' adoption of Judaean law fits not only general ancient discourse, but also the biblical tradition made famous by Ruth, the Moabite, when she joined the people of Israel: "Your people will be my people and your God my God. Where you die I will die, and there I will be buried" (Ruth 1:16-17). The Adiabenians offer a clear example of such re-affiliation—something like new citizenship in our world.

All Josephus' descriptions of what we call conversions make the best sense, it seems to me, within the same paradigm and on the familiar assumptions. A revealing tic throughout his corpus is Josephus' use of Greek *par' hēmin* ("with/among us") to highlight what is characteristic of Judaean customs in relation to others, a phrase that incidentally highlights the generic nature of the categories.[70] One third of the occurrences fall in the

69. Her sarcophagus, most scholars agree, now reposes in the Louvre in Paris.

70. He uses the phrase 50 times, most often in strategic places such as prologues and epilogues: *War* 1.6; *Ant.* 1.5, 9, 11; 3.172, 248, 318, 320; 20.198, 264; *Life* 1, 7, 10; *Apion* 1.1.

brief *Against Apion*, which might be considered an essay in comparative ethnography. It programmatically sets Judaean laws and customs alongside those of other peoples. Josephus contrasts Judaean and Egyptian traditions with the greatest energy because Egypt is home to the fiercest critics of the Judaeans. The world's alleged emulation of Judaean laws has been for the good, he offers, whereas a comparable enthusiasm for Egyptian ways would have been disastrous (*Apion* 2.139, 279-295).

Against a key target, Apion, Josephus turns a classic statement of ethnic loyalty: "It is the duty of thoughtful men to devote themselves to the scrupulous maintenance of their domestic laws in relation to piety, and not to malign those of others"—before accusing Apion of failing on *both* sides: disloyalty to his own and slander of others' (2.144). Similarly in 2.237: "Now I have no intention of making an examination of others' customs/ ordinances. It is our tradition to the maintain our own, and not to denigrate those of aliens." His whole discussion assumes the inter-ethnic discourse that is broadly familiar from Herodotus through Strabo, Plutarch, Lucian, Dio, and Julian.

Whereas Judaean communities everywhere fit the model of an *ethnos* with a great mother-*polis* and sacrificial cult, the people with an urgent interest in dismantling that paradigm were, I have proposed, the early Christians. Their need was clear. Although they had come from some *ethnos* and usually a *polis*—Thessalonica Corinth, Rome—they did not, as Christians, constitute an *ethnos*. They lacked a place of origin, a *polis*, sacrificial cult, temples, altars, priests, and sacrifices. In opting to follow Christ, depending on their teacher and sub-group, they often found themselves radically at odds with *polis* and *ethnos* loyalties, unwilling any longer to participate fully in public duties, festivals, sacrifices, and entertainments, and rather in peril as bad citizens.

For some Christians, having no established place in the world did not matter greatly, if they believed that "this age" was rapidly ending and there was no time for entanglement in it.[71] What were such Christ-followers, in the categories of the ancient paradigm? They were inescapably a voluntary association (previous chapter), but a fairly new one that was liable to be misunderstood and vulnerable to local harassment.[72] Other Christ-followers through the first three centuries advocated cleaving to the Judaean commu-

---

71. The Pauline-Marcan trajectory is most noticeable here. See 1 Thess 1:10; 4:13-18; 5:3-11, 23; 1 Cor 1:18-25; 2:6-16; 7:26-31; 15:35-57; Mark 9:1; 13:2-37.

72. See Pliny's puzzlement about Christians in Bithynia-Pontus, which does not deter him from harsh punishment, and the emperor Trajan's response ca. A.D. 110 (*Ep.* 10.96-97). Cf. the *polis* harassment experienced by the itinerant Paul, perhaps in Ephesus (Phil 1:12-14).

nities of the eastern Mediterranean, citing as warrants the Judaean context of Jesus and his first students.[73] Others tried to identify with the prestige of philosophical schools, seeing Jesus as founding moral philosopher. This also made some sense in view of the Christians' quasi-philosophical (even utopian) discipline of life in certain respects, but the disdain of other philosophers for such a "faith" impaired this appeal.[74]

When the Christians finally had sufficient unity of organization, numbers, and security from long existence in various places, and had leaders with the requisite education and social standing, they began gradually to rework the classical paradigm in the direction of categories and assumptions more congenial to their views of the world. The single most important figure in this creative process was the erudite Tertullian, who wrote in Carthage, North Africa, from the end of the second century A.D. Although Tertullian borrowed much from his classical education, he was clear about his program. He recognized that Christians were vulnerable precisely from those who saw themselves as "protectors and preservers of laws and ancestral usages" (*Apol.* 6.1), and that they were not considered Romans because they rejected Roman sacrificial cult, which was embedded in society (24.9). He is clear in response about Christian views:

> So this is what our project is against: it is against the arrangements made by the ancestors, authoritative opinions [or models] passively received, the laws of those in power, and the reasonings of the wise; it is against antiquity, custom, coercion; it is against precedents, marvels, and wonders—all of which conspired to create your [non-Christian] corrupt view of the Deity.[75]

He is, in other words, rejecting the norms of the *ethnos-polis* paradigm, which have been so injurious to Christians, who found no place among them. This is not to say that it never occurred to Christian authors

---

73. This direction is found among our earliest texts: Paul's opponents in Philippi (Phil 3:2–21) and Galatia (e.g., 2:14; 3:1—5:12); Matt 5:17–20; the opponents of Ignatius (*Magn.* 8.1; 10.3; *Phil.* 6.1); the pseud-Clementines; *Gospel of the Hebrews*; the Ebionite movement among others in Eusebius (*Hist. eccl.* 3.27; 6.17); and John Chrysostom's anti-Judaean sermons in fourth-century Antioch.

74. The idea that Jesus founded a philosophical school appears in Justin Martyr (e.g., *Apol.* 2.1–2; 3.2–3; 4.8; 7.3; 2 *Apol.* 3.2, 6; 15.2; *Dial.* 1.1–6) and some later apologists. This tendency may be found already in the hypothetical sayings-source Q, a lost early version of Coptic *Thomas*, and Paul's opponents in Corinth (1 Cor 4:8–12). It may go back to aspects of Jesus' own self-presentation, as a teacher among his students.

75. *Ad nat.* 2.1.7: Aduersus haec igitur nobis negotium est: aduersus institutiones maiorum, auctoritates receptorum, leges dominantium, argumentationes prudentium; aduersus uetustatem, consuetudinem, necessitatem; aduersus exempla, prodigia, miracula, quae omnia adulterinam istam diuinitatem [istam] corroborauerunt.

to try out, suggest, or imply *ethnos* language (with anti-*ethnos* force) for Christ-followers.[76] But this kind of word-play or sermonizing made no impact on the common lexical bank, and Christian authors themselves did not pursue it.

The essential step for Tertullian and his constituency was to declare their hitherto anomalous group—defined by faith, belief, and creed—*normative*. Styling it *Christianismus* (above), Tertullian could reconfigure the cultures that had excluded Christians as competing and defective *-isms*. Following the lead of Paul, who had reduced all that was not Christ to "Greek" and "Judaean," a tendency elaborated by the apologists of the late second century, Tertullian and his many successors compressed these great civilizations into the capsules *pagan-ism* or *Hellenism* and *Juda-ism*, as though they were mere belief systems. In that form they could readily be measured against *Christianismus*, and on Christian terms found wanting for their supposedly inferior beliefs about God.[77] From Tertullian's time onward, notwithstanding the ever-more universal efforts to impede the spread of this faith, Christians grew in confidence and increasingly rejected their peripheral status. A century after Tertullian this fundamental shift would find concrete political expression as Constantine decided to sponsor and embrace Christianity.

As Christian-ish emperors took power from Constantine onward, they gave flesh to the new discourse by gradually but methodically eviscerating ancient *ethnos-polis* culture. They banned animal sacrifice and incrementally shut down public altars, temples, priesthoods, along with the most characteristic features of *polis* life connected with calendar, festivals, dramatic and sporting events.[78] Taking the place of these age-old forms were Christian values and structures, which were inherently trans-local, non-ethnic, and non-*polis*-based. Indeed the new structures leeched resources and vitality from the *poleis* in favor of rapidly expanding churches under regional (diocesan) hierarchies.[79] The growing Christian monastic movement enticed

76. See Johnson 2006 and the works cited in p. 184 n. 19 above.

77. See also Eusebius (Greek, early 4th century: *Praep. ev.* 1.5.12; *Dem. ev.* 1.2.1–2). Cf. Victorinus, *Comm. Gal.* 1.1.20; Filastrius of Brescia, *Div. haer.* 29.15–20.

78. After decades of partial legal moves in this direction, and widespread freelance attacks on temples by newly-favored Christian monks, Theodosius I banned the practice of traditional rituals in 391 and 392, closing the temples—animal sacrifice had already been proscribed—and excluding anyone who persevered in such practices from public office. See Bury 1958: 1.365–77 and the pithy take on Theodosius' motives in Gerald Bonner, "The Christianization of the Roman Empire: inspiration or warning for contemporary Christians?" in Ford, Destro, and Dechert 2005: 74–84.

79. On Late Antiquity as the crucial period of *polis* decline, see in general (with partly different emphasis) Hansen 2006: 48–50.

men who would formerly have constituted the *polis* elites away to solitary desert lives. Diocesan leaders found their prestige from status-criteria that bore no relation to the *polis*.[80]

Perhaps the clearest indication that Christianity's rise dissolved the *ethnos-polis*-cult paradigm is the career of the young emperor who bent every effort to halt and reverse that development. Julian (ruled A.D. 361–363), known as "the apostate" from the Christian perspective, had escaped the massacre of his family by Christian relatives and was not impressed by their ethical credentials or their philosophical ideas. He chose to target both the rational and the political foundations of the new order. A Platonist philosopher, among many other things, Julian wanted to restore that world in which Christians had no place, to force them back to the margins and irrelevance—or better, to proper *ethnos-* and *polis*-loyalty with some form of sacrificial cult.

Julian believed deeply in the old world of established *ethnē*, each with its characteristic laws and customs expressing its nature, realized in the life of the *polis* and centered in an ancestral regimen of animal sacrifice—the heart of the system.[81] His version of the classical paradigm was conditioned by the distinctive features of *neo*-Platonism of the third and fourth centuries, such as the notion that each *ethnos* was supervised by a tutelary god[82] and the mystical-magical practice of theurgy. He was also no doubt unconsciously affected by aspects of his Christian upbringing.[83] But still Julian saw himself as a traditionalist through and through, determined to recover the venerable ways of the ancient past that underlay classical society.

These views led Julian to see the Judaeans as fully part of the proper ancient scene, in spite of their peculiarities (C. *Gal.* 306b):

> The Judaeans agree with the [other] *ethnē*, except in supposing that there is only one God. That is their peculiar thing, alien to us, but *all other matters are in common with us: the sanctuaries, sacred spaces, sacrificial altars, purifications, and particular*

---

80. See Libanius, *Or.* 30 (*For the Temples*), a lament to the emperor Theodosius I about the decline of these crucial centers.

81. E.g., Julian, *C. Gal.* 176a–c. Like most anti-Christian writings or texts deemed heretical, Julian's work did not survive as such (because medieval monks did not copy it out). His *Against the Galileans* has to be reconstructed, chiefly from the rebuttal by the 5th-century Christian Patriarch of Alexandria, Cyril. The reference system I use is that of Spanheim's 1696 edition of Cyril, which was adopted by K. J. Neumann for his 1880 edition of Julian's reconstituted work and then taken over by Wilmer C. Wright in the Loeb edition and translation (1923).

82. For the tutelary deities over each *ethnos*, see *C. Gal.* 141c–d, 143a–b.

83. So Belayche 2002.

THE END OF THE CLASSICAL PARADIGM 215

observances, concerning which we [and the Judaeans] differ from one another *either not at all or only trivially.*

Evoking Aristotle, by contrast, Julian complained to a sympathetic priest of the old-fashioned *polis* kind about the condition of the *poleis* after decades of Christian inroads:

> There are some men who even pursue life in the deserts instead of the *poleis*, though the human is by nature a *polis*-based animal and civilized (ὄντος ἀνθρώπου φύσει πολιτικοῦ ζῴου καὶ ἡμέρου); they [Christians] have given themselves up to malign spirits, by whom they are led into the hatred of humanity (μισανθρωπία).[84]

Julian aimed to bring back the *status quo ante* as he understood it: restoring the *poleis* and their traditional sources of funding, requiring Christians to devote themselves loyally to *polis* life,[85] re-establishing the prestige of philosophy and rhetoric above church theology, and reconstituting the temples, altars, and animal sacrifices of the ancient *polis* and *chōra*.

It is telling that when Julian discussed the Judaeans, as far as we can tell from surviving fragments, he used neither the Christian construct *Ioudaismos* (*Judaism*) nor any conception of faith systems or "religions."[86] In keeping with his general outlook, he understood the *Ioudaioi* as an ancient *ethnos* comparable to other *ethnē*. He preferred "the *ethnos* of the Hebrews," perhaps to emphasize their antiquity.[87] He calls Christians, by contrast, *Galileans*, apparently to stress that being a Christ-follower gives one no place in the world. If they were to have an *ethnos*, it would be the inglorious one of their undistinguished Galilean founder.

Julian's *ethnos-polis* perspective led him to see the Judaeans as laboring under a huge liability, in having been deprived of their mother-*polis* and temple—the only place where they could follow their laws fully and offer public sacrifice in accord with ancestral law (*C. Gal.* 306a). From his Christian education, moreover, Julian understood the importance of their loss

---

84. Julian, *Ep.* 89b (= 288b), *Fragment of a Letter to a Priest*. The misanthropy charge had attached to Christians from the start, because of their withdrawal from full *polis* life. A similar accusation had been leveled at Judaeans for their perceived aloofness, and going against the Greek spirit of mutual respect. But they were an established *ethnos*; the charge against Christians, who opted out of the whole *polis* paradigm, was more concrete and more serious in the first two centuries of Christianity.

85. Cf. Ammianus Marcellinus 25.4.15 on Julian's measures.

86. For Julian on the Judaeans in particular, along with much insight into related issues, see Finkelstein 2011.

87. On ethnic diversity and comparison (largely unfavorable to Judaeans), see *C. Gal.* 116a–b, 131b–d, 168b–c, 171a, d–e, 176a–c, 184b–c, 198b; 99e for τὸ τῶν Ἑβραίων ἔθνος.

of Jerusalem for *Christians*, who presented it as incontrovertible proof of divine punishment and transfer of favor to Christians.[88] To undermine that theological edifice, he intended to rebuild the Judaean temple in Jerusalem, reinstate their sacrificial system, and reconstitute their *mētropolis*.[89] Doing so would restore the crucial components of the classical world. The discomfited Christians would then face a crystal-clear choice: either become upstanding citizens of their native (and superior) Greek *poleis*[90] or, if they were determined to follow an exclusivist barbarian culture, have the courage of their convictions and follow Judaean law: become Judaeans.[91]

Julian's untimely end while on military campaign in Persia meant that his vision never materialized, and the new Christian social-political lexicon would stand. Its novelty is clear from the fat lexicon of Christian Greek created as a necessary companion to the standard classical-Greek lexicon, which had excluded most Christian authors and with them distinctively Christian word use.[92] Although Christian authors were individuals who wrote in many styles and registers, their shared discourse featured Church and churches—reworking the *ekklesia* (assembly) of the *polis*—sin, (the) faith, the gospel, salvation, scripture, dogma, liturgy—reconfiguring public *polis* duties to church service—apostle, bishop, elder, diocese (*doikēsis*: originally household management), right-thinking or *orthodoxia* (all but exclusively in Christian authors), heresies, religions, and -isms. The fourth-century Latin Vulgate translation canonized such language, sometimes transliterating Greek words as technical Christian vocabulary (*Christus, apostolus, ekklesia, evangelium*). The lexicon grew steadily, as individual authors (since Paul) pushed Greek terms in new directions until eventually all members of the linguistic community—ultimately all members of Christianized society—understood the new significations.

This lexicon would continue to evolve through the mediaeval and early modern periods. With good reason, many or most scholars now see the generic category "religion"—as a voluntary identity-shaping association, grounded in a system of belief about divine-human relations and ritual practice, separable in principle from politics, business, art, entertainment,

---

88. Matt 22:1–7; 23:37–24:2; Luke 19:41–44. For gentile Christians as replacements grafted on the Judaean heritage see Paul in Romans chapters 9 to 11.

89. Julian, *Ep.* 51 (298a) and the fragment 295c. On this initiative in the context of Julian's life, see Theodoret, *Ecclesiastical History* 3.2–4, 15–22. For illuminating analysis see Bowersock 1978.

90. *C. Gal.* 42e–43b, 100e–106e, 194d–202a.

91. *C. Gal.* 49a–c, 96c–e, 253a–e, 305d, 314c–e, 319d–20c, 343c–58e.

92. Lampe 1961, supplementing Liddell, Scott, Jones 1990 (reprint of 9th ed., from the early 19th century).

and all other aspects of life—as a product of (roughly) the Age of Discovery, the western colonization of the East, and the Enlightenment.[93] Wilfred Cantwell Smith agreed, but long ago proposed that fourth-century Christians were on the verge of "an elaborate, comprehensive, philosophic concept of *religio*," which they did not pursue and so it lay dormant for a millennium until modernity.[94] Daniel Boyarin has argued that Christians did in fact create *religion*, to serve their needs, and finally forced the separation with Judaism because the rabbis refused to conform to the category.[95] Perhaps there is no need to decide between these positions. In the early third century Tertullian of Carthage had already pushed Latin *religio*, which he used 45 times in one modest essay, away from its vague and varied uses as solemn obligation, vow, or taboo to become a catch-all term for comparing Christian, Judaean-Jewish, and Roman *religion*, or even as a criterion ("true religion") for assessing each system.[96] Greek-speaking Christians continued to press *thrēskeia* (cultic worship), *eusebeia* (piety), and *theosebeia* (piety toward God) in the same way. So Boyarin is right, but so is Smith. For although Christian discourse came to pervade western society from the fourth century, sustained encounter with other "religions" had to await the modern period.

I have argued that the pre-Christian classical paradigm had no need or place for Egyptism, Romism, Samaritism, or Judaism, and that such categories were Christian creations. A work that appeared a decade after Julian's death, by the Judaean-born bishop of Salamis (Cyprus), Epiphanius, appears to confirm this. His little guide for Christians who wished to be "Well-Anchored" reduces the world's cultures to eighty barren and decrepit intellectual systems (*Ancoratus* 12.7–9):

> Of these there are five 'mothers', namely: Barbarism, Scythism, Hellenism, Judaism, and Samaritism (Βαρβαρισμὸς Σκυθισμὸς

93. E.g., Harrison 1990, Asad 1993, Smith 1998: 269, Masuzawa 2005, Josephson 2012, Nongbri 2013; cf. Barton and Boyarin 2016 on the absence of ancient religion.
94. Smith 1963: 28.
95. Boyarin 2004: 202–25.
96. Tertullian, *Apol.* 6.1, 9; 9.5; 13.1, 6; 14.5; 15.4; 16.2–3 (Judaean religion, to which Christians may be presumed to be close), 6, 8 (Roman religion), 13 ("our religion"); 19.1; 21.1 (*Iudaei* have a very famous religion, *insignissimae religionis*); 21.27, 29; 24.1–2, 6, 9 ("We alone are forbidden a religion of our own"); 25.2, 12–17; 28.3; 29.5; 33.1 (Christians are full of *religio*, religious awe, toward the emperor); 34.3; 35.5, 8 (Roman *religio*: Christians are charged with not celebrating holidays / festivals of Caesar); 36.1; 39.1 ("We are a society with a shared sense of religion, unity of life-regimen, and common hope"; *corpus sumus de conscientia religionis et disciplinae unitate et spei foedere*), 5 (Christian religion), 17 ("duty of religion" as criterion); 42.8 (Roman religion). Cf. *Spec.* 1 for the criterion.

Ἑλληνισμὸς Ἰουδαϊσμὸς Σαμαρειτισμός). Of these, four systems [or schools, factions: αἱρέσεις] come from Hellenism: Pythagoreans, Platonists, Stoics, and Epicureans. Of those [that came] after the Law and before Christ's coming in the flesh, there are eleven. Seven are from the Judaeans—Scribes, Pharisees, Sadducees, Ossaeans, Nasarenes, Daily-dunkers [Hemerobaptists], and Herodians—while four are from the Samaritans: Gorothenes, Sebouaeans, Essenes, and Dositheans. Since the [giving of the] Law, then, eleven factions have grown out of the Judaeans and Samaritans together.

With such a systematic heresy-chart based on mother *-isms* and their derivatives (no longer flourishing mother-*poleis*), the classical model was broken through. There was no longer a place for the vibrant cultures that had once fascinated Herodotus, Strabo, and Pliny, each belonging to an *ethnos*, most centered in a *polis* and maintaining a sacrificial cult. Judaean civilization had been replaced by a Juda-ism.

Conclusions: Withdrawals and Deposits at the Ancient Lexical Bank

In this chapter and the preceding one, I have tried to show that the ancient world knew an already ancient and flourishing Judaean culture, with a renowned mother-*polis* and colonies of long standing in many other Mediterranean *poleis*. Speaking of *Judaeans* this way, in continuity with the Israel and Yahud of the preceding centuries, should not be seen as injurious to Jewish tradition. This kind of analysis has worried some scholars because calling ancient Jews "Judaeans" might seem to remove "Jews" from the ancient world.[97] Others find in the distinction between Judaeans as an *ethnos-polis*-cult and Christians lacking these a potential revival of Marcion, F. C. Baur, or Adolf von Harnack, who exalted what they saw as transcendent and spiritual Christian universalism over a *merely* local, physical, or racial Judaism.[98] I hope that the foregoing investigation has obviated both kinds of postulated consequence. In case any shred of doubt lingers, let me respond explicitly to each.

First, this is a historical exploration of Jews, the community that has followed the Torah of Moses from antiquity until now, in the Graeco-Roman period. My argument that the ancient Greek and Latin terms that evolved into English "Jew" (*Ioudaios* / *Iudaeus*) had connotations fitting their times,

97. Reinhartz 2014.
98. Horrell 2016: 4404–43 for an overview and sharp statement of the charge.

THE END OF THE CLASSICAL PARADIGM 219

in the ancient lexical bank, could not possibly be understood to remove Jews from the ancient world. That would stand everything I have argued on its head and pull it inside-out.

Second, what is physical or spiritual in religion is not my concern; all the terms and their possible oppositions elude me. It should be clear by now, however, that ancient Judaean authors who wrote in Greek participated fully in the shared, public discourse of their time. In this they differed dramatically from their Christian contemporaries, who appeared to outsiders a strange, obscurantist, inward group. The second-century philosopher Celsus captures well, with neo-Platonist spice, the contrast between Judaeans and Christians from the perspective of common categories (in Origen, *C. Cels.* 5.25):

> The *Ioudaioi*, having become a unique *ethnos* [i.e., after leaving Egypt], enacted laws in keeping with their local conditions, and protect them until even now. In preserving their way of worship—which, whatever its actual form, is ancestral—they act *just like other people*: each deals with its ancestral ways, no matter what kind happen to have been established.[99] ... and it is not pious to dissolve what has become customary/legal in each place from the beginning.

This leaves Christians in a perplexing and anomalous position, as Origen summarizes Celsus' view. They cannot clarify their "ancestral laws" or their originator, because they have completely defected from the Judaeans (5.33). The Christians' own ideas, about Christ's awaited return from heaven to roast "like a cook" everyone on earth except these few believers, hardly deserves respect (5.14). It is an arrogant and ignorant view (5.51,65). In short (5.35):

> All people ought to live according to their ancestral ways, and are never blamed for this. But the Christians have abandoned their ancestral ways. And since they are not[100] a distinct *ethnos* like the Judaeans, associating themselves with the teaching of [the Judaean] Jesus *is* blameworthy.

Given the long and sordid history of Christian characterizations and repressions of Jews, these concerns about possible Christian manipulation of the differences between Judaean culture and Christ-following deserve a full

99. Ἰουδαῖοι μὲν οὖν ἔθνος ἴδιον γενόμενοι καὶ κατὰ τὸ ἐπιχώριον νόμους θέμενοι καὶ τούτους ἐν σφίσιν ἔτι νῦν περιστέλλοντες καὶ θρησκείαν ὁποίαν δή, πάτριον δ' οὖν, φυλάσσοντες ὅμοια τοῖς ἄλλοις ἀνθρώποις δρῶσιν, ὅτι ἕκαστοι τὰ πάτρια, ὁποῖά ποτ' ἂν τύχῃ καθεστηκότα, περιέπουσι. . . παραλύειν δὲ οὐχ ὅσιον εἶναι τὰ ἐξ ἀρχῆς κατὰ τόπους νενομισμένα.

100. Origen, summarizing defensively, says "they happen not to be..."

hearing. But it was Tertullian and Origen who tried to turn the Christian predicament to a virtue. Here we are trying to understand not their theological maneuvers but the general shared discourse, in which the Judaeans and not the Christians were fully at home. The greater risk to historical understanding, in my view, comes in retrojecting Christian categories into classical discourse. Imagining Judaism and Christianity as two religions runs the serious risk of skewing academic discussion toward the supposed nature of Jewish religion (Legal? Protected? Legalistic? Missionary? Many Judaisms or one?) or of abstracting elements in Judaean texts that lend themselves to comparison with Christianity: theology, soteriology, messianism, eschatology.

These tendencies drain the vitality from living Judaean civilization in all of its dimensions—politics, hereditary aristocracy, economics, local and distant trade, temple functions, relations with local *poleis*, relations with Judaeans abroad, accommodations for Judaean and non-Judaean visitors. This chapter is an effort to help students, in particular, break free of that traditional framework, to think new thoughts about the ways in which Judaeans actually lived among their contemporaries and appeared to them. Perhaps the most important thing to say here is that I may be wrong. Other scholars of good will disagree. Students may at least read, compare, and choose the best course for their needs.[101]

In venturing a glance over the complex events of later centuries I am simplifying greatly, perhaps unforgivably in the eyes of some specialists. I dare to do so, again, in order to emphasize that the overthrow of the classical paradigm came only with the ascent of Christianity, which had clear motives for such a change and demonstrably effected it. Before the rise of Christianity there was no perceptible need, in spite of such dramatically changing circumstances as the destruction of Jerusalem and (temporary-seeming?) loss of the temple, for such distinct categories as *religion* or *Judaism*. Both Judaean authors and non-Christian observers continued to communicate in the same way, about this ancient *ethnos* with its laws and customs— even when the Judaean *mētropolis* had been destroyed for a time and the sacrificial cult was suspended.

101. D. R. Schwartz (2007: 5–6) finds the use of "Judaean" in modern Christian-theological contexts nobly motivated, insofar as it seeks to deprive hatred of Jews (e.g., as children of Satan in the Gospel of John) of canonical warrant, but thinks that *historical* principles nonetheless recommend "Jews." Translating the NT *Ioudaioi* as Judaeans, however, has usually gone with an assumption that there *were* Jews at the time, but these canonical strictures were not against them. Without exploring the in-house invective of early Christian authors, or trying to remedy its effects today by translation, I have simply argued that Judaeans were a populous, widespread, and well-known *ethnos* of antiquity with an ancient civilization admired by many. Their thriving existence was always a problem for Christians who would not Judaize.

7

Geography: The World, the Homeland, the Mother-*Polis*

In this chapter we turn to the physical geography of Judaea and Jerusalem in the context of the ancient mapping of peoples and their places. Before discussing Judaea, we need to reconsider our own profound mapping instincts in critical-historical perspective.

Did the Romans Depend on Maps, or Have a Map Complex?

In the nineteenth and twentieth centuries, as modern maps became ever more faithful to earth's physical reality, scholars rejoiced that we in the modern west were finally able to study the Mediterranean world as the Greeks and Romans knew it. We had liberated ourselves from the colorful but rather cartoonish maps of the medieval and early modern periods. In the past century and more, ancient history has come to depend on good maps. Our books and lecture halls are filled with them. I cannot get enough of them, and they fill a good proportion of my shelf and disk space. How exciting they are! Instead of trying to follow in our minds the numbing references to cities, rivers, mountains, and valleys by Polybius, Pliny, or Josephus, we can study the terrain and put ourselves in the picture. A detailed map geared to ancient conditions, such as the magnificent *Barrington Atlas*,[1] can seem almost like a poor person's time machine. As Kai Brodersen puts it, using the past tense for a naïve view we have all inclined

---

1. Talbert 2000.

to share, "Mapping the Ancient World was considered inseparable from Mapping *in* the Ancient World."[2]

When we enquire into the Romans' view of their own world, we may be surprised to find scant evidence that they thought about maps in the way we do, and plenty of evidence that they did not and could not have done so. Appreciatively reviewing a book that assembled virtually all known evidence for Greek and Roman map use, Richard Talbert concluded "that the majority of Greeks and Romans had only the most limited use for maps." He elaborated:

> Once an empire-wide network of main roads was established by the Romans, their invention of 'strip' maps met all the practical needs of most long-distance travellers, who rode or drove just from one city to another. It was duly recognized that to go further and prepare accurate maps of wide expanses (let alone reproduce them) presented immense obstacles... Even so, such difficulties were hardly the decisive influence; it was the necessary attitude of mind that was missing. Seafarers, soldiers and historians concentrated upon written accounts, not maps, while even among so-called experts there was regularly complacent repetition of outdated, muddled or inadequate geographical information.[3]

His next paragraph explores the "general absence of a 'map consciousness' among Greeks and Romans."

Since around the time of Talbert's review, a growing company of scholars have been cautioning us about that warm feeling of "being there" we get when we examine accurate modern maps.[4] As Brodersen advises above, we need to make a distinction between the way we study the ancient world, with maps at almost any desired level of detail, and what was possible for residents of the Roman world.[5] However they saw their world, and without prejudging that question, it must have been different from the way we see ours, after Copernicus, modern exploration and cartography, aerial and satellite photography. Again, we need to be open to the challenges and surprises of investigating a culture that could never conceive of our dependence on maps, partly because they were not available.

2. On the old assumptions (with documentation) and the state of the recent discussion, see Brodersen 2004; the quotation is from p. 185.

3. Talbert 1987: 211.

4. E.g., Bekker-Nielsen 1988; Isaac 1992: 401–8; Mattern 1999: 41–87; Talbert (leading cartographer of the ancient world) 1990, 2010; Brodersen 1995, 2001; Whittaker 2004: 63–87; Talbert and Brodersen 2004.

5. Brodersen 2004.

To make the general point it is enough to read an ancient expert on geography. Pliny the Elder tirelessly researched his *Natural History* and wrote it up in Rome at about the same time that Josephus was composing his *Judaean War* there. Pliny attempts to describe the world in terms of seven parallels or circles of latitude. For each one he begins in the east, moving northward at intervals from the south of India to the Caspian Sea, listing major sites on the same latitude as he moves west. This might all sound tolerably modern—until we read his lists and try to imagine the mental picture that his description would create.

To begin with, he puts the south of India (about 10° north of the Equator, we know) on the same latitude as North Africa (30° N). On his second latitude, beginning from central India, are: central Parthia (Iran), Persepolis, Persis, Arabia, and then "Judaea and nearby Mt. Lebanon." This band also "encompasses Babylon, Idumaea, Samaria, Jerusalem, Ascalon, Ioppa [Jaffa], Caesarea, Phoenicia, Ptolemais, Sidon, Tyre, Berytus [Beirut], Botrys, Tripoli, Byblos, Antioch, Laodicea, Seleucia, coastal Cilicia..." (*Nat.* 6.213). From Ascalon onward, the list of sites on the coast of southern Syria actually heads *northward*, though maps until the nineteenth century put the Levant on a northeast line. My point is not that Pliny was a fool. Far from it. He used the best information available to him, in a project that he himself understood to be somewhat boring, but correct and valuable for serious men in the Roman tradition (*Nat.* pr. 13; 3.7).

In modern discussion of Romans and maps, as in other problems we have discussed, there is ample room for miscommunication. The question of what was technologically possible, in particular, has become intertwined with debatable larger issues connected with Roman conceptions of empire, frontiers, strategy, and much else.[6] A recurring question, in various guises, is whether they planned their empire, its administration, and military posture, or whether they mainly reacted to crises. If they had planned, did they work from a grand map? Those who favor an unplanned Rome tend to be more comfortable with an absence of maps or a map mentality.

Slippery terminology can derail communication. When Talbert denied a Graeco-Roman "map consciousness," he seems not to have meant—given that he was reviewing a book on ancient maps—that Greeks and Romans had never experienced any mapping instincts or made efforts at representation. Whatever they might have liked, they did not have usable maps and therefore could not seek them out or depend upon them. Brodersen, similarly,

---

6. See the studies mentioned in n. 4 for doubts, Scott and Greatrex below for more positive views. The larger debate about Roman strategy was framed largely by Luttwak 1976 (describing grand strategy) and Millar 1977 (no grand strategy).

was well aware of surviving ancient representations when he stated: "We simply lack the evidence for 'map consciousness' in the ancient world."[7]

But James M. Scott, after making the plausible case that a neglected epigram by one Philip of Thessalonica, describing a certain tapestry as "a precise depiction of as much of the harvest-bearing earth . . . as obeys Caesar,"[8] was a gift from King Agrippa I's wife Cyprus to Gaius Caligula, concludes that this *objet d'art* "would seem to indicate more 'map consciousness' than is often admitted."[9] Similarly, in arguing for the Romans' ability to formulate large-scale strategy in late antiquity, Geoffrey Greatrex concludes from "numerous references to maps" (about half a dozen, ranging over several centuries), that "it is at least plausible, if not highly probable, that the Romans *had access* to maps."[10] In such cases, scholars appear to be talking about different things while appearing to disagree.

If we are to get to the nub of this issue, we might restrict our question to the possibility of map *dependence* in Roman (or Judaean) political and military planning. Did the ancients act, or could they have acted, on the basis of *data* provided by visual images of their world? Today we unquestionably depend on precise and detailed maps, from for travel or hiking to international diplomacy, intelligence gathering, and military planning. But we can depend on maps only because we have them: accurate representations of all the world's regions, even of the ocean floor, at virtually any level of desired detail and including minute topographical indications above and below sea level. As long as these maps remain accurate (a road has not been closed, a harbor not destroyed by tsunami), we can map routes by land, air, or sea and anticipate the terrain through which we will cross—or would have crossed in antiquity if the terrain has remained stable. Did the ancients have anything like these data-providing maps to assist their planning? Did they desire them and conceive of the world in this spatially accurate way?

Let us return to Talbert's comment above. Modern thinking and expectation have naturally evolved over the centuries, in dialogue with the gradual development of mapping precision. Sitting in my study I have topographical maps, at a large enough scale for hiking, of every part of northern Israel. But did a Roman senator dispatched to Antioch as the emperor's legate, such as Cestius Gallus, have any such guide when he led an expedition to Jerusalem in the autumn of 66? Did the equestrian official in Caesarea,

---

7. Brodersen 2004: 185.

8. The epigram is in the *Greek Anthology* (9.778), a collection of short poems and sayings from classical through Byzantine times.

9. Scott 2002: 15.

10. Greatrex 2007: 135–36; emphasis mine.

such as Pontius Pilate or Gessius Florus, have anything comparable for the areas under their purview?

The answer is plainly *No*. Modern soldiers spend much time learning to navigate, with detailed contour maps and compasses. Knowing precisely where they are in relation to other tactical elements is a crucial part of their training. Did Roman legionaries have something similar? Again, no. Any of us can draw a schematic impression of the globe or our neighborhood or street. A few lines here or there will give an *impression*, enough to make a point or win an argument. That sort of thing was undoubtedly possible for ancient Romans, and it is a "map" in some sense. But lacking scale, accurate relationships, or completeness, it would have no value for the purposes we associate with maps.

This is not, again, to suggest that the ancients had no *curiosity* about the land they walked, that they did not speculate about what it might look like from above, or that they attempted no graphical representations. Herodotus relates that a ruler of Miletus (mod. western Turkey) named Aristagoras, who was itching to throw off Persian rule as the Ionian Revolt was taking shape (Chapter 1), travelled to Sparta to request the support of that famously martial *polis*. He took with him a bronze tablet or plate on which were engraved—there was no word for map—"the course [or route, march, circuit: *periodos*] of the whole earth and every sea and all the rivers" (5.49.1).

In his discussion with the Spartan king, Cleomenes I, Aristagoras uses this forerunner of Power Point to count off the *ethnē* situated between the Milesians and the Persian king, in Anatolia up to Syria. Downplaying the military capability of trouser-wearing, towel-headed easterners (5.49.3), he encourages his host to envision the bountiful lands that the Spartan army will liberate, which will make Cleomenes as rich as God (5.49.7). Cleomenes duly ponders the request for a couple of days. But when he asks how much real space is represented by the engraving, and how long it will take him to reach the Persian king from Ionian shores, the Milesian puts aside his spin and gives an honest answer: about three months. Cleomenes orders him to leave Sparta by sunset (5.50.2–3). Herodotus leaves no doubt about the deficiencies of Aristagoras' representation or about the potential for manipulation by a self-serving man, unlike the historian himself, who tells the truth about both the distances and the character of the Persians.[11] The geographical question, importantly, turns on the length and course of the royal road from Ionian Sardis to Persian Susa, suggesting that the Milesian's engraved representation consisted of lines representing routes (5.52–54).

---

11. See Branscome 2010 for the function of the episode in Herodotus.

Here we have some kind of visual representation of the earth, then, and one might say that it was used in military planning (or non-planning). But what use did it have by itself? Herodotus' vignette depends on the novelty of using such a prop. The Milesian could not say to an attendant, "Bring a *map*." He took a purpose-made work of art as a visual aid for his rhetoric. The Spartans' own military reputation had been earned without maps, and they were supposed to be impressed by the novelty. Obviously, the image did not indicate *all* the world's rivers and seas, even the few known at the time. The Milesian used it to indicate a route and count off the rich *ethnē* along it—some of their names perhaps being inscribed on the routes—to facilitate his dissembling. The story assumes that Cleomenes gained no impression of how far away the Persians were, and that he was none the wiser after staring at the plate. His shock at the answer to his question implies that it either conveyed no such information or gave a grossly misleading impression. It could not have portrayed terrestrial features with an accuracy useful for planning because those details were not known. And that was not its purpose.

After Herodotus' time, Greek thinkers including Aristotle, Eratosthenes of Cyrene, Hipparchus of Nicaea, and Poseidonius of Apamaea (fourth to second centuries B.C.) experimented with representations of the whole earth and what they understood to be its three continents: Europe, Asia, and Africa or Libya. They discovered that the earth was roughly a sphere, devised ways of calculating its circumference with rough accuracy, and began linking up places—haphazardly—on latitudinal parallels (above). Locating sites on the same longitude was even harder.[12] All of this thinking was well established by the time the Romans extended their empire in the second and first centuries B.C.[13] But even if the Romans had shown a keen interest in developing this Greek tradition (apparently they did not), that was not enough to inculcate a *map-based* mentality of the kind that we imbibe in classrooms surrounded by Mercator projections: the mentality that undergirds our understanding of the world.

Four and a half centuries after Herodotus, Strabo still sounds much like him when he describes current geographical sensibilities. If anyone

---

12. The Latin words *longitudo* and *latitudo* meant simply "length" and "width" (we still speak of giving someone a "wide latitude"). In Pliny longitude tends to be the longer of two geographical dimensions (whether east-west or north-south in a given case). Ptolemy, however counted degrees from the empire's western end and up from the equator.

13. On ancient developments see Bunbury 1879 (with extraordinary erudition and detail); Crone 1953: 15–28; Tozer 1971 (intended as a more accessible Bunbury); Dilke 1985, 1987: 35–39 (remarkably concise).

knew about the learned cosmological-geographical tradition, Strabo did. But even such progress as the Greeks had made, this Rome-friendly writer from Syria acknowledged (3.4.19), was of little interest to Romans because it was not practically useful.[14] For his part, having declared that a geographer has use only for places that are worthy of note and "well defined," he elaborates on the meaning of the latter term (2.1.30):

> A place is well-defined when it can be so [defined] by rivers or mountains or a sea, and by an *ethnos* or *ethnē* and a certain size and shape—where this is possible. At all events, rather than [reckoning] by means of rigorous measurement it is enough to go with the simple and rough (ἀντὶ τοῦ γεωμετρικῶς τὸ ἁπλῶς καὶ ὁλοσχερῶς ἱκανόν): as for size, it is enough if you should mention its *greatest length and breadth* . . . ; as for shape, if you should compare it either to one of *the geometrical shapes*—Sicily to a triangle, for example—or to one of the other familiar shapes: Iberia to an animal hide, maybe, or the Peloponnesus to a plane-tree leaf. The greater the territory that is being carved up [e.g., Syria?], the more roughly it is acceptable to make the segments.

Missing here is the modern axiom that the geography must first of all represent accurate spatial relationships, what is actually in the ground, which Strabo had no way of knowing. Strabo's recommendations are just the sort of principles that he exemplifies when he describes southern Syria and its constituent *ethnē* (Chapter 5a).

G. R. Crone long ago made this observation: "The Romans seem to have been singularly unconcerned with Greek achievements in scientific cartography. For them a map remained a practical aid to the journeys of their officials and the campaigns of their legions. If we were to judge from the sole surviving example of any size [i.e., the Peutinger Table, below], we would conclude that they were little more than *graphical renderings of written itineraries*."[15]

Itineraries were lists of place names and stations along a given route. Within a certain region, authors would say, one encounters first X, then Y, and after that Z. We have many Roman-period lists and they are largely accurate when they follow a coastal road or river as a linear guide. When they depart from these routes, however, the information becomes difficult or impossible to square with the known terrain. We find such lists often in the geographical section (Bks 3–6) of Pliny's *Natural History*, for example in

14. Crone 1953: 22.
15. Crone 1953: 22 (emphasis mine).

barrages of names along the course of the Nile (6.177–182) or in southern Syria (5.66–73).

Pliny realizes that listing "naked names"—especially barbarian names—with such vague connectors as "after that, next, from there," may be off-putting ("My subject is a barren one," pr. 13), but he makes a virtue of necessity by flattering his Roman readers that Romans can take this hard going, unlike Greeks who need soothing words (pr. 24–28; cf. 3.2). Anyway, he will leaven his dry lists with fascinating tales of the weird, wonderful, and grotesque (1.7). With Strabo-like vagueness, Pliny gives the dimensions of the Dead Sea (Asphaltites) as more than 100 Roman (92 imperial) miles by 75 (69 imperial), but "6 [5.5 imperial] where smallest" (5.72)—wherever that should be. Since the Dead Sea was at most about 48 imperial miles by 11 (today shrunk to 42 x 10), Pliny has nearly doubled its length and multiplied its width more than six times, creating a mammoth body of water. He plainly has no sense of the spatial reality.

None of this information could have produced a map usable for finding one's way if one left the established routes. Henry Tozer long ago noted Pliny's "complete ignorance of scientific geography; and in describing the leading features of countries, such as mountains and rivers . . . he contents himself with lists of names, and in like manner the cities of any particular region he simply catalogues without remarking on their relative position."[16]

Pliny is important for understanding Roman conceptions. In dedicating his work to the future emperor Titus (pr. 1–5), who had acquired extensive experience in the east from A.D. 67 to 70, he was writing potentially (if Titus cared to look) for discriminating readers. He outlines the research he has undertaken, claiming to have consulted the best authorities—100 authors and 2,000 volumes (pr. 17). His first volume actually lists his sources. These include Marcus Agrippa: the emperor Augustus' well-travelled colleague, fleet admiral, and son-in-law. Pliny is the one who tells us most clearly about a display of the inhabited earth (*orbis terrarum*) that was in Rome, built on the basis of Agrippa's geographical notes after his death, by his sister and the emperor.[17]

That representation, perhaps completing an earlier effort by Julius Caesar, was located along a decorative portico that formed one edge of Agrippa's Field, which was part of the Campus Martius on Rome's north end. It is probably the most frequently cited example of a Roman map,

16. Tozer 1971 [orig. 1876]: 264.

17. For the map and Pliny's use of it see Pliny *Nat.* 3.17; 6.139 with Tierney 1962–1964; Dilke 1985: 39–54. Strabo is usually thought to be citing this map when he cites "the [anonymous] chorographer" (Strabo 5.2.7, 8; 6.1.11, 2.1, 11, 3.10; 8.3.17; 10.3.5; cf. Tierney 1962–1964: 152).

though no one has a clue what it looked like.[18] J. J. Tierney argued that its intended contribution must have been its officially recorded distances, rather than any advance in spatial cartography or representation.[19] The works that depended on Agrippa, including Pliny's, take the form of written expositions, not visual maps, and Pliny himself discusses problems with Agrippa's *numbers* (3.16–17).

When Roman authors attempt to portray a large land mass and its proportions with words, which is rare, their adherence to the kind of advice given by Strabo can make them seem childishly naïve, even if they have undergone considerable hardship in visiting sites.[20] A famous example is Julius Caesar's description of Britain as a triangle with a perimeter of about 2,000 Roman miles (*Bell. gall.* 5.13). So far, so good.[21] That perimeter was roughly measurable in the standard way, by navigating the linear route around the island. But the mind-bending triangle he describes—if we try to imagine it in view of our knowledge of the real geography—has a 700-mile side *facing Spain and Ireland*, an 800-mile side facing the open north seas (rather than northwestern Europe and Scandinavia), and a 500-mile side facing Gaul (France).[22] The well-informed Tacitus similarly locates Spain to the west of Britain (*Agric.* 10). More disconcertingly, he may have been so innocent of Greek cosmology that he assumed the world to be basically flat.[23]

The geographer Ptolemy (mid-second century A.D.) is rightly hailed as a genius for his remarkably accurate calculations of the earth's circumference and proportions. His *Handbook of Geography* gave the latitudinal and longitudinal coordinates for some 8,000 locations, and he wrestled intelligently with the problem of representing the earth's globe in two dimensions. Although he may not have drawn a corresponding map, many others would later try their hands on the basis of his work, especially after it was translated into Latin in the fifteenth century, when exciting geographical discoveries were underway and astronomical study was gaining in confidence.

---

18. Brodersen (2004: 185) exposes the many contradictory claims with evident relish.

19. Tierney 1962–1964: 164–65; cf. 155, 160.

20. See Mattern (1999: 24–80); Dilke 1985: 112–29.

21. The coastline of the United Kingdom is a much longer 7,767 mi (12,500 km), http://www.webcitation.org/5RSu3AP6O, but that includes the coastlines of the 1000 islands and the contours of the mainland. A rough triangle along the southern, western, and eastern coasts could be close to Caesar's figure.

22. See Mattern 1999: 52–53; Brodersen 2001: 7–21.

23. So Romm 1992: 4, citing Tacitus, *Agr.* 12.4.

Ptolemy's work had an enormous impact on geography in the Byzantine East and the Arab world, from which it was recovered for the West.[24]

But as maps based on Ptolemy's work show, his impression of the world scarcely matched the reality. It may have been a Greek attachment to symmetry that led him to imagine the Indian Ocean as enclosed by land and matching the Mediterranean.[25] Although he did a decent job with latitudes, for his longitudes he depended on known itineraries and travellers' reports,[26] which caused major errors. H. S. Cronin began his 1905 study: "The first condition of any study of Ptolemy's map is to disabuse our minds completely of the notion that we have in it a map which is accurate according to modern standards of accuracy, or which was constructed along modern lines."[27] Ptolemy imagined Scotland as a giant eastward protrusion from Britain. Leading astray generations of later cartographers, he portrayed the Syrian coast as angled northeastward, instead of almost due north.[28] The latter mistake may have been in Agrippa's "map" or already in Eratosthenes in the third century B.C.[29] It would not be corrected until systematic surveying of the Levant by French, Russian, and British navies in the eighteenth and nineteenth centuries.[30] Obviously it was not possible to acquire a usable map of southern Syria (including Judaea) from such a skewed orientation, seriously compounded by Pliny-like misunderstandings of the major bodies of water.

The only surviving map-like artifact widely regarded as a more or less direct copy of a Roman model is the so-called Peutinger Table (*tabula peutingeriana*). Named after the sixteenth-century antiquarian who once owned it, it is a colorful twelfth- or thirteenth-century reproduction of a

---

24. Dilke 1985: 72–86, 154–66. On Ptolemy's lack of influence in the Latin West before the 15th century see Crone 1953: 21–22. Ptolemy's estimate of the earth's circumference was as much as 18% too small, depending on the length of his *stadion* standard, and Eratosthenes' (3rd cent. B.C.) had been at least 15% too large (Berggren and Jones 2000: 20–21)—though some scholars rescue him by positing a the shortest known (Egyptian) *stadion* (Crone 1953: 18; Dilke 1985: 33).

25. So Crone 1953: 17.

26. Crone 1953: 21–22.

27. Cronin 1905: 429.

28. See the (15th-cent.) interpretation in Berggren and Jones 2000: plate 2.

29. For Agrippa see Tierney 1962–1964: 164 ("Agrippa regarded the Syrian coast running north-east from the boundary of Egypt"). For Eratosthenes see the map in Dilke 1985: 33.

30. Carmody 1976: 601–609: Ptolemy did not create a visual map, as far as we know, but a book of theoretical considerations and coordinates. For the modern surveys, see Gavish 2005: 3–20 (6).

GEOGRAPHY: THE WORLD, THE HOMELAND, THE MOTHER-*POLIS* 231

much earlier map,[31] perhaps modeled on the one in Agrippa's Portico. One scholar prefers a ninth-century origin under Charlemagne, when the explosion in map-making first created the need for a word for "map": an old Latin word for towel or cloth (*mappa*) was pressed into service for the newfangled image.[32] The Peutinger Table's eleven surviving parchment sheets used to be part of a continuous roll, with one or more additional sheets at the beginning. The surviving document is about a foot high (0.34 m) but an astonishing 23 ft (6.75 m) in length.

Some have argued that because it could not practically be read in sections, unlike a scroll book, this map must rather have been created for unrolled display as a continuous whole.[33] However that may be, its extraordinary proportions confirm that its creator was not even aiming at scale representation. Although it visually depicts rivers, lakes, and other features, from France (in the lost section from Spain) to India, it remains basically a representation of itinerary routes. In one section we see a kind of west-east progression in the upper part, with Cappadocia above Lycia and Cilicia, which are in turn above a river-like Mediterranean hosting a gigantic Cyprus. Although Antioch is about where we would expect it, to the right of that, southern Syria is then bent around beneath it, such that the Sea of Galilee is left of Damascus, the Dead Sea and Jerusalem left of that, and Philadelphia (Amman) still further left—none of this bearing any relationship to physical reality. The Peutinger Table thus represents a Roman, itinerary-based image of the empire. It is a visual impression of something like the ca. third-century *Antonine Itinerary*, a written list of roads, stations, and distances.[34] A growing awareness of Roman political discourse inclines scholars to suspect that it was actually designed as a symbol of Roman *imperium*, and meant to be ornamental rather than practically useful like the portable written itineraries.[35]

Before we leave antiquity I shall mention two other famous maps with some claim to follow older models. The first is the mosaic floor built in

31. The Peutinger Map is available online in at least two helpful formats. Richard Talbert has it in color and with selectable overlays, as an accompaniment to his 2010 study: http://peutinger.atlantides.org/map-a. His introduction and analysis are particularly helpful, at the publisher's site: http://www.cambridge.org/us/talbert. Euratlas has a serviceable version at http://www.euratlas.net/cartogra/peutinger. For a downloadable copy see http://en.wikipedia.org/wiki/File:TabulaPeutingeriana.jpg.

32. Albu 2005, 2008.

33. Salway 2005: 122.

34. For the *Antonine Itinerary* see Reed 1978 (a basic tour, arguing that it was an official text authorized by the emperor for the grain tax). Small 2010 applies cold criticism to a related issue: the map transmitted with the Artemidorus Papyrus.

35. Salway 2005; Talbert 2010.

the sixth-century Byzantine cathedral of Madaba, 30 km (18.6 mi) south of Amman in Jordan. The Madaba map was uncovered in the late nineteenth century by Christians resettling from Kerak as they were building the current St. George's Church, which incorporated this ancient floor.[36] What remains of the famous mosaic depicts an area from Palestine to the Nile River in a highly impressionistic way. It may be the most broadly accurate representation of this region before nineteenth-century cartography, but if so it shows the serious limitations of ancient map-making.

The other example is a colorful painting of the world on a large piece of vellum parchment (calfskin), signed by one Richard of Holdingham and dating to about A.D. 1290. It is owned by Hereford Cathedral in Britain. This round *mappa*, as such representations were called from the ninth century, stretches over an oak board 1.58 m by 1.33 m (5 ft 2 in by 4 ft 4 in). In Christian-mediaeval style, the world looks eastward (i.e., east is up), because that is where salvation will come from. Although it is a wholly Christian map, centered in Jerusalem as navel of the earth, it stands out from more than a thousand other mediaeval maps for its level of detail, which is commonly attributed to a Roman original.[37] For all its intrinsic interest, however, even this late thirteenth-century "map" shows the serious limitations of all such efforts at visual representation of the world before modern tools were available.

To sum up thus far, surviving evidence suggests that in the Roman world no one imagined accurate maps, which could not be produced for the provinces anyway, to be a necessary basis for either provincial administration or military campaigns. It was the Romans' experience of the world through trade, conquest, and combat in various regions that led to occasional efforts at graphic representation; the activities had not themselves required accurate maps. For small-scale mapping, it should be noted, the Romans had highly effective surveying tools, perfected from Egyptian and Greek precursors, as well as expert technicians (*agrimensores*).[38] These enabled them to build their famous roads, aqueducts, and cities, and to mark out settlements or even fairly large agricultural fields. But this was very different from what they would have needed to produce accurate maps of provinces such as Egypt or Syria.

36. Donner 1992: 11–12. It seems impossible to take a good photograph of the whole sprawling map in surviving fragments. The annotated replica on site is reproduced at https://en.wikipedia.org/wiki/Madaba_Map#/media/File:Madaba_Map_reproduction.jpg.

37. See Harvey 1996: 21–39.

38. See the drawings of Roman surveying equipment in Rowland and Howe 1999: 170–71; for analysis, Olson 2008: 560–62; cf. 296–302.

Nothing that I have said above suggests that the Romans had *no idea* where their provinces were, or which harbors and roads they needed to use to reach them. It is only that they depended on established sea routes and road systems where these existed, the latter annotated with carefully recorded distances and landmarks, and supplemented this knowledge when necessary with the aid of expert local guides—as in the Judaean War.

It is often said nowadays that men gravitate to maps, whereas women tend to remember routes and landmarks.[39] *If* that is so, though they may not have been pleased to hear this, Roman men thought like (modern) women.

Modern Mapping of Judaea and Environs

In 1564 the Flemish father of modern cartography, Abraham Ortelius, produced a world map that looks not too strange at first glance.[40] But closer views of the dozens of sheet maps in his 1570 atlas expose problems. His impression of the Holy Land shows a dramatically saw-toothed coastline running northeast, gigantic blobs for the Dead Sea and Kinneret, the former a rectangle with a sizeable external protrusion, and a Jordan River that runs as far east as south in its northern half.[41] Maps produced by the Dutch Blaeu family in the mid-1600s, influenced even more by that age of rapid discovery, were also beautiful and highly prized, but not remotely accurate. Their representation of the Holy Land (ca. 1630) sports a nearly quadrilateral Sea of Galilee, on a line somewhat east of the Dead Sea, a position that requires the Jordan River to lurch southwest on its journey to the southern lake. The Dead Sea, for its part, looks like a long Yorkshire Terrier, much skinnier than Ortelius' impression but no more accurate, with projections eastward at both ends.[42]

To get a sense of the challenges involved in surveying even linear routes over difficult terrain, one might profitably read Andrew Jampoler's *Sailors in the Holy Land* (2005). It is a gripping account of a U.S. Navy crew's 1848 attempt at the first methodical survey of the Jordan River and Dead

39. E.g., Rahman, Andersson, and Govier 2005.

40. See the Wikimedia version at https://upload.wikimedia.org/wikipedia/commons/e/e2/OrteliusWorldMap1570.jpg.

41. The Abraham Ortelius map (ca. 1560) may be viewed, before and after restoration, at http://www.rmg.co.uk/discover/behind-the-scenes/blog/conserving-copper-green-degradation-maps.

42. A downloadable Blaeu map is at https://commons.wikimedia.org/wiki/File:Willem_Blaeu._Terra_Sancta_quae_in_Sacris_Terra_Promissionis_olim_Palestina._ca._1650.jpg.

Sea. They were trying to ascertain, on scientific principles, both the course of the Jordan and the previously guessed-at shape, level, and depth of the mysterious deadly southern lake—while, in the spirit of the time, searching for biblical Sodom and Gomorrah. Even with the latest scientific equipment, their expedition was harrowing. They lost their lead surveyor to deadly fever, and a boat to the Jordan River's torrents, which existed at the time. They faced constant peril from local tribesmen, injury, and illness.[43] And all of this was only to establish key *linear* routes and their elevations. Recent western visitors to the site had made grossly incorrect estimates of the Dead Sea's elevation and shape, even as they looked at it. Lynch's team still did not attempt to draw spatially accurate maps, except of the Dead Sea itself and its floor, which they could carefully measure both by daily criss-crossing and constant visual checking.

For decades after Lynch's expedition, therefore, cartographers even still lacked a precise understanding of the land. The map from an 1873 edition of the standard *Mitchell's Ancient Atlas* (original 1844) shows a highly erratic course for the Jordan River and sets the Dead Sea at a sharp angle in an unrecognizable shape (Figure 2). Notice the placement of En Gedi at the south end, whereas in reality it sits about half-way along the western shore.[44] Notice also the mistaken locations of sites around the Sea of Galilee (Magdala, Tiberias, Bethsaida, Hippos, and Pella) and that lake's unreal orientation. The fifth edition of another standard, Shepherd's *Historical Atlas* (1911), which brings us to the eve of World War I (Figure 3), showed dramatic improvements, though small errors abound still.[45]

43. Jampoler 2005: 217–52.
44. Mitchell 1873 (1844) map 8.
45. Shepherd 1926 (1911): 6–7.

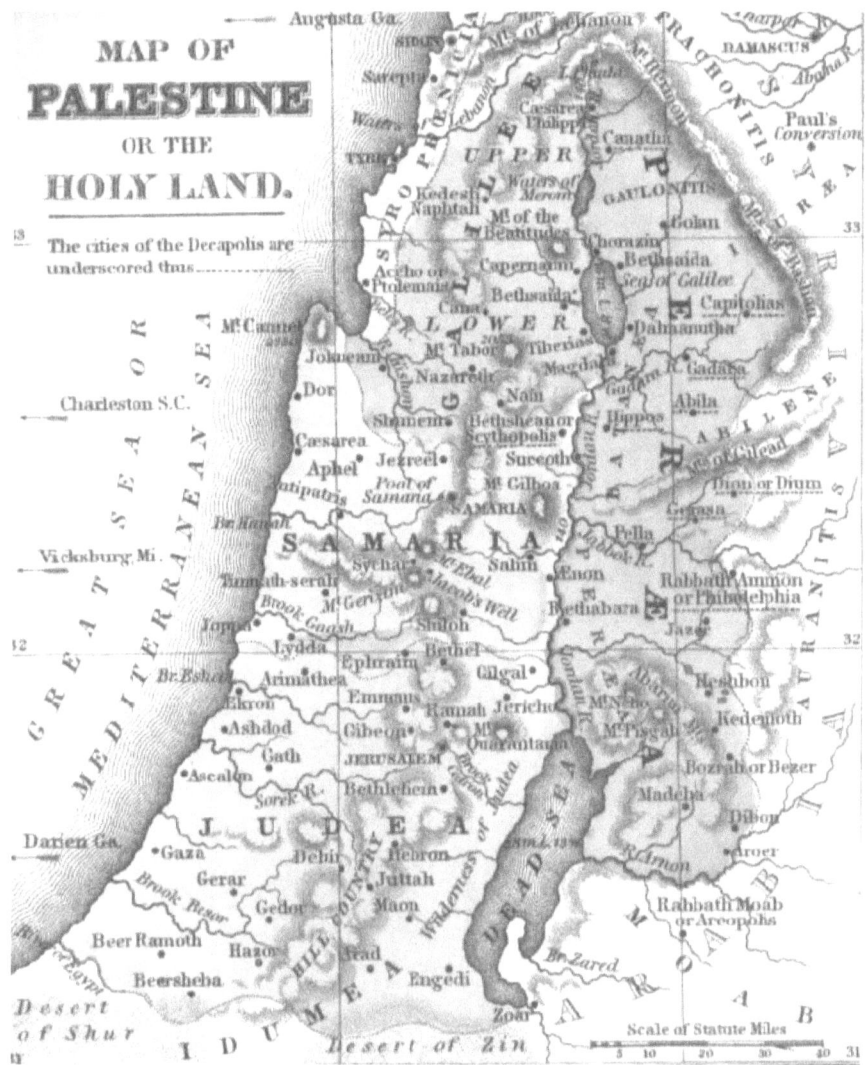

Figure 2. Map of Palestine (Map 8) from S. A. Mitchell, *Mitchell's Ancient Atlas, Classical and Sacred*. Philadelphia: Butler, 1873 (1844 original). Public domain.

Figure 3. Map of Palestine (pp. 6–7) from W. R. Shepherd, *Historical Atlas*, 5th ed. New York: Holt, 1926 (1911 original).

Before the late nineteenth century and the Palestine Exploration Fund's *Survey of Western Palestine* published in 1880,[46] it was the unavoidable reality that even the most curious had no way of knowing the lie of the land.[47] That is why the *Survey* was initiated: curious biblically-interested Britons wanted the truth. Accurate spatial geography would require the use of triangulation: calculating distances with the aid of trigonometry from various directions, reckoned from established baselines, knowable angles, and their lines of intersection.[48] Such techniques had not been systematically applied even in Britain until the eighteenth century.[49] So maps from the sixteenth to eighteenth centuries, though made with intelligence and all the science then available, are so misleading as to be useless for practical purposes.[50] The Romans had no chance.

Thus far we have been elaborating the first part of Talbert's opening quotation, that the Greeks and Romans did not possess the kind of maps that could have been useful to them in the way ours are valuable to us. We conclude this part of the chapter with a briefer consideration of his second and related point: a different *mentality*.

Because we have learned to fuse our experience as walkers, drivers, and travellers with the bird's-eye picture of our world available in maps of all sizes, we are apt to assume that any representation of territory that lacks the accuracy of spatial maps would therefore be useless. We may therefore assume that the Romans *must* have had good maps (they were not stupid), and recoil from suggestions that they thought so differently.[51] But perhaps we can find modern analogies for representations of the world that do not attempt spatial accuracy and yet can be at least as helpful as those that do.

---

46. Conder and Kitchener 1880. C. R. Conder and H. H. Kitchener were lieutenants in the British Army's Corps of Royal Engineers.

47. See Ben-Arieh 1979: 121–32 (124): "Scientifically, the region of the Jordan valley was completely unknown until the beginning of the nineteenth century"; also Goren 2002: 87–110.

48. See Gavish 2005: 8–12, 49–103, the latter section on the development of a comprehensive triangulation net in Palestine under the British Mandate.

49. See Hewitt 2010.

50. For Palestine see Tishby 2001: 82–107; Bartlett 2009.

51. E.g., Moreland and Bannister 1983: 4 (emphasis added): "[T]here is little direct evidence of their [the Romans'] interest in cartography. All the same, considering their highly developed administrative abilities, it is *hard to believe that maps were not in common use* even though so few have survived." I owe the reference to Talbert 1987: 211. He himself quotes from Johnston 1967: 92, who argues from what he considers a relief map of the Ephesus region on the back of a coin that the ancients must have had "really practical, detailed maps"—"particularly for fiscal, military and navigational purposes."

Britain's *Telegraph* newspaper has an online feature provocatively called *The Atlas of the Real World*.[52] But the real world turns out not to be the one that corresponds to physical territory. Although it begins with a standard satellite-based map, it offers users eighteen criteria for viewing the world: demographic, economic, military, "ecological footprint," or other such issues. The representation of the world then varies dramatically, as different states become much larger or smaller from one map to the next, according to the chosen criterion. This ingenious atlas drives home the reality, and it is the reality, that we have always viewed the world according to our needs and interests, and not simply as it is. Our shared image of the "real world" typically shrinks the vast territories of the Russian steppe or sub-Saharan Africa, while it enlarges the U.S. in relation to northern Canada. As a pupil in Australia, having moved from Canada, I recall noticing immediately that Australian projections of the world placed that country in the middle and North America to the right.

Britain offers a much more familiar illustration. Brodersen has pointed out that the creators of the world-famous and now indispensable London Underground (Tube) map, in the 1930s, deliberately abandoned earlier attempts at spatial correctness. They decided that it was much more useful for travellers to represent only the sequence of stops and transfers, in a diagram of rectilinear and oblique lines, without trying to indicate realities on the ground. The resulting map quickly won out over geographical correctness, because it was indeed far more useful.[53]

The designers of the Tube map understood that, where such routes exist—rail lines, roads, shipping channels, as also aircraft waypoints—the greatest value for the user lies in knowing how to get from A to B. Taking in the surrounding topography and geography, even though we can do this today, would be a massively pointless distraction.[54] Drivers understand the same point. On a highway it is more important to know which exit to take, and the distances before turns, than to visualize the terrain all around. Satellite-navigation systems work by the same principle, focusing all our attention on a single route rather than overwhelming us with a tangle of information. Likewise it is more important for a ship's pilot to know where the safe channel lies. The larger underwater scene is irrelevant.

So, recognizing that Greeks and Romans made do with itineraries, describing the routes that would take them and their armies where they

---

52. http://www.telegraph.co.uk/travel/picturegalleries/3109042/The-Atlas-of-the-Real-World.html.

53. Contrast the 1909 real-terrain map of tube lines with the current map at https://en.wikipedia.org/wiki/Tube_map.

54. Brodersen 2001: 18–19.

needed to be, and the distances between stops and turns, is no insult to their intelligence. Although we feel dependent on accurate maps, even we do not need them for practical purposes, and they were a long time coming.

The Geography of Ancient Judaea: Reality and Ancient Impressions

In keeping with the discourse we have been considering all along, ancient authors thought more in terms of peoples, tribes, or nations (Greek *ethnē*, *genē*; Latin *nationes*, *gentes*) than of *territories* with fixed borders. They assumed that tribes and cities dominated certain areas, which might be defined by such a natural marker as a river or mountain range, but these were vaguely and provisionally indicated. *Ethnos* and *polis chōrai* were in constant flux, expanding or contracting under changing political conditions. This was as true of Rome itself and its provinces as of other *poleis* or petty kingdoms. No *ethnos* or *polis* had the resources for securing and maintaining borders in the modern sense.

The ancients spoke of Greece (*Hellas*) as a vague region—including parts of Asia Minor or not—and Greek ways as cultural facts, but in any case Hellas was not a political entity like the modern state of Greece. When describing actual events, writers from Herodotus and Thucydides to Pausanias in the second century A.D. referred usually to Athenians, Spartans, Corinthians, Thebans, Argives, Ephesians, Milesians, or Pergamenians—the people or *ethnē* of the *poleis*. These peoples constructed changing leagues and alliances (Boeotian, Delian, Peloponnesian, Achaean), but these were far from being states. Even the mighty Rome was a *polis* with massive power (*imperium*), never a country like modern Italy—Italy itself being a fairly recent creation (1861) from independent city-states.

The Romans also knew their enemies, even in such a small area of Britannia as East Anglia, by nation or tribe: the Catuvellauni, Trinovantes, Corieltavi, and Iceni. Each Celtic tribe or nation was known to have its own clans and leaders, town bases, and unique relations (frequently hostile) with neighboring peoples. The tribes had independent stances toward Roman leaders. Thus eleven British kings reportedly submitted to the emperor Claudius on his arrival in A.D. 43, each representing his people, whereas other nations on the island resisted long afterward. There was no political entity of *Britain*, or of course anything like a border security service.[55]

The ethnographic understanding of the world we have been discussing since Chapter 2 is important also for understanding the Judaeans in their

55. Webster 1978: 38–53.

contexts. It is easy for us, when looking at maps of "ancient Israel / Judaea / Palestine" in biblical or classical atlases to imagine that these were more or less coextensive with modern Israel and the Palestinian territories. Such an assumption would badly skew our understanding first-century realities and prevent us from thinking clearly about the relations among Judaeans, their neighbors, and Roman administrators. As we have seen, ancient Judaea was the *chōra* of Jerusalem, the size of which varied considerably over time and for long periods imposed on the neighbors, including hostile Samaria to the north, while Idumaea was a quasi-independent *ethnos* to the south. Just as Attica was the *chōra* of Athens, and Laconia the hinterland of Sparta, Judaea was above all the *chōra* of the renowned mother-*polis* Jerusalem.

The actual ground indicated by such labels was subject to constant change, as we have noted. And even when used of the same moment, geographical terms could have simultaneous narrow (or "proper") and broad meanings. Homer called the mainland Greeks fighting at Troy Achaeans, though Achaea proper was the small northern-most region of the Peloponnese. The Romans would later borrow the word for their large Greek province, which included the whole Peloponnese plus areas northeast. Strabo gives two senses of Coele-Syria: the narrow or proper one—Lebanon's Bekaa Valley, from which it takes its name (*coelē* meaning hollow)—and a much more capacious use encompassing all of southern Syria: Judaea, Samaria, Idumaea, and the many Greek cities (16.2.21). Judaea was not unusual, therefore, in having the clear sense of Jerusalem's countryside or hinterland, which the Hasmoneans hugely extended in all directions and the Romans shrank again, and a lingering use as one of several informal terms for much of southern Syria. In this sense it overlapped with Coele-Syria or Palestine (see Chapter 3), which each also had a narrow and broader meaning. Unsurprisingly, the Flavians chose Judaea as the name for their signature trophy province after the war with Jerusalem (chiefly) that vaulted them to power—or so I have argued.[56]

Josephus normally uses Judaea in a narrower sense, for Jerusalem's ethnic territory: east of the coastal plain, south of Samaria, north of Idumaea, and west of the Jordan River. Attributing other nations' lack of knowledge about his people to a paucity of trade, he observes: "Now, we do not inhabit a coastal territory [*chōra*] . . . , but our [Judaean] *poleis* have been constructed far from the sea" (*Apion* 1.60). His main geographical overview (*War* 3.51–58) comes as an apparent afterthought to a longer description of Galilee that is required by the narrative of *War* 3, set in Galilee (3.35–45). Perhaps his decision to compare Galilee with Peraea across the Jordan led

56. *HJW* 239–45.

him to throw in Samaria (3.48–50) and then Judaea while he was at it. In any case his description of Judaea, which puts the *polis* Jerusalem at its physical center (3.52), makes clear the highland environment. Judaea is not deprived of "the delights of the sea," he says, *because* its ridge declines (in the *shephela*) toward the sea, apparently meaning that one can see the blue water from the hills (3.52). Although he mentions coastal Joppa as Judaea's westernmost point, he then includes it with the *other* places that should be named *alongside Judaea* (3.56: μεθ' ἅς), as far away as Mt. Lebanon, presumably because they have sizeable Judaean populations: coastal Joppa and Jamnia plus various parts of King Agrippa's kingdom in the Golan and far north.

Josephus' description sharpens the difference between Judaea and modern Israel, which includes the coastal cities from Ashkelon and Ashdod to Acco. In the first century these were, like Gaza and Raphia further south, emphatically non-Judaean *poleis* with distinctive constitutions, cultures, calendars, and coinage. Ashkelon (Ascalon), inhabited from at least 5000 B.C. and a flourishing Canaanite, later Philistine port, was already Jerusalem's enemy in biblical times. That deep hostility remained on both sides throughout the first century.[57]

Looking at a map of modern Israel (including the Golan Heights) and the Palestinian territories, then, we need to make some basic adjustments to understand the ancient landscape. To begin with, nearly the southern half of Israel, from a line between Masada and Beer-Sheva to Eilat, was never part of Judaea (Josephus, *War* 3.51). Through the first century that desert region belonged to the Nabataean Arab tribes and their king, an ally (or client) of Rome, based in the famous pink-stone city of Petra, 80 km (50 mi) south and just east of the Dead Sea. The northern half of modern Israel and Palestine runs about 200 km (125 mi) from that line to the Lebanese border at the edge of Upper Galilee. Extending to 220–225 km (137–140 mi) reaches the Litani River—on a line from the Golan Heights across Lebanon north of Tyre (mod. Sur). The width of this parcel from the Mediterranean to the Jordan River narrows dramatically as we proceed northward, from 120 km (75 mi) in the south to less than 40 km (25 mi) in the north. Adding 25 km (15.5 mi) east of the Jordan River takes in the Golan Heights. Although the whole area is tiny by North American and even European standards,[58] in the Roman period it hosted many different *ethnē* and *poleis*, of which the Judaeans were one.[59]

---

57. Philo, *Legat.* 205; Josephus, *War* 3.9–10.

58. This area is ca. 10,500 km2: half the size of Slovenia or New Jersey, a third of Canada's Vancouver Island. Austria has 84,000 km2, Slovakia 49,000.

59. See *HJW* 226–38, with maps.

In the southernmost three quarters of the strip just described, a fertile plain adjoins the Mediterranean coast, extending between 30 and 20 km (19 to 12.5 mi) inland, to the foothills of the dominant south-to-north range of hills. The eastward slope from the plain begins gently, coming up through the foothills known as the *shephela*, and then rises more steeply to a plateau, roughly on the longitude of inland Jerusalem. East of this rugged south-north range is a much more abrupt decline into the Jordan River valley and the Dead Sea, a rift that extends all the way south to east Africa. The Jordan River, perhaps named for its north-to-south descent (*Yarden* from *yarad*: "to fall"?), empties into what we know today, thanks to Lynch's 1848 expedition, as the lowest point on earth, more than 400 m (1,300 ft) below sea level. This is the mineral-rich Dead Sea, called Asphaltites in antiquity because of the bitumen (cf. English *asphalt*) that it produces.

This coastal plain rising gradually eastward towards rugged hills, with a sharp decline east into the Jordan valley, continues northward almost as far as Mt. Carmel on the coast. Inland, the south-north range of hills dissipates at the end of Samaria, flattening out into the broad transverse Jezreel Valley. This extends from Beit-Shean (Scythopolis) near the Jordan River northwest towards Carmel, bottle-necking as it nears the Carmel range before opening again into the plain that surrounds Ptolemais-Acco on the coast. This important Phoenician center, later beloved of Greek and Roman rulers, was entirely non-Judaean. It dated its Year 1 from a visit by Julius Caesar in 48 B.C. and by A.D. 54 it had been re-established as a colony for veterans of the four legions based in Syria.[60]

North of the Jezreel Valley and inland is Galilee, whose hills now create an east-west orientation, rather than the south-north ridge of Judaea and Samaria. In Galilee's southern half, which is anchored on the east side by the Kinneret Lake (Sea of Galilee), most hills are rolling and gentle, and separated by a series of fertile east-west valleys. The largest of these is the Beit-Netofa Valley, which runs from Tiberias (after a protective rim of high hills) toward Carmel in the west. Upper Galilee, although it also happens to be north of this, is named for its *higher* elevation and more rugged hill country. It too is green and fertile, but lacking the wide valleys of Lower Galilee.

Across the Kinneret Lake to the east, past a narrow dagger of flat shoreline, the Golan Heights rise abruptly to a plateau. South of the Golan, past the intervening east-west Yarmuk River Valley, the eastern Jordan valley roughly mirrors the western side. But the mountains on the east, today in the Hashemite Kingdom of Jordan, are higher. On both sides, a flat valley cradles the river before the steep rise of the hills.

60. Strabo 2.5.39; 14.4.2; 16.2.25–26, 4.7; 17.3.20; Pliny, *Nat.* 5.75.

GEOGRAPHY: THE WORLD, THE HOMELAND, THE MOTHER-*POLIS*   243

Such diverse topography in a small area created both a variety of micro-climates and widely varied situations for secure settlement: from well-watered cities with temperate climates to inaccessible caves and desert fortresses on precipitous cliffs; from the rich coastal plain to the terraces of the Judaean and Samarian hills; from the fertile Jordan Valley to the desert conditions just east and west of it, especially around the Dead Sea. Ancient Jericho was built, for example, on an oasis nestled in the Judaean desert. Though only 24 km (15 miles) from Jerusalem, its climate was so different that rulers based in Jerusalem would build winter palaces there, to facilitate a quick escape from the capital's cold, rain, and occasional snow. Whereas Galilee and the Golan are temperate regions with moderate rainfall between October and April, and their high northern spots can be very cold (Mt. Hermon being snow-capped), summer temperatures in the south of this small parcel are extremely hot, whether accompanied by humidity on the coast or almost perfectly dry around the Dead Sea. The Dead Sea zone has a brief but intense period of winter rain, which creates torrents in the *wadis* (winter riverbeds) but then is gone for at least ten months.

This tiny land bridge between massive Africa and Asia, with such varied possibilities for habitation, regularly fell under the domination of a great empire. By the first century B.C. these changes, along with the Hasmonean expansion of Judaea's *chōra* and its removal by Rome in the 60s, had left many diverse peoples and settlements. In southern Syria not all the settled areas were marked by walled *poleis* and their dependent territories. Regions such as Peraea east of the Jordan, Galilee, Samaria, and Trachonitis east of the Kinneret consisted largely of villages without a dominant *polis*, though inevitably some villages assumed prominence over the others.

First-century authors such as Strabo and Pliny attempted to describe the varied conditions and peoples of southern Syria in the early Roman period, from the best sources available. They understood the region as a kaleidoscope of ethnic-tribal regions and territories around individual *poleis*. Here I can only sketch the main components. Looking northward from the baseline mentioned above (Beer-Sheva to Masada), three large ethnic regions sat in the hill country, from south to north: Idumaea, with its *poleis* of Marisa and Adora toward its north end; Judaea, the large *chōra* of Jerusalem with several *poleis* as regional centers (toparchies);[61] and Samaria, whose leading city of the same name, badly damaged by the Hasmonean

---

61. Josephus (*War* 3.55) gives an occasionally puzzling list, which may have been mangled in the manuscript transmission. It should be compared with the one in Pliny, *Nat.* 5.70. They agree on the most plausible sites: Jerusalem plus Jericho, Emmaus, Gophna, Thamna, Lydda, Acrabeta, Herodium.

John Hyrcanus (ca. 110 B.C.), Herod rebuilt soon after 30 B.C. as Sebastē in honor of Augustus.

Along the western coast was a series of independent *poleis*, each with its own identity, history, laws, calendar, and customs, and a surrounding *chōra* that reached inland for perhaps 6 to 10 km (3.7 to 6 mi). From south to north, these *poleis* were Raphia, Gaza, Ascalon, Azotus, Jamnia, Joppa, Apollonia, Strato's Tower, Dora, Ptolemais, and Tyre. Some inland territories of dependent villages were large indeed, that of Tyre reaching all the way to the Jordan River. Ptolemais, the thoroughly Greek *polis* turned somewhat Roman after 54 (above), and its dependent villages dominated the coastal plain immediately west of Lower Galilee.

Northeast of Samaria were ten independent Greek cities, one just west of the Jordan but the others in a jagged line to the east, in modern Jordan. Although the ancients called them the *Decapolis* ("The Ten-City [group]"), they seem not to have been a political federation.[62] Like the coastal *poleis*, each one had its distinctive history, in some cases already ancient, and its own deities, laws, and calendar. Nowadays it is a two-hour drive from Jerusalem to Beit-Shean, but in the first century it was days of walking and a world away. This was the proudly independent and wealthy *Scythopolis*, which Josephus calls the largest *polis* of the Decapolis (*War* 3.446). This "House of (the god) Shan" dated to ca. 5000 B.C. and archaeology has uncovered both Canaanite remains and some from its time as an Egyptian administrative center, centuries before King David entered Jerusalem. These highly distinctive *poleis*, including Hippos on the western ridge of the Golan Heights, Gadara south of that, Pella, Esebonitis (Heshbon), Gerasa (Jarash) from ca. 3000 B.C., and Philadelphia (mod. Amman), played crucial roles in the local conflicts that led to the war of 66.

This picture of distinct *ethnē* living in close proximity is confirmed in every direction from Jerusalem. Sebastē, just 50 km (30 mi) north of Jerusalem, was a very different place from the Judaean mother-*polis*, boasting large entertainment facilities in Graeco-Roman style and temples to Augustus and Rome as well as other gods. Coastal Caesarea, 120 km (72 mi) away, had the same features on a much grander scale: temples, theatres, markets, statues, palatial buildings.[63] The modern visitor to the fragmentary remains

62. Cf. Mark 5.20; 7.31; Matt 4.25; Pliny, *Nat.* 5.74 for a list of *poleis*. Josephus mentions only Scythopolis (*War* 3.446). Aelius Herodian mentions it in connection with Gerasa (*Pros. cath.* under names ending in *son/sa*). He and Herennius Philo, cited in Stephanus' *Ethnica* ("Gerasa"), both locate Gerasa and the Decapolis in Coele-Syria, showing the elasticity of this term. Ptolemy, *Geog.* 5.15.22–24, lists 18 *poleis* of Coele-Syria and Decapolis without distinction.

63. Aerial distance in both cases. One should add nearly 20 km for the road trip to

of these *poleis* or to Scythopolis, Gadara, or Gerasa, can easily imagine the pride and confidence their citizens felt, just as we can appreciate the pride of Judaeans for Jerusalem, according to Pliny "the most famous *urbs* of the east and not Judaea alone" (*Nat.* 5.70).

One important consequence of the picture we are developing is that the standard framework of "(Eretz-) Israel and Diaspora," another staple of scholarly discussion,[64] becomes impossible to sustain from ancient texts. In the nineteenth century, it is worth noting, Graetz did not use this modern frame in writing about antiquity, but preferred the ancient categories: Judaea and its colonies.[65] Although the category is rarely interrogated,[66] Diaspora seems mainly to be understood as "not at home," but (a) removed from regular contact with Jerusalem and temple and (b) a minority population among pagans.

We can now see some problems with such a conception. Judaeans were minority populations and for practical purposes far removed from Jerusalem if they lived in Gaza, Ascalon, Caesarea, or Scythopolis, among majority populations following entirely different calendars and worshipping other gods. As for distance, it normally took at least as long to travel from Judaean centers in Galilee to Jerusalem, through hostile territory, as it did on a possibly pleasant cruise-plus-hike from Alexandria.[67] Caesarea

---

Caesarea, under 10 for Sebastē.

64. E.g., Kraabel 1982; Lightstone 1984; Kasher 1990 (for Eretz-Israel as a concept including the non-Judaean *poleis*); Barclay 1996, 2004; Gafni 1997; Gruen 2002; Rajak 2009; Tuval 2013.

65. Graetz (1914:1.295) "Judaea was surrounded on all sides by a Greek-speaking population"; cf. 1862: 2.2.207, 215, 231–32; 3.24–27.

66. Price 1994 is the main exception I know. In a devastating assault on these categories he mentions among other things that the term *Eretz-Israel* first appears in the third-century Mishnah and later rabbinic literature. On that I would add: (a) *halakha* used this language to facilitate discussion, after both the fall of Jerusalem (70) and ban of Judaeans from its immediate territory (136), to settle questions about tithing, sabbatical year, divorce; (b) that this language does not map onto political realities of the period 200 B.C. to A.D. 200; and (c) that Mishnah's definitions of Eretz-Israel and "outside" can be flexible and paradoxical. Flexible: *Shev.* 6:1; *Hal.* 4:8; *Git.* 1:2. Paradoxical: *BabaQ* 7:7 ("not in the Land of Israel . . . but in the wildernesses that are in the Land of Israel").

67. Philo mentions his travel through Ascalon (NB: "a *polis* of Syria") on a journey to Jerusalem; this was the port most directly en route from Alexandria (*Prov.* 2.64). Josephus (*War* 2.335) notes that a tribune dispatched from Antioch met up with King Agrippa II at Jamnia, in the coastal plain NE of Ashdod/Azotus, as the latter was returning from Alexandria, which would also make sense if he were coming from Ascalon (or Azotus), before the pair turned inland at Lydda. The roughly 300 nmi from Alexandria to Ascalon could be covered in 3.5 days (@ 4 nmi / hour), and a 2+-day walk inland from there followed. Caesarea was nearly twice the distance of Ascalon (120 km by

was far enough away, the better part of four days' walking, to make them practically isolated worlds, as Herod well understood in establishing an imperial cult there. The Israel-Diaspora frame is historically harmless if it is a mere entry point for the study of particular sites and evidence, as is often the case. It can become a conceptual problem and foreclose historical understanding, however, if we either imagine a shared Diaspora-Jewish identity[68] or ignore local dynamics around Jerusalem's hinterland, from a mistaken impression that modern Israel and Palestine map onto a "homeland" province of Judaea or Eretz-Israel.

A final consideration that drives home the absence of a states-with-borders mentality is that when *poleis* and their territories and revenue changed hands, they did not need to be contiguous with a larger political entity. Marc Antony took many individual *poleis* from King Herod for his lover Queen Cleopatra, removing even fertile Jericho from his disgruntled royal friend (*War* 1.361). On Herod's death, Augustus presented the coastal *poleis* of Ascalon, Azotus (Ashdod), and Jamnia, along with Phasaelis in the Jordan valley, to the king's sister Salome (*War* 2.98). Salome's will, in turn, bequeathed them to Augustus' wife Livia (*War* 2.167). When she died, they passed to the emperor Tiberius, since he was her son, and he promptly dispatched a financial agent to consolidate the revenue (*Ant.* 18.158). Again, Nero would grant King Agrippa II the lakeside *poleis* of Tiberias and Taricheae, irrespective of the rest of Galilee, along with Julias across the Jordan River: "Julias, a *polis* in Peraea, and the fourteen villages around it"—that is, the city with its *chōra* (Josephus, *Ant.* 20.159). This gifting of *poleis* here and there drives home the absence of any notion of political territory as a country with a border.

To be sure, such changes of ownership may have had little practical effect on the day-to-day operation of a *polis* internally. After its transfer to Agrippa II, Tiberias continued to be administered by a local assembly and Council of Ten. But new ownership by Agrippa from A.D. 54/55 and the diversion of revenue to his coffers presumably affected customs barriers on goods entering and leaving these now-royal zones. And the addition

---

road) requiring perhaps 4 days normally. One could reportedly reach Jerusalem from southern Galilee in 3 days of hard going, but only by hazarding the dangerous route through Samaria. More common was the detour via the Jordan Valley and Jericho, even though it doubled the travel time (6–7 days?) and faced the lower-grade but perpetual risk of banditry (Josephus, *Life* 269 [the rapid route]; Cf. *War* 2.125 [banditry]; 2.232–235 [ongoing hostility and violence]; Luke 9:51–56 [Samaria a problem]; 10:30; 17:11; 18:35 [going the long way]).

68. So especially Lightstone 1984 and Tuval 2013, both arguing that life far away from the temple cult (in "Diaspora") required other modes of mediating the divine, in which Jerusalem and its temple were at best notional.

of proud Tiberias to Agrippa II's growing kingdom may have been felt as a sharp drop in status, aside from any direct economic liabilities, causing resentment against him (*Life* 37–39).[69]

Such inter-*polis* antagonism was common throughout the eastern empire. It was entirely different from the usually good-natured competition of cities and their sports teams inside a modern country, to which citizens may relocate while retaining all their rights and privileges. Citizen status today issues from the higher level of the state and encompasses all the territory within it, and the cities and towns are mainly economic creations.[70] In a world without such states, one's identity—and "citizen-ship" or political rights—still came from the *polis*. Inter-*polis* rivalry was serious, and conflict within a *polis*, citizens against minorities with limited rights, had the potential to turn lethal.

King Herod and the Mother-*Polis* Jerusalem

Since everything we have seen to this point underscores the importance of Jerusalem for Judaean identity in the classical paradigm, we conclude our study with a closer look at the mother-*polis*. When the Elder Pliny called Jerusalem, recently destroyed by his young imperial friend Titus, "by far the most distinguished city of the East, and not of Judaea alone" (*Nat.* 5.70), he was referring essentially to the *polis* built by King Herod. Indeed, we cannot separate the king and his descendants from the *polis*, in terms of either its built environment or its significance for both local and Roman officials. Jerusalem and its royal family—Herod and his descendants—would remain close to emperors and legates through and past the war of 66–70. From a couple of decades after Rome's arrival in Syria, Herodians and Jerusalem come to form a conceptual unit, the status of each enhanced by the other. Roman Jerusalem was in important ways Herodian Jerusalem. Both strengthened the primacy of Judaea in southern Syria, over the other *ethnē* and *poleis*, and both seem to have been helpful to Judaeans elsewhere at times.

---

69. See *HJW* 372–75.

70. The speeches of Dio Chrysostom from around the turn of the second century A.D. were almost all made to cities of the east. They are filled with references to antagonism, resentment, and the struggle for primacy within each region. Dio constantly pleads for calm, partly for the practical purpose of not annoying the Roman overlords. When Pliny the Younger was sent as imperial legate to Bithynia-Pontus in A.D. 110, one of his primary tasks was to calm inter-*polis* rivalry in that province (in northern Anatolia, modern Turkey).

If we think back to the debate about whether individuals matter in history (Chapter 2), this appears to be a case in which Jerusalem's future was decisively shaped by a unique personality. With all allowance for the situation that spawned him and might have produced others like him in certain ways, it would be hard to argue that Herod simply embodied the spirit of his age or that someone like him would have done similar things if he had not existed.

A quarter-century after Pompey's capture of Jerusalem in 63 B.C., a new generation of legionaries found themselves besieging the city in the spring of 37 B.C. Commanded by Marc Antony's general and proconsul of Syria, Gaius Sosius, they were struggling to install an allied king, whom the Senate and People of Rome had recognized in 40 B.C. as their friend. King Herod would have to fight, nevertheless, with the help of his powerful allies for all the territory Rome had allotted him, especially for his ancient capital Jerusalem. In total the fight seems to have required two years, from 39 to 37 B.C.[71]

That was because, while Herod was away in Rome receiving his authority from the Senate under the sponsorship of both Antony and Octavian Caesar, a Hasmonean named Antigonus had staged a bloodless coup with the aid of the Parthians. Julius Caesar had confirmed Pompey's choice of Hyrcanus II as high priest, and Antigonus, the son of Hyrcanus' deposed brother Aristobulus II (now dead), tried unsuccessfully to undermine Hyrcanus II and his supporter Antipater, Herod's father.[72] Now in 40 B.C. he had another chance.[73] According to Josephus, a petty king in the north offered a Parthian official a massive sum if he would remove Hyrcanus II and his strong-man backer Antipater, Herod's father, and replace them with Antigonus as both high priest and king. This initiative attracted huge public support, perhaps from affection for the late Aristobulus II, who was considered a more vigorous champion of the people than the docile Hyrcanus II. The Parthian force reached Jerusalem and in a display of fake kindness

71. Josephus, *War* 1.290–357.

72. Josephus, *War* 1.195–200.

73. I follow the generally accepted chronology. In recent years nearly every important date in our field—Herod's reign and that of his descendants, the opening and closing years of the first war with Rome, the Diaspora Revolt, and the Bar-Kochba Revolt—have been challenged. They are not givens, and remain always open to dispute. The most comprehensive revision for the Herodians is Mahieu 2012, which puts the siege of Jerusalem in 36 B.C. and the king's death in A.D. 1. She may be correct, but I have not had a chance to work through all the extremely tangled connections that would need to be lined up, and some of her interpretations of Josephus appear to me too restrictive. I stay with conventional dates, but the reader should not take this to mean that such dates are settled.

persuaded both Hyrcanus II and Herod's brother to leave for consultations, a pretext for installing Antigonus.[74]

Judaea's position between Rome and the nearby Parthian world is easily to forget because we habitually think of Judaea only as part of the Roman empire. But we should remember Parthia's constant background presence, in both Judaean and Roman thinking, not least as a factor in the Judaean revolt.[75]

Why were the Parthians on the scene now? Through the preceding two centuries their empire had come gradually to control the enormous territories east of the Euphrates, centered in Iran and then equally Iraq, once held by the Seleucids. In the 40s B.C. they were apparently feeling particularly strong, having recently dealt a blow to Roman pride. In 53 B.C. the obscenely rich 60-year-old senator M. Licinius Crassus—political ally of Pompey and rising star Julius Caesar—took seven legions across the Euphrates River in search of military glory. He did not get far into Parthian territory, at its northwest extremity in Carrhae (Harran, modern Turkey), before he met total defeat, the loss of tens of thousands of soldiers, and a horrible death.[76]

Energized and offended in equal measure by this Roman incursion, as we may imagine, and perhaps by news of a planned follow-up by Julius Caesar in 45 B.C., the Parthians were willing to press their advantage in forays across the Euphrates into Roman Syria. They may have regarded Syria or even Anatolia (western Turkey) as the eventual western limit of an Asian power based in Mesopotamia, given the reach of the Persians and Seleucids before them. If so, they did not test the issue until the Romans had provoked them so seriously. Even then they might have let it lie.

According to Dio (48.24–26), it was paradoxically a Roman senator and commander, Q. Atius Labienus, who stirred them to action. Labienus had been a supporter of Julius Caesar's assassins (on March 15, 44 B.C.), Brutus and Cassius, who had also received support from the Parthians. In the confusion after Caesar's death in March 44, Cassius briefly established himself with Senate support as proconsul of Syria. But he soon lost his life in the contest with Antony and Octavian at Philippi (42 B.C.). With those victors now in pursuit of all the remaining sympathizers of Caesar's assassins, Labienus fled to the Parthians. This happened to coincide with Antony's famous infatuation with Queen Cleopatra, so he departed for a stay in Egypt. Labienus, seeing himself in a position to fuse Parthian and Roman-Republican interests, urged the Parthian king Orodes to move into Syria

74. Josephus, *War* 1.248–62.
75. See *HJW* 155–66 with bibliography and ancient references.
76. Plutarch, *Crassus* 16–33.

at once, while Rome's power looked vulnerable there. During his invasion in 40 B.C. alongside the son of the Parthian king, named Pacorus, many Roman garrisons went over to Labienus without a fight, seeing him not as a foreigner but as a virtuous Roman commander.

The Parthians' alliance with Antigonus was part of this regional picture. It is not hard to speculate as to why the Parthian king agreed to Labienus' proposal, especially as it concerned southern Syria. Parthia's huge Judaean population, which as far as we know had lived in peace and prosperity since the sixth-century B.C., would have made Jerusalem an ideal *polis* for Parthia to hold. Mass pilgrimages to Jerusalem from Parthian territory for the festivals of Passover, Booths/Pentecost, and Sukkot/Tabernacles, and the annual caravans bringing support for the temple maintained Parthia's tight bond with Jerusalem.[77] With a willing ally of prestigious descent in Aristobulus' son Antigonus, it might have seemed the perfect moment to recover the mother-*polis* for the eastern Judaeans, in whose orbit it had been for most of the preceding half-millennium: under Babylonians, Persians, and Hellenistic kings, even perhaps Hasmoneans. If we may indulge a counterfactual scenario for a moment: if Jerusalem had remained under Parthian influence, it seems unlikely that it would have been destroyed a century later.[78]

The contest between Herod and Antigonus for kingship in Jerusalem was thus a proxy war. Parthia's presence in Syria and Jerusalem and its entanglement in the Roman civil war immeasurably raised the stakes. Whatever the possibilities may have been, Labienus fell to Roman arms in 39 B.C., and Pacorus died in 38. So Marc Antony remained the towering figure in the east, strengthened locally by his merger with Queen Cleopatra, and Antigonus was isolated in Jerusalem. When Antony offered his client Herod all the military assistance he needed, the prospects for Rome's recovery of Jerusalem became bright. Like the Flavians a century later, he took his time and consolidated Galilee, Idumaea, and the rest through 39–37 B.C., reaching the early in the spring of 37.[79] Although Herod's army, with two legions under the proconsul Sosius assisting him, faced a struggle there, after

---

77. For the Parthian contribution to the temple see Josephus, *Ant.* 18.311–313. For Parthians (with Medes, Elamites, and residents of Mesopotamia) at Jerusalem festivals see Acts 2.5–9. The language may well be stylized, but it seems broadly to reflect real expectations.

78. Although the regional animosities in southern Syria might have been much the same under Parthia, that empire's highly diffuse and loose administration makes it unlikely that they would have sent an official such as Gessius Florus to raid temple funds for central needs as Nero did.

79. Josephus, *War* 1.295–342.

GEOGRAPHY: THE WORLD, THE HOMELAND, THE MOTHER-*POLIS* 251

perhaps three months Antigonus surrendered and was executed.[80] Herod's rebuilding of Jerusalem would include greatly strengthening its natural fortress-like qualities, and memories of 37 must have been the best guide about what he needed to do.

Antigonus' defeat marked the end of serious Hasmonean or Parthian ambitions in Judaea. But Herod would need to remain sensitive to still-strong Hasmonean sympathies among the populace if he wished to rule in peace. His marriage already during the siege to the young Mariamme, grand-daughter of *both* Aristobulus II and Hyrcanus II (captive in Parthia), in addition to flaunting his confidence of success and along with whatever true love it represented, was evidently an effort to co-opt pro-Hasmonean sentiment.[81] The proximity of Parthia would remain a political concern for generations to come, however. For Judaeans disgruntled with their regional status or their position in relation to Rome, dreaming eastward would remain an irresistible temptation.

The rule of King Herod (effectively 37–4 B.C.), like that of the Hasmoneans before him, had a considerable impact on Judaea's immediate neighbors. When he became king he was given Judaea, Idumaea, Samaria, and Galilee. To these were soon added the Greek coastal *poleis* as well as large territories east of the Sea of Galilee, granted by Augustus between 30 and the mid-20s B.C.: Trachonitis, Batanaea, and Auranitis (*Ant.* 15.343). Herod found himself with responsibility for several *poleis* of the Decapolis (Hippos, Gadara, and Esebonitis). On a modern map, which he lacked, this kingdom resembles a snub-nosed revolver pointed towards the Parthian empire.

His eventual territory was even larger than that controlled by the Hasmoneans at their height, but the two Jerusalem-based regimes had very different visions of governance, which were apparent to outsiders. Strabo, a younger contemporary of Herod, expressed serious indignation at what he considered Hasmonean belligerence. King Herod he assessed very differently (16.2.46):

> Now Pompey clipped off some of what the Judaeans had appropriated by force and assigned the priesthood to Hyrcanus [II]. Later a certain Herod, a local man and one of the race who had sneaked into the priesthood,[82] *distinguished himself so*

---

80. Josephus, *War* 1.327, 343–357. *War* (1.351) has the siege end in its fifth month. The parallel in *Ant.* 14.476, 487 gives around two months or possibly three (depending on what the third month in the second refers to)—in any case, concluded in the summer of 37.

81. Josephus, *War* 1.344 with 241–242: "Even those who did not take to him in the past accepted him as family then, because of his marriage connection with Hyrcanus."

82. This is an understandable mistake for an outsider who had heard that the

much from those before him, especially in his relationship with the Romans and in his mode of government, that he was even styled 'king'—Antony giving him this authority first, and later also Caesar Augustus.

Through his long reign, indeed, Herod became famous around the empire as *the* Judaean king. Notwithstanding complaints brought against him, from antiquity to the present, he did a great deal to enhance the position of Judaeans. Yet as far as we can tell he became neither a model for nationalist aspiration nor an object of abiding hatred among Judaea's neighbors.

The mother-*polis* Jerusalem was a principal beneficiary of Herod's vision. He greatly enhanced its infrastructure, appearance, and reputation. The following description is not meant to provide an original account of Jerusalem's appearance under Herod. A number of distinguished archaeologists and architects have done this work, and the rest of us are in their debt.[83] Naturally, these scholars disagree on various points, such as the precise location and shape of the Antonia fortress, the Pool of Israel, or the second wall, or the orientation of the central temple shrine. Since I am not attempting to resolve these matters, there is no point opening them up. Agreement on one point, following one author's logic, might have knock-on effects with other matters. I am content here to follow the Ritmeyers' synthetic work, to which they bring archaeological experience, from the early days of digging in Jerusalem, as well as architectural and artistic expertise. Their lavishly illustrated work is easily accessible to readers. This does not imply my agreement with every point, and I mention a few debates in the notes, but for our purposes here most of these do not matter. Rather than footnoting every sentence, then, I leave the reader to consult the Ritmeyers' work along with the other bibliography mentioned.

Herod's construction of two dominating structures, like bookends on Jerusalem's east and west sides, required him also to rebuild much of the rest (Figure 4). On the eastern side he boldly re-envisioned the central shrine and its hill-top platform: the 500-year-old "second temple," as we call it, though one could argue that his renovations made this a third temple. The original had been built with Persian support, after they permitted Judaean exiles to return around 538 B.C. That post-exilic temple apparently sat on a 500-cubit (= 861 ft, 262.5 m) square platform around the summit of

---

Judaean leaders, down to Herod's contemporary Hyrcanus II, had been high priests and political leaders. Herod had no claim to priestly ancestry.

83. E.g., Avigad 1976, 1983; Gibson and Jacobson 1994; Geva 1994, 2000; Levine 2002; Netzer and Laureys-Chachy 2006; Ritmeyer 2006a, 2006b, 2011; Steinberg 2008; Bahat 2009; Grabar and Kedar 2009; Patrich 2009a; Galor and Avni 2011.

Jerusalem's eastern hill, where the Dome of the Rock is today. The Hasmoneans extended the square nearly 50 m (164 ft) to the south, after destroying the Seleucid "Akra" fortress (Figure 5).

Herod's project was vastly more ambitious: he doubled the size of the original temple platform by extending it to the south, west, and north. In order to achieve this his workers dug down to bedrock and laid enormous limestone ashlars—perfectly cut stones often weighing 70 tonnes (80 tons) each, to form a retaining wall. They either filled in or arched the interior space below to support the platform.[84] The lower courses of the outer retaining wall were so solid that the Romans, despite their otherwise thorough demolition in A.D. 70, could not dislodge them. On the western side, the lower courses have survived in modern Jerusalem as the Western Wall or *ha-kotel* (Figure 6).

Since the dimensions of the central shrine (comprising the "Holy Place" and "Holy of Holies") were established by precedent, Herod's large expansions of the temple platform mainly accommodated a massive new Court of the Nations (or "gentiles"), which was lined around its edges with high porticoes, created by rows of columns. These provided welcome shade beneath their wooden roofs. The immense columns were in the Ionic and Corinthian styles of contemporary Graeco-Roman architecture. In the vast outer courtyard, non-Judaeans could mingle with the locals, pray together to the Judaean god, and arrange for animal sacrifices. Sacrifices were offered by priests in the central slaughtering area before the shrine, which was strictly off limits to foreigners.

Although Herod's design incorporated many eastern elements—such a large square, for example, was not common with Greek or Roman temples—the spirit of the structure accorded with Hellenistic-Roman attitudes toward the gods. When visiting the mother-*polis* of a foreign people, it was normal to pay one's respects to the local deity. This was not seen as disloyal, because each *ethnos* and *polis* was assumed to have distinctive and in principle respectable ancient traditions. When travelling it was common decency, and perhaps necessary for one's safety, to give honor to the local god.

Suetonius relays a revealing anecdote about Augustus' comment-worthy distaste for rituals not traditionally Graeco-Roman. He avoided stopping to offer sacrifice at the sanctuary of the bull Apis in Egyptian Memphis, and

---

84. See Ritmeyer's (2006a–b) fully illustrated books. The largest stone is often estimated to have weighed 517 tonnes (570 tons), but Ritmeyer, challenging the usual assumption about its thickness (p. 32), estimates a maximum of 159 tonnes (175 tons). See also Netzer and Laureys-Chachy 2006: 137–78. Bahat (2009) independently reached conclusions similar to those of Ritmeyer concerning the phases of temple-mount expansion.

commended his grandson Gaius for not visiting Jerusalem to offer sacrifice (*Aug.* 93.1). These uniquely powerful Romans were exceptional, however. The story gets its force from the assumption that lesser public figures *would* make a respectful effort to worship at other sacred sites. Augustus' close friend and son-in-law Marcus Agrippa, for example, had no such qualms. Josephus describes him visiting Jerusalem and joyfully offering a hecatomb (properly, 100 animal victims) at the temple, then providing a lavish feast for the delighted populace (*Ant.* 16.14). Josephus tells of a Roman tribune visiting Jerusalem decades later, gathering the people "in the temple" (i.e., the outer court) for a talk, and then making obeisance—humbly prostrating himself, or something in that vein—to God before departing (*War* 2.341). When Josephus mentions the many costly gifts from foreigners that were visible around the temple precincts, he assumes and implies that it was normal for them to give such honors and pay for sacrifices—though they could not themselves approach the inner court.[85]

Herod could well argue that such openness was a Judaean tradition, as old as King Solomon a millennium earlier.[86] Since the inability of (most) Judaeans to reciprocate such devotion in other peoples' temples had led to accusations of misanthropy or even atheism,[87] it may have been particularly important to Herod that Jerusalem conspicuously welcome strangers. When some young priests decided to refuse "gifts and sacrifices from foreigners" in the summer of A.D. 66, amidst seriously inflamed regional tensions, Josephus presents this as a "foundation of war" (*War* 2.409). Jerusalem's elders complain that it will make Judaeans appear uniquely hostile to the world, and lead to a condemnation for impiety (*War* 2.413–414).

Despite this welcoming of foreigners, in Herod's temple Judaean law and tradition were visibly and emphatically respected. A 1.5-m (4.5-ft) balustrade surrounding the interior courts warned foreigners to advance no farther or face the risk of their own death.[88] Although Greek-style col-

85 See *War* 2.409, 413–414; 4.180–182.

86 King Hiram of Tyre (1 Kgs 7:13–45; 9:11–14) and the Queen of Sheba (2 Kgs 10:1–10) had famously sent lavish gifts. Josephus' Solomon, when dedicating the first temple to God, elaborates the biblical claim (1 Kgs 8:41–43) that supplicants from the ends of the earth were welcome in the temple (*Ant.* 8.116–117).

87. Josephus summarizes the accusations of one anti-Judaean writer: "In one place he abuses us as *atheists* and *misanthropes*" (*Apion* 2.148). Cf. Cicero, *Flac.* 66–69; Juvenal 5.14.96–106; Tacitus, *Hist.* 5.4–5. For discussion see Sevenster 1975; Smallwood 2001 [1981]: 120–43; Daniel 1979; Gager 1983; Whittaker 1984; Feldman 1993; Schäfer 1997.

88. See *War* 5.193–94. At 6.124–125, Josephus has Titus refer to these warnings, inscribed in both Greek and Latin, and the extraordinary privilege granted the Judaeans to kill even a Roman citizen who trespassed. Remarkably, two copies of the Greek tablet

umns surrounded the open courts, and both Greek and Roman architectural features were abundant in the surrounding walls and vaults, the Bible's prescriptions for the central buildings, the lack of figural representation on the temple itself, and the use of local materials and design elements gave the structure a different look from its Greek and Roman counterparts.[89] An eagle that Herod reportedly erected over the temple's "great gate" (*War* 1.649–50), which caused enormous controversy, remains an anomaly and a puzzle.[90] His general concern to maintain Judaean law in both Jerusalem and the *chōra* Judaea is reflected in his coinage. He and later his son Archelaus would use traditional Judaean symbols on their Jerusalem-minted coins. They were also careful to avoid representing human or animal forms. The Tyrian coins bore such images, to be sure, but they were required by priestly authorities until the 60s, because of their stable value.[91]

Herod's renovations around Jerusalem's eastern hill necessitated the redesign of much else in its environment (Figure 4). On the temple's vulnerable north side, he relocated the fortress that had guarded the north end of the smaller Hasmonean temple mount, naming this "Antonia" in tribute to Marc Antony. This massive stronghold, occupying more than a third of the 316 m (1038 ft) north wall, added greatly to the security of that open side—and would indeed become a major obstacle to Titus' army when it approached from the north. Towering over the new temple mount, its garrison helped to ensure order at crowded festivals. On the eastern end of the same northern temple wall was the deep "Pool of Israel," whose eastern wall was a northern extension of the temple mount's own formidable eastern wall. This pool served a double purpose: occupying another third of the northern wall, it was effectively a defensive moat nearly 40 m (131 ft) in width. For everyday purposes it was a reservoir for the *polis*. Several other reservoirs

---

have been discovered, one—virtually complete—found in 1871 (*CIJ* 2.1400, kept in the Istanbul Archaeology Museum), the other, a fragment from the middle section, found in 1935 (*OGIS* 2.598, kept in the Rockefeller Museum, Jerusalem).

89. See the reconstructions in Ritmeyer 2006.

90. We are unsure of what the eagle was supposed to signify (Roman legions? Divine protection coupled with Herod's royal power?), when Herod erected it (perhaps shortly before his death?), or how most of the populace reacted to it. Josephus relates only that two "sophists" with a reputation for precision in the laws took advantage of reports that Herod was near death to stir up their young students to pull the eagle down. Underlying all this is the larger problem of interpreting the second commandment: van Henten 2008; von Ehrenkrook 2011. Centuries later, Ashkenazi synagogues in Europe would make extensive use of eagle imagery: Szkolut 2002: 1–11; Rodov 2004.

91. Herod produced a few eagle coins, which might be connected with his gift of the eagle to the temple, the cause of a notorious incident near the end of his life that caused problems also for Archelaus (*War* 1.648–655; 2.5). See Meshorer 2001: 61–72, 322.

were cut from bedrock to the north of the temple mount, one on the west side (the Struthion pool) specifically to serve the needs of soldiers in the Antonia.

To the south of the temple mount, Herod's redesign required a change in the landscape of the Lower City and the temple's access points from that direction. These included a monumental staircase, which was now cut into the bedrock, leading up to double and triple gates and into the temple complex. All of this was surrounded by abundant facilities for purification, especially in large immersion pools, and for visitors' other needs. The western side of the temple mount needed to be transformed, with vaulted bridges over the Tyropoeon Valley, which continued north to a location beneath the modern Damascus Gate, a monumental staircase, and rows of shops along the road beside the temple platform. This was paved with admirably thick stones, which have been uncovered and restored. Visitors to the modern city may walk on them again.

The other bookend project in Herod's Jerusalem was on the city's western hill (inward from the modern Jaffa Gate): a magnificent palace compound for the king, with internal courtyards, gardens, colonnades, and fountains. At the north end Herod built three multi-story towers, dedicated respectively to the wife he had killed out of jealousy and then deeply mourned (Mariamme), the loyal brother who had fallen victim to the Parthians before Herod took power (Phasael), and an unknown friend named Hippicus ("Equestrian") who had died in battle.[92] Josephus, though he had travelled widely by the time he wrote of these things, could still describe the towers as "for their size, beauty, and sturdiness, unique in the entire world" (*War* 5.161).

These western structures were located on the summit of Jerusalem's higher hill, which hosted the Upper City (Figure 7). This housed the wealthiest citizens, including many of the upper priests. Archaeology has uncovered the remains of palatial homes, some of which enjoyed a view of the temple mount to the east. The Upper City also hosted an upscale (Upper) Market and a Hasmonean palace, across the valley from the temple (*War* 5.137). On the slope beneath that palace was, if not an actual gymnasium (a Greek cultural-educational-athletic facility for male teens and alumni), at least the open courtyard with gardens called the *xystus* that typically accompanied a gymnasium in other cities (*War* 2.344).

The mass of poorer citizens lived in much more densely packed housing on the hill south of the temple and on its slopes. As Jerusalem continued to grow, residential expansion was mainly to the north of the wealthier area and of the temple—beyond the walls of Herod's time in the New City. In the early 40s A.D., Herod's grandson Agrippa attempted to enclose this with

92. On the elusive Hippicus see Rocca 2008: 95–96.

GEOGRAPHY: THE WORLD, THE HOMELAND, THE MOTHER-*POLIS* 257

a sturdy protective wall, the so-called Third Wall, but had to abandon the project because of Roman suspicions of conspiracy. Thus, just as Augustus had set about rebuilding Rome in his image after the long period of civil war that produced his regime, a model later followed by the Flavians (Chapter 1), so too in the east Augustus' friend Herod rebuilt Jerusalem to imprint his personality and his new vision of stability and grandeur for all posterity.[93]

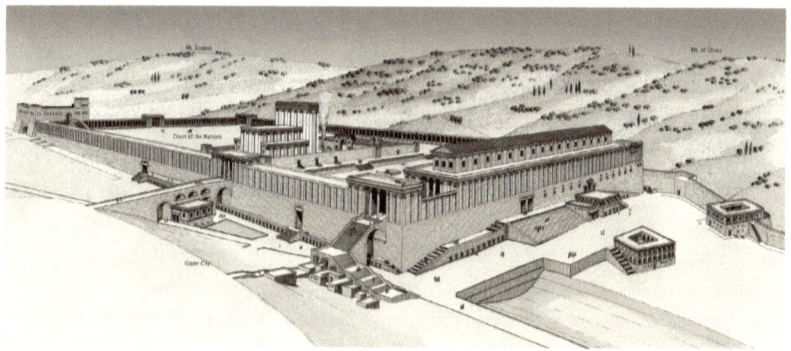

Figure 4. The classic reconstruction of first-century Jerusalem's Herodian temple mount. © and rights reserved by L. Ritmeyer, used with permission.

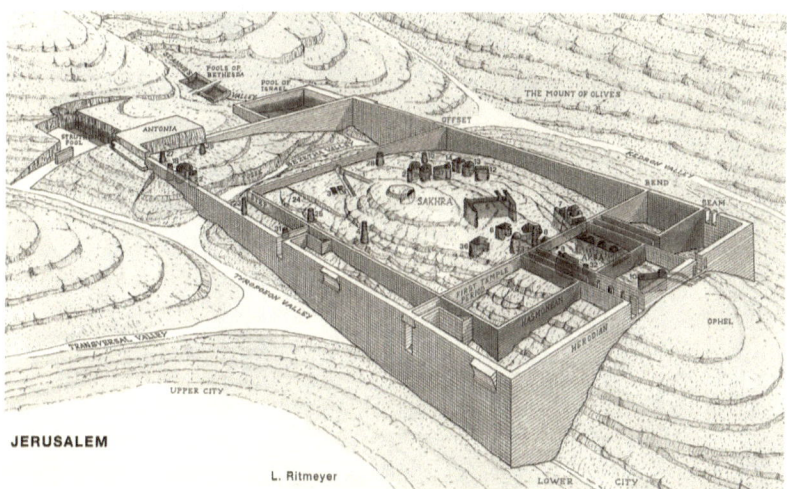

Figure 5. Cutaway view of the building stages of the temple mount, the largest area being Herod's retaining wall, showing the bedrock. © and rights reserved by L. Ritmeyer, used with permission.

---

93. For a comparison between Augustus and Herod see Galinsky 1996: 29–42 and Geiger 2009: 157–70.

Figure 6. Model of first-century Jerusalem at the Israel Museum, from the south: Lower City and temple with Antonia in the background to the right, Upper city centre left, and New City in the distance northward. Author 2013.

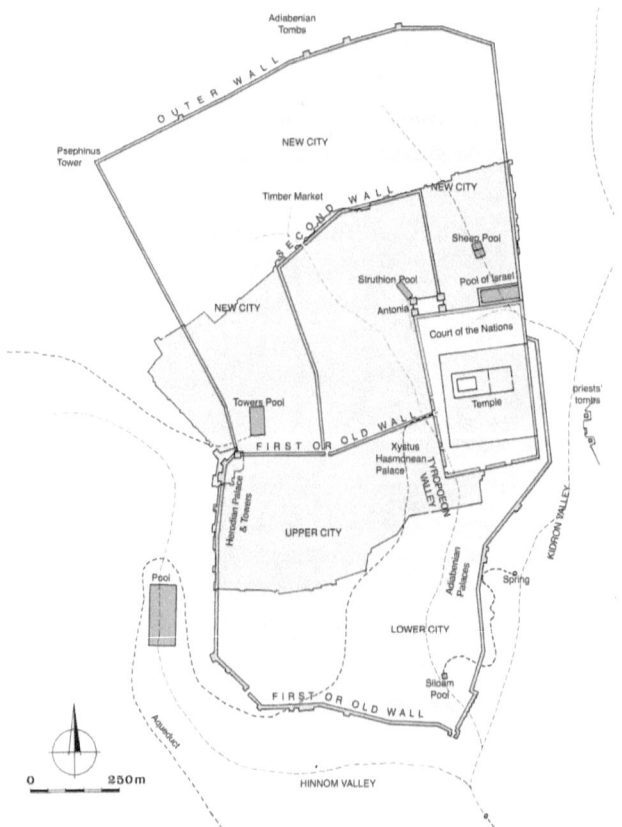

Figure 7. Plan of Jerusalem ca. A.D. 66, with the area of the modern Old City shaded more darkly. The diagram is © with rights reserved by L. Ritmeyer. Annotations are by the author with Ritmeyer's permission.

If Herod was so obviously solicitous for his adopted capital, however, he was equally careful to cultivate the distinctive characters of other *poleis*, both those under his rule and others in the region. Josephus, in a passage defending the uniqueness of Judaean tradition, admired "the magnanimity and moderation of the Romans in not expecting their subjects to violate their ancestral laws" (*Apion* 2.73). Perhaps Herod was influenced by Rome's approach, for it was the same style of governing (*politeia*), in contrast to the Hasmoneans' overtly Judaizing approach, that attracted Strabo's respectful notice above.

We see the starkest contrast in the case of Samaria, the region north of Judaea that had been traditionally hostile. John Hyrcanus had destroyed both the Samarians' mother-city and their temple in 111 B.C. Herod, by contrast, made the re-foundation of Samaria as *Sebastē* ("Augustus-City") a high priority. This was a *polis* to which he often turned for refuge and support, especially during his war with Antigonus and the Parthians (39–37 B.C.) before he took control of Jerusalem. It was in Samaria that he married Mariamme and minted his first coins—bearing standard Roman images, without concern for Judaean sensibilities—in the same period. The Samarians offered provisions and fighters to help him seize Jerusalem.[94] A later wife (Malthacē) would actually come from Samaria (*War* 1.562), and near the end of his life the tortured king would return there to kill two of his sons (1.551).

So it was that in Samaria, even before he started the rebuilding of Jerusalem, Herod began in 27 B.C. to establish a very different kind of urban space. A large temple platform was constructed on the central summit, and next to that a palace. Although similar to those of the redesigned Jerusalem, however, Sebastē's temple and altar were devoted to the emperor Augustus. Prominent Samarian men could compete for the signal honor of priesthoods in the imperial cult. Significantly smaller than Jerusalem's rebuilt temple precinct, Sebastē's was nevertheless the fourth-largest of the fifteen surviving temples to Augustus, and among the first to be constructed after Augustus (as Octavian Caesar) became supreme by defeating Antony and Cleopatra, in 31/30 B.C.[95] It was only in 27 B.C. that the Senate bestowed the cultic title "Augustus" on him, so Herod wasted no time in honoring the ruler in this most exalted way. Settling some 6,000 veterans of his army there, he privileged them with a favorable political constitution and prime

---

94. Safety during war and marriage: *War* 1.303, 314, 344, 551; *Ant.* 14.284, 467. A later wife, Malthace, would originate from Samaria (*War* 1.562). On Herod's Samarian coins see Meshorer 2001: 61–65. On provisions during the war, *Ant.* 14.408; on additional fighters, 14.468.

95. On the design, structure, and meaning of this temple, Bernett 2007: 66–98 has many valuable insights.

parcels of land in Sebastē's *chōra* (*War* 1.403; *Ant.* 15.296–298), creating a lasting bond between the Samarians and their sovereign.

All of this furnished important if remote conditions for the war a century later. Sebastene fighters, along with others recruited from Caesarea, formed the hard core of Herod's army. Their successors would continue to be the base of his son Archelaus' army and then of the Roman auxiliary forces, following the area's annexation under direct Roman rule in A.D. 6. The anti-Judaean sentiments of these forces would become an aggravating factor in the outbreak of war (*Ant.* 19.355–366). Herod recruited his army not only from around his large kingdom, however. He also had specialist guard units from Gaul and Germany, and his total force may have reached 30,000 or more. It appears that he kept units largely distinct according to their ethnic composition.[96]

Having mentioned Herod's temple to Augustus in Sebastē, I pause to consider some features of the imperial cult. It seems clear from the evidence that this was not something normally imposed by Rome or the emperor on the provinces, but was rather a natural outgrowth, from the bottom up, of eastern populations who had been accustomed to worshipping their rulers as divine: from Egyptian Pharaohs to Hellenistic monarchs. This was a world in which the lines between humans, demigods, and gods were blurred, to be sure. The Greeks recognized a number of heroes who were born mortals, and in general great men were understood to have a spiritual force (*daimōn*, *genius*) animating their actions that was worthy of reverence; after death their shades were assumed to live on.[97]

In spite of a common perception that Roman emperors demanded worship from their subjects,[98] the initiative in imperial cult most often

96. See Saddington 2009: 313 on ethnic separation.

97. One example of how a highly educated thinker and speaker could see such matters is Cicero's speech in favor of the extension of Pompey's powers, *Man.* 27–50, celebrating his unparalleled accomplishments, wisdom, and valor in bringing the whole world to heel, especially 36 ("... the divine and incredible virtue of that general").

98. The famous first-century exception was during the brief reign of Gaius Caligula, who ordered his colossal statue erected in Jerusalem's temple (Josephus, *War* 2.185–203). Gaius may have been mentally unstable at that point, but even hostile sources agree he was reacting to a perceived insult. Josephus has an Alexandrian delegation persuading Gaius that Judaeans were generally refusing to accept his images or swear oaths of loyalty (*Ant.* 18.256–309). Philo claims that Judaeans in coastal Jamnia had knocked down altars in his honor. As far as we know, Gaius would otherwise have not undertaken the statue initiative. His reported logic was: "If you are going to interfere with efforts to honor me in other cities, we'll see how you like it when I put my statue in Jerusalem!" For judicious efforts to reconstruct the events, see Smallwood 1961: 31–6, 267–325; 2001 [1981]: 174–80, 235–50, and Barrett 1989: 182–91. Philo presents Gaius' petulant move as a sharp break from the understanding established between Augustus

came from prominent men in the empire's eastern *poleis* who were eager to establish themselves and their home cities as supremely loyal. They vied for the privilege of serving as priests of Augustus. There was considerable vagueness, however, about any theology behind these arrangements. To judge from coins and inscriptions, emperors themselves were most often concerned to be seen *as chief priests*—reverently leading the people in sacrificing to the gods—rather than as objects of worship.[99] In Rome, although divine ancestry and afterlife among the gods presented no conceptual problems, tradition did not tolerate even kingship, let alone the assumption of divine status by a living ruler.

In Augustus' personal account of his achievements, rather than making himself a god he was eager to record his *service in* Rome's top priestly colleges. He was also an initiate in Greek cults, and reportedly accepted temples devoted to himself reluctantly—only in the provinces and only if they were also dedicated *to Rome*.[100] He formulated his responses as a *concession* to the provinces' desire to express their loyalty, in ways consonant with their eastern traditions of "slavery" under kings and tyrants. Augustus' successor Tiberius famously forbade the dedication of temples and priests in his honor, or even statues, without his express permission (Suetonius, *Tib*. 26.1). And in the letter of Claudius to Alexandria of 41 (Chapter 2), that emperor politely declines the Alexandrians' *request* to build shrines or establish a priesthood for his cult. He does not want to make himself tiresome to others, he says. Anyway, temples are for gods![101] Vespasian's reported dying words—"Uh oh: Looks like I am becoming a god!" (Suetonius, *Vesp*. 23.4)—assume both the Roman tradition of divinization only after death and that emperor's distaste for that status.

Both Philo and Josephus understood that the making of statues to honor exceptional humans and the imperial cult, though alien to Judaean custom, was part and parcel of *polis* culture elsewhere.[102] The problem arose

---

and Herod, that a daily sacrifice in Jerusalem's temple for the emperor's well-being would more than suffice to express loyalty (*Leg*. 188–348).

99. See Price 1980; 1984. Notice the frequent representation of Augustus and other emperors with togas pulled over their heads as they offered reverent sacrifice.

100. On his priesthoods, *RG* 7; initiation into the Eleusinian mysteries, Suetonius, *Aug*. 93.1; limitation of imperial cult, Suetonius, *Aug*. 52; Dio 51.20.7.

101. Letter of Claudius to the Alexandrians (A.D. 41), *CPJ* vol. 2, pp. 40–42, col. III, lines 48–50.

102. Josephus, *Apion* 2.74: "The Greeks and various others reckon it a good thing to make statues . . ." Philo speaks at some length of the honors paid to Augustus, and the competition to honor him, not least in Philo's own city of Alexandria (*Leg*. 140–51), the beauty and appropriateness of which he concedes. He has no objection to the temple of Augustus in Caesarea (*Leg*. 305). He insists, however, that neither Augustus nor his

that, if other *poleis* were jockeying to build temples for the imperial cult, the reluctance of Judaeans could make Jerusalem's inhabitants and émigrés look disloyal—even if emperors had not required worship. Josephus reports that Judaeans were accused by their neighbors (*not* normally by emperors or Roman officials) on this point: "Apion attempted to denounce us because we do not erect statues of the emperors" (*Apion* 2.73). His response was that the Judaeans did something more meaningful but in keeping with their ancestral laws, and that this had always been accepted by the emperors. Namely, they offered a special daily sacrifice in Jerusalem's temple "for the emperors" (*Apion* 2.76-77). This arrangement was worked out between Herod and Augustus and continued by subsequent emperors, who reciprocated the expression of loyalty with generous gifts to Jerusalem's temple.[103]

The Judaean arrangement appears to have fit well enough, from the perspective of the emperors themselves, within the general requirements of imperial loyalty. While governing Bithynia-Pontus (modern Turkey) in the early second century, Pliny the Younger reported to Trajan that his provincials had taken their oaths of loyalty to Trajan and were competing in demonstrations of loyalty. He continued: "We have petitioned the gods to preserve you and the commonwealth . . . especially because of your sanctity, reverence, and piety." Trajan responded with gratitude and apparent satisfaction that his subjects had made their "vows *to the immortal gods* for my safety" (*Ep.* 10.100-101). He does not seem to have expected more, certainly not worship of himself.

In his new Augustus-City (Sebastē), nevertheless, we see Herod's effort to share in the more common gestures of loyalty by doing what he could not do in nearby Jerusalem: be first and biggest in the provincial cult of Rome and Augustus. We do not know how the native Samarians aligned his project with their ancestral laws, which shared much (including the Pentateuch) with the Judaeans, but apparently they found a way to deal with it, just as they had not protested vigorously at Antiochus IV's commonality initiative. Even Josephus, who abhors violation of Judaean law in Jerusalem and is eventually critical of Herod's behavior on many fronts, speaks of the beauty and size of the temple to Augustus at Sebastē, much as Philo describes the remarkable facilities of Alexandria (*Legat.* 150-51). The well-situated

---

successors ever expected any such treatment from the Judaeans, whose distinctive traditions they respected (*Leg.* 152-61).

103. The arrangement is described by Philo, who lived in Alexandria through much of Herod's reign (*Leg.* 280) and by Josephus (*Apion* 2.73-77), who also emphasizes that the termination of this sacrifice in 66 was a foundation of the coming war (*War* 2.409-414). On Roman rulers' gifts and admiration, see Philo, *Leg.* 291-98, 309-311.

Sebastē was, Josephus remarks, conceived as a monument to the king's humanity and love of beauty (*Ant.* 15.298).

Another Herodian city that would play a pivotal role in the Judaean War featured a large temple to Augustus and Rome.[104] In coastal Caesarea the contrast between his policies and those of the Hasmoneans could not have been starker. The Judaeans' need for access to the sea had led Simon to seize Joppa to the south and colonize it with Judaeans. Herod also needed a reliable port, but his approach was different. He undertook to transform the old Greek town of Strato's Tower into a world-class port, with an artificial harbor resembling Alexandria's and larger than Athens' renowned Piraeus (*War* 1.410). He enthusiastically dedicated the *polis* to Augustus, invoking the emperor's family name *Caesar* rather than the title *Sebastos* (Greek for Augustus), as a synonymous alternative to Sebastē. Lying some 54 km (33.5 miles) north of now-Judaean Joppa, and described by Josephus as part of the Phoenician coast (*Ant.* 15.333), Caesarea would be a prominent center for sailors, trade, and Roman provincial administration, outside the orbit of the ethnic laws and traditions that characterized the Judaean capital Jerusalem.

Archaeology confirms important parts of Josephus' glowing descriptions (*War* 1.413–416; *Ant.* 15.331–341). Using the latest technology of his day, Herod overcame nature itself by sinking a massive breakwater and, inside the space thus created, constructing a safe double harbor. This was big enough for the largest cargo ships headed to and from Egypt along the Mediterranean coast, which had previously been forced to lie at anchor offshore when bad weather arose. Every aspect of both harbor and city declared the king's own greatness as well as his loyalty to Augustus. Ships entering the harbor from its protected north side passed a massive circular tower on the left, with three column-mounted colossal statues above it, and an even higher rectangular stone structure on the right, also topped with giant statues. The left tower (Druseion) was named for Augustus' stepson Drusus, who had died tragically young; the other may have been called the Tibereion,[105] named after his other stepson, the future emperor Tiberius.

---

104. Herod built yet another center for Augustus' imperial cult, with a spectacular white temple, near the northern extremity of his kingdom, by the sources of the Jordan River in the slopes of Mt. Hermon (*War* 1.404–406), on a site that had long before been dedicated to the nature cult of the God Pan—hence its name Panias (modern Banias). Under Herod's son Philip this would become yet another "Caesar-city," often known by the Latinized name Caesarea Philippi (i.e. "of Philip").

105. A famous partial inscription was found in the excavations of Caesarea, recording Pontius Pilate's dedication (or something) of a *Tiberieum*, and scholars have long debated what the structure was. Since Pilate had been sent by Tiberius, scholars imagined that Pilate authorized a new honorific structure of some kind. Alföldy (1999) has argued that the name would make best sense as a counterpart to the Drusion tower. So

The most striking part of this shining white city of broad streets was the central temple to Augustus and Rome, angled so as to face new arrivals in the harbor, and containing a colossal statue of the emperor (modeled on Olympian Zeus) alongside one of Roma (modeled on Hera at Argos). The city was fitted with all the accouterments of a prosperous *polis*: an aqueduct, baths, vaulted underground structures and storage houses, an effective sewer system, a large theatre and multifunction hippodrome along the seashore, and between these two a magnificent palace built on a promontory that projected into the sea.[106] The hippodrome hosted international games, every four years after the city's foundation, which were supported by Augustus and his wife Livia (*Ant.* 16.136–141). A modern visitor to the well-excavated site can easily believe Josephus' claim that Herod "dedicated the *polis* to the Roman province of Syria, the harbor to those sailing this coast, and the honor of the foundation to Caesar" (*War* 1.414).

In these diverse parts of his kingdom Herod fundamentally altered the physical landscape, as he did also in his fortress-mausoleum complex at Herodium and his palaces at Jericho, Machaerus, and Masada. His reach extended to foreign cities. Those west and north of Judaea (Ascalon, Ptolemais, Damascus, Tyre, Sidon, Berytus, Antioch) he furnished with basic elements of *polis* infrastructure: gymnasia, markets, colonnades, theatres, temples, aqueducts, and baths. His liberality apparently reached even Asia Minor (Turkey) and the Greek mainland, including the *poleis* of Rhodes, Athens, and Sparta, to which he extended his largesse on personal visits. He perpetually endowed the famous quadrennial Games at Olympia, himself serving as games president for one season (*War* 1.422–428). Inscriptions indicate that Herod was honored as a benefactor (one of many), directly and indirectly, by the citizens of Athens, Cos, and Delos—indirectly when they honored his son Antipas or great-granddaughter Berenice as a descendant of *the great king*.[107]

As a product of regional politics himself, Herod came by this un-Hasmonean approach honestly. His grandfather Antipas had risen to

---

Pilate may have repaired and rededicated a structure that was by then, nearly a half-century after construction, badly weathered.

106. There is some debate as to whether this palace goes back to Herod. Even if it does not, since Josephus refers to Herod's "sumptuous royal grounds" in the city, there must have been palaces elsewhere (*Ant.* 15.331). See Patrich 2009b.

107. Herod appears as "lover of Rome," honored for his benefactions, in *OGIS* 415 (= *IG* 2.3440), and is praised for his virtue, possibly after visiting the city in 14 B.C. and donating money for a gymnasium (Segre 1993: 87). Berenice is the descendant of "great kings" in *OGIS* 428 (= *IG* 2.3449). Antipas is honored as "the son of King Herod" in *OGIS* 416 (= *Inscriptions of Cos*, ed. Paton and Hicks, no. 75) and 417 (= *Inscriptions de Délos* no. 1586).

prominence when Alexander Jannaeus chose him to govern recently Judaized Idumaea.[108] Antipas used his position to cultivate friendships with Gaza and Ascalon to the west, as with Nabataean Arabia to the south and east (*Ant.* 14.10). He arranged for his son Antipater to marry a Nabataean princess, Cyprus, who became Herod's mother. When we first meet Antipater in Josephus (*War* 1.123–124; *Ant.* 14.10), we learn that he had a long-standing dislike of Aristobulus II, the one who (following Alexandra's death in 67 B.C.) had persuaded his older brother Hyrcanus II to retire from the high priesthood in his favor.

It was therefore with the support of the Idumaean Antipater and the Nabataean King Aretas III that Pompey and later Gabinius reinstated Hyrcanus II. Aretas was on board partly because of Antipater's assurances that this quieter Hasmonean would return a dozen cities that the aggressive Alexander (son of Aristobulus II) had taken from the Arabs (*Ant.* 14.18). But this personal connection with Pompey created serious problems a few years later, when the Roman civil war forced Pompey along with much of the Senate to flee Rome (49 B.C.), ahead of Julius Caesar's advancing army. Seeing an opportunity, the Hasmonean Aristobulus II made his final bid for power by winning Julius Caesar's support: *he* would be the new dictator's ally in Judaea. Pompey was having none of it. In his final desperate days, he used his network of friends to kill both Aristobulus and his son Alexander (*War* 1.183–185).

Now came Antipater's master-stroke, which would define Herodian policy thereafter. Seeing the new political realities after Pompey's death in Egypt (48 B.C.), Antipater urged Hyrcanus to throw his support behind Julius Caesar, who still had to fight against Roman troops ensconced in Egypt. Antipater and Hyrcanus not only facilitated the passage of forces coming from the north to support Caesar; Antipater himself led 3,000 Judaean fighters into battle for Caesar's cause, while using his diplomatic skill to bring over the Judaeans of Egypt and Alexandria to that cause. This forever endeared him to Caesar, who, after magnanimously affirming his support for his enemy Pompey's client Hyrcanus, made Antipater his chief agent in the region.[109]

108. On the history and cultural complexity of Idumaea, see Kokkinos 1998: 36–139. An intriguing early Christian tradition that the family's roots were in Ascalon is explored by Kokkinos (100–39), who finds it supportable on other historical grounds, including parallels in coinage.

109. *War* 1.187–199; *Ant.* 14.127–144. Greek *epitropos* was used by ancient writers for Latin *procurator*. Both terms indicated an official who took care of someone else's interests, including but not exclusively financial ones: his agent or steward. It is not clear from Josephus' account *whose* agent Antipater was supposed to be: Caesar's, Hyrcanus', or both. Since Caesar appointed him, and it was normal (in later times) for emperors to

The striking thing here is Antipater's contentedness, as it seems, to enjoy his power *indirectly*, through the pliable figurehead Hyrcanus: a Judaean high priest considered legitimate by the people because of his Hasmonean ancestry. As the muscle behind Hyrcanus, Antipater reportedly went around the countryside persuading and threatening various groups to align their fortunes with the high priest and his Roman patrons (*War* 1.201–203). We see the effects of this strategy in the many decrees that Josephus cites from Caesar, the Senate, and other city councils (under their orders) in support of Judaean rights in the eastern Mediterranean (*Ant.* 14.186–265). Although these are predicated on the assistance that Caesar received from the Judaeans (14.192–93), Antipater—engineer of that assistance—does not appear by name. The high priest and ethnarch (i.e., ruler of an *ethnos*—the Judaeans) Hyrcanus is the featured leader. (Caution: in some cases this is apparently because the document accidentally reflects its origin in the time of John Hyrcanus I.[110]) Still, Antipater quietly got on with his agenda. He made his son Phasael "general" of Jerusalem and its territory, and sent the 27-year-old Herod to deal with Galilee, where Sepphoris and its environs had become home to significant disaffection.

Herod, then, had been schooled from his youth in an approach to regional politics that differed sharply from the Hasmonean model. In spite of being "the Judaean king," he would be no Judaizer. He was a pragmatic ruler in his dealings with Rome and with non-Judaean centers in his kingdom. His father Antipater had proven a nimble politician by working through Hyrcanus, but that shadowy position cost him his life in 43 B.C. The Nabataean king Malichus, becoming increasingly alarmed at Antipater's hidden power and worried about its potential to push aside Hyrcanus in favor of Antipater's sons, arranged for his old ally to be poisoned, hoping that this would end the family's ambitions (*Ant.* 14.277–284). He was wrong. Young Herod soon had his revenge (*Ant.* 14.288–293).

After Herod was appointed king by the Roman Senate in 40 B.C., there was no longer any need for him to work through a Hasmonean high priest. In 37 he married the Hasmonean Mariamme, granddaughter of both Hyrcanus II and Aristobulus II (her parents were cousins), and made Mariamme's young brother Aristobulus III high priest (37 B.C.), also inviting her aged grandfather Hyrcanus II back from his Parthian exile (36 B.C.). But these Hasmonean connections would not last. He decided to have Aristobulus III drowned (35 B.C.) and a few years later murdered not

---

have their own procurators working in areas governed by others, I tend to the view that Antipater understood himself above all to be Caesar's man.

110. See Eilers 2004: 6–22.

GEOGRAPHY: THE WORLD, THE HOMELAND, THE MOTHER-*POLIS* 267

only Hyrcanus II (30 B.C.) but even wife Mariamme (29/28 B.C.). His sons by Mariamme, and the Hasmonean lineage they represented, would not survive his reign either.[111]

In presenting Herod as promoting the ethnic diversity within his kingdom, Roman-style, I am unavoidably simplifying matters for the sake of a big picture. Before we leave this important king, I should mention three significant complications of the simple picture.

First, Herod blundered spectacularly when he initially tried to locate in Jerusalem the sorts of entertainments that he would later establish in Caesarea and fund in other *poleis* (*Ant.* 15.267–291). For the new "quinquennial" (= quadrennial)[112] Jerusalem games, he reportedly built a theatre and amphitheater in the capital, invited athletes and musicians from far and wide, and imported exotic animals to fight each other or to be hunted. What blatantly violated Judaean law, people felt, was Herod's decoration of "trophies" in honor of Augustus. In the Graeco-Roman context, trophies were displays of armor arranged as though worn by a man, each one a symbolic representation of a place the emperor had conquered. According to Josephus, Herod was caught off guard by the indignant reaction. After failing to "dispel their superstition" with soothing words (*Ant.* 15.277), he eventually realized that they were objecting because they assumed that actual human figures—mannequins—stood beneath the suits of armor. When the exasperated Herod ripped off the armor to show that only wooden stick-frames stood underneath, they all had a good laugh and the opposition dissipated—except that a group of ten remained resolved on a plot to kill the king. (Is this simply what happened or a moralizing tale meant to highlight the folly of rash judgment?)

According to Josephus, Herod built Sebastē as and where he did, close to Jerusalem and with strong walls and an ex-military population, for insurance against uprisings in the Judaean heartland (*Ant.* 15.292–293). However that may be, he evidently learned to be more careful about Jerusalem's laws and customs, shifting the Roman-style games and institutions to sites outside the capital and its immediate *chōra*.

The second incident involved Costobar, husband of Herod's sister Salome. Costobar was a prominent Idumaean like Herod, but before their Judaization under the Hasmoneans this man's ancestors had been priests of the Idumaean deity Kozē (*Ant.* 15.253)—or Cos/Qos as in the first part of

---

111. The dates are by no means straightforward to calculate. See the analysis in Kokkinos 1998: 211–15.

112. Since the Romans counted inclusively, if a festival fell in Year 1 then Year 5 would come four years later.

Costobar's name.[113] Early in his rule Herod appointed this brother-in-law as subordinate ruler of Idumaea and Gaza. Attributing to Costobar the basest motives of self-aggrandizement and hubris, Josephus claims that he used his new position to attempt a break from Herod's kingdom. He includes the possibly revealing pretext, however, that it was not proper for Idumaea to be subject to Judaeans or for Costobar, the noble descendant of (Idumaean) priest-aristocrats, to take direction from a commoner such as Herod. In the story Costobar saw his best chance with Queen Cleopatra, who allegedly had an insatiable desire for property, and wrote to offer his services as her governor. Cleopatra was keen, but unable to persuade Antony, Herod's staunch supporter. When Herod's sister Salome learned of her husband's disloyalty she divorced him, though Josephus notes that the divorce itself violated Judaean law (*Ant.* 15.253–266).

We do not know what really happened here. It has been speculated that Costobar hoped from the start to create a Hasmonean-Idumaean alliance, based in an independent Idumaea under the aegis of Cleopatra's Egypt (before 31/30 B.C.).[114] That is an intriguing possibility. However that may be, Josephus' story at least reflects the attempt of some Idumaean nobles to dissolve their nearly century-old identity as *Judaeans*, in spite of the fact that one of their own was ruling Judaea. We know much less than we would like about Idumaean social stratification and the motives behind this initiative.

A third incident we know even less about. The Decapolis city of Gadara across the Jordan River, which Alexander Jannaeus had destroyed and Pompey had rebuilt and repopulated after 63 B.C. (above), was given to Herod in 30 B.C. It was part of a much larger gift from Octavian (soon to be Augustus) that included the late Cleopatra's bodyguard of 400 Gauls, her former holdings in the region, Samaria, Hippos, Gaza, and several other Greek cities (*War* 1.396; *Ant.* 15.217). The acquired cities now had to pay Herod an annual tribute—the established revenue stream for whichever ruler was in power, possibly continuing assessments made by Ptolemies and Seleucids long before.[115] Herod must have dispatched financial agents to

113. It has been suggested that his name was actually *Cos-gever* ("Cos's man"), on the analogy of *Cos-melekh* (Cos's king) attested in an inscription: see Ronen 1988: 214–15.

114. See Ronen 1988.

115. Josephus occasionally mentions the assessed worth of particular cities and their territories, especially when they changed hands: *War* 1.362; 2.95–98. A substantial city such as Jerusalem, Caesarea, or Sebastē seems to have produced about 100 talents of annual revenue for a ruler, when 50 talents was (were?) considered suitable annual income for a king-designate (*Ant.* 17.97). A single talent was somewhat more than the entire career earnings of a legionary soldier. So, the attraction of owning such cities is obvious.

these areas, and he may even have established residences in some. Samaria and Strato's Tower were exceptional cases because he decided to transform them from small towns into the showpiece cities of Sebastē and Caesarea. The more established *poleis* may have experienced little interference in their day-to-day operations. We do not know.

Josephus singles out the Gadarenes for extreme restlessness under Herod's rule. When Augustus' lieutenant Marcus Agrippa visited western Anatolia in about 22 B.C., the Gadarenes sent a delegation all that way to accuse Herod. Refusing even to hear them, however, loyal Agrippa shackled the delegates and sent them back to Herod, who reportedly released them without a grudge (*Ant.* 15.351). But they were not finished. When Augustus visited Syria two years later, "most" Gadarenes rushed to him to complain that Herod "was being too harsh in his orders, and tyrannical" (15.354, monarchical tyranny being a theme of the *Antiquities*). They were supported by neighboring rulers who had their own grievances against Herod: the Nabataeans as well as a petty chieftain named Zenodorus, who had lost territory north of Galilee to Herod, by Augustus' decision. Gadarenes were the only plaintiffs from within Herod's kingdom, however, who complained so strenuously.

Whatever the precise causes of discontent were, these cases are enough to suggest that in spite of his political astuteness and energetic efforts to promote local cultures, which Strabo applauded, Herod's success was far from complete. Some indeterminate numbers of Judaeans, Idumaeans, and Gadarenes were deeply unhappy with him at certain times. We should remember, however, that even today any political leader who lasts more than a decade in office is likely to have cultivated a vigorous opposition. A ruler who remained firmly in power for more than three decades, and an absolute ruler who could exercise the power of the sword at will, would certainly have created enemies, no matter how beneficial his policies might have been. It is impossible now to determine how much animosity clung to Herod for who he was and what he represented, such as perceived impiety, and how much reflected the inevitable animosities that such a long rule would create. More importantly, we do not know *that* any opposition he faced outweighed, in popular sentiment, the pride that most Judaeans felt in being a regional capital with a glorious *polis*.

For foreigners under Herod's jurisdiction, even if they preferred his style to that of the Hasmoneans, the humiliation of being ruled from Jerusalem by a *Judaean* may have been a nagging problem. Nevertheless, some of his policies and benefactions toward Judaeans and foreigners alike won him admirers, among those who found employment in his extensive public-works projects at home, or among foreigners who saw their *poleis* enhanced by his generosity.[116]

The Settlement following Herod's Death (4 B.C.)

Since allied kings such as Herod were an integral part of the Roman imperial system, each appointment was subject to review when the ruler died. According to Josephus, Augustus granted Herod the right to name his own heirs (*War* 1.454), but the king, in shrewd posthumous diplomacy, insisted that his heir-designate travel to Rome with a sealed parcel containing the royal ring and documents needed for rule, for Augustus' ratification (1.668-669). Designating his heirs had turned out to be complicated because Herod had so many wives, who bore him some fifteen children in total, two-thirds of whom were male. As each one came into or fell out of favor, he would prepare a new will or add a codicil to promote or exclude someone.[117] Near the end of his life he killed his three oldest sons in exasperation at their intrigues, the last one just days before he himself expired. At one point near the end he named Antipas his heir, by-passing the slightly older Archelaus and Philip because they were in his bad books (*War* 1.646). But at the last moment he changed his mind again and designated Archelaus king, with Antipas and Philip "tetrarchs" or "rulers of a quarter" (1.664, 668). When he died in 4 B.C., therefore, these three oldest surviving sons, each still in his early twenties, prepared cases before Augustus. Each had the support of some family members and each could cite a version of the will in his favor (*War* 2.1-38).

The Herodian factions were not the only ones who travelled to Rome. A fragment preserved from Herod's aide and biographer, Nicolaus of Damascus,[118] tells of a serious conflict that broke out on Herod's death, as the Judaean *ethnos* rose up against Herod's young sons *and* against the neighboring *poleis*. Josephus does not mention the latter but does describe the Judaean civil strife in some detail (*War* 2.39-79). Tacitus notes a Judaean revolt in passing (*Hist.* 5.9). Josephus has Judaean rebels fighting only Romans (based in Syria, now present in Judaea) and Herodians. Nicolaus,

---

116. See Richardson 1996: 8-10, 315-17; Rocca 2008: 259-61, 370-78.

117. See Richardson 1996: 33-38; Kokkinos 1998: 243-45.

118. The fragment of Nicolaus' autobiography is preserved only in a tenth-century collection *On Virtues and Vices*, by the emperor Constantine VII ("Born-to-the-Purple"). We are concerned with the passage in Dindorf 1870: 143-44 (= latter half of frag. 5, lines 70-102 in Müller 1841-1870: vol. 3: 354).

however, says that Judaeans came into violent confrontation with the other *poleis* and that the latter caused disproportionate Judaean casualties. Clearly, the old hostilities had not abated.

In Rome, therefore, both Judaean and Greek leaders were present according to Nicolaus, alongside the Herodian cliques on which Josephus focuses, making their various appeals to Augustus. The *poleis* that had been under Herod pressed the emperor for *their* freedom—from the Judaeans (αἱ ὑφ' Ἡρώδῃ Ἑλληνίδες πόλεις αἰτούμεναι τὴν ἐλευθερίαν παρὰ Καίσαρος).[119] Paradoxically, these Judaean leaders wanted a similar freedom—from the Herodian family. Both preferred to be under Roman rule, freed from local monarchs perceived as tyrants. If this should not be possible, the Judaean contingent preferred the younger brother Antipas to Archelaus. Everyone reportedly hated Archelaus, a point on which Nicolaus (this man's advocate in Rome) and Josephus agree.

Josephus adds that a separate delegation of fifty Judaean elders, supported by the Judaeans of Rome, arrived to accuse Herod himself: he was the cruelest tyrant ever, who had killed his own people, destroyed their prosperity, and trampled on their laws while lavishing generosity on foreigners. The prospect of Archelaus as king was horrifying to this group: he had killed 3,000 Judaeans before he was even confirmed (*War* 2.80–87). They begged to give up their notional independence under a monarch and be joined to the Roman province of Syria—the default position of *poleis* not otherwise governed—under a Roman legate, and be permitted to follow their ancestral laws in Jerusalem (*War* 2.91–92).

After much deliberation, Augustus honored the spirit of Herod's final wishes against those of the emissaries, but with qualifications. He divided Herod's former territory at least five ways, revealing his sensitivity to the appeals, perhaps, but also his lack of confidence in any of the young Herodians. Because Archelaus received the part that included the heartland Judaea, he would be styled not king but "ethnarch"[120]—with kingship possible later if he governed well (*War* 2.93). Nicolaus presented this as his own rhetorical triumph as advocate, who had made a successful pitch against overwhelming hostility. (It is not clear that he personally liked Archelaus.) In addition

119. Dindorf 1870: 143 lines 13–18.

120. This position (ruler of an *ethnos*), which Hyrcanus II had also held, did not reflect a Roman administrative term in Latin. It was used especially in Egypt and the Near East. Strabo observed that clever Roman diplomacy gave the title to local rulers over "affairs of no great importance" (17.1.13). In the 9,000 or so texts of the *Thesaurus Linguae Graecae* (www.tlg.uci.edu), the term first appears in Judaean texts (1 Macc. 14.47; 15.1–2), and Josephus accounts for 20 of the first 28 occurrences; it appears only once, also of an eastern ruler (Lucian, *Macr.* 17), between Josephus and the mid-third century.

to Judaea proper, Archelaus received the port of Joppa, by now recognized as Judaean, along with his father's showcase *poleis* of Sebastē with its territory Samaria, Caesarea, and the family's homeland of Idumaea.

Although Josephus does not mention the delegation from the Greek *poleis*, his notice about Augustus' decision to return Gaza, Hippos, and Gadara to the great province of Syria suggests that *their* appeal for freedom from Judaean rule was successful. Herod's sister Salome received prime coastal *poleis* (Ascalon, Azotus, and Jamnia) along with Phasaelis in the Jordan valley (*War* 2.97–98). Archelaus' brothers, to be styled "tetrarchs" (rulers of a quarter), received the outer districts of Herod's kingdom: Galilee and Peraea across the Jordan going to Antipas, with the more remote areas north and east of that going to Philip. The only ones who were completely disappointed, then, were the council delegates from Jerusalem. Judaea would not be annexed to Syria as they had requested—not yet.

This fragmentation of Herod's kingdom shows how heterogeneous its constituent parts really were, and how deep the divisions remained.

Given that Archelaus was the only one reported to have had the possibility of future kingship mentioned, it is remarkable that he was the first of the sons to fall. Antipas and Philip remained in power for four decades or more, but he was gone within ten years (A.D. 6). Josephus says almost nothing about his reign, except that he managed to alienate both of his main constituencies: Samarians and Judaeans. When both communities dispatched delegations to Augustus, to complain of his brutality, the emperor exiled Archelaus to the far end of the empire (*War* 2.111). We might wish that we had a Samarian Josephus, to learn their perspective on this and much more.

In *A History of the Jewish War*, I have proposed that the evidence sketched above would make the best sense on the following hypotheses. From the Roman point of view it was simplest to administer southern Syria, with its diverse cultures, through a Herodian monarch ruling from Jerusalem. Successive emperors remained close to Herod's heirs and continued testing them in power, seemingly finding a winner in Agrippa I and his son before that man's sudden death in 44. Otherwise they installed equestrians in Caesarea, sometimes for long terms (Pilate and Felix), with a mandate to mind the Judaean portfolio and keep the peace. The nearby *poleis*, eager for Rome's eye and advancement, resented being under Jerusalem's domination and wished to be ordinary *poleis* with equal opportunity for advancement in the province of Syria. The Judaeans were divided. Many priestly aristocrats resented monarchical rule because it severely limited their prospects, and they could make common cause with popular pietists. Many business people, traders, and artisans, however, would have walked taller as citizens of the region's most prominent city and so favored monarchical rule.[121]

Conclusions

This chapter offers another perspective on the theme of mapping peoples in the ancient world. Here we have moved from abstract notions and discourse to the limited physical means of representing the earth's populations. I have argued that, although educated people living under the Roman empire were no doubt as curious as anyone else, and although they surely would have been pleased to have something like modern maps for trade, military purposes, and provincial administration, such things were not conceivable. It is only relatively recently, since the late nineteenth century, that we have been able to create maps accurately representing spatial relations and elevations. It seems a necessary consequence that the Romans could never have had the opportunity to develop the kind of map consciousness that we take for granted.

In the final section I reconsidered the region we often loosely call Judaea with ancient realities and perspectives in mind. Rather than any sort of country or even province with clear borders, we find in this small region (today the northern half of Israel and Palestine) a large number of independent and sometimes antagonistic *ethnē* and *poleis*. Judaea was, we see again, the territory of Jerusalem, whose laws and traditions Judaeans everywhere were known to follow. But other *poleis*, of similar age or much older, and famous for their great human exports, were equally proud and deeply unhappy during periods of Judaean domination. These antagonisms are explored in *HJW* as major contributing factors in the tensions that brought Roman forces to Judaea in late 66.

121. *HJW* 225–60.

Summary and Conclusions

This book is neither a history in the usual senses nor an argument about past events or specific texts. Its companion volume *HJW* is largely devoted to those things. This *Orientation* has instead addressed two large and preliminary problem sets: the nature of historical inquiry and the language ancient historians use to describe societies and peoples. In both cases the main drift of my argument is that we need to be open to every kind of question. Indeed, the most important—the only indispensable—part of history is the framing and pursuit of questions.

Part I is an exercise in scraping off the encrustations around history, from school experience through adult life in society and history's manipulation for politics, to lay bare its basic idea: the methodical investigation of questions concerning the human past. Chapter 1 thus recalls the origins of history, over against pervasive traditions in Herodotus' Ionia, and argues that his (perhaps not original) insight about the need to investigate the past remains fundamental. This simple observation overthrows much of the burden placed on history: to teach lessons or to be accurately learned, for example. Most often, as we see in debates about the kind of history that should be taught in schools, or in internet trolls' ferocious exhortations to go and learn our history, we see traditions impersonating history.

The second chapter explores the roots of enduring fissures among academics who do history differently, especially the division between social-scientific and humanist tendencies, to make the case that we all need to get along. Singing Kumbaya and holding hands are not obligatory, thankfully, but the inescapable reality is that historians may investigate anything they wish about the human past, as long as they do so responsibly. Working responsibly means making clear their questions, criteria, and interpretations of evidence so that others may offer critique *on those bases*. Too often we talk past each other, either disdaining what others do because it does not fit our interests or assimilating their questions to ours—and rejecting their answers because they do not solve *our* questions. We should stop doing that, and try to listen more carefully to what each historian is actually doing. The social or social-scientific and humanistic trajectories in historical research are both important, and to pursue either alone would skew our perceptions of the past, given that no single truth could cover its chaotic riches. Tragic-ironic approaches temper all of our methods and systems.

Chapter 3 works through some peculiarities of historical work in Hellenistic-Roman Judaea, which arise from a range of causes, from our uniquely large public and often religious constituencies to the central role of Josephus and archaeology to the political import of such work. For reasons possibly having to do with the heritage of religion and faith commitments or perceived religious stakes, the field also has a propensity to generate warring camps. Since most of this rests on the failure to understand others' questions (above), I again recommend—tritely—openness. There is plenty for all of us to do, with our chosen questions, methods, and issues, and no need to register people in camps. One might object that I seem to have done this in distinguishing social-scientific from humanistic history, but I hope it is clear that this was not my purpose. Some scholars work in both areas, or migrate from one to the other. They need not be hermetically sealed, and we need both. The distinction was an ordering principle, to help identify some underlying rationales driving each direction—given that it is not obvious, after all, *how* we should investigate the human past.

Chapter 4 tries to extract from these reflections a way of going about ancient history, after a section that stresses the differences between the material conditions facing ancient and modern historians, and their consequences for our ambitions. Misunderstanding may arise again if we hold ancient historians to standards elaborated by modern counterparts in relation to confidence and facts. The sort of procedure I recommend has a pyramid shape, in that the weight lies in what we control: our questions and research. It is a kind of Stoic approach to history. The amount of evidence that fate has left us is not in our power to control, and is therefore a matter of indifference. We do what we can, pursuing our questions, but we are not required to make commitments that depend on matters outside our control. We are not, as historians, required to believe anything about the past.

The three chapters constituting Part II take up the second problem set. This can be considered a basic sort of historical question, namely: How did the ancients talk among themselves about human life and society? What categories did they use to communicate about social-political-religious life? Here again there is ample room for confusion, with social-scientific historians rejecting such a question as invalid or humanists arguing that if a given writer or small group (arguably) used certain language then it existed, and claims that it was not part of the common discourse are wrong. My recommendation is again that we allow each other to pursue our different questions, and in each case try to divulge ours and its criteria and evidence as clearly as possible.

Chapter 5 takes the biggest risk, perhaps, in trying to sketch a "classical paradigm" or common "lexical bank." Though meant to be a coherent whole, the chapter was too long and so I divided it in two.

The chapter isolates four anchor points in the shared discourse, for reasons given there, which undoubtedly invite debate, but essentially hinge on frequency of appearance across a wide range of authors. The categories are: *ethnos*-belonging and all that goes with it (place, customs, laws, way of life, cult), *polis*-belonging and its correlatives (territory, calendar, festivals, constitution, citizenship, leadership, cult), bloody sacrificial cult (with temples, altars, priests, attendants, rituals, sacred and profane, polluted and consecrated), whether given by the *ethnos* and *polis* or voluntarily chosen, and voluntary associations in the *poleis*, including philosophical schools. These were not meant to be exhaustive, and they certainly are not carefully defined. They are, simply, terms the ancients used. The first three parts are mainly descriptive of the terminology (with Latin counterparts) that appears in ancient texts (whether Herodotus, Polybius, Diodorus, Strabo, Pliny, Plutarch, Tacitus, Pausanias, Celsus, Cassius Dio, and Julian or *Aristaeas*, Philo, and Josephus). In the case of voluntary associations, given their largely sub-elite constituencies, one must take fuller account of inscriptions to balance the rather negative elite discourse—though the categories were understood by all and were used in a wide range of texts.

Chapter 6 follows up with the question of how this classical paradigm met its end. Following the same method as Chapter 5—reading surviving material and examining key terms—one can see that it was eventually replaced with a paradigm that marginalized or even expunged *ethnos, polis*, and animal sacrifice in favor of faith or right belief, religions, -isms, heresies, churches, and bishops—in other words, a discourse that turned the tables on society from a Christian vantage-point. In this paradigm, which becomes prominent from the fourth century, those terms that were not discarded along with athletic contests, staged plays, festivals, temples, and priesthoods were sublimated or spiritualized as *polis* assemblies became churches, *polis* duties became liturgies, and sacrifice and libation became mental or spiritual operations. That much is demonstrable, and the emperor Julian's late attempt to reverse it all did not succeed.

The question has arisen, surprisingly perhaps in connection with the translation of *Ioudaios*, whether there was not a clear rupture of the classical paradigm before the ascent of Christianity, in which the "meaning" of *Ioudaios* changed in some basic way. I propose that it is difficult to track such a change in the common lexical bank. This is *not* to say that individual and communal views did not change over the centuries, but only that writers outside the Christian orbit in the late first, second, third, and fourth centuries, whether Judaean or outside observers, appear to be communicating in much the same way. The people-place or *ethnos-polis*-cult bond remains intact as a fundamental aspect of ancient thought and rhetoric (origins matter), and decidedly to the advantage of the Judaeans over against the anomalous Christians. This appears to be an area in which different questions and criteria have become conflated—an essence of Jewishness, internal communal perceptions at various times, social-scientific models of ethnicity, religion, and conversion, particular authors' presentations, common elite discourse—perhaps by a lack of clarity on my part as much as anyone's.

On the specific question of translating (or transliterating) *Ioudaios*, I have stressed in every way possible that, although I have unwillingly become a flag-bearer for "Judaean" in a debate about how one *should* translate this word, I see no need for a debate and never desired one. This is not because everyone *should* adopt Judaean. At a time in which Jew(s) was the accepted standard, it seemed necessary to justify on philological-historical grounds my preference for *Judaean*. For my specific tasks as a researcher and teacher, I prefer to translate *Judaean*. This has to do with my situation and questions, which are not exactly paralleled even among close colleagues. If they will permit the use of *Judaean*, which I would never claim is *the appropriate* translation or one that should be followed by others, then "we're good."

The final chapter turns to another relatively neglected aspect of common ancient discourse: geographical representation. Perhaps all geography is mental, in that the earth's nature did not declare itself, but required centuries of exploration and technical refinement to map. But my goal here is to contrast what we know of Israel and Palestine today with what the ancients perceived. Living somewhere does not mean that you understand its geography, of course, from above or in elevation: you only experience what you need.

So Chapter 7 moves from general considerations about ancient geography to the southern or Coele-Syria as it was in the first century. This included Judaea as the upland *chōra* of the mother-*polis* Jerusalem, but it was surrounded by many other *poleis* and *ethnē*. The ongoing attention to Jerusalem as ancestral home (*patris*) and defining locus of the Judaean *ethnos* in ancient writers suggested a final quick tour of the *polis*. There I highlight the role of King Herod, builder of the most famous and enduring version of Jerusalem, and his successors as its external face. A brief consideration of Jerusalem's regional dominance and the resulting resentments, favor with Rome, and divided internal assessments lead back to *HJW* for the history of the first century and the war with Rome.

An inevitable criticism of any such big sketch will be that it is too "sweeping." I would agree if it is taken in unintended ways, as some kind of master blueprint of ancient society. In some ways this book runs up against my own historicist-particularist instincts, and the fact that most of my teachers shared them may explain why it took me so long to reflect on these matters. (Or they might simply be appalled at the result.) But whether we like it or not, we all live among dialectics between various wholes and parts, and even the interpretation of a particular word drives us back to the big canvas. Eventually it seemed to make a case, no matter how ramshackle and inadequate, for the way ancient writers customarily communicated about their world. My preliminary effort in 2007, focused negatively (on the absence of religion and Judaism as current categories of discourse), prompted a more constructive consideration of what they did, demonstrably, talk about.

That said, I am at least partly aware of how wrong I might be on any number of points, from the choice of anchor terms and clustering with correlatives to interpreting a nineteenth-century German thinker to adequately capturing any Greek or Latin term. This book is about the inquiry, and if it helps advanced students (especially) to gain clarity about their work, it will have succeeded. If it can throw light on debated matters in scholarship and extract some of the heat, all the better.

Two points I feel reasonably confident in advocating are these. First, since history exists only in inquiries into the human past, in the absence of which there is no history, each investigator needs to be as clear as possible about the specific question under study, its criteria, and its evidence. Second, in the course of pursuing our inquiries we must of course take account of others that have at least superficial bearing, so as to situate our intended contribution. Since it rarely happens, at least in the humanist stream of history, that two of us will pursue exactly the same question—even when our interests overlap in the translation of certain words—we should guard against judging others' conclusions according to our interests, assumptions, and criteria, and focus our energies rather on understanding their questions, criteria, and interpretations.

Bibliography

Adams, M. B., ed. 1990. *The Wellborn Science: Eugenics in Germany, France, Brazil, and Russia*. Oxford: Oxford University Press.
Albu, E. 2005. "Imperial Geography and the Medieval Peutinger Map." *Imago Mundi* 57:136–48.
———. 2008. "Rethinking the Peutinger Map." In R. J. A. Talbert and R. W. Unger, eds., *Cartography in Antiquity and the Middle Ages: Fresh Perspectives, New Methods*, 111–20. Leiden: Brill.
Alcock, S. E. 2002. *Archaeologies of the Greek Past: Landscape, Monuments, and Memories*. Cambridge: Cambridge University Press.
Alcock, S. E., J. F. Cherry, and J. Elsner. 2001. *Pausanias: Travel and Memory in Roman Greece*. Oxford: Oxford University Press.
Alföldy, G. 1999. "Pontius Pilatus und das Tiberieum von Caesarea Maritima." *Scripta Classica Israelica* 18:85–108.
Alston, R. 1995. *Soldier and Society in Roman Egypt: A Social History*. London: Routledge.
Ames, R. T., and H. Rosemont. 1998. *The Analects of Confucius: A Philosophical Translation*. New York: Ballantine/Random House.
Ando, C. 2000. *Imperial Ideology and Provincial Loyalty in the Roman Empire*. Berkeley: University of California Press.
———. 2008. *The Matter of the Gods: Religion and the Roman Empire*. Berkeley: University of California Press.
[Anonymous] Ex-Attaché. 1914. "Tragedy Will Bring Peace for Austria? Francis Ferdinand has been Disturbing Factor of Nation." *Chicago Daily Tribune*, Monday June 29, 1914, 1, 4.
Arnaoutoglou, I. N. 2002. "Roman Law and *Collegia* in Asia Minor." *Revue internationale des droits l'antiquité* 49:27–44.
———. 2005. "*Collegia* in the Province of Egypt in the First Century CE." *Ancient Society* 35:197–216.
Asad, T. 1993. *Genealogies of Religion: Discipline and Reasons of Power in Christianity and Islam*. Baltimore: Johns Hopkins University Press.
Ascough, R. S., P. A. Harland, and J. S. Kloppenborg. 2012. *Associations in the Greco-Roman World: A Sourcebook*. Waco, TX: Baylor University Press.

Ashmole, B. 1956. "A Relief of Two Greek Freedmen." *British Museum Quarterly* 20:71–73.
Assmann, J. 1988. "Collective Memory and Cultural Identity." In J. Assmann and T. Hölscher, eds., *Kultur und Gedächtnis*, 9–19. Frankfurt: Suhrkamp.
Atkinson, K., and J. Magness. 2010. "Josephus's Essenes and the Qumran Community." *Journal of Biblical Literature* 129:317–42.
Attridge, H. W. 2004. "Pollution, Sin, Atonement, Salvation." In S. I. Johnston, ed., *Religions of the Ancient World: A Guide*, 71–83. Cambridge: Harvard University Press.
Avigad, N. 1976. "How the Wealthy Lived in Herodian Jerusalem." *Biblical Archaeology Review* 2.1:23–32, 34–35.
———. 1983. *Discovering Jerusalem: Recent Archaeological Excavations in the Upper City*. Nashville: Nelson.
Bacon, F. 1605. *The Two Books of Francis Bacon, of the Proficience and Advancement of Learning, Divine and Human: To the King*. London: Tomes.
Bagnall, R. S., ed. 2009. *The Oxford Handbook of Papyrology*. Oxford: Oxford University Press.
Bahat, D. 1994. "The Western Wall Tunnels." In H. Geva, ed., *Ancient Jerusalem Revealed*, 177–90. Jerusalem: Israel Exploration Society.
———. 2009. "The Architectural Origins of Herod's Temple Mount." In D. M. Jacobson and N. Kokkinos, eds., *Herod and Augustus: Papers Presented at the IJS Conference, 21st–23rd June 2005*, 235–45. IJS Studies in Judaica 6. Leiden: Brill.
Baines, J. 2004. "Egyptian Elite Self-Representation in the Context of Ptolemaic Rule." In W. V. Harris and G. Ruffini, eds., *Ancient Alexandria between Egypt and Greece*, 33–62. Columbia Studies in the Classical Tradition 26. Leiden: Brill.
Baker, J. N. L. 1963. *The History of Geography: Papers*. Oxford: Blackwell.
Baltrusch, E. 2002. *Die Juden und das römische Reich: Geschichte einer konfliktreichen Beziehung*. Darmstadt: Wissenschaftliche Buchgesellschaft.
Bambach, C. R. 1995. *Heidegger, Dilthey, and the Crisis of Historicism*. Ithaca: Cornell University Press.
Bar-Kochva, B. 1976. "Seron and Cestius at Beith Horon." *PEQ* 108:13–21.
———. 1992. *Pseudo-Hecataeus on the Jews*. Berkeley: University of California Press.
Barclay, J. M. G. 1996. *Jews in the Mediterranean Diaspora: from Alexander to Trajan (323 BCE–117 CE)*. Edinburgh: T. & T. Clark.
———, ed. 2004. *Negotiating Diaspora: Jewish Strategies in the Roman Empire*. Library of Second Temple Studies 45. London: T. & T. Clark.
———. 2006. *Against Apion*. Flavius Josephus: Translation and Commentary 10. Leiden: Brill.
Barrett, A. A. 1989. *Caligula: The Corruption of Power*. New Haven: Yale University Press.
Barth, F. 1969. *Ethnic Groups and Boundaries: the Social Organization of Culture Difference*. Boston: Little, Brown.
Bartlett, J. R. 2009. "Early Printed Maps of Galilee." In Z. Rodgers, M. Daly-Denton, and A. Fitzpatrick-McKinley, eds. *A Wandering Galilean: Essays in Honour of Seán Freyne*, 187–204. Journal for the Study of Judaism Supplements 132. Leiden: Brill.
Barton, C. A., and D. Boyarin. 2016. *Imagine No Religion: How Modern Abstractions Hide Ancient Realities*. New York: Fordham University Press.
Batten, S. Z. 1908. "The Redemption of the Unfit." *American Journal of Sociology* 14:233–60.

Baumgarten, A. I., ed. 2002. *Sacrifice in Religious Experience*. Studies in the History of Religions 93. Leiden: Brill.
Beall, T. S. 1988. *Josephus' Description of the Essenes Illustrated by the Dead Sea Scrolls*. Society for New Testament Studies Monograph Series 58. Cambridge: Cambridge University Press.
Beard, M. 2007. *The Roman Triumph*. Cambridge: Belknap/Harvard University Press.
Beard, M., J. North, and S. Price. 1998. *Religions of Rome*. 2 vols. Cambridge: Cambridge University Press.
Beckett, F. 2010. "Remembering the Blitz: Was It an Avoidable Tragedy?" *Guardian G2 Special Supplement*, Sept. 7.
Beeson, S. D. 2007. "Historiography Ancient and Modern: Fact and Fiction." In G. J. Brooke and T. Römer, eds., *Ancient and Modern Scriptural Historiography—L'Historiographie Biblique, Ancienne et Moderne*, 3–11. Bibliotheca Ephemeridum theologicarum Lovaniensium 207. Leuven: Peeters.
Beiser, F. C. 2011a. *The German Historicist Tradition*. Oxford: Oxford University Press.
———. 2011b. "Hegel and Ranke: A Re-examination." In S. Houlgate and M. Baur, eds., *A Companion to Hegel*, 332–50. London: Wiley-Blackwell.
Bekker-Nielsen, T. 1988. "*Terra Incognita*: The Subjective Geography of the Roman Empire." In A. Damsgaard-Madsen, E. Christiansen, and E. Hallager, eds., *Studies in Ancient History and Numismatics Presented to Rudi Thomsen*, 148–61. Aarhus: Aarhus University Press.
Belayche, N. 2002. "Sacrifice and the Theory of Sacrifice during the 'Pagan Reaction': Julian the Emperor." In A. I. Baumgarten, ed., *Sacrifice in Religious Experience*, 101–26. Studies in the History of Religions 93. Leiden: Brill.
Ben-Ami, D., and Y. Tchekhanovets. 2011. "Has the Adiabenian Royal Family 'Palace' been Found?" In K. Galor and G. Avni, eds., *Unearthing Jerusalem: 150 Years of Archaeological Research in the Holy City*, 231–39. Winona Lake, IN: Eisenbrauns.
Ben-Arieh, Y. 1979. *The Rediscovery of the Holy Land in the Nineteenth Century*. Jerusalem: Magnes.
Benko, S. 1984. *Pagan Rome and the Early Christians*. Bloomington: Indiana University Press.
Bentley, M., ed. 1997. *Companion to Historiography*. London: Routledge.
———. 1999. *Modern Historiography: An Introduction*. London: Routledge.
Ben Zeev, M. P. 1993. "The Reliability of Josephus Flavius: The Case of Hecataeus' and Manetho's Accounts of Jews and Judaism. Fifteen Years of Contemporary Research (1974–1990)." *Journal for the Study of Judaism* 24:215–34.
———. 1998. *Jewish Rights in the Roman World: The Greek and Roman Documents Quoted by Josephus Flavius*. Texte und Studien zum Antiken Judentum 74. Tübingen: Mohr/Siebeck.
Berggren, J. L. and A. Jones. 2000. *Ptolemy's Geography: An Annotated Translation of the Theoretical Chapters*. Princeton: Princeton University Press.
Berlin, I. 2002. *Liberty: Incorporating Four Essays on Liberty*. Edited by H. Hardy. Oxford: Oxford University Press.
Bernett, M. 2007. *Der Kaiserkult in Judäa unter den Herodiern und Römern*. Wissenschaftliche Untersuchungen zum Neuen Testament 203. Tübingen: Mohr/Siebeck.
Bernhardi, F. von. 1914 [1912]. *Germany and the Next War*. Translated by A. H. Powles. New York: Eron.
Beyer, K. 1986. *The Aramaic Language, Its Distribution and Subdivisions*. Translated by J. F. Healey. Göttingen: Vandenhoeck & Ruprecht.

Bickerman, E. J. 1979. *The God of the Maccabees: Studies on the Meaning and Origin of the Maccabean Revolt.* Studies in Judaism in Late Antiquity 32. Leiden: Brill.
———. 1980 [1968]. *Chronology of the Ancient World.* London: Thames and Hudson.
———. 1988. *The Jews in the Greek Age.* New York: Jewish Theological Seminary.
Bilde, P. 1988. *Flavius Josephus between Jerusalem and Rome: His Life, His Works and Their Importance.* Journal for the study of the Pseudepigrapha Supplements 2. Sheffield: Sheffield Academic.
Birnbaum, E. 1996. *The Place of Judaism in Philo's Thought: Israel, Jews, and Proselytes.* Brown Judaic Studies 290. Atlanta: Scholars.
Birnbaum, M. 2010. "Historians Speak out against Proposed Texas Textbook Changes." *Washington Post,* March 18, 2010.
Bloch, M. 1992 [1941]. *The Historian's Craft.* Translated by P. Putnam. Manchester: Manchester University Press.
Bloch, R. S. 2002. *Antike Vorstellungen vom Judentum: der Judenexkurs des Tacitus im Rahmen der griechisch-römischen Ethnographie.* Historia 160. Stuttgart: Steiner.
Boatwright, M. T. 2000. *Hadrian and the Cities of the Roman Empire.* Princeton: Princeton University Press.
Bowersock, G. W. 1978. *Julian the Apostate.* Cambridge: Harvard University Press.
———. 1994. *Fiction as History: Nero to Julian.* Berkeley: University of California Press.
Bowie, E. L.1970. "The Greeks and Their Past in the Second Sophistic." *Past and Present* 46:3–41.
Boyarin, D. 2004. *Border Lines: The Partition of Judaeo-Christianity.* Philadelphia: University of Pennsylvania Press.
Boyle, A. J. 2003. "Introduction: Reading Flavian Rome." In W. J. Dominik and A. J. Boyle eds., *Flavian Rome: Culture, Image, Text,* 1–68. Leiden: Brill.
Boynton, H. W., ed. 1896. *Selections from Carlyle* Boston: Allyn & Bacon.
Branscome, D. 2010. "Herodotus and the Map of Aristagoras." *Classical Antiquity* 29:1–44.
Braudel, F. 1958. "Histoire et science sociale: la longue durée." *Annales: Economies, Sociétés, Civilisations* 13:725–53.
Braund, D. 1984. *Rome and the Friendly King: The Character of the Client Kingship.* London: Croom Helm.
———. 1998. "Cohors: The Governor and His Entourage in the Self-Image of the Roman Republic." In R. Laurence and J. Berry, eds., *Cultural Identity in the Roman Empire,* 10–24. London: Routledge.
Bricault, L., M. J. Versluys, and P. G. P. Meyboom, eds. 2007. *Nile into Tiber: Egypt in the Roman World. Proceedings of the IIIrd International Conference of Isis Studies, Leiden, May 11–14 2005.* Religions in the Graeco-Roman World 159. Leiden: Brill.
Brighton, M. 2009. *The Sicarii in Josephus's Judean War: Rhetorical Analysis and Historical Observations.* Early Judaism and Its Literature 27. Atlanta: Society of Biblical Literature.
Brodd, J., and J. L. Reed, eds. 2011. *Rome and Religion: A Cross-Disciplinary Dialogue on the Imperial Cult.* Society of Biblical Literature Writings from the Greco-Roman World Supplement Series 5. Atlanta: Society of Biblical Literature.
Brodersen, K. 1995. *Terra Cognita: Studien zur römischen Raumerfassung.* Spudasmata 59. Hildesheim: Olms.
———. 2001. "The Representation of Geographical Knowledge for Travel and Transport in the Roman World." In C. E. P. Adams and R. Laurence, eds., *Travel and Geography in the Roman Empire,* 7–21. London: Routledge.
———. 2004. "Mapping (In) the Ancient World." *Journal of Roman Studies* 94:183–90.

BIBLIOGRAPHY   285

Broshi, M. 1982. "The Credibility of Josephus." *Journal of Jewish Studies* 33:379–84.
Buckle, H. T. 1903 [1857]. *History of Civilization in England*, 3 vols. London: Frowde.
Buell, D. K. 2005. *Why this New Race: Ethnic Reasoning in Early Christianity*. New York: Columbia University Press.
Bunbury, E. H. 1879. *A History of Ancient Geography among the Greeks and Romans from the Earliest Ages till the Fall of the Roman Empire*. 2 vols. London: Murray.
Burke, E. 1790. *Reflections on the Revolution in France*. London: Dodlsey.
Burkert, W. 1985. *Greek Religion*. Translated by J. Raffan. Cambridge: Harvard University Press.
Burleigh, M. 2010. *Moral Combat: A History of World War II*. London: HarperCollins.
Burnett, A., M. Amandry, and P. P. Ripollès. 1992. *Roman Provincial Coinage*. Vol. 1, Pt. 1. London: British Museum.
Bury, J. B. 1930. *Selected Essays*, ed. H. Temperley. Cambridge: Cambridge University Press.
———. 1958. *History of the Later Roman Empire from the Death of Theodosius I to the Death of Justinian*. 2 vols. New York: Dover.
Caddick-Adams, P. 2013. *Monte Cassino: Ten Armies in Hell*. London: Arrow.
Campbell, J. B. 1984. *The Emperor and the Roman Army: 31 BC–AD 235*. Oxford: Clarendon.
Caponigri, A. R. (1953). *Time and Idea: the Theory of History in Giambattista Vico*. London: Routledge and Kegan Paul.
Capponi, L. 2004. "The *Oikos* of Alexandria." In W. V. Harris and G. Ruffini, eds., *Ancient Alexandria between Egypt and Greece*, 115–24. Columbia Studies in the Classical Tradition 26. Leiden: Brill.
———. 2005. *Augustan Egypt: The Creation of a Roman Province*. London: Routledge.
———. 2007. *Il tempio di Leontopoli in Egitto: Identità Politica e Religiosa dei Giudei di Onia (c. 150 a.C–73 d.C.)*. Pisa: ETS.
———. 2011. *Roman Egypt*. Classical World Series. Bristol: Bristol Classical Press.
Carlsson, S. 2010. *Hellenistic Democracies: Freedom, Independence and Political Procedure in Some East Greek City-States*. Historia Einzelschriften 206. Stuttgart: Steiner.
Carlyle, T. 1900–1901. *Critical and Miscellaneous Essays*. 5 vols. New York: Scribner.
Carmody, F. J. 1976. "Ptolemy's Triangulation of the Eastern Mediterranean." *Isis* 67:601–9.
Carr, E. H. 1950–78. *A History of Soviet Russia*. 14 vols. London: Macmillan.
———. 2001 [1961]. *What Is History?* 50th anniversary ed. Introduction by R. J. Evans. Notes for second ed. R. W. Davies. London: Palgrave Macmillan.
———. 1917. *The Philosophy of Benedetto Croce: The Problem of Art and History*. London: Macmillan.
Carradice, I., and M. J. Price. 1988. *Coinage in the Greek World*. London: Spink.
Cartledge, P. 2002a. *The Greeks: A Portrait of Self and Others*. Oxford: Oxford University Press.
———. 2002b. *The Spartans: An Epic History*. New York: Pan Macmillan.
Carus, P., ed. 1909 [1783]. *Kant's Prolegomena to Any Future Metaphysics*. Chicago: Open Court.
Cary, E. 1914–1927. *Dio's Roman History*. 9 vols. Cambridge: Harvard University Press.
Chabris, C., and D. Simons. 2010. *The Invisible Gorilla, and Other Ways Our Intuition Deceives Us*. New York: Crown.
Chamberlain, H. S. 1909. *Foundations of the Nineteenth Century*. Translated by J. Lees. Introduction by Lord Redesdale. 2 vols. London: Lane.

Champion, C. B. 2004. *Cultural Politics in Polybius's Histories.* Berkeley: University of California Press.
Chapman, H. H. 1998. "Spectacle and Theater in Josephus's *Bellum Judaicum.*" Ph.D. diss., Stanford University.
———. 2006. "Paul, Josephus, and the Judean Nationalistic and Imperialistic Policy of Forced Circumcision." *Ilu Revista de Ciencias de las Religiones* 11:131–55.
Cheesman, G. L. 1914. *The Auxilia of the Roman Imperial Army.* Oxford: Clarendon.
Chilton, B., and J. Neusner. 2004. *Classical Christianity and Rabbinic Judaism: Comparing Theologies.* Grand Rapids: Baker.
Churchill, R. S., and M. Gilbert. 1966–86. *Winston S. Churchill.* 8 vols. London: Heinemann.
Clark, E. A. 2004. *History, Theory, Text: Historians and the Linguistic Turn.* Cambridge: Harvard University Press.
Clark, L. 2006. *Anzio: The Friction of War. Italy and the Battle for Rome 1944.* London: Headline Review.
Clark, M. 2007 [1950]. *Calculated Risk.* New York: Enigma Books.
Clarke, K. 1999. *Between Geography and History: Hellenistic Constructions of the Roman World.* Oxford: Clarendon.
———. 2008. *Making Time for the Past: Local History and the Polis.* Oxford: Oxford University Press.
Clarysse, W., and D. J. Thompson. 2006. *Counting the People in Hellenistic Egypt.* 2 vols. Cambridge Classical Studies. Cambridge: Cambridge University Press.
Cohen, E. E. 2000. *The Athenian Nation.* Princeton: Princeton University Press.
Cohen, S. J. D. 1979. *Josephus in Galilee and Rome: His Vita and Development as a Historian.* Columbia Studies in the Classical Tradition 8. Leiden: Brill.
———. 1982. "Masada: Literary Tradition, Archaeological Remains, and the Credibility of Josephus." *Journal of Jewish Studies* 33:385–405.
———. 1999. *The Beginnings of Jewishness: Boundaries, Varieties, Uncertainties.* Hellenistic Culture and Society 31. Berkeley: University of California Press.
Colautti, F. M. 2002. *Passover in the Works of Josephus.* Journal for the Study of Judaism Supplements 75. Leiden: Brill.
Coleman, K. M. 2003. "Euergetism in Its Place." In K. Lomas and T. Cornell, eds., *Bread and Circuses: Euergetism and Municipal Patronage in Roman Italy,* 61–88. London: Routledge.
Collingwood, R. G. 1994 [1946 posth.]. *The Idea of History.* Rev. ed. Edited by J. van der Dussen. Oxford: Oxford University Press.
Collins, J. J., and P. W. Flint, eds. 2001–2002. *The Book of Daniel: Composition and Reception.* 2 vols. Vetus Testamentum Supplements 83. Leiden: Brill.
Colvin, D., and R. Hodges. 1994. "Tempting Providence: the Bombing of Monte Cassino." *History Today* 44:13–20.
Comte, A. 1830–42. *Cours de Philosophie Positive.* 6 vols. Paris: Bachelier.
———. 1896. *The Positive Philosophy of Auguste Comte.* 3 vols. Translated and condensed by Harriet Martineau. London: Bell & Sons.
Concannon, C. W. 2014. *"When You Were Gentiles": Specters of Ethnicity in Roman Corinth and Paul's Corinthian Correspondence.* New Haven: Yale University Press.
Conder, C. R. and H. H. Kitchener, with C. Wilson. 1881–1884. *The Survey of Western Palestine,* 4 vols. with 26 sheet maps. London: Palestine Exploration Fund.
Condor, J. E. 2010. "The Tomb of the *Haterii*: The Significance of the Sacra Via Relief." Paper presented in Meeting of the Classical Association of the Middle West and South, March 26, 2010, Oklahoma City.

Cowey, J and Maresch, K. 2001. *Urkunden des Politeuma der Juden von Herakleopolis (144/3–133/2 v. Chr.) (P. Polit. Iud.)*. Wiesbaden: Westdeutscher.

Cribiore, R. 2001. *Gymnastics of the Mind: Greek education in Hellenistic and Roman Egypt*. Princeton: Princeton University Press.

Croce, B. 1921. *Theory & History of Historiography*. Translatd by D. Ainslie. London: Harrap.

Crone, G. R. 1953. *Maps and Their Makers: An Introduction to the History of Cartography*. London: Hutchinson House.

Cronin, H. S. 1905. "Ptolemy's Map of Asia Minor: Method of Construction." *Geographical Journal* 25:429–41.

Dalberg-Acton, J. E. E. 1907. *The History of Freedom and Other Essays*. Edited by J. N. Figgus and R. V. Laurence. London: Macmillan.

Daley, G. 2002. *The Experience of Battle in the Second Punic War*. London: Routledge.

Dawson, J. 1984. *The Unusable Past: America's Puritan Tradition, 1830–1930*. Scholars Press Studies in the Humanities Series 4. Chico, CA: Scholars.

Debevoise, N. C. 1938. *A Political History of Parthia*. Chicago: University of Chicago Press.

Delia, D. 1991. *Alexandrian Citizenship during the Roman Principate*. American Classical Studies 23. Atlanta: Scholars.

den Hollander, W. 2012. "From Hostage to Historian: Josephus, the Emperors, and the City of Rome." Ph.D. diss., Graduate Program in History, York University, Toronto.

———. 2014. *Josephus, the Emperors, and the City of Rome: From Hostage to Historian*. Ancient Judaism and Early Christianity 86. Leiden: Brill.

Derks, T., and N. Roymans, eds. 2009. *Ethnic Constructs in Antiquity: The Role of Power and Tradition*. Amsterdam Archaeological Studies 13. Amsterdam: Amsterdam University Press.

Dignas, B., and K. Trampedach, eds. 2008. *Practitioners of the Divine: Greek Priests and Religious Officials from Homer to Heliodorus*. Hellenic Studies 30. Washington, DC: Center for Hellenic Studies.

Dilke, O. A. W. 1985. *Greek and Roman Maps*. Ithaca, NY: Cornell University Press.

———. 1987. *Mathematics and Measurement*. London: British Museum.

Disraeli, B. 1832. *England and France: A Cure for the Ministerial Gallomania*. London: Murray.

Dodd, C. H. 1935. *The Bible and the Greeks*. London: Hodder & Stoughton.

Dominik, W. J., and A. J. Boyle, eds. *Flavian Rome: Culture, Image, Text*. Leiden: Brill.

Donner, H. 1992. *The Mosaic Map of Madaba: An Introductory Guide*. Kampen: Kok Pharos.

Douglas, M. 2002. *Purity and Danger: An Analysis of Concept of Pollution and Taboo*. London: Routledge.

Droysen, J. G. 1875. *Grundriss der Historik*. 2nd ed. Leipzig: von Veit.

———. 1893 [German source of this translation: 1881]. *Outline of the Principles of History*. Translated by E. B. Andrews. Boston: Ginn & Company.

Dunn, J. D. G. 2003. *Jesus Remembered. Christianity in the Making* 1. Grand Rapids: Eerdmans.

Dyson, S. L. 1971. "Native Revolts in the Roman Empire." *Historia: Zeitschrift für alte Geschichte* 20:239–274.

Eckstein, A. M. 1995. *Moral Vision in the Histories of Polybius*. Hellenistic Culture and Society 16. Berkeley: University of California Press.

———. 2006. *Mediterranean Anarchy, Interstate War, and the Rise of Rome*. Hellenistic Culture and Society 48. Berkeley: University of California Press.

Edmondson, J. C. 1987. *Two Industries in Roman Lusitania: Mining and Garum Production.* Oxford: Archaeopress / B.A.R.
Edmondson, J., S. Mason, and J. Rives, eds. 2005. *Flavius Josephus and Flavian Rome.* Oxford: Oxford University Press.
Ehrenkrook. J. von. 2011. *Sculpting Idolatry in Flavian Rome: (An)Iconic Rhetoric in the Writings of Flavius Josephus.* Society of Biblical Literature Early Judaism and Its Literature 33. Atlanta: SBL.
Eilers, C. 2004. "Josephus' Caesarian *Acta*: History of a Dossier." *SBL Seminar Papers* 2003:189–213.
Elliott, J. H. 2007. "Jesus the Israelite Was neither a 'Jew' nor a 'Christian': On Correcting Misleading Nomenclature." *Journal for the Study of the Historical Jesus* 5:119–54.
Ellis, J. 1984. *Cassino, the Hollow Victory: The Battle for Rome, January–June 1944.* London: Aurum.
Ely, R. G., R. Gruner, and W. H. Dray. 1969. "Mandelbaum on Historical Narrative: A Discussion." *History and Theory* 8:275–94.
Esler, P. S. 2003. *Conflict and Identity in Romans: The Social Setting of Paul's Letter.* Minneapolis: Fortress.
Evans, R. J. 2005. *The Third Reich in Power.* London: Penguin.
———. 2000. *In Defence of History.* Rev. ed. London: Granta.
Farmer, W. R. 1973 [1956]. *Maccabees, Zealots, and Josephus.* New York: Columbia University Press.
Faraone, C. A., and F. S. Naiden, ed. 2012. *Greek and Roman Animal Sacrifice: Ancient Victims, Modern Observers.* Cambridge: Cambridge University Press.
Faulkner, N. 2004. *Apocalypse: The Great Jewish Revolt against Rome AD 66–73.* Stroud: Tempus.
Feeney, D. 2007. *Caesar's Calendar: Ancient Time and the Beginnings of History.* Sather Classical Lectures 65. Berkeley: University of California Press.
Feldherr, A. 1998. *Spectacle and Society in Livy's History.* Berkeley: University of California Press.
Feldman, L. H. 1993. *Jew and Gentile in the Ancient World: Attitudes and Interactions from Alexander to Justinian.* Princeton: Princeton University Press.
———. 2000. *Flavius Josephus: Translation and Commentary,* ed. S. Mason, vol. 3: *Judean Antiquities 1–4.* Leiden: Brill.
Ferguson, N. 1998. *The Pity of War.* London: Penguin.
Ferris, I. 2009. *Hate and War: The Column of Marcus Aurelius.* Stroud: History Press.
Ferro, M. 2003. *The Use and Abuse of History, or How the Past Is Taught to Children.* Translated by N. Stone and A. Brown. Rev. ed. London: Routledge.
Finkelstein, A. B. 2011. "Julian among Jews, Christians and 'Hellenes' in Antioch: Jewish Practice as a Guide to 'Hellenes' and a Goad to Christians." Ph.D. diss., Harvard University.
Force, P. 2009. "Voltaire and the Necessity of Modern History." *Modern Intellectual History* 6:457–84.
Ford, J. T., R. A. Destro, and C. R. Dechert, eds. 2005. *Religion in Public Life,* vol. 2: *Religion and Political Structures: from Fundamentalism to Public Service.* Washington, DC: Council for Research in Values and Philosophy.
Foucault, M. 1972. *The Archaeology of Knowledge and The Discourse on Language.* Translated A. M. Sheridan Smith. New York: Pantheon.

Fowler, R. 2006. "Herodotus and his Prose Predecessors." In C. Dewald and J. Marincola, eds., *The Cambridge Companion to Herodotus*, 29–45. Cambridge Companions to Literature. Cambridge: Cambridge University Press.

Fraser, P. M. 1972. *Ptolemaic Alexandria*, 3 vols. Oxford: Clarendon.

Frerichs, E. S., W. S. Green, and J. Neusner. 1987. *Judaisms and their Messiahs at the Turn of the Christian Era*. Cambridge: Cambridge University Press.

Freyne, S. 2009. Review of S. Mason's *Josephus, Judaea, and Christian Origins: Methods and Categories*." *Review of Biblical Literature* 11/27 2009: http://www.bookreviews.org/bookdetail.asp?TitleId=7010&CodePage=4130,6945,7010,1649,4648,481.

Friedlander, H. 1995. *The Origins of Nazi Genocide: From Euthanasia to the Final Solution*. Chapel Hill: University of North Carolina Press.

Fuks, A. 1970. "The Bellum Achaicum and its Social Aspect." *Journal of Hellenic Studies* 90:78–89.

Fuks, G. 1985/1988, "Some Remarks on Simon bar Giora." *Scripta Classica Israelica* 8–9:106–119.

Fung, Y.-L. 1948. *History of Chinese Philosophy*, ed. D. Bodde. New York: Macmillan.

Funke, P., and N. Luraghi, eds. 2009. *The Politics of Ethnicity and the Crisis of the Peloponnesian League*. Washington, DC: Center for Hellenic Studies.

Fustel de Coulanges, N. D. 1877 [1864]. *The Ancient City: A Study on the Religion* [NB: *le culte*], *Laws and Institutions of Greece and Rome*. 3rd ed. Translated by W. Small. Boston: Lee and Shepard.

Gadamer, H.-G. 1989. *Truth and Method*. 2nd rev. ed. Edited by J. Weinsheimer and D. G. Marshall. London: Continuum.

Gafni, I. M. 1997. *Land, Center, and Diaspora: Jewish Constructs in Late Antiquity*. Journal for the Study of the Pseudepigrapha Supplements 21. Sheffield: Sheffield Academic.

Gager, J. G. 1972. *Moses in Greco-Roman Paganism*. Nashville: Abingdon.

———. 1983. *The Origins of Anti-Semitism: Attitudes toward Judaism in Pagan and Christian Antiquity*. Oxford: Oxford University Press.

Gaifman, M. 2008. "The Aniconic Image of the Roman Near East." In T. Kaizer, ed., *The Variety of Local Religious Life in the Near East in the Hellenistic and Roman Periods*, 37–72. Religions in the Graeco-Roman World 164. Leiden: Brill.

Galinsky, K. 1996. *Augustan Culture: An Interpretive Introduction*. Princeton, NJ: Princeton University Press.

Galor, K., and G. Avni, eds. 2011. *Unearthing Jerusalem: 150 Years of Archaeological Research in the Holy City*. Winona Lake, IN: Eisenbrauns.

Galton, F. 1869. *Hereditary Genius: An Inquiry into its Laws and Consequences*. London: Macmillan.

Gambetti, S. 2009. *The Alexandrian Riots of 38 C.E. and the Persecution of the Jews: A Historical Reconstruction*. Journal for the Study of Judaism Supplements 135. Leiden: Brill.

Gardiner, J. 2010. *The Blitz: Our Cities under Attack 1940–1941*. London: Harper Collins.

Garfinkel, Y. 2011. "The Birth and Death of Biblical Minimalism." *Biblical Archaeology Review* 37.3:46–53, 78.

Garraghan, G. J., and J. Delanglez. 1946. *A Guide to Historical Method*. New York: Fordham University Press.

Gavish, D. 2005. *A Survey of Palestine under the British Mandate, 1920–1948*. London: Routledge.

Geiger, J. 2012. "Ptolemy of Ascalon, Historian of Herod." *Scripta Classica Israelica* 12:185-90.

———. 2009. "Rome and Jerusalem: Public Building and the Economy." In D. Jacobson and N. Kokkinos, eds., *Herod and Augustus: Papers Presented at the IJS Conference, 21st-23rd June 2005*, 157-69. IJS Studies in Judaica 6. Leiden: Brill.

Gellner, E. 1973. *Cause and Meaning in the Social Sciences*. Edited by I. C. Jarvie and J. Agassi. London: Routledge & Kegan Paul.

Geva, H., ed. . 2000. *Ancient Jerusalem Revealed*. Rev. and exp. ed. Jerusalem: Israel Exploration Society.

———. 2014. "Jerusalem's Population in Antiquity: A Minimalist View." *Tel Aviv* 41:131-50.

Gibson, S., and D. M. Jacobson. 1994. "The Oldest Datable Chambers on the Temple Mount in Jerusalem." *BA* 57:150-60.

Gichon, M. 1981. "Cestius Gallus's Campaign in Judaea." *Palestine Exploration Quarterly* 113:39-62.

Gilbert, M. 1991. *Churchill: A Life*. London: Heinemann.

Gilderhus, M. T. 2010. *History and Historians: A Historiographical Introduction*. 7th ed. Upper Saddle River, NJ: Pearson.

Ginzburg, C. 1991. "Checking the Evidence: The Judge and the Historian." *Critical Inquiry* 18:79-92.

Gobineau, A. 1915 [1853]. *The Inequality of Human Races*. London: Heinemann.

Goldfus, H., Y. Avni, R. Albag, and B. Arubas. 2016. "The Significance of Geomorphological and Soil Formation Research for Understanding the Unfinished Roman Ramp at Masada." *Catena* http://dx.doi.org/10.1016/j.catena.2016.04.014. In press.

Goldstein, D. S. 1977. "J. B. Bury's Philosophy of History: A Reappraisal." *American Historical Review* 82:896-919.

Goldstein, J. A. 1984. *II Maccabees*. Anchor Bible 41A. Garden City, NY: Doubleday.

Goldstein, L. J. 1976. *Historical Knowing*. Austin: University of Texas.

Goldsworthy, A. K. 1996. *The Roman Army at War 100 BC –AD 200*. Oxford: Oxford University Press.

Goren, H. 2002. "Sacred, but not Surveyed: Nineteenth-Century Surveys of Palestine." *Imago Mundi* 54:87-110.

Grabar, O. and B. Z. Keda, eds. 2009. *Where Heaven and Earth Meet: Jerusalem's Sacred Esplanade*. Jerusalem: Yad Ben-Zvi.

Graetz, H. 1862. *Die Geschichte der Juden von ältesten Zeiten bis auf die Gegenwart*. 11 vols. 2nd ed. Leipzig: Leiner.

———. 1914 [1888]. *Volkstümliche Geschichte der Juden*. 3 vols. 3rd ed. Leipzig: Leiner.

———. 1956 [1891]. *History of the Jews*. Translated by B. Löwy. 6 vols. Philadelphia: Jewish Publication Society of America.

Graf, F. 2004. "Myth." In S. I. Johnston, ed., *Religions of the Ancient World: A Guide*, 45-58. Cambridge: Harvard University Press.

Grant, M. 1916. *The Passing of the Great Race, or, The Racial Basis of European History*. New York: Scribner.

———. 1936. *The Passing of the Great Race, or, The Racial Basis of European History*. 4th ed. New York: Scribner.

Greatrex, G. 2007. "Roman Frontiers and Foreign Policy in the East." In R. Alston and S. Lieu eds., *Aspects of the Roman East*, 103-73. Turnhout: Brepols.

Green, P. 1990. *Alexander to Actium: The Historical Evolution of the Hellenistic Age.* Berkeley: University of California Press.
Grenfell, B. P., and A. S. Hunt. 1916. *The Oxyrhynchus Papyri.* 15 vols. London: Egypt Exploration Fund.
Grieb, V. 2008. *Hellenistische Demokratie: politische Organisation und Struktur in freien griechischen Poleis nach Alexander dem Grossen.* Stuttgart: Steiner.
Gruen, E. S. 1976. "The Origins of the Achaean War." *Journal of Hellenic Studies* 96:46–69.
———. 1984. *The Hellenistic World and the Coming of Rome,* 2 vols. Berkeley: University of California Press.
———. 2002. *Diaspora: Jews amidst Greeks and Romans.* Cambridge: Harvard University Press.
———. 2011. *Rethinking the Other in Antiquity.* Princeton: Princeton University Press.
Grünenfelder, R. 2003. *Frauen an den Krisenherden: eine rhetorisch-politische Deutung des Bellum Judaicum.* Münster: LIT.
Guérin, V. 1868–1880. *Description géographique, historique et archéologique de la Palestine: accompagnée de cartes détaillées,* 3 parts in 7 vols. Paris: à l'imprimerie impériale [repr. 1969, Amsterdam: Oriental Press].
Günther, H. F. K. 1930a. *Rassenkunde des deutschen Volkes.* 14th ed. Munich: Lehmann.
———. 1930b. *Rassenkunde des jüdischen Volkes.* 2nd ed. Munich: Lehmann.
Gussmann, O. 2008. *Das Priesterverständnis des Flavius Josephus.* Texte und Studien zum antiken Judentum 124. Tübingen: Mohr/Siebeck.
Habicht, C. 1998 [1985]. *Pausanias' Guide to Ancient Greece.* Berkeley: University of California Press.
Hacking, I. 1975. *The Emergence of Probability: A Philosophical Study of Early Ideas about Probability, Induction and Statistical Inference.* Cambridge: Cambridge University Press.
Halbwachs, M. 1950. *La Mémoire Collective.* Edited by J. Alexandre. Paris: Presses Universitaires de France.
Hale, J. R., ed. 1967. *The Evolution of British Historiography from Bacon to Namier.* London: Macmillan.
Hall, E. 1989. *Inventing the Barbarian: Greek Self-Definition through Tragedy.* Oxford: Clarendon Press.
Hall, J. M. 1997. *Ethnic Identity in Greek Antiquity.* Cambridge: Cambridge University Press.
———. 2002. *Hellenicity: Between Ethnicity and Culture.* Chicago: University of Chicago Press.
Hall, L. J. 2004. *Roman Berytus: Beirut in Late Antiquity.* London: Routledge.
Hallote, R. S., and A. H. Joffe. 2002. "The Politics of Israeli Archaeology: Between 'Nationalism' and 'Science' in the Age of the Second Republic." *Israel Studies* 7:84–116.
Hamilton, P. 2003. *Historicism.* 2nd ed. New Critical Idiom. London: Routledge.
Hannah, R. 2005. *Greek and Roman Calendars: Constructions of Time in the Classical World.* London: Duckworth.
Hansen, M. H., ed. 1993a. *The Ancient Greek City-State: Symposium on the Occasion of the 250th Anniversary of the Royal Danish Academy of Sciences and Letters, July, 1–4 1992.* Acts of the Copenhagen Polis Centre 1. Copenhagen: Munksgaard.
———. 1993b. "The *Polis* as a Citizen-State." In Hansen, ed., 1993a, 7–29.

———. 2006. *Polis: An Introduction to the Ancient Greek City-State*. Oxford: Oxford University Press.
Hansen, M. H., and T. H. Nielsen, eds. 2004. *An Inventory of Archaic and Classical Poleis: An Investigation Conducted by The Copenhagen Polis Centre for the Danish National Research Foundation*. Oxford: Oxford University Press.
Hanson, K. C., and D. E. Oakman. 2008 [1998]. *Palestine in the Time of Jesus: Social Structures and Social Conflicts*. 2nd ed. Minneapolis: Fortress.
Hapgood, D., and D. Richardson. 2002. *Monte Cassino: The Story of the Most Controversial Battle of World War II*. Cambridge, MA: Da Capo.
Harker, A. 2008. *Loyalty and Dissidence in Roman Egypt: The Case of the Acta Alexandrinorum*. Cambridge: Cambridge University Press.
Harland, P. A. 2003. *Associations, Synagogues, and Congregations: Claiming a Place in Ancient Mediterranean Society*. Minneapolis: Fortress.
———. 2006. "The Declining *Polis*? Religious Rivalries in Ancient Civic Context." In L. E. Vaage, ed., *Religious Rivalries in the Early Roman Empire and the Rise of Christianity*, 21–49. Studies in Christiantiy and Judaism 18. Waterloo, ON: Wilfrid Laurier University Press.
———. 2009. *Dynamics of Identity in the World of the Early Christians: Associations, Judeans, and Cultural Minorities*. London: T. & T. Clark.
Harlow, M., and R. Laurence. 2002. *Growing Up and Growing Old in Ancient Rome: A Life Course Approach*. London: Routledge.
Harris, M. 1976. "History and Significance of the Emic/Etic Distinction." *Annual Review of Anthropology* 5:329–50.
Harris, W. V. 1985. *War and Imperialism in Republican Rome, 370–70 B.C.* Oxford: Clarendon.
———. 1989. *Ancient Literacy*. Cambridge: Harvard University Press.
Harrison, P. 1990. *'Religion' and Religions in the English Enlightenment*. Cambridge: Cambridge University Press.
Harrison, T., ed. 2002. *Greeks and Barbarians*. Edinburgh: Edinburgh University Press.
Hartog, F. 1998. *The Mirror of Herodotus: The Representation of the Other in the Writing of History*. Translated by J. Lloyd. Berkeley: University of California Press.
Harvey, P. D. A. 1996. *Mappa Mundi: the Hereford World Map*. London: Hereford Cathedral and the British Library.
Hastings, M. 2009. *Finest Years: Churchill as Warlord 1940–45*. London: Harper.
Hegel, G. W. F. 1900 [1822–1831]. *The Philosophy of History*. Edited by C. Hegel. Translated by J. Sibree. New York: Colonial.
Hempel, C. G. 1942. "The Function of General Laws in History." *Journal of Philosophy* 39:35–48.
Hengel, M. 1989 [1961]. *The Zealots: Investigations into the Jewish Freedom Movement in the Period from Herod I until 70 A.D.* Translated by D. Smith. Edinburgh: T. & T. Clark.
———. 2011. *Die Zeloten: Untersuchungen zur jüdischen Freiheitsbewegung in der Zeit von Herodes I. bis 70 n. Chr.* 3rd ed. Edited by R. Deines and C.-J. Thornton. Tübingen: Mohr/Siebeck.
Henig, R. B. 2002. *The Origins of the First World War*. 3rd ed. Lancaster Pamphlet. London: Routledge.

Herz, P. 2002. "Sacrifice and Sacrificial Ceremonies of the Roman Imperial Army." In A. I. Baumgarten, ed., *Sacrifice in Religious Experience*, 81-100. Studies in the History of Religions 93. Leiden: Brill.

Hewitt, R. 2010. *Map of a Nation: A Biography of the Ordnance Survey*. London: Granta.

Heylbut, G. 1887. "Ptolemaeus ΠΕΡΙ ΔΙΑΦΟΡΑΣ ΛΕΞΕΩΝ." *Hermes* 22:388-410.

Hitchcock, D., and B. Verheij, eds. 2006. *Arguing on the Toulmin Model: New Essays in Argument Analysis and Evaluation*. Dordrecht: Springer.

Hodge, C. E. J. 2007. *If Sons, then Heirs: A Study of Kinship and Ethnicity in the Letters of Paul*. New York: Oxford University Press.

Hoffman, D. C. 2008. "Concerning *Eikos*: Social Expectation and Verisimilitude in Early Attic Rhetoric." *Rhetorica* 26:1-29.

Hölkeskamp, K.-J. 1996. "Exempla und *mos maiorum*: Überlegungen zum kollektiven Gedächtnis der Nobilität." In H.-J. Gehrke and A. Möller, eds., *Vergangenheit und Lebenswelt: soziale Kommunikation, Traditionsbildung und historisches Bewusstsein*, 301-38. ScriptOralia 90. Tübingen: Narr.

Honigman, S. 2003. "*Politeumata* and Ethnicity in Ptolemaic and Roman Egypt." *Ancient Society* 33:61-102.

Hope, V. M., and E. Marshall, eds. 2000. *Death and Disease in the Ancient City*. London: Routledge.

Hopkins, K. 1983. *Death and Renewal*. Sociological Studies in Roman History 2. Cambridge: Cambridge University Press.

Hornblower, S. 1987. *Thucydides*. London: Duckworth.

Horrell, D. G. 2016. "Ethnicisation, Marriage and Early Christian Identity: Critical Reflections on 1 Corinthians 7, 1 Peter 3 and Modern New Testament Scholarship." *New Testament Studies* 62:439-60.

Horsley, R. A. 1979a. "Josephus and the Bandits." *Journal for the Study of Judaism* 10:37-63.

———. 1979b. "The *Sicarii*: Ancient Jewish 'Terrorists.'" *Journal of Religion* 59:435-58.

———. 1993. *Jesus and the Spiral of Violence: Popular Jewish Resistance in Roman Palestine*. Minneapolis: Fortress.

———. 1995. *Galilee: History, Politics, People*. Valley Forge, PA: Trinity.

———. 1996. *Archaeology, History, and Society in Galilee: The Social Context of Jesus and the Rabbis*. Valley Forge, PA: Trinity.

———. 2002. "Power Struggle and Power Vacuum in 66-7 C.E." In A. M. Berlin and J. A. Overman, eds., *The First Jewish Revolt: Archaeology, History, and Ideology*, 87-109. London: Routledge.

———. 2003. *Jesus and Empire: the Kingdom of God and the New World Disorder*. Minneapolis: Fortress.

———. 2008. "Jesus and Empire." In R. A. Horsley, ed., *In the Shadow of Empire: Reclaiming the Bible as a History of Faithful Resistance*, 75-96. Louisville: Westminster John Knox.

Horsley, R. A., and J. S. Hanson. 1988. *Bandits, Prophets, and Messiahs: Popular Movements at the Time of Jesus*. New Voices in Biblical Studies. New York: Harper & Row.

Houlgate, S. 2011. "G. W. F. Hegel: An Introduction to his Life and Thought." In S. Houlgate and M. Bauer, eds., *A Companion to Hegel*, 1-20. Blackwell Companions to Philosophy 48. Chichester, UK: Wiley-Blackwell.

Howard, T. J. 2000. *Religion and the Rise of Historicism: W. M. L. de Wette, Jacob Burckhardt, and the Theological Origins of Nineteenth-Century Historical Consciousness.* New York: Cambridge University Press.

Hoyt, E. P. 2002. *Backwater War: the Allied Campaign in Italy, 1943–1945.* London: Praeger.

Hudon, W. 1996. "Religion and Society in Early Modern Italy—Old Questions, New Insights." *American Historical Review* 101:783–804.

Hughes, D. J., ed. 2009. *Moltke on the Art of War: Selected Writings.* New York: Random House.

Hughes-Warrington, M. 2008. *Fifty Key Thinkers on History.* 2nd ed. London: Routledge.

Hume, D. 1870. *Essays, Literary, Moral, and Political.* London: Alex, Murray & Son 1870.

Hume, R. D. 1999. *Reconstructing Contexts: The Aims and Principles of Archaeo-Historicism.* Oxford: Oxford University Press.

Iggers, G. G. 1968. *The German Conception of History: The National Tradition of Historical Thought from Herder to the Present.* Middletown, CT: Wesleyan University Press.

Iggers, G. G. 1997. *Historiography in the Twentieth Century: From Scientific Objectivity to the Postmodern Challenge.* Hanover, NH: Wesleyan University Press.

Isaac, B. H. 1992. *The Limits of Empire: The Roman Army in the East.* Rev. ed. Oxford: Clarendon.

Jacobson, D. M., and N. Kokkinos, eds. 2009. *Herod and Augustus: Papers Presented at the IJS Conference, 21st–23rd June 2005.* IJS Studies in Judaica 6. Leiden: Brill.

James, E. O. 1963. *Seasonal Feasts and Festivals.* New York: Barnes & Noble.

Jampoler, A. C. A. 2005. *Sailors in the Holy Land: the 1848 American Expedition to the Dead Sea and the search for Sodom and Gomorrah.* Annapolis, MD: Naval Institute Press.

Jaschik, S. 2015. "Thomas Jefferson is Next Target." *Inside Higher Ed.* 23 November: https://www.insidehighered.com/news/2015/11/23/thomas-jefferson-next-target-students-who-question-honors-figures-who-were-racists

Jenkins, K. 1991. *Re-thinking History.* London: Routledge.

Jenkins, K. 1995. *On "What is History?" From Carr and Elton to Rorty and White.* London: Routledge.

Jenkins, K., ed. 1997. *The Postmodern History Reader.* London: Routledge.

Jeremias, J. 1969. *Jerusalem in the Time of Jesus: An Investigation into Economic and Social Conditions during the New Testament Period.* Translated by F. H. Cave and C. H. Cave. Philadelphia: Fortress.

Johnson, A. J. 1864. "Palestine." In R. S. Fisher, ed., *Johnson's New Illustrated (Steel Plate) Family Atlas, with Physical Geography, and with Descriptions Geographical, Statistical, And Historical,* 93. New York: Johnson & Ward.

Johnson, A. P. 2006. *Ethnicity and Argumentation in Eusebius' Praeparatio Evangelica.* Oxford: Oxford University Press.

Johnston, A. E. M. 1967. "The Earliest Preserved Greek Map: A New Ionian Coin Type." *Journal of Hellenic Studies* 87:86–94.

Johnston, K. 1894. *Classical Atlas.* Boston: Ginn.

Joint Association of Classical Teachers (JACT). 1984. *The World of Athens.* Cambridge: Cambridge University Press.

Jones, A. H. M. 1940. *The Greek City: from Alexander to Justinian.* Oxford: Clarendon.

―――. 1971. *The Cities of the Eastern Roman Provinces*. 2nd ed. Oxford: Clarendon.
Jones, B. W. 1989. "Titus in Judaea, A.D. 67." *Latomus* 48:127–34.
Jones, C. P. 1996. "ἔθνος and γένος in Herodotus." *CQ* 46:315–20.
Jones, S. 1997. *The Archaeology of Ethnicity: Constructing Identities in the Past and Present*. London: Routledge.
Josephson, J. A. 2012. *The Invention of Religion in Japan*. Chicago: University of Chicago Press.
Kadman, L. 1960. *The Coins of the Jewish War of 66 to 73*. Tel Aviv: Schocken.
Kalmar, I. D., and D. J. Penslar, eds. 2005. *Orientalism and the Jews*. Hanover, NH: Brandeis University Press.
Kammen, M. 1991. *Mystic Chords of Memory: The Transformation of Tradition in American Culture*. New York: Knopf.
Kant, I. 1881 [1781]. *Critique of Pure Reason*, 2 vols. Translated by F. M. Müller. London: Macmillan.
―――. 1950 [1783]. *Prolegomena to Any Future Metaphysics*. Edited and translated by L. W. Beck. Indianapolis: Bobbs-Merrill.
Kasher, A. 1985. *The Jews in Hellenistic and Roman Egypt: The Struggle for Equal Rights*. Texte und Studien zum antiken Judentum 7. Tübingen: Mohr/Siebeck.
―――. 1990. *Jews and Hellenistic Cities in Eretz-Israel: Relations of the Jews in Eretz-Israel with the Hellenistic Cities during the Second Temple Period (332 BCE—70 CE)*. Texte und Studien zum antiken Judentum 21. Tübingen: Mohr/Siebeck.
Keegan, J. 1976. *The Face of Battle*. New York: Viking.
Kennedy, G. A. 1994. *A New History of Classical Rhetoric*. Princeton: Princeton University Press.
Keyes, C. W. 1931. "Syntaximon and Laographia in the Arsinoite Nome." *AJP* 3:263–69
Klawans, J. 2012. *Josephus and the Theologies of Ancient Judaism*. Oxford: Oxford University Press.
Kloppenborg, J. S., and S. G. Wilson, eds. 1996. *Voluntary Associations in the Graeco-Roman World*. London: Routledge.
Kloppenborg, J. S., R. S. Ascough, and P. A. Harland. 2011. *Greco-Roman Associations: Texts, Translations, and Commentary*. Berlin: de Gruyter.
Klauck, H. J. 2003. *The Religious Context of Early Christianity: A Guide to Graeco-Roman Religions*. Minneapolis: Fortress Press.
Knust, J. W. and Z. Varhelyi, eds. 2011. *Ancient Mediterranean Sacrifice*. Oxford: Oxford University Press.
Koenen, L. 1968. "Die Prophezeiungen des 'Töpfers.'" *ZPE* 2:178–209.
Kokkinos, N. 1998. *The Herodian Dynasty: Origins, Role in Society and Eclipse*. Journal for the Study of the Pseudepigrapha Supplements 30. Sheffield: Sheffield Academic.
Konstan, D. 1997. "Defining Ancient Greek Ethnicity." *Diaspora* 6:97–110.
Korhonen, K., ed. 2006. *Tropes for the Past: Hayden White and the History / Literature Debate*. Amsterdam: Rodopi.
Kraabel, A. T. 1982. "The Roman Diaspora: Six Questionable Assumptions." *Journal of Jewish Studies* 33:445–64.
Kraeling, C. H. 1938. *Gerasa, City of the Decapolis: An Account Embodying the Record of a Joint Excavation Conducted by Yale University and the British School of Archaeology in Jerusalem (1928-1930), and Yale University and the American Schools of Oriental Research (1930-1931, 1933-1934)*. New Haven: American School of Oriental Research.

Kraft, R. A., and G. W. E. Nickelsburg, eds. 1986. *Early Judaism and Its Modern Interpreters*. Philadelphia: Fortress.
Kraus, C. S., and A. J. Woodman. 1997. *Latin Historians*. Greece & Rome: New Surveys in the Classics 27. Oxford: Oxford University Press.
Krause, J.-U., and C. Witschel, eds. 2006. *Die Stadt in der Spätantike—Niedergang oder Wandel?* Geschichte. Stuttgart: Steiner.
Kreissig, H. 1970. *Die sozialen Zusammenhänge des judäischen Krieges: Klassen und Klassenkampf im Palästina des 1. [ersten] Jarhunderts vor Unserer Zeit*. Schriften zur Geschichte und Kultur der Antike 1. Berlin: Akademie-Verlag.
Krieger, L. 1968. "Review of M. White's *Foundations of Historical Knowledge*." *American Historical Review* 73:1092–94.
Kushner, H. S. 1981. *When Bad Things Happen to Good People*. New York: Random House.
———. 1986. *When All You've Ever Wanted Isn't Enough*. New York: Simon & Schuster.
Kwiek, M. 2006. "The Classical German Idea of the University Revisited, or On the Nationalization of the Modern Institution." *Centre for Public Policy Studies, Research Paper Series* 1:1–59.
Landau, T. 2006. *Out-Heroding Herod: Josephus, Rhetoric, and the Herod Narratives*. Arbeiten zur Geschichte des antiken Judentums und des Urchristentums 63. Leiden: Brill.
Lape, S. 2010. *Race and Citizen Identity in the Classical Athenian Democracy*. Cambridge: Cambridge University Press.
Lampe, G. W. H. 1961. *A Patristic Greek Lexicon*. Oxford: Clarendon.
Larson, J. 2007. *Ancient Greek Cults: A Guide*. London: Routledge.
Laurence, R., and J. Berry, eds. 1998. *Cultural Identity in the Roman Empire*. London: Routledge.
Le Bohec, Y. 1994. *The Imperial Roman Army*. Translated by R. Bate. London: Batsford.
Lee, R. Y. T. 2012. "Diaspora Judaeans and Proselytes in Early Roman Palestine: A Study of Ethnic, Social, and Cultural Boundaries." Ph.D. diss., University of Aberdeen.
Leiter, B. 2004. "The Hermeneutics of Suspicion: Recovering Marx, Nietzsche, and Freud." In B. Leiter, ed., *The Future for Philosophy*, 74–105. Oxford: Clarendon.
Leon, H. 1960. *The Jews of Ancient Rome*. Morris Loeb Series. Philadelphia: Jewish Publication Society.
Levine, L. I. 2002. *Jerusalem: Portrait of the City in the Second Temple Period (538 B.C.E.–70 C.E.)*. Philadelphia: Jewish Publication Society / Jewish Theological Seminary of America.
Lewis, N. 1983. *Life in Egypt under Roman Rule*. Oxford: Clarendon.
Liddell, H. G., R. Scott, H. S. Jones et al. 1990. *A Greek-English Lexicon*. Reprint of 9th ed. Oxford: Clarendon.
Lightstone, J. L. 1984. *The Commerce of the Sacred: Mediation of the Divine among Jews in the Graeco-Roman Diaspora*. Brown Judaic Studies 59. Chico, CA: Scholars.
Lomas, K. 1998. "Roman Imperialism and the City in Italy." In R. Laurence and J. Berry, eds., *Cultural Identity in the Roman Empire*, 64–78. London: Routledge.
Luce, T. J. 1977. *Livy: The Composition of His History*. Princeton: Princeton University Press.
Luraghi, N. 2006. "Meta-*historiē*: Method and Genre in the *Histories*." In C. Dewald and J. Marincola, eds., *The Cambridge Companion to Herodotus*, 76–91. Cambridge Companions to Literature. Cambridge: Cambridge University Press.

Macaulay, T. B. 1989. "History." In H. M. M. Trevelyan, ed., *The Works of Lord Macaulay*, 7:167–220. 20 vols. London: Longmans, Green.
Macfie, A. L. 2002. *Orientalism*. London: Pearson.
MacMullen, E. 1966. *Enemies of the Roman Order: Treason, Unrest, and Alienation in the Empire*. London: Routledge.
Mader, G. 2000. *Josephus and the Politics of Historiography: Apologetic and Impression Management in the Bellum Judaicum*. Mnemosyne Supplements 205. Leiden: Brill.
Magness, J. 2002. *The Archaeology of Qumran and the Dead Sea Scrolls*. Studies in the Dead Se Scrolls and Related Literature. Grand Rapids: Eerdmans.
Mahieu, B. 2012. *Between Rome and Jerusalem: Herod the Great and His Sons in Their Struggle for Recognition*. Orientalia Lovaniensia Analecta 208.Leuven: Peeters.
Majdalany, F. 1957. *Cassino: Portrait of a Battle*. London: Cassell.
Malkin, I. 2001. *Ancient Perceptions of Greek Ethnicity*. Center for Hellenic Studies Colloquia 5. Washington, DC: Center for Hellenic Studies.
Mandelbaum, M. 1967. "A Note on History as Narrative." *History and Theory* 6:413–19.
Manning, W. H. 1964. "A Relief of Two Greek Freedmen." *British Museum Quarterly* 29:25–28.
Marincola, J. 2001. *Greek Historians*. Oxford: Oxford University Press.
Marx, K. 1904 [1859]. *A Contribution to the Critique of Political Economy*. Translated by N. I. Stone. Chicago: Kerr.
Mason, S. 1991. *Flavius Josephus on the Pharisees: A Composition-Critical Study*. Studia Post-Biblica 39. Leiden: Brill.
———. 1999. "Revisiting Josephus's Pharisees." In J. Neusner and A. J. Avery-Peck, eds., *Judaism in Late Antiquity, Part 3. Where We Stand: Issues and Debates in Ancient Judaism*, 2:23–56. Handbuch der Orientalistik: Nahe und der Mittlere Osten 16. Leiden: Brill, 1999.
———. 2000. "Introductory Essay." In L. H. Feldman, ed. and trans., *Flavius Josephus: Translation and Commentary. Judean Antiquities 1–4, Translation and Commentary*, xiii–xxxv. Leiden: Brill.
———. 2001. *Flavius Josephus: Translation and Commentary*, vol. 9: *Life of Josephus*. Leiden: Brill.
———. 2003. *Josephus and the New Testament*. 2nd ed. Peabody, MA: Hendrickson.
———. 2007. "Jews, Judaeans, Judaizing, Judaism: Problems of Categorization in Ancient History." *Journal for the Study of Judaism* 38:1–56.
———. 2008. *Flavius Josephus: Translation and Commentary*, vol. 1b: *Judean War 2*. Leiden: Brill.
———. 2009. *Josephus, Judea, and Christian Origins: Methods and Categories*. Peabody, MA: Hendrickson.
———. 2011a. "What Is History? Using Josephus for the Judaean-Roman War." In M. Popović, ed., *The Jewish Revolt against Rome: Interdisciplinary Perspectives*, 155–240. Journal for the Study of Judaism Supplements 154. Leiden: Brill.
———. 2011b. "The Historical Problem of the Essenes." In P. W. Flint, J. Duhaime, and K. S. Baek, eds., *Celebrating the Dead Sea Scrolls: A Canadian Contribution*, 201–51. Early Judaism and Its Literature 30. Atlanta: Society of Biblical Literature.
———. 2014a. "The Priest Josephus away from the Temple: A Changed Man?" *Revue de Qumran* 26:375–402.
———. 2014b. "Why Did Jews Go to War with Rome in 66–67 C.E.? Realist–Regional Perspectives." In P. J. Tomson and J. Schwartz, eds., *Jews and Christians in the First*

and Second Centuries: How to Write Their Histories, 126–206. Compendia Rerum Iudaicarum ad Novum Testamentum 13. Leiden: Brill.

———. 2016. *A History of the Jewish War, A.D. 66–74*. New York: Cambridge University Press. [Abbreviated *HJW*.]

Mason, S., and T. Robinson, 2013. *Early Christian Reader: Christian Texts from the First and Second Centuries in Contemporary English Translations including the New Revised Standard Version of the New Testament*. Atlanta: Society of Biblical Literature. Original pub. Peabody, MA: Hendrickson, 1994.

Masuzawa, T. 2005. *The Invention of World Religions, or, How European Universalism Was Preserved in the Language of Pluralism*. Chicago: University of Chicago Press.

Mattern, S. P. 1999. *Rome and the Enemy: Imperial Strategy in the Principate*. Berkeley: University of California.

McCarney, J. 2000. *Hegel on History*. Routledge Philosophy Guidebooks. London: Routledge.

McClellan, S. 2008. *What Happened: Inside the Bush White House and Washington's Culture of Deception*. New York: Public Affairs.

McEvedy, C. 2011. *Cities of the Classical World: An Atlas and Gazetteer of 120 Centres of Ancient Civilization*. Edited by D. S. Oles. London: Allen Lane.

McInerney, J., ed. 2014. *A Companion to Ethnicity in the Ancient Mediterranean*. Chichester, UK: Wiley.

McLaren, J. S. 1998. *Turbulent Times? Josephus and Scholarship on Judaea in the First Century CE*. Journal for the Study of the Pseudepigrapha Supplements 29. Sheffield: Sheffield Academic.

———. 2003. "The Coinage of the First Year as a Point of Reference for the First Jewish Revolt (66–70 CE)." *SCI* 22:135–52.

Meimaris, Y. E. et al., eds. 1992. *Chronological Systems in Roman-Byzantine Palestine and Arabia: The Evidence of the Dated Greek Inscriptions*. Athens: The National Hellenic Research Foundation/Research Centre for Greek and Roman Antiquity. Paris: Diffusion de Boccard.

Meinecke, F. 1972 [1936]. *Historism: The Rise of a New Historical Outlook*. Translated by J. E. Anderson and H. D. Schmidt. London: Routledge & Kegan Paul.

Mellor, R. 1993. *Tacitus*. London: Routledge.

———. 1999. *The Roman Historians*. London: Routledge.

Meshorer, Y. 2001. *A Treasury of Jewish Coins from the Persian Period to Bar Kokhba*. Jerusalem: Yad ben-Zvi.

Mettinger, T. N. D. 1995. *No Graven Image? Israelite Aniconism in its Ancient Near Eastern Context*. Coniectanea Biblica: Old Testament Series 42. Stockholm: Almqvist & Wiksell International.

Meyer-Zwiffelhoffer, E. 2002. *Politikōs Archein: zum Regierungsstil der senatorischen Statthalter in den kaiserzeitlichen griechischen Provinzen*. Historia: Enzelschriften 165. Stuttgart: Steiner.

Michaud, G. 1908. "Shall We Improve Our Race?" *Popular Science Monthly* 72:75–78.

Michel, O. 1968. "Studien zu Josephus: Simon bar Giora." *New Testament Studies* 14:402–8.

Miles, G. B. 1995. *Livy: Reconstructing Early Rome*. Ithaca, NY: Cornell University Press.

Milgrom, J. 2004. *Leviticus: A Book of Ritual and Ethics*. Continental Commentaries. Minneapolis: Fortress.

Mill, J. S. 1891 [1865]. *Auguste Comte and Positivism*. 4th ed. London: Kegan Paul.

Millar, F., ed. 1967. *The Roman Empire and its Neighbours*. New York: Delacorte.
———. 1977. *The Emperor in the Roman World, 31 BC—AD 337*. Ithaca, NY: Cornell University Press.
———. 1993. *The Roman Near East, 31 B.C.—A. D. 337*. Cambridge: Harvard University Press.
Miller, D. M. 2010. "The Meaning of *Ioudaios* and Its Relationship to Other Group Labels in Ancient 'Judaism.'" *Currents in Biblical Research* 9:98–126.
———. 2012. "Ethnicity Comes of Age: An Overview of Twentieth-Century Terms for Ioudaios." *Currents in Biblical Research* 10:293–311.
———. 2014. "Ethnicity, Religion and the Meaning of *Ioudaios* in Ancient "Judaism.'" *Currents in Biblical Research* 12:216–65.
Mitchell, S. A. 1873 (1844). *Mitchell's Ancient Atlas, Classical and Sacred*. Philadelphia: Butler.
Modrzejewski, J. M. 1995. *The Jews of Egypt: from Rameses II to Emperor Hadrian*. Translated by R. Cornman. Philadelphia: Jewish Publication Society.
Moehring, H. R. 1957. "Novelistic Elements in the Writings of Flavius Josephus." Ph.D. diss., University of Chicago.
———. 1984. "Joseph ben Matthia and Flavius Josephus." In *ANRW* 2.21.2:864–917.
Moltke, H. von. 1907. *The Franco-German War of 1870-71*. Translated by A. Forbes. London: Harper & Brothers.
Momigliano, A. 1966. *Studies in Historiography*. New York: Harper & Row.
———. 1974. "Le regole del giuoco nello studio della storia antica." *Annali della Scuola Normale Superiore di Pisa*, Cl. Lett. e Fil., Serie III, vol. 4: 1183–1192 = *Introduzione bibliografica alla storia greca fino a Socrate* (Florence: La Nuova Italia, 1975), 1–12. Translated in Schwartz, *Reading the First Century* (2013), 181–89, and in K. W. Yu, "The Rules of the Game in the Study of Ancient History." *History and Theory* 55 (2016) 39–45.
———. 1976. Review of T. D. Barnes' *Tertullian: A Historical and Literary Study*. *Journal of Roman Studies* 66:273–76.
———. 1977. "Historicism Revisited." In A. Momigliano, *Essays in Ancient and Modern Historiography*, 365–73. Oxford: Blackwell.
———. 1981. "The Rhetoric of History and the History of Rhetoric: on Hayden White's Tropes." In E. S. Shaffer, ed., *Comparative Criticism: A Yearbook*, 3:259–68. Cambridge: Cambridge University Press.
Montesquieu, C. de Secondat, Baron de. 2001 [1752]. *The Spirit of Laws*. Translated by T. Nugent. Kitchener, ON: Batoche.
Moreland, C., and D. Bannister. 1983. *Antique Maps*. London: Phaidon.
Morgan, C. 2003. *Early Greek States Beyond the Polis*. London: Routledge.
———. 2009a. "Ethnic Expression on the Early Iron Age and Early Archaic Greek Mainland: Where Should We Be Looking?" In T. Derks and N. Roymans, eds. *Ethnic Constructs in Antiquity: The Role of Power and Tradition*, 11–36. Amsterdam: Amsterdam University Press.
Morgan, C. 2009b. "The Archaeology of *Ethnē* and Ethnicity in the Fourth-Century Peloponnese." In P. Funke and N. Luraghi, eds., *The Politics of Ethnicity and the Crisis of the Peloponnesian League*, 148–82. Washington, DC: Center for Hellenic Studies.
Morgan, G. 2006. *69 A.D.: The Year of Four Emperors*. Oxford: Oxford University Press.
Mortimer, G. 2010. *The Blitz: An Illustrated History*. Oxford: Osprey.

Müller, K., ed. 1841–1870. *Fragmenta Historicorum Graecorum (FHG)*. 5 vols. Paris: Didot.
Munslow, A. 1997. *Deconstructing History*. London: Routledge.
Murphy, T. M. 2004. *Pliny the Elder's Natural History: The Empire in the Encyclopedia*. Oxford: Oxford University Press.
Musurillo, H. 2000 [1954]. *The Acts of the Pagan Martyrs = Acta Alexandrinorum*. Oxford: Clarendon.
Myers, E. A. 2010. *The Ituraeans and the Roman Near East: Reassessing the Sources*. Society for New Testament Studies Monograph Series 147. Cambridge: Cambridge University Press.
Myres, J. L. 1953. *Herodotus: Father of History*. Oxford: Clarendon.
Naiden, F. S. 2013. *Smoke Signals for the Gods: Ancient Greek Sacrifice from the Archaic through Roman Periods*. Oxford: Oxford University Press.
Nanos, M. D., and M. Zetterholm. 2015. *Paul within Judaism: Restoring the First-Century Context to the Apostle*. Minneapolis: Fortress.
Navy League of the United States. 1915. *Seven Seas* (now *Seapower*) 2: November, 27–28.
Nearing, S. 1912. *The Super Race: An American Problem*. New York: Huebsch.
Netzer, E., with R. Laureys-Chachy. 2006. *The Architecture of Herod, the Great Builder*. Texts and Studies in Ancient Judaism 117. Tübingen: Mohr/Siebeck.
Neusner, J. 1973. *From Politics to Piety: The Emergence of Pharisaic Judaism*. Englewood Cliffs, NJ: Prentice-Hall. Reprinted, Eugene, OR: Wipf & Stock, 2003.
———. 1991. *Studying Classical Judaism: A Primer*. Louisville: Westminster John Knox.
———. 1993. *Rabbinic Literature and the New Testament: What We Cannot Show, We Do not Know*. Philadelphia: Trinity.
Neusner, J., and B. Chilton, eds. 2007. *In Quest of the Historical Pharisees*. Waco, TX: Baylor University Press.
Neitzel, S., and H. Welzer. 2011. *Soldaten: Protokolle von Kämpfen, Töten und Sterben*. Frankfurt: Fischer.
Neumann, K. J. 1880. *Iuliani imperatoris Librorum contra Christianos quae Supersunt*. Scriptorum Graecorum qui Christianam Impugnauerunt Religionen quae Supersunt 3. Leipzig: Teubner.
Neyrey, J. H. 1994. "Josephus' *Vita* and the Encomium: A Native Model of Personality." *JSJ* 25:177–206.
Nickau, K., ed. 1966. *Ammonii Qui Dicitur Liber de Adfinium Vocabulorum Differentia*. Bibliotheca Scriptorum Graecorum et Romanorum Teubneriana. Leipzig: Teubner.
———. 2000. "Schiffbruch in der Wüste des Sinai: Zu Herennios Philon, Neilos von Ankyra und dem Ammonioslexikon." *Hermes* 128:218–26.
Nock, A. D. 1933. *Conversion: The Old and the New in Religion from Alexander the Great to Augustine*. London: Oxford University Press.
Nolan, P., and G. Lenski. 2015. *Human Societies: An Introduction to Macrosociology*. 12th ed. New York: Oxford University Press.
Nongbri, B. 2013. *Before Religion: A History of a Modern Concept*. New Haven: Yale University Press.
Noy, D. 2000. *Foreigners at Rome: Citizens and Strangers*. London: Duckworth.
Oakeshott, M. 1999. *"On History" and Other Essays*. Indianapolis: Liberty Fund.

Oliver, J. H. 1932. "The Augustan Pomerium." *Memoirs of the American Academy in Rome* 10:145–82.

———. 1953. *The Ruling Power: A Study of the Roman Empire in the Second Century after Christ through the Roman Oration of Aelius Aristides*. Philadelphia: American Philosophical Society.

Olson, J. P. 2008. *The Oxford Handbook of Engineering and Technology in the Classical World*. Oxford: Oxford University Press.

Olson, R. S. 2010. *Tragedy, Authority, and Trickery: The Poetics of Embedded Letters in Josephus*. Washington, DC: Center for Hellenic Studies.

Parker, M. 2003. *Monte Cassino: The Story of the Hardest-fought Battle of World War Two*. London: Headline.

Parker, R. 1983. *Miasma: Pollution and Purification in Early Greek Religion*. Oxford: Clarendon.

———. 2005. *Polytheism and Society at Athens*. Oxford: Oxford University Press.

Parkin, T. G. 1992. *Demography and Roman Society*. Baltimore: Johns Hopkins University Press.

Pascal, B. 1846. *Thoughts of Blaise Pascal*, ed. E. Craig. Andover: Allen, Morrill, and Wardwell.

Pasto, J. 2002. "The Origin, Expansion and Impact of the Hasmoneans in Light of Comparative Ethnographic Studies (and Outside of its Nineteenth-Century Context)." In P. R. Davies and J. M. Halligan, eds., *Second Temple Studies III: Studies in Politics, Class and Material Culture*, 166–201. Journal for the Study of Old Testament Supplements 340. Sheffield: Sheffield Academic.

Patrich, J. 2009a. "538 BCE—70 CE: The Temple (*Beyt Ha-Miqdash*) and Its Mount." In O. Grabar and B. Z. Keda, eds., *Where Heaven and Earth Meet: Jerusalem's Sacred Esplanade*, 36–71. Jerusalem: Yad Ben-Zvi.

———. 2009b. "Herodian Entertainment Structures." In D. M. Jacobson and N. Kokkinos, eds., *Herod and Augustus: Papers Held at the IJS Conference, 21st–23rd June 2005*, 181–213. IJS Studies in Judaica 6. Leiden: Brill.

Pearce, S. 2004. Review of S. Mason, ed., *Flavius Josephus: Translation and Commentary*. *Journal of Jewish Studies* 55:169–70.

———. 2007. *The Land of the Body: Studies in Philo's Representation of Egypt*. Wissenschaftliche Untersuchungen zum Neuen Testament 208. Tübingen: Mohr/Siebeck.

Pelz, S. 1990. "Essay and Reflection: On Systematic Explanation in International History." *International History Review* 12:762–81.

Pickard-Cambridge, A. 1988. *The Dramatic Festivals of Athens*. 2nd ed. Revised by J. Gould and D. M. Lewis. Oxford: Clarendon.

Pike, K. L. 1954. *Language in Relation to a Unified Theory of the Structure of Human Behavior*. Glendale, CA: Summer Institute of Linguistics.

Plass, P. 1988. *Wit and the Writing of History: the Rhetoric of Historiography in Imperial Rome*. Madison: University of Wisconsin Press.

Platner, S. B. 1911. *The Topography and Monuments of Ancient Rome*. 2nd ed. Boston: Allyn & Bacon.

Pois, R. A. 1970. "Two Poles within Historicism: Croce and Meinecke." *Journal of the History of Ideas* 31:253–72.

Pompa, L. 1993. "The Inaugural Address: The Possibility of Historical Knowledge." *Proceedings of the Aristotelian Society, Supplementary Volumes* 67:1–16.

Popper, K. 1957. *The Poverty of Historicism*. Boston: Beacon.

Potter, D. S. 1996. "Emperors, Borders, and Their Neighbours: The Scope of Imperial *Mandata*." In Kennedy, ed., *Roman Army*, 49–66.
Price, J. J. 1994. "The Jewish Diaspora of the Graeco-Roman Period." *Scripta Classica Israelica* 13:169–86.
Price, S. R. F. 1980. "Between Man and God: Sacrifice in the Roman Imperial Cult." *Journal of Roman Studies* 70:28–43.
———. 1984. "Gods and Emperors: the Greek Language of the Roman Imperial Cult." *Journal of Hellenic Studies* 104:79–95.
Pritchett, W. K. 1974. *The Greek State at War*. Berkeley: University of California.
Pugsley, C. 2004. *The Battle for Monte Cassino, Central Italy, 12 January—5 June 1944*, Second World War 60th Anniversary Series. London: Central Office of Information.
Purvis, A. L. 2007. *The Landmark Herodotus: The Histories*. New York: Pantheon.
Rabinovich, A. 2011. "At Yadin's Side." *The Jerusalem Post Magazine*, April 28, 2011. http://www.jpost.com/Magazine/Features/Article.aspx?id=218262.
Rahman, Q., D. Andersson, and E. Govier. 2005. "A Specific Sexual Orientation-Related Difference in Navigation Strategy." *Behavioral Neuroscience* 119:311–16.
Rajak, T. 1983 [repr. 2002]. *Josephus: the Historian and His Society*. London: Duckworth.
Rajak, T. 2009. *Translation and Survival: The Greek Bible of the Ancient Jewish Diaspora*. Oxford: Oxford University Press.
Rand, C. G. 1964. "Two Meanings of Historicism in the Writings of Dilthey, Troeltsch, and Meinecke." *Journal of the History of Ideas* 25:503–18.
Ranke, L. von. 2011. *The Theory and Practice of History*. Edited by G. G. Iggers. London: Routledge.
Rappaport, U. 1982. "John of Gischala: from Galilee to Jerusalem." *Journal of Jewish Studies* 33:479–93.
———. 1994. "Where was Josephus Lying—in his *Life* or in the *War*?" In F. Parente and J. Sievers, eds., *Josephus and the History of the Greco-Roman Period: Essays in Memory of Morton Smith*, 279–89. Studia Post-Biblica 41. Leiden: Brill.
———. 2013. *John of Gischala: From the Mountains of Galilee to the Walls of Jerusalem*. The author's electronically circulated translation, by R. Toueg (with J. Pastor and G. Silberman), of his *Yohanan mi-Gush Halav: me-Hare ha-Galil el Homot Yerushalayim*. Haifa: University of Haifa Press [Hotsa'at ha-Sefarim], 2006. [Hebrew].
Rashdall, H. 2010 [1895]. *The Universities of Europe in the Middle Ages*. 2 vols. in 3. Cambridge: Cambridge University Press.
Reed, N. 1978. "Pattern and Purpose in the Antonine Itinerary." *American Journal of Philology* 99:228–54.
Reinhartz, A. 2014. "The Vanishing Jews of Antiquity: How Should One Translate the Greek *Ioudaios*?" http://marginalia.lareviewofbooks.org/vanishing-jews-antiquity-adele-reinhartz.
Revell, L. 2009. *Roman Imperialism and Local Identities*. Cambridge: Cambridge University Press.
Reynolds, D. 2006. *From World War to Cold War: Churchill, Roosevelt, and the International History of the 1940s*. New York: Oxford University Press.
Rhoads, D. M. 1976. *Israel in Revolution, 6–74 C.E.: A Political History Based on the Writings of Josephus*. Philadelphia: Fortress.
Richardson, J. 2008. *The Language of Empire: Rome and the Idea of Empire from the Third Century BC to the Second Century AD*. Cambridge: Cambridge University Press.

Richardson, P. 1996. *Herod: King of the Jews and Friend of the Romans. Studies on Personalities of the New Testament*. Columbia: University of South Carolina Press. Reprinted, Minneapolis: Fortress, 1999.
Ricoeur, P. 1970. *Freud and Philosophy*. New Haven: Yale University Press.
Ridder-Symoens, H. D., and W. Rüegg, eds. 1992–2010. *A History of the University in Europe*. 4 vols. Cambridge: Cambridge University Press.
Rigsby, K. J. 1996. *Asylia: Territorial Inviolability in the Hellenistic World*. Berkeley: University of California Press.
Ripley, W. Z. 1898–1899. "The Racial Geography of Europe XII: The Aryan Question," and "XV: Supplement, the Jews of Europe" (Lowell Institute Lectures 1896), *Popular Science Monthly* 52:49–68; 54:163–75, 338–51.
Ritmeyer, L. 2006. *The Quest: Revealing the Temple Mount in Jerusalem*. Jerusalem: Carta.
———. 2011. "The Architectural Development of the Western Wall of the Temple Mount in Jerusalem." Blog 23 November 2011: http://www.ritmeyer.com/2011/11/23/the-architectural-development-of-the-western-wall-of-the-temple-mount-in-jerusalem.
Ritmeyer, L., and K. Ritmeyer. 2006. *Secrets of Jerusalem's Temple Mount*. Rev. ed. Jerusalem: Washington, DC: Biblical Archaeology Society.
Ritner, R. K. 1998. "Egypt under Roman Rule: The *Legacy* of Ancient Egypt." In C. F. Petry, ed., *The Cambridge History of Egypt*, 1:1–33. Cambridge: Cambridge University Press.
Ritter, B. 2015. *Judeans in the Greek Cities of the Roman Empire: Rights, Citizenship and Civil Discord*. Journal for the Study of Judaism Supplements 170. Leiden: Brill.
Rives, J. B. 1999. *Tacitus: Germania*. Oxford: Oxford University Press.
———. 2007. *Religion in the Roman Empire*. Oxford: Blackwell.
———. 2010. "Graeco-Roman Religion in the Roman Empire: Old Assumptions and New Approaches." *Currents in Biblical Research* 8:240–99.
Roberts, A. 2008. *Masters and Commanders: The Military Geniuses who led the West to Victory in WW II*. London: Penguin.
———. 2009. *The Storm of War: A New History of the Second World War*. London: Penguin.
Roberts, C. 1996. *The Logic of Historical Explanation*. University Park: Pennsylvania State University Press.
Rocca, S. 2008. *Herod's Judaea: A Mediterranean State in the Classical World*. Texte und Studien zum antiken Judentum 122. Tübingen: Mohr/Siebeck.
———. 2009. *The Army of Herod the Great*. Oxford: Osprey.
Rodov, I. 2004. "The Eagle, its Twin Heads and Many Faces: Synagogue Chandeliers Surmounted by Double-Headed Eagles." *Studia Rosenthaliana* 37:77–129
Rogan, J. 2011. *Roman Provincial Administration*. Stroud: Amberley.
Roller, D. W. 1998. *The Building Program of Herod the Great*. Berkeley: University of California Press.
Romm, J. 2011. "Among the Barbarians." *London Review of Books* 33.24:26–27.
Ronen, I. 1988. "Formation of Jewish Nationalism among the Idumaeans." In A. Kasher, ed., *Jews, Idumaeans, and Ancient Arabs: Relations of the Jews in Eretz-Israel with the Nations of the Frontier and the Desert during the Hellenistic and Roman Era (332 BCE—70 CE)*, 214–20. Texte und Studien zum antiken Judentum 18. Tübingen: Mohr/Siebeck.

Roth, C. 1960. "Simon bar Giora: Ancient Jewish Hero. A Historical Reinterpretation." *Commentary* 29.1:52-8.
Rowland, I. D., and T. N. Howe, eds. 1999. *Vitruvius: Ten Books on Architecture*. Cambridge: Cambridge University Press.
Runesson, A., D. D. Binder, B. Olsson. 2008. *The Ancient Synagogue from Its Origins to 200 C.E.: A Source Book*. Ancient Judaism and Early Christianity 72. Leiden: Brill.
Rüpke, J. 2007. *Religion of the Romans*. Translated by R. Gordon. Malden, MA: Polity.
Saddington, D. B. 2009. "Client King's Armies under Augustus: The Case of Herod." In D. Jacobson and N. Kokkinos, eds., *Papers Presented at the IJS Conference, 21st-23rd June 2005*, 303-23. IJS Studies in Judaica 6. Leiden: Brill.
Said, E. W. 1978. *Orientalism*. New York: Random House.
Saldarini, A. J. 1988. *Pharisees, Scribes and Sadducees in Palestinian Society: A Sociological Approach*. Wilmington, DE: Glazier. Reprinted, Biblical Resource Series. Grand Rapids: Eerdmans, 2001.
Saller, R. P. 1982. *Personal Patronage under the Early Empire*. Cambridge: Cambridge University Press.
———. 1983. "Martial on Patronage and Literature." *Classical Quarterly* 33:246-57.
———. 1994. *Patriarchy, Property, and Death in the Roman Family*. Cambridge Studies in Population, Economy, and Society in Past Time 25. Cambridge: Cambridge University Press.
Salles, C. 1992. *Lire à Rome*. Paris: Les Belles Lettres.
Salway, B. 2005. "The Nature and Genesis of the Peutinger Map." *Imago Mundi* 57:119-35.
Samuel, A. E. 1972. *Greek and Roman Chronology: Calendars and Years in Classical Antiquity*. Handbuch der Altertumswissenschaft part 1, vol. 7. Munich: Beck.
Sanders, E. P. 1992. *Judaism: Practice & Belief, 63 BCE—66 CE*. London: SCM.
Sandgren, L. D. 2010. *Vines Intertwined: A History of Jews and Christians from the Babylonian Exile to the Advent of Islam*. Peabody: Hendrickson.
Santayana, G. 1920 [1906]. *The Life of Reason, or the Phases of Human Progress*, 5 vols. Vol. 1: *Reason in Common Sense*. New York: Scribner.
Sardar, Z. 1999. *Orientalism*. Buckingham: Open University Press.
Saussure, F. de. 1959. *Course in General Linguistics*. Translated by W. Baskin, ed. C. Bally, A. Sechehaye, and A. Reidlinger. New York: Philosophical Library.
———. 1993. *Troisième Cours de Linguistique Générale (1910-1911) d'après les cahiers d'Emile Constantin; Saussure's Third Course of Lectures on General Linguistics from the Notebooks of Emile Constantin*, ed. E. Komatsu and R. Harris. New York: Pergamon.
Schäfer, P. 1997. *Judeophobia: Attitudes toward the Jews in the Ancient World*. Cambridge: Harvard University Press.
Schätzl, L. 2003. *Wirtschaftsgeographie: Theorie*. Paderborn: Schöningh.
Scheid, J. 2003. *An Introduction to Roman Religion*. Translated by J. Lloyd. Bloomington: Indiana University Press.
———. 2012. "Roman Animal Sacrifice and the System of Being." In Faraone and Naiden, eds., *Greek and Roman Animal Sacrifice: Ancient Victims, Modern Observers*, 84-98. Cambridge: Cambridge University Press.
Scheidel, W. 2001. *Death on the Nile: Disease and the Demography of Roman Egypt*. Mnemosyne Supplements 228. Leiden: Brill.
———. 2004. "Creating a Metropolis: A Comparative Demographic Perspective." In W. V. Harris and G. Ruffini, eds., *Ancient Alexandria between Egypt and Greece*, 1-32. Columbia Studies in the Classical Tradition 26. Leiden: Brill.

———. 2005. "Real Slave Prices and the Relative Cost of Slave Labor in the Greco-Roman World." *Ancient Society* 35:1–17.
Scheidel, W., and S. J. Friesen. 2009. "The Size of the Economy and the Distribution of Income in the Roman Empire." *Journal of Roman Studies* 99:61–91.
Schimmeck, T. 2013. "Der ewige Diktator." *Berliner Zeitung*, 22 February, p. 3.
Schwartz, D. R. 1983. "Josephus and Nicolaus on the Pharisees." *Journal for the Study of Judaism* 14:157–71.
———. 1990. *Agrippa I: The Last King of Judaea*. Texte und Studien zum antiken Judentum 23. Tübingen: Mohr/Siebeck.
———. 1992. *Studies in the Jewish Background of Christianity*. Wissenschaftliche Untersuchungen zum Neuen Testament 60. Tübingen: Mohr/Siebeck.
———. 2005. "Herodians and *Ioudaioi* in Flavian Rome." In J. Edmondson, S. Mason, and J. Rives, eds., *Flavius Josephus and Flavian Rome*, 63–78. Oxford: Oxford University Press.
———. 2007. "'Judaean' or 'Jew'? How Should We Translate IOUDAIOS in Josephus?" In J. Frey, D. R. Schwartz, and S. Gripentrog, eds., *Jewish Identity in the Greco-Roman World: Jüdische Identität in der Griechisch-römischen Welt*, 3–28. Ancient Judaism and Early Christianity 71. Leiden: Brill.
———. 2008. *2 Maccabees*. Commentaries on Early Jewish Literature. Berlin: de Gruyter.
———. 2013. *Reading the First Century: On Reading Josephus and Studying Jewish History of the First Century*. Wissenschaftliche Untersuchungen zum Neuen Testament 300.Tübingen: Mohr/Siebeck.
———. 2014. *Judeans and Jews: Four Faces of Dichotomy in Ancient Jewish History*. Kenneth Michael Tanenbaum Series in Jewish Studies. Toronto: University of Toronto.
Schwartz, S. 1990. *Josephus and Judaean Politics*. Columbia Studies in the Classical Tradition 18. Leiden: Brill.
———. 1993. "A Note on the Social Type and Political Ideology of the Hasmonean Family." *Journal of Biblical Literature* 112:305–9.
———. 2006. "Political, Social, and Economic Life in the Land of Israel, 66–c. 235." In S. T. Katz, ed., *Cambridge History of Judaism*, 4:23–50. 4 vols. Cambridge: Cambridge University Press.
———. 2010. *Were the Jews a Mediterranean Society? Reciprocity and Solidarity in Ancient Judaism*. Princeton: Princeton University Press.
———. 2011. "How Many Judaisms Were There? A Critique of Neusner and Smith on Definition and Mason and Boyarin on Categorization." *Journal of Ancient Judaism* 2:203–38.
Scott, J. M. 2002. *Geography in Early Judaism and Christianity: The Book of Jubilees*. Society for New Testament Studies Monograph Series 113. Cambridge: Cambridge University Press.
Sechrest, L. L. 2009. *A Former Jew: Paul and the Dialectics of Race*. Library of New Testament Studies 410. London: T. & T. Clark.
Segev, T. 2000. *One Palestine, Complete: Jews and Arabs under the British Mandate*. Translated by Haim Watzman. London: Abacus.
Segre, M. 1993. *Iscrizioni di Cos*. Rome: L'Erma di Bretschneider.
Semenchenko, L. 2002. "Hellenistic Motifs in the *Jewish Antiquities* of Flavius Josephus." Ph.D. diss., Department of History, Russian Academy of Sciences [Russian].
Sevenster, J. N. 1975. *The Roots of Pagan Anti-Semitism in the Ancient World*. Novum Testamentum Supplements 41. Leiden: Brill.

Seward, D. 2009. *Jerusalem's Traitor: Josephus, Masada, and the Fall of Judea*. Cambridge, MA: Da Capo.
Shatzman, I. 2010. Review of J. Richardson's *The Language of Empire: Rome and the Idea of Empire from the Third Century BC to the Second Century AD*. *Scripta Classica Israelica* 29:128-32.
Shenoy, S. 2006. "Josephus' *Jewish War* as a Narrative Five-Act Tragedy." Ph.D. diss., Australian Catholic University, School of Theology.
Shepherd, W. R. 1926 (1911). *Historical Atlas*. 5th ed. New York: Holt.
Sherman, N. 2005. *Stoic Warriors: the Ancient Philosophy behind the Military Mind*. Oxford: Oxford University Press.
Shorey, P. 1921. "Τύχη in Polybius." *Classical Philology* 16:280-83.
Shotwell, J. T. 1922. *An Introduction to the History of History*. New York: Columbia University Press.
Siggelkow-Berner, B. 2011. *Die jüdischen Feste im Bellum Judaicum des Flavius Josephus*. Wissenschaftliche Untersuchungen zum Neuen Testament 2/306. Tübingen: Mohr/Siebeck.
Small, J. P. 2010. "Maps within Texts: The Artemidorus Papyrus." *Quaderni di Storia* 71:51-76.
Smallwood, E. M. 1961. *Philonis Alexandrini Legatio ad Gaium*. Leiden: Brill.
———. 2001 [1981]. *The Jews under Roman Rule from Pompey to Diocletian: A Study in Political Relations*. Studies in Judaism in Late Antiquity 20. Leiden: Brill Academic.
Smith, J. Z. 1998. "Religion, Religions, Religious." In M. C. Taylor, ed., *Critical Terms for Religious Studies*. Chicago: University of Chicago Press.
Smith, R. R. R. 1988. "*Simulacra Gentium*: The *Ethne* from the Sebasteion at Aphrodisias." *Journal of Roman Studies* 78:50-77.
Smith, W. C. 1963. *The Meaning and End of Religion: A New Approach to the Religious Traditions of Mankind*. New York: Macmillan.
Sordi, M. 1986. *The Christians and the Roman Empire*. Translated by A. Bedini. Norman: University of Oklahoma Press.
Spencer, H. 1872. "The Study of Sociology." *Popular Science Monthly* 1:1-17.
———. 1879. *The Data of Ethics*. New York: Crowell.
———. 1896. *The Study of Sociology*. New York: Appleton.
Sprague, R. K. 1972. *The Older Sophists*. Columbia: University of South Carolina Press.
Stambaugh, J. E. 1988. *The Ancient Roman City*. Baltimore: Johns Hopkins University Press.
Steinberg, A. 2008. "Secret Passage Discovered under Ancient Jerusalem." *Biblical Archaeology Review* 34.4:20.
Sterling, G. E. 1992. *Historiography and Self-Definition: Josephus, Luke-Acts, and Apologetic Historiography*. Novum Testamentum Supplements 64. Leiden: Brill.
Stern, F. R. 1973. *The Varieties of History: From Voltaire to the Present*. Rev. ed. New York: Vintage.
Stern, M., ed. 1974. *Greek and Latin Authors on Jews and Judaism*. 3 vols. Jerusalem: Israel Academy of Sciences and Humanities.
Stevenson, D. 1999. "War by Timetable? The Railway Race before 1914." *Past & Present* 162:163-94.
Stewart, D. 1989. "The Hermeneutics of Suspicion." *Journal of Literature and Theology* 3:296-307.
Stoll, O. 2007. "The Religions of the Armies." In P. Erdkamp, ed. *A Companion to the Roman Army*, 451-76. Blackwell Companions to the Ancient World: Ancient History. Oxford: Blackwell.

Stone, T. 2016. "History Tells Us What Will Happen with Trump and Brexit." *Newsweek Europe* online, 25 July 2016: http://europe.newsweek.com/history-tells-us-what-will-happen-brext-trump-483671.
Strong, S. A. 1914. "A Note on Two Roman Sepulchral Reliefs." *Journal of Roman Studies* 4:147–56.
Swain, S. 1996. *Hellenism and Empire: Language, Classicism, and Power in the Greek World, AD 50–250*. Oxford: Clarendon.
Swarney, P. R. 1970. *The Ptolemaic and Roman Idios Logos*. Toronto: Hakkert.
Syme, R. 1958. *Tacitus*. 2 vols. Oxford: Clarendon.
———. 1970. *Ten Studies in Tacitus*. Oxford: Clarendon.
Szkolut, P. 2002. "The Eagle as the Symbol of Divine Presence and Protection in Ancient Jewish Art." *Studia Judaica* 5:1–11.
Taillardat, J. 1967. *Suétone*. Περὶ βλασφημιῶν. Περὶ παιδιῶν. Nouvelle Collection de Textes et Documents. Paris: Les Belles Lettres.
Talbert, R. J. A. 1987. Review of O. A. W. Dilke, *Greek and Roman Maps*. *Journal of Roman Studies* 77:210–12.
———. 2000. *Barrington Atlas of the Greek and Roman World: Map-by-Map Directory*. Princeton: Princton University Press.
———. 2010a. *Rome's World: The Peutinger Map Reconsidered*. Cambridge: Cambridge University Press.
———. 2010b. "The Roman Worldview: Beyond Recovery?" In K. Raaflaub and R. J. A. Talbert, eds., *Geography and Ethnography: Perceptions of the World in Pre-Modern Societies*, 252–72. Oxford: Blackwell.
Talbert, R. J. A., and K. Brodersen, eds. 2004. *Space in the Roman World: Its Perception and Presentation*. Münster: LIT.
Talbert, R. J. A., and R. W. Unger, eds. 2008. *Cartography in Antiquity and the Middle Ages: Fresh Perspectives, New Methods*. Technology and Change in History 10. Leiden: Brill.
Taylor, A. J. P. 1969. *War by Time-Table: How the First World War Began*. New York: American Heritage.
———. 1972. *Beaverbrook*. London: Hamilton.
———. 1979. *How Wars Begin*, London: Hamilton.
———. 2009 [1963]. *The First World War: An Illustrated History*. London: Rainbird.
Tcherikover, V. A., and A. Fuks, eds. 1957–1963. *Corpus Papyrorum Judaicarum*. 3 vols. Cambridge: Harvard University Press.
Thackeray, H. St. J. 1929. *Josephus: The Man and the Historian*. New York: Jewish Institute of Religion.
Thomas, R. 2000. *Herodotus in Context: Ethnography, Science and the Art of Persuasion*. Cambridge: Cambridge University Press.
———. 2006. "The Intellectual Milieu of Herodotus." In C. Dewald and J. Marincola, eds, *The Cambridge Companion to Herodotus*, 60–76. Cambridge Companions to Literature. Cambridge: Cambridge University Press.
Thompson, D. J. 2001. "Alexandria: The City by the Sea." *Bulletin of the Archaeological Society of Alexandria* 46:73–79.
Tierney, J. J. 1962–1964. "The Map of Agrippa." *Proceedings of the Royal Irish Academy. Section C: Archaeology, Celtic Studies, History, Linguistics, Literature* 63:151–66.
Tishby, A., ed. 2001. *Holy Land in Maps*. Jerusalem: Israel Museum.
Todd, M. 1999. *Roman Britain*. 3rd ed. Oxford: Blackwell.
Toulmin, S. E. 2003. *The Uses of Argument*. Updated ed. Cambridge: Cambridge University Press.

Tozer, H. F. 1971. *A History of Ancient Geography*. New York: Biblio & Tannen.
Trevelyan, G. M. 1913. *Clio, a Muse and Other Essays Literary and Pedestrian*. London: Longmans, Green.
Turcan, R. 1996. *The Cults of the Roman Empire*. Oxford: Blackwell.
Turda, M., and P. Weindling, eds. 2007. *"Blood and Homeland": Eugenics and Racial Nationalism in Central and Southeast Europe, 1900–1940*. Budapest: Central European University Press.
Turner, E. W. 1954. "Tiberius Iulius Alexander." *Journal of Roman Studies* 44:54–64.
Tuval, M. 2013. *From Jerusalem Priest to Roman Jew: On Josephus and the Paradigms of Ancient Judaism*. Wissenschaftliche Untersuchungen zum Neuen Testament 2/357. Tübingen: Mohr/Siebeck.
Ulf, C. 2009. "The Development of Greek Ethnê and Their Ethnicity: An Anthropological Perspective." In P. Funke and N. Luraghi, eds. *The Politics of Ethnicity and the Crisis of the Peloponnesian League*, 215–49. Washington, DC: Center for Hellenic Studies.
Ullmann-Margalit, E. 2008. "Spotlight on Scroll Scholars: Dissecting the Qumran-Essene Hypothesis." *Biblical Archaeology Review* 34.2:63–67, 86.
van der Horst, P. W. 2003. *Philo's Flaccus: The First Pogrom. Introduction, Translation and Commentary*. Philo of Alexandria Commentary Series 2. Leiden: Brill, 2003.
van Henten, J. W. 2008. "The Demolition of the Golden Eagle in Josephus' *Antiquities*." Paper presented at the colloquium "Flavius Josephus." Netherlands Institute for Advanced Study in the Humanities and Social Sciences, Wassenaar, 4 June.
Veeser, H. A., ed. 1989. *The New Historicism*. London: Routledge.
Verboven, K. 2011. "Professional Collegia: Guilds or Social Clubs?" *Ancient Society* 41:187–95.
Vico, G. 1990 [1708]. *On the Study Methods of Our Time*. Translated by E. Gianturco. Ithaca: Cornell University Press.
———. 1993 [1699–1707]. *On Humanistic Education (Six Inaugural Orations, 1699–1707)*. Translated by G. A. Pinton and A. B. Shippee. Ithaca: Cornell University Press.
———. 2002 [1725]. *The First New Science*. Edited by L. Pompa. Cambridge: Cambridge University Press.
Vlassopoulos, K. 2007. *Unthinking the Greek Polis: Ancient Greek History beyond Eurocentrism*. Cambridge: Cambridge University Press.
———. 2015. "Ethnicity and Greek History: Re-Examining our Assumptions." *Bulletin of the Institute of Classical Studies* (University of London) 58:1–13.
Voltaire. 1901. *A Philosophical Dictionary*. 5 vols. Trans. W. F. Fleming. = vols. 5–14 of *Voltaire: A Contemporary Version*. Paris: DuMont.
Walbank, F. W. 1972. *Polybius*. Sather Classical Lectures 42. Berkeley: University of California Press.
———. 2002. *Polybius, Rome and the Hellenistic World: Essays and Reflections*. Cambridge: Cambridge University Press.
Warren, R. 2007. *The Purpose-Driven Life*. Grand Rapids: Zondervan.
Weber, M. 1958 [1921]. *The City*. Translated and edited by D. Martindale and G. Neuwirth. New York: Macmillan/Free Press.
Webster, G. 1978. *Boudica: The British Revolt against Rome AD 60*. London: Routledge.
———. 1985. *The Roman Imperial Army of the First and Second Centuries A.D.* 3rd ed. London: A. & C. Black.
Wells, G. L., and E. F. Loftus. 1984. *Eyewitness Testimony: Psychological Perspectives*. Cambridge: Cambridge University Press.

Wheeler, C. N. 1916. "Fight to Disarm His Life's Work, Henry Ford Vows." *Chicago Daily Tribune*, Thursday May 25, p. 10.
White, H. 1973. *Metahistory: The Historical Imagination in Nineteenth-Century Europe*. Baltimore: Johns Hopkins University Press.
———. 1978. *Tropics of Discourse: Essays in Cultural Criticism*. Baltimore: Johns Hopkins University Press.
———. 1987. *The Content of the Form: Narrative Discourse and Historical Representation*. Baltimore: Johns Hopkins University Press.
White, M. 1965. *Foundations of Historical Knowledge*. New York: Harper & Row.
White, P. 1975. "The Friends of Martial, Statius, and Pliny, and the Dispersal of Patronage." *Harvard Studies in Classical Philology* 79:265–300.
———. 1978. "*Amicitia* and the Profession of Poetry in Early Imperial Rome." *Journal of Roman Studies* 68:74–92.
Whitmarsh, T. 2016. *Battling the Gods: Atheism in the Ancient World*. London: Faber & Faber.
Whittaker, C. R. 2004. *Rome and Its Frontiers: The Dynamics of Empire*. London: Routledge.
Whittaker, M. 1984. *Jews and Christians: Graeco-Roman Views*. Cambridge: Cambridge University Press.
Wilamowitz-Moellendorff, U. von. 1982 [1921]. *History of Classical Scholarship*. Translated by A. Harris, ed. H. Lloyd-Jones. Baltimore: Johns Hopkins University Press.
Wilken, R. L. 1984. *The Christians as the Romans Saw Them*. New Haven: Yale University Press.
Williams, D. S. 1992. *Stylometric Authorship Studies in Flavius Josephus and Related Literature*. Jewish Studies 12. Lewiston, NY: Mellen.
———. 1994. "Josephus and the Authorship of War 2.119–161 (on the Essenes)." *Journal for the Study of Judaism* 25:207–21.
Woodman, A. J. 1988. *Rhetoric in Classical Historiography: Four Studies*. London: Croom Helm.
Woolf, G. 2006. "Pliny's Province." In T. Bekker-Nielsen (ed.) *Rome and the Black Sea Region: Domination, Romanization, Resistance*, 93–108. Aarhus: Aarhus University Press.
Yadin, Y. 1966. *Masada: Herod's Fortress and the Zealots' Last Stand*. London: Phoenix.
Yardley, J. C. and R. Develin. 1994. *Justin: Epitome of the Philippic History of Pompeius Trogus*. Atlanta: Scholars.
Yegül, F. K. 1992. *Baths and Bathing in Classical Antiquity*. New York: Architectural History Foundation/MIT Press.
Yegül, F. K. 2010. *Bathing in the Roman World*. Cambridge: Cambridge University Press.
Zerubavel, Y. 1994. *Recovered Roots: Collective Memory and the Making of Israeli National Tradition*. Chicago: University of Chicago Press.
Zuber, T. 2002. *Inventing the Schlieffen Plan: German War Planning, 1871–1914*. Oxford: Oxford University Press.

www.ingramcontent.com/pod-product-compliance
Lightning Source LLC
Chambersburg PA
CBHW021345300426
44114CB00012B/1089